Failed God

Also by JOHN A. RUSH

*Spiritual Tattoo: A Cultural History of
Tattooing, Piercing, Scarification, Branding, and Implants*

*The Twelve Gates: A Spiritual Passage
through the Egyptian Books of the Dead*

Failed God

Fractured Myth in a Fragile World

JOHN A. RUSH

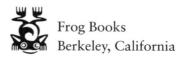

Frog Books
Berkeley, California

Published by Frog Books
Frog Books' publications are distributed by
North Atlantic Books
P.O. Box 12327
Berkeley, California 94712

Cover photography by John A. Rush
Cover and book design by Suzanne Albertson

Printed in the United States of America on 30% post-consumer-waste paper

Failed God: Fractured Myth in a Fragile World is sponsored by the Society for the Study of Native Arts and Sciences, a nonprofit educational corporation whose goals are to develop an educational and cross-cultural perspective linking various scientific, social, and artistic fields; to nurture a holistic view of arts, sciences, humanities, and healing; and to publish and distribute literature on the relationship of mind, body, and nature.

North Atlantic Books' publications are available through most bookstores. For further information, call 800-733-3000 or visit our website at www.northatlanticbooks.com.

Library of Congress Cataloging-in-Publication Data

Rush, John A.
  Failed God : fractured myth in a fragile world / John A. Rush.
    p. cm.
  Includes bibliographical references and index.
  Summary: "Presents idea that the three major world religions developed through the use of mind-altering drugs. Examines each religion individually, concluding that beneath each lies an irrational system that is incongruent with today's world"—Provided by publisher.
    ISBN 978-1-58394-274-1 (alk. paper)
  1. Psychotropic drugs. 2. Religion. 3. Religions. 4. Judaism. 5. Christianity. 6. Islam. I. Title.

BL65.D7R87 2008
200—dc22   2008032974

    2   3   4   5   6   7   8   9   United   16   15   14   13   12   11

TABLE OF CONTENTS

Humanity has always existed in troubled times; there has always been a challenge. In the process of evolution we opted for brains, not brawn, for coping with or overcoming what nature tossed our way. We developed big brains with a type of consciousness that allows us to be part of nature yet step back, observe, imagine, and ask "What if?" and "How come?" Without this ability to imagine beyond the moment, our kind, like all other animals, would passively accept what nature provides and our existence would be no different from that of chimpanzees.

All of us are equipped with imagination; we can think things that no one has ever thought before. This leads to an unexpected problem and that is keeping people on the same page of imagination for some communal effort. This is where storytelling and myth come in, as it is through our stories that we curb creative anarchy and settle for a group myth, providing reference points and expectations through ritual.

Studied at a distance, biblical scholars, Middle Eastern historians, and others understand the Bible and Qur'an by examining the stories in conjunction with social circumstances (famine, war, plagues, technology, etc.), and what we know about behaviors and beliefs. What we select as focal points for explaining history and our current circumstances varies from author to author, some looking at technology, others at warfare, and still others analyzing myth and various art forms. And, naturally, each author believes his position as perhaps most significant, because that is what he or she knows or hears from experts, and feels competent to share with others. In the process of selecting a point of view or a model for explaining, we often neglect that which appears insignificant, and do not notice it or cannot comprehend it (perhaps out of political correctness). If I, for example, tried to discuss ancient warfare without including politics, economics, or the motives of warring tribes, the "why" of events would be unanswerable, outside of saying humans are violent. A conscious or subconscious ordering of symbols (thought) precedes human action, with these symbols and thoughts being the product of combined experiences. Action flows from this in terms of what we think and believe, as beliefs structure behaviors.

The reader will agree that what we call religion—for example, Judaism, Christianity, and Islam—matured from beliefs about experiences and the experiences of others a long, long time ago, in a different place, under different circumstances. Keep in mind that these traditions, their beliefs and experiences, emerged within an entirely different culture than the one Westerners experience today.

The reader would also concur that our experiences of the world come to us through information presented and how we interpret it, for all people can look at the moon and see something different. Also, when you are in a good mood, the world is experienced much differently than when you are in a bad mood. Behavior, then, is very complex, but our behaviors are directly related to what we believe about our observations and experiences of the world through group consensus, or simply through what we are told to believe. This creates predictability in human behavior, and without predictability no stability and forward motion (evolution) can occur. Culture is based on predictable and shared outcomes orchestrated through our stories, our myths.

Following this, when a person purposely alters his or her consciousness through cannabis, alcohol, Prozac, cocaine, LSD, and so on, such behavior can have a profound effect on perception, action, and actions and reactions of others. For example, if a person gets drunk, drives a car, and runs down a pedestrian, we don't exclude alcohol from understanding why the event occurred. This is the purpose of laws about drinking and driving; there is recognition that certain substances alter thought and behavior and can have severe effects on many people. Think of how the world would be if Princess Diana wasn't riding in a car driven by a drunk. If a person smokes cannabis and drives thirty miles an hour in a sixty-five-mile-per-hour zone, we can explain this behavior in terms of the effects of THC. We don't simply say he was driving slowly. If a person chews on datura leaves, suffers extreme anxiety, and believes that demons are chasing him, the psychiatrist at the local hospital does not conclude that the individual was actually possessed by demons—nor does he or she ignore the consumption of datura, which led to the thoughts and behavior.

How do we explain, then, the behaviors of personalities in the Bible and Qur'an? Where did the ideas come from that shaped much of Western Civilization? Are we to believe that clever individuals made up stories that became layered over time with new twists and turns, and all these people were just normal, everyday people? The ancients explain many of their conversations, experiences, and directives for action as the result of a deity having a special person or group to whom this deity delivers the laws or rules of government. How would we explain this today? As individual or cultural psychosis? Perhaps lead poisoning, malnutrition, and stress are responsible. Certainly no reputable scholar can possibly believe that an external, creator god came down out of the sky and spoke to special people who were then to relay the message to all mankind. So what would be the best and most obvious choice to explain the experiences of Abraham, Moses, Jacob, Paul, Apollinarius, Muhammad, popes, and many other saints and sinners, experiences that led to the shaping of Western Civilization?

The most reasonable and highly volatile conclusion would be mind-altering fungi and plants. Many scholars avoid the subject because these experiences have been demonized and restricted to a small few. Perhaps this avoidance is out of political correctness or to protect a career. The ancients who constructed Judaism, Christianity, and Islam were doing what had gone on for thousands of years, and that is communicating with their ancestors using mind-altering substances, with ancestors who became their gods. To leave mind-altering fungi and plants out of discussions and interpretations of these traditions, and the development of Western Civilization in general, leaves biblical history without an explanation outside of cultural psychosis.

On July 13, 2001, I entered St. Mark's Basilica in Venice, Italy, and was overwhelmed by the beauty of the mosaics. As I moved along, I noticed an arch with a curious scene (see front cover). There was Jesus with the cap of *Amanita muscaria,* the sacred mushroom, in his hand. Throughout the basilica there are images of angel-mushrooms and tree- or plant-mushrooms (many explained in Chapter Three). When I returned to the entrance of the basilica, I looked up at the ceiling and into the domes to my right and left. I could see the story of Creation and other stories in Genesis, but not very well, as this space was roped off. An elderly woman saw I was interested and ask, "You want to see?" She took down the cord and I could clearly see the biblical story of Creation.

When I returned to California and viewed in detail these photos and others from cathedrals in Italy, France, and England, I was stunned. There was no doubt that Allegro (1970) was correct—the sacred mush- room was indeed a central feature in the development of Judaism and Christianity. With respect to Christianity, Jesus and the mushroom are one and the same. He is the portal to the other side, the way, "and he who believeth in me shall have everlasting life." One of the images from St. Mark's (the Tree of Good and Evil) was included in *Spiritual Tattoo* (see Rush 2005, 217); it is a tree-mushroom. At the same moment I realized the importance of this, and the future of Judaism and Christianity, and by default, Islam. St. Mark's was only the tip of the ice- berg; the mushroom, in one form or another, is present in every piece of Christian art.

Since 2001, numerous books (referenced in the text) have appeared associating Jesus with mushrooms, but historians and biblical scholars either ignored this or wrote it off as "artistic anomalies" and of little sig- nificance in the construction of Judaism and Christianity. These books also include references to mind-altering plants and fungi in the Old and New Testament and Greek myth, as well as auxiliary texts. Yet this was still ignored by many scholars. The use of mind-altering substances is undeniable; the pope and most high-level religious clerics obviously know about these images and their reference—their predecessors com- missioned the art. The altered reality that flows from mind-altering substances certainly had an effect on how rulers and religious clerics saw their world, determined how many angels could stand on the head of a pin, and consequently enacted public policy. How these systems (Judaism, Christianity, and Islam) were generated is extremely important in understanding the evolving images and thoughts that changed the world. Since that discovery in 2001, I have collected hundreds of images from stained glass, mosaics, manuscripts, wall paintings, and woodcuts, from the fifth century to the present, which show without doubt the symbolic importance of *Amanita muscaria* (and other mind-altering substances) in the Christian tradition as expressed in Christian art. The fact that the use of mind-altering substances and their connection to religion has been "overlooked" certainly does not mean they are unimportant, just overlooked. Philosophy, music, visual arts, theater, technology, and so on would have been directly or indirectly influenced by plant/mushroom use, in both ritual and recreational settings.

The Bible and Qur'an cannot be understood (outside of cultural psychosis) without reference to mind-altering substances. They help to explain the contact between special humans, supernatural forces, and attitudes, policies, and laws evolving from them. They help us to understand the ranting of Paul in the New Testament and why he could propose that he was an apostle (the "least apostle") of Jesus. These plants and fungi are crucial in understanding his convoluted discussion of "the body of Christ" or to be "in Christ" (1 Corinthians:10, 11, 15—see Chapter Three and front cover), references to "bread" (obviously an analogue of *Amanita muscaria*), and Paul's overall magical and disturbed thinking that went into the construction of Christianity. They help to explain some of the ritual paraphernalia, the red and white caps worn by Catholic clerics, the wine and the wafer, the halo, dove, book, and chalice. They help us to explain Muhammad's contact with Gabriel or Samael in the cave, and they help us to understand the disturbed and angry messages from al Liah and Yahweh—these were troubled times and a troubled god tumbled from these adventures with the mushroom.

Without reference to mind-altering substances, the scholarly interpretations regarding how and why the Bible and Qur'an (as well as auxiliary works) were written cannot be adequately addressed. Beginning with Allegro (1970) the religious scholars were alerted to the use of *Amanita muscaria*, but they chose political correctness and ruined his career (see Irvin 2008). These substances brought people to action. They influenced thought patterns and the construction of Western Civilization. It is perhaps easy to understand why magic mushrooms were left out of the analysis, and it is not because they were an insignificant ingredient. On the contrary, the real reasons are politics and political correctness. Recognition of ritual drug use by important scholars would show that Judaism, Christianity, and Islam were born on drug-assisted dreams—drug-assisted psychosis, if you will—that served to control and justify social process and social action. Whole departments in prestigious universities would close for lack of enrollment and churches would be empty if this secret truth was revealed to the world. These drug-induced states led to drug-induced beliefs, which led to decisions and social action. Mind-altering fungi and plants take center stage for touching the supernatural, and once and for all discredit these traditions as stemming from actual contact with supernatural powers.

More importantly, they force a rewriting of history, a rewriting of people, places, and outcomes, of why our culture evolved as it did. People during biblical times believed that gods resided in plants and fungi; they are to be forgiven for this, but not in today's world. They used gods as third-person reference points for constructing oppressive rule and oppressive political systems, while, at the same time, restricting supernatural access to a special few. Current religious clerics approach this with denial, but any reasonable person cannot ignore the evidence. Yet the evidence is neglected in scholarly books and articles. Most of the scholars referenced in this work have very interesting and important things to say, but they are also silent about drugs, and without that element in their analyses, although interesting in themselves, the presentations are wanting in terms of explanations as to who, why, and what.

For example, how would our understanding of the Jesus and Christ cults change if mind-altering substances are computed into cause and effect? How might we explain the communal meal, a central feature of these cults, and the necessity of going to church to receive the sacrament, when mind-altering substances, especially *Amanita muscaria,* are added to the formula of explanation? How does our understanding of Abraham, Moses, Ezekiel, and Daniel change when we realize that drugs were the conduits to supernatural entities? Were they really communicating with a deity? No serious scholar believes this, so we are left with reports of psychotic episodes, or auditory and visual hallucinations brought on by stress, illness, or malnutrition. Without mind-altering substances, the supernatural evaporates into cultural psychosis. So, either the Bible and Qur'an are examples of cultural psychosis, or drug-induced, altered forms of awareness best explain these stories.

Fundamentalists, and many scholars included, will not accept or even consider this. How many sociologists or historians, when researching the 1960s or youth culture today, would fail to mention the impact of tobacco, alcohol, LSD, DMT, cannabis, cocaine, amphetamines, designer drugs, caffeine, and so on? How does current drug usage affect relationships, use of spare time, sexual activity, technology, health issues, religious beliefs, art, music, and commercial advertising? Mind-altering substances had a great deal to do with the music of Jimi Hendrix, Janice Joplin, the Beatles, the Rolling Stones, and many, many others, and their music altered the history of the world. Our culture cannot be properly understood without computing mind-altering substances into the formula. Allegro's (1970) proposal that *Amanita muscaria* was central to Judaism and Christianity certainly had little impact on the popular and scholarly discussions of these traditions since that time. To exclude mind-altering fungi and plants without proper research does not produce good scholarship. There are only two ways to go: Either Abraham, Isaac, Moses, Jesus, Paul, and Muhammad were psychotic, or they were on drugs. These are the only reasonable explanations. Either way, without including psychosis in one form or another, the events in the Bible and Qur'an become incomprehensible.

Some say the discussion of drugs and religion is a form of insensitivity. I am not concerned with political correctness, for that amounts to a lie, and it would appear that politics has corrupted many in the academic community. This book is about myth, how the Bible and Qur'an were constructed, and the use of very powerful mind-altering substances in the building of the myths and associated pronouncements (cosmic laws) for social action. It is what it is; truth many times does not bring peace.

Chapter One is an overview of the problem of myths in collision, the myths supporting Judaism, Christianity, and Islam, and the story provided by science. Within this discussion I define who and what we are and where we came from using an anthropological, scientific model. The reader can then decide which story is more rational, reasonable, and useful for continued survival on this planet and beyond.

Chapter Two is an analysis of Judaism, showing how the Old Testament represents a mythical charter for a special people with special privileges given by God. I outline how at least some of the charter was constructed using prevailing stories from other cultural groups, and how the adventures of Abraham, Moses, and so on, were brought on by mind-altering substances.

Chapter Three is about John the Baptist and how he morphed into Jesus once his ministry abruptly ended. John came with a simple message that did not require a church or priest, only human decency. The sentiments of John, possibly a renegade of the Essenes, were perverted once Paul (perhaps a fictional character) entered the scene. Paul was converted during a drug-induced experience, and continued to use cannabis and other more powerful substances, as he composed what we know today as Christianity. If there is such a thing as the "anti-Christ," then Paul and his continuers are it.

Chapter Four is about Islam and its construction some time after 700 CE. As with Jesus, there is no historical visibility for Muhammad, the hero of the Islamic community. Muhammad was modeled after Moses and thus the Islamic poets must have been aware of and undoubtedly used the mind-altering substances that placed Muhammad in contact with al Liah, Gabriel or Samael, and Shaytan. I show that similar literary techniques are used in the construction of the Qur'an as in the Old Testament. In fact, if the Qur'an were written today it would be considered plagiarism. The real downfall of the Qur'an stems from that which it attempted to emulate—if the Old Testament is a concocted mythical charter stemming from drug-induced romps (Abraham, Moses, etc.) with the supernatural, then the same applies to the Qur'an.

Chapter Five offers a review and accentuation of specific points brought up in the preceding chapters. For example, is there such a thing as freedom of religion in the West, seeing that most children aren't allowed to choose their religion? Because adventures with the gods in the Bible and Qur'an were drug induced, should we continue to believe these stories as fact, as real conversations with God? Or, should maintaining these beliefs, in the spite of the evidence, be considered forms of neurosis or psychosis? Once we understand that Jesus is a personification of *Amanita muscaria,* having "faith" in his physical existence and supernatural powers rapidly evaporates in the rational mind. Should the psychiatric community take a more active interest in reprogramming those individuals pushed, bullied, and threatened by religious clerics? Should religious clerics be cautioned about emotional abuse and fear stemming from negative incantations of hellfire and damnation if people don't believe their drug-generated fantasy? Should parents be cautioned about exposing their children to these irrational, oppressive systems? As a social statement, how do we reconcile women's rights in today's world when compared to that presented by fundamental Judaism, Christianity, and Islam? They are terribly at odds. Do women really want their daughters growing up thinking they are inferior to men?

Finally, morality stems from social necessity, not religious observance. Morality stems from self-responsibility, emotional responsibility, and plain and simple human decency, not gods, temples, and religious clerics. Judaism, Christianity, and Islam are responsible for promoting some of the most immoral, horrendous acts perpetrated against humanity, all done in the name of their respective gods.

Many individuals were involved in the composition of this work—too many to mention personally. Special mention, however, goes to Jan Irvin, for editorial assistance and comments on technical issues, Brian Haley, for his assistance in translating some troublesome Medieval Latin, Al Desetta, for his patience and persistence in editing this work, the staff at North Atlantic Books/Frog Books (Emily Boyd, Paula Morrison, Suzanne Albertson, and Richard Grossinger), and my wife, Katie, for her support and encouragement during this project.

Lastly, there is a sequel to this work entitled *The Mushroom in Christian Art,* in which I review approximately fifty images (and reference many others) taken from stained glass and mosaics, in both Europe and North America, as well as manuscripts, wall paintings, and wood-cuts. These images stand as representatives of mushrooms in Christian art, spanning a time period of 1,500 years. Not all Christian art contains mushrooms per se, but they always take center stage in one form or another. Within this I have collected statistics as to frequencies of specific imagery in relation to certain players in the Old and New Testaments. This ensemble graphically shows the influence of *Amanita muscaria, Psilocybin* species, and other plant mind-altering substances as central ingredients surrounding the development of Christianity and Judaism. The work also shows the alteration of the mushroom symbol through time, that is, in some time periods it is obvious while at others there are numerous stand-ins. This, as I suggest, represents a more open as opposed to a more closed depiction of the mystery and repressive attitudes of the Church. In any case, through the use of magic mushrooms special people could commune with the godhead, obtain rules and directives, justify events, and promote social action. Judaism, Christianity, and Islam, in my opinion, are based on a type of mushroom worship (animism), a tradition that reaches back thousands of years into our prehistoric past.

CHAPTER ONE

Introduction

Overview

The world is in the midst of a paradigm shift, brewing for about two thousand years, but the basic elements fueling the shift can be traced back to earlier times, especially to the philosophy of the ancient Greeks. We are in a clash of philosophies as to how humans should think and live their lives. This was not a problem in isolated communities, where one's world extended to a river, a grove of trees, or a mountain range. That has all changed and we are threatened with new ideas, concepts, and spiritual awareness. We are into the politics of truth and a struggle for power over people, territory, and resources.

Because none of the monotheistic traditions (Judaism, Christianity, and Islam) can prove their stories as historical, unambiguous fact, there is great tension and insecurity about the continuation of their beliefs. People and groups will kill and persecute any or all who point to different truths. Social scientists can understand the processes and the psychology involved, and simply from an anthropological perspective all is as it should be—this is what humans do. We cling to life, we eat and engage in sex to maintain life, and we need to be accepted at some level in the group. Clinging to life at the biological level is the same as clinging to one's beliefs at the social level. When groups are separated geographically with little information flow between them, this is a local problem. In today's world, however, clinging to life means clinging to one's philosophies and myths. It is difficult to maintain mythic themes in the midst of rapid technological change, which, in itself, prompts very different views of the world. The advances in science over the past 150 years are mind-boggling and have cast doubt upon and negate the very foundations of Judaism, Christianity, and Islam. When you begin your assumption that two and two equals five, what follows is merely an elaboration on a false assumption.

The world, thus, is poised between a paradigm promoting a logical/rational approach to cause and effect on the one hand (Greek), and the competing model that promotes a more magical/irrational approach to life and its meaning (Judaism, Christianity, and Islam) on the other. This is as things should be; such opposition is normal and identifiable in daily life. What appears to be happening in the world today is polarity, with those heavily invested in the logical/rational approach aligning against those more magical/irrational belief systems. These paradigms are incompatible; therefore, these are perilous times. Let me make clear that neither approach is good or bad, right or wrong. These are simply ways of approaching explanations of what and who we are. To clarify the two paradigms in the pages below means saying things that some will applaud, while others will feel offended. Some will say that I am being disrespectful to the people who uphold these monotheistic traditions; this is not true. However, I have no respect for these pseudo-religious or political systems in themselves, for to have respect would mean that I condone lying, deception, and the use of emotional and physical violence as a method of instilling and maintaining certain archaic and medieval beliefs and practices. Moreover, the scholars—historians, biblical scholars, and so on—have neglected to factor in the use of mind-altering drugs as creating the inspiration for the storyline in both the Bible and Qur'an. Had these same scholars tasted the powerful experience that goes with these drugs, we would have a very different perspective on the development of Western civilization and most certainly on our understanding of Judaism, Christianity, and Islam.

Introduction

Humanity is awakening from a long, long sleep; our awakening began between six and two and a half MYA (Million Years Ago). This awakening involved a specific type of consciousness (or a significant part of it) that allowed us to participate in nature much the same as other animals. But it also allowed us to step back from nature and become active participants (see Rush 1996). We take ideas from nature and incorporate them into our culture, as evidenced by our science and technology. Stone knives, watercraft, fire, the wheel, aircraft, and spaceships all represent analogues in nature. All that we know and all that we experience come from nature—even our gods, which represent aspects of nature that we did not or do not understand. Other animals participate in nature and some make and use tools, but we actively participate in everything through our magic, religion, and science. We even participate in that which cannot be known with our current knowledge base and probably our intelligence as well. Through active participation we stand back and observe the environment and classify everything; we are all scientists in that respect, deeply involved in the scientific process. Everything has to have a name and/or purpose. We step back from our everyday world of work, school, eating, sex, and so on, and examine it. We ask, "Why does it rain? Why does the sun rise? Why do I get an erection? How does a seed grow into a tree? Who am I? Where did I come from? What will happen when I die?"

"Why" questions open possibilities, for without speculation there are no stories to tell. We get into trouble when our stories stagnate and fracture away from the demands of the moment or the world as it is today. They become remnants, potshards of an ancient time, and once fractured they can never come back together in their original form. Judaism, Christianity, and Islam are fractured traditions clinging to life. Good examples of fractured traditions altering and changing in order to stay alive are some of the ultra-liberal protestant groups, who bring into their services entertainers, musicians, comedians, and famous speakers. They draw a crowd because no one is cramming Jesus down people's throats; for the most part, their services are a celebration of life. Of course they charge a fee, just like you pay a fee to go to the movies or the California State Fair. This approach to the "spiritual" is likely to continue into the twenty-second century because it is entertaining, more personal, accords the individual a great deal of freedom, and certainly does not tell people what to think with the threat of hellfire, damnation, and/or physical violence. Many ministers and some priests have taken a more philosophical approach to the meaning of Christ, rather than seeing the death and resurrection of Jesus as a historical fact. Unless Islam radically reforms its story and repents its own sins, it will not move into the twenty-second century. Of course, Judaism is unlikely to reform much further from where it is. Judaism is not a proselytizing system, does not desire converts, and just wants to be left alone in the land of "milk and honey," least they acquire a spiritual disease.

The Stories We Tell

By first using proto-language and eventually language as we know it today, we have been telling stories about ourselves and the universe within which we live for at least 50,000 years (see Bickerton 1990; Klein and Edgar 2002), and perhaps a million or more years before that (see Rush 1996). We tell stories about who, what, where, and how. Until recent times, our stories were in step with what we understood about nature. Thunder and lightening were gods at war with each other or pissed at the sinful and wicked, you and me. You might wonder why an all-knowing god would create such wicked, evil animals. In any event, few people in the Western world would seriously believe that thunder, lightening, earthquakes, and so on are anything more than natural, explainable, reproducible (at least in miniature) events, rather than God waging war with sinful humans. So we have a different story, but many people believe very seriously that natural events depicted in the Bible *were* supernatural, caused by a god to deal with unruly humans. Similar events today get connected to a different story, more in line with what we understand about the world around us. With a proper introduction to science prior to any religious indoctrination, few people would accept what is presented as truth by contemporary monotheists and pagans alike. There have been recent attempts to teach intelligent design (creationism) in public schools, but when asked if biologists could teach evolution in bible schools, the answer is clearly and violently "No." Most religious clerics, because it is their livelihood, take the supernatural very seriously and see evil as an entity that controls our actions. For example, the pope recently exonerated Hitler by emphatically stating that poor little Adolph was possessed by the Devil! Harry Potter enthusiasts are possessed by the Devil as well. Failing to understand our basic animal nature, the pope thinks that all evil is a product of demonic activity—"The devil made me do it." The pope neglected to mention that the Harry Potter series has created a renaissance in reading among young and old alike. As we will see, literacy is a problem for despots because literate people might read things that question religious/political authority and privilege. Censorship is a major priority in Christianity and Islam, just as it is in theocratic, communistic, and fascist governments. Although Judaism, Christianity, and Islam are political systems, they are certainly not democracies.

Humans, like all other hunting, gathering, and predatory animals, must, in some way, classify and organize the universe around them. We find patterns in nature and/or invent them. These patterns include the rising and setting of the sun, the phases of the moon, the seasons of the year, and so on. A reasonable thinking person would conclude that there must be something that controls the patterns, for just as a person can throw a stone, break a branch, or otherwise alter the landscape (micro-patterns), a more powerful entity can lift the sun in the sky. Or such an entity can carve the moon in concentric rings, similar to the way concentric flakes were removed from stone cores to produce the stone tools of our ancient ancestors. The early stories about why, what, where, how, and who were necessary for us to organize our world and take an active part in it. As time went on the stories became more and more complex, mirroring the cultural systems that invented them, from hunter-gatherers and their organization of the world, all the way to nation-states and the need to control the energy of people for building hydraulic and temple projects. Again, the beliefs and practices tend to coincide with technology and our beliefs about cause and effect.

Rapid technological change, however, and different ideas about cause and effect, have brought many of the old stories into doubt. Systems maintaining these stories, such as fundamental Judaism, Christianity, and Islam, can only thrive in a climate of ignorance. Because of the competing metaphor presented by the scientific community, this has led to a great deal of insecurity. Both Islam and Christianity turned away from science because science opens the door to more questions. Questions eventually lead to analyzing our beliefs about where we come from; questions generate new questions about old ideas, and this is very, very dangerous for the maintenance of fundamental monotheistic traditions. Judaism, unlike Christianity and Islam, never actively attempted to shut off critical thinking and curiosity. They have, however, maintained that portion of the myth, which, through a covenant with a deity, gives them special privileges, land holdings, and an attitude of superiority for which they are despised. This tells us something about human nature, about something deep in our psyches. We are a small-group animal; we do not like the difference that status brings. For hunter-gatherers, leadership was contingent on who was best, who was respected for his/her opinion, or perhaps who owned the rabbit net. For hunter-gatherers, there are as many levels of status as people to fill them. Division of labor was by sex, age, experience, and perhaps expertise. We lived in this type of an arrangement for at least a million years. So when people show up and claim to be superior to all others "because we are Daddy's favorite children," this is not a measurable or reasonable statement. "You think you are superior, prove it!" So we go about beating each other up. Identity as a people is the base of the Jewish family tree; this is a political tradition and not a religion. But in a larger sense, the story of creation has to be true; we materialized out of something, but creation is a little more complicated than the overly simplistic notions presented in the Bible and Qur'an. Most people, when asked outside a religious context, do not believe that there is a god in the clouds with a white beard and a nasty disposition. This image alters with Jesus, of course, but most fundamentalists insist on this image of wrathful power because it represents obedience to authority—*male* authority, *their* authority. This is part of the storyline added after the mythic hero Jesus was murdered by the Romans. Jesus was saying some interesting things; his method of delivery was very different from that presented in the Old Testament, more similar to that of a Buddhist monk. In the Old Testament you are told not to do this, not to do that, to do this on certain days, and on this day do nothing. Then there is what to eat, when to eat, with whom you can eat, the clothes you should wear, and on and on. This emphasis on explicit rules changes in the New Testament. Instead of "Thou shall not," you get a story indirectly telling you not to sin and cause problems for others: "Eat what you want, just be a decent human being."

Science proposes questions that raise doubts about the validity of the older stories, a god in the sky to whom one should submit, creation in six days, and so on. The politics and economics connected to these stories is such that those who run these systems will do what is necessary—censorship, shunning, deception, persecution, torture, and murder—in order to maintain their power over body and soul. These systems, medieval in content, attempt to spin-doctor scientific explanations. Do things really change and evolve, or is this illusion and scientific fraud? Are we simply products of evolution like all organic life, or is there something more divine and special that separates us from the other plants and animals? When we die, will we really go to hell because we do not accept Jesus as our savior or Allah as our god? These are important questions, and they have been answered with stories told, retold, modified, amplified, and simplified over the millennia. Just like biological evolution, these stories change. This is inevitable for Islam as well; they evolve to fit the times, even under great protest.

Stories are clusters of symbols designed to direct our energies in a way similar to how clusters of genes direct our biological development. Our stories bring people to social action, just as genes bring us to physical action. Because our stories have this power (as does DNA), there must be something inherent in the symbols themselves. Symbols in this sense have a life of their own. The ancient Egyptians understood the literal power of symbols; the Pharaoh issued an edict and it was acted upon—"So it is written, so it shall be"—and all the images/symbols on the tomb walls could come to life. I pick up a book, turn to the first page, and magically I'm in touch with the author. Symbols can protect and encourage the mind to explore the universe. But they can likewise oppress and imprison, especially when our stories are out of step with the world as it is. When such stories are not recalibrated, they *fracture* with those groups adhering to certain parts of the storyline, while others have their favorites. These groups attempt to maintain the relevance of their storyline in today's world—often violently. Any "religion" within which the stories originated eventually morphed from a personal experience with the deity to a political system designed to control the minds and energies of the populace. Judaism, Christianity, and Islam have never been religions systems; they were born and raised as political entities with a paper-thin religions veneer, with their gods having an unquestionable right to rule.

Evolution: Storytelling and the Explanation of Life

Stories evolve just as biological life evolves, and this is a significant problem for monotheists with their texts representing the revealed word of God. If these stories changed from their originals in any way, it removes the possibility that they represent the divine and unalterable word from an infallible god. Even Muhammad said, "New prophecies replaced old prophecies."

Moreover, if we can find similar myths connected to surrounding cultural groups, this suggests sharing, diffusion, borrowing, and reworking to meet sociopolitical needs. It is difficult (not impossible) for fundamentalists to draw the connection between a myth and its political analogue ("as above, below"). Most Christians, when reading the Lords Prayers (Matthew 6:9–13), don't seem to comprehend the meaning of the second line:

> Our Father who art in heaven, Hallowed be thy name.
> Thy kingdom come. Thy will be done on earth as [it is] in
>   heaven.
> Give us this day our daily bread . . .

"Thy kingdom come. Thy will be done on earth as [it is] in heaven."
This means that there is a heaven-based world constructed out of papier-mâché and glitter by priest-poets, and the earth-based world is obliged to be a mirror of this. That is to say, priest-kings envision the sacred geography of heaven, and because of their power to tell people what to think, this sacred geography is transplanted to the world of humans. "The sun does its duty, the moon does the same, and so should you!" The priests then invent duties and, at the same time, attempt to secure their own future through the exclusion of non-relatives or those without some genealogical connection or technological/artistic worth. They construct a mythical charter (politics begins early) validating their right to rule. From ancient Mesopotamia and Egypt and right up to the present, we find charters connecting back to a patron deity who perhaps brought them to this place, paid special favors to a group in war, or helped in some other manner. This connection to or interface with the deity can be by way of a "chosen people," as in the case of the Hebrews, by way of seduction of a mortal by a god (Mary's "virgin birth"), as is the case with Jesus, and through submission and slavery to a deity, as in the case of Muhammad and Islam. You need a royal connection, time depth, and the chosen deity on your side. The "deity taking our side" is the religious veneer in Judaism, Christianity, and Islam; all the ritual (praying, washing, etc.) is calculated political action encasing the individual's mind in an inescapable story-net that follows him or her to the hereafter. Pulling the weeds and thorny brambles sown by these traditions, especially when the indoctrination is early and intense, is near impossible and will require a monumental event. Logic and reason are of little use.

The first kings evolved from warrior chiefs and/or magician priests (shamans), and, in some cases, the warrior chief and magician-priest might rule as co-equals (e.g., Moses and Aaron). In either fashion, a mythic charter adds credibility. The warrior chief articulates with the secular world through the advice of the magician priest, who communes with the supernatural world. In these early dynasties, "as above, below" was the mantra that justified maintaining the status quo. Then we add the concept of succession, father to son, which makes this process a static "given," for just as the god never dies, neither does the king— "The King is dead. Long live the King." Mythical charters and succession also hold true for the early mother-goddess cults. This does not mean that women were accorded a higher status than men. In fact, we don't exactly know about the status of women in these traditions (see Eller 2000; Godison and Morris 1998). What we know is that when the male energy predominates, the female energy becomes less and less important, and when we encounter monotheism the female energy is sublimated or eliminated. Monotheism can be defined as an exclusive emphasis on the male energy. We know that the status of women in ancient Egypt was relatively high, and this is, no doubt, connected in some way to years and years of stability with everyone "employed." Those immense building projects controlled the minds and bodies of Egyptians year after year. The point, however, is that stability promotes an equality between male and female energies around which the universe revolves. Let me begin my storytelling with how anthropologists conceptualize social organization of early human groups and how this relates to magical-religious thinking.

Hunter-Gatherers

Modern humans emerge in Africa around 130 KYA (Thousand Years Ago). One of the defining characteristics of modern humans is the presence of a chin. It isn't brain power or the presence of religion, but the chin. Why the chin? Well, we do not rely on our jaws and contiguous muscles as we once did. Beginning with *Homo habilis* and *Homo erectus*, tools are used more and more frequently, rather than strictly teeth, to process food. Heavy jaws and large molars are not necessary for processing when roots and tubers can be chopped up and eaten in small portions. Mutations promoting smaller jaws and teeth would survive and pass on to succeeding generations. Teeth are very important in tracking human evolution because they are conservative in shape and cusp pattern, and usually last longer than other parts of the body. As our jaws decreased in size with a corresponding flattening of the face (as the skull case becomes more rounded), we still support some pretty powerful chewing muscles. A chin would appear to be a crimping of bone to add strength. Creationists say that humans as they are today were zapped into existence, chin and all, with no precedents, as was the case for all life on this planet. Evolution, according to creationist philosophy, is to be seen as an illusion constructed by science to test faith. The problem creationist-intelligent design people face is that we have the physical remains—our relics, if you will—and their significance is grounded in self-correcting science.

But just as we have physical evolution, we have social evolution. For probably six million years or more, hominids (bipeds) lived in small groups or bands that scavenged for food, with the individual consuming what he or she collected. Around two and a half MYA our ancestors added stone tools and meat scavenging to their lifestyles, a style of living that lasted for over two million years. Around 300 KYA we see a change in technology (the throwing spear), and now hunting is added to scavenging and gathering. Hunter-gatherers, at least from our understanding of contemporary groups, are small bands, perhaps twenty-five to one hundred individuals, who do not see themselves as much different from the animals they are killing and eating. There are few of these nomadic groups existing in the world today, but they are good models for small-group behavior (50 +/- individuals). Each member is a carrier of the culture and all are in face-to-face contact on a day-to-day basis. There are few levels of status, no full-time specialists, and no strangers. This level of social organization leads to stories that connect the individual and the group to animal ancestors. This is an early form of evolution, with our ancient ancestors evolving from animal forms—the wolf, lion, and so on. We see remnants of this thinking when we name our football and other sports teams after ancient "ancestors" who represent power. Hunter-gatherers do not have prophets, sin-atoning saviors, priests, or popes. The question is, "Why not?" The answer lies in the fact that hunter-gatherers do not live in stratified societies, and saviors, popes, mullahs, priests, temples and mosques do not fit this level of social organization. They do not need all these trappings in their world; their explanations and rituals work for them. What we call "Western Religions" today are in reality political systems designed to control the populace through judgment and fear; hunter-gatherers have little need for such micromanagement.

Hunter-gatherers, however, have part-time specialists, generally called *shamans,* who act as conduits between the living and the supernatural world. Here is the origin of what original religion was all about, that is, personal and group contact and identity with the energy that informs all.

Our early ancestors were animists who personified unseen forces (wind, lightning, rain, etc.) and worshipped ancestors. It is well known that shamans often use hallucinogenic plants and mushrooms to commune with unseen forces, and the use of these plants, perhaps more than anything else, served to validate a world beyond—a spirit world unseen yet connected to the workings of the world as they knew it. If you have never been on a guided trip with a mind-altering plant or mushroom, you cannot appreciate how powerful the experience can be.

The animals they hunted—the deer, pig, elk, and so on—were respected and thanked, for not to do so could result in the animal's spirit enacting revenge on the hunter. He could be attacked in his sleep, made ill, or perhaps injured during the next hunt. This way of life and magical thinking was the human condition for hundreds of thousands of years. Why had these people not found Jesus? Why were these people from the beginning not building temples and mosques and bowing down to Yahweh and Allah? Contrary to the Islamic community, who claim that only Allah has existed forever ("the religion before Allah is Islam"), these types of deities can only materialize out of stress-ridden, state-based societies, and these are comparatively recent.

The types of stories a little more familiar to us emerge around ten KYA (and at varying times all over the world) with the development of sedentary agriculture. The idea of agriculture, or planting seeds and protecting plants, is a time-honored practice, and probably dates to the late Paleolithic (13–12,000 BCE—Before Current Era). The first to do this were shamans, probably female, who experimented (through analogy with their own bodies) with seeds. Hunter-gatherers usually do not stay in one spot unless game and other provisions are readily available. Planting seeds in diverse areas would allow a shaman or healer some predictability as to where certain plants will be found. One of the easiest shamanic plants to grow over a vast geography is cannabis, and its use in a variety of medicinal procedures and magical practices is very old and well documented.

Sedentary Agriculture

No one is sure who was first to take a plant out of its natural setting and make the connection between burying seeds in the ground in anticipation of new plants, but it certainly did not one day materialize with people clearing land and planting crops. I do like the shaman story above, however. The primary stage—an experimental stage—probably had more to do with specific plants not used for food but instead for altering consciousness, communing with the gods, or medicinal purposes (see Johns 1999; Rudgley 1994; Devereux 1997; McKenna 1992). In fact, the development of more extensive agricultural pursuits in Southeast Asia and the Middle East may have had more to do with attracting and feeding sheep, goats, and fowl rather than for human consumption. Moreover, as suggested by many anthropologists, the use of mind-altering substances was a pivot point for developing more elaborate myths and rituals regarding supernatural forces and entities (see McKenna 1992; Rush 1996, 2007).

Sedentary agricultural is a shift in behavior from a less secure nomadic existence to one wherein plants are moved from one location and transplanted in well-watered areas where they can be tended and selected, the original Garden of Eden. Animal husbandry, as suggested above, is closely connected to agriculture and begins at about the same time. We also encounter a different story or myth relating the people to the land, animals, and forces of nature. Both transplanting plants and tending animals, as mentioned, have their beginnings among hunter-gatherers.

Animal husbandry may have been modeled after the domestication of the dog from various canine species, and the model for transplanting is possibly connected to the cultivation and use of cannabis (or some other very useful plant). Sedentary people tend to worship what is local—a special rock, a tree, or a stream, and of course the sun, moon, and stars, because they appear locally (and predictably) as well. The moon and stars become connected to ritual events—especially planting and harvesting—because of their predictability, which must have been observed for over one million years. The ability of our ancient hunting-gathering ancestors to predict animal migrations through the movements of the sun, moon, and stars would have great survival value, as it creates predictability.

Agricultural people rely upon the fertility of nature for survival, and their magical beliefs revolve around calendrical systems and the gods and goddesses associated with the daily, monthly, and yearly rounds. Out of this evolve cosmic laws created by the priest-kings; their beliefs and relationship to nature is very different from that of hunter-gatherers. Cults emphasizing fertility, no doubt carried over from earlier people, and the mother-goddess as well as male gods, were prominent. Both represented the forces of nature. You and/or your family would be involved in the practical, daily, and personal (health, progeny, and crop fertility) worship or recognition of specific patron deities, with the spiritual connection reached through group (multi-family) mystery initiation rites of one type or another. These are the rites of passage and intensification also carried over from our hunter-gatherer ancestors but inflected to meet the new symbolic needs of the community. Mystery cults were common in the Mediterranean area throughout the Greek and Roman period, only subsiding with Constantine (330 CE—Current Era) and then Theodosius the Great (386 CE). After Theodosius, who banned all non-Catholic traditions, these esoteric rites were available to only a special few, while disallowed groups took their rites and rituals underground.

Going from hunting and gathering to agriculture requires a new myth or storyline for directing the energies of the group. In the hunting-gathering tradition the animals hunted represented life, and at some point there is a recognition that the animals had to be respected or they would not return. Hunting, and the sacrifice it represents, is dangerous and uncertain. This is the origin, I believe, of the covenant or sacred relationship between the group and animals so they would return. This was later transferred to ancestors and then finally to powerful, less personal creator beings, for example, Abraham's covenant with Yahweh (personal) or Moses with the Plant God (more impersonal). It seems that the more we learn about the world around us through science, the less personal the deity becomes. Which brings us to *Neteru* of the Egyptian and *Atman* of the Hindu; the power that informs this universe cannot be named and is as impersonal as impersonal can be.

The myth connected to hunting and gathering changes in a more sedentary and food-secure environment, and out of this emerges the idea that out of death (planting "dead" seeds) comes life, and the more death you create the more life you can support. This leads to human and animal sacrifice, as well as wrathful gods and sin-atoning saviors. Why? Here is my story.

Around ten KYA little communities begin to emerge in the Tigris-Euphrates River valleys. Originally based on extended family groups, they tended to collect in areas capable of sustaining many people per acre. In these areas crops were originally grown to attract and feed animals, as they had continued their old ways of hunting, but instead of going to the animals the animals now came to the hunters. The origins of agriculture had more to do with continuing a way of life but changing the rules. These hunter-agriculturists must have learned early on that by blowing one's breath (several times a day for several days) into the nostrils of a baby dog, sheep, or goat, the animal fixates on you just as he would its mother. This knowledge was gained and lost over the millennia. This may be one of the connections to the "breath of life," as found in the ancient Egyptian and Hebrew texts.

Humans cannot eat grains without processing, and only with great difficulty could a modern human eat enough dry grain, processing it with his teeth and jaws, to sustain life. Try it. Your jaw muscles will be extremely tired after grinding up enough grain to derive perhaps fifty to sixty calories, with most of the grain passing through your alimentary system unchanged. If you have ever eaten corn-on-the-cob, you know that to which I refer. You would expend more energy than you received in return and starve to death in a field of grain. The use of grain as human foodstuffs was a lucky accident, as most anthropologists would agree. Perhaps grain storage pits filled with water and grain were allowed to soak for a while, perhaps a day or so. The sheep or goats might still consume it in this form, but children most certainly experimented—they put everything in their mouths at least once. This isn't bread yet—bread is a complicated issue because it means combining nature. So, the first use of grain for human consumption was a gruel that the children probably experimented with. Perhaps you would take a handful of soaked gruel and throw it at your friend. Or press it into a ball-shape and let it dry in the hot sun; this could lead to a sort of hardtack. Then again, if you threw the gruel into a fire, the result was an instant cracker. Certainly this gruel, if left past a few days, would ferment, and eating it would lead to slight intoxication, or at least until they started boiling the grains to speed up the process of softening the protective coating. This altered consciousness would lead to a story or explanation, and raise grains to the status of "food of the gods." The connection of bread to *manna* must date back to this early time period. But there are different types of "breads" and different types of manna, as we will see, all leading to the same result—that is, communion with the gods.

By pressing the liquid from fermented grain, you could then dry the mush by placing it in the sun or on rocks in a fire, and then you have crackers or cake. The liquid could then be consumed by itself, with the bitter taste probably more appealing to children because of its connection to fermented dried milk or the mother's breast. Beer is born.

Eventually we learn how to grind dried grain to make flour, which was mixed with water and either immediately (or perhaps after sitting a while) baked in the form of little thin cakes on rocks in a fire. With this you get unleavened bread. Eventually, perhaps by accident, animal fat was added—probably because early bakers learned that bread dough sticks to everything, but when you add fat the dough does not as easily stick to your hands or the rocks. Yeast is ubiquitous, so with the ground grain, water, and animal fat, all that is required is a little heat from the sun for the bread to rise and an easier to eat product emerges. We also know from the ancient Egyptians that wherever there is a bakery, next door is a brewery.

Agriculture can support more people per square mile than hunting-gathering, and this results in a number of unexpected problems (population growth being one of them) and changes in the storyline. One unique problem is that all members of the group are not in face-to-face contact on a day-to-day basis. Face-to-face contact on a day-to-day basis is a most effective method of social control and curbing deviance. As face-to-face contact decreases, the probability of deviant behavior increases; this type of personal contact decreases rapidly as groups increase in size past 150 individuals. Moreover, there are strangers in town—other family groups engaged in the same agricultural pursuits. This results in social stress (murders, rape, land disputes, etc.) and pushes into existence another type of politics. Now remember, these people I'm discussing were very, very superstitious, which in itself has a profound effect on behavior. But more than superstition is necessary. Strong leaders emerge (some were certainly bullies) and invent for themselves a mythical charter, giving them privilege, a right to lead, and the use of supernatural sanctions or perhaps force to discourage "deviant" behavior. These leaders in many cases were the shamans of the hunting-gathering tradition. They were, for the most part, respected individuals who presented themselves as models of behavior and acted as mirrors for all to see. As the leader moved throughout the community, he or she communicated the rules for all to follow, even though all were not in face-to-face contact on a day-to-day basis. This individual, or perhaps a number of family members, would help resolve disputes or help work through crises symbolically, using ritual rather than with physical violence. In this experimental stage, the destruction of a neighbor's crop (either maliciously or by the will of the gods) or murder could be disastrous for the whole community, and thus social accord was a necessity. Communal rituals and marriages also kept social chaos at a minimum. We see a type of morality that spontaneously arises from social necessity and biological survival. There have to be agreed upon rules of relationships (see Rush 1999); no deity need apply.

Mythical charters—essentially ancestor worship and the privileges that go with having *special* ancestors—are the model upon which modern religions/political systems are based; that is, a cosmic pantheon as a representation or extension of the ruling king and/or priest. Mythical charters, once in place, ritualized, and accepted by the populous, validate a bloodline of kings, queens, and sheiks, and invalidate anyone else's claim to the throne or interpretation of the will of deities. Rules of succession are absolutely necessary because bumpy transitions result in massive social stress. Mythical charters and the right to rule—this is the politics of truth. Just as kings judge subjects, so the gods judge humans—through the kings. This is a very powerful method of control, and anyone who doubts this need only look at the influence religion has on politics today, especially in the United States and the Middle East. Mythical charters reflect the body politic and justify its existence. Myth connected to time depth equals legitimacy, especially when there are ancient written records, for these are the "tangible" laws of the ancestors. And, because they are in print, they must be true—"So it is written, so it shall be." The inequities in these systems are well known. In most of these systems the individual is trapped at some level, usually in the poor, lower classes. This breeds resentment, and there is the inevitable challenge with word, sword, or both. Judaism, Christianity, and Islam grew out of extreme social stress. All constructed mythical charters as their means of promoting legitimacy, and all used violence, including torture and murder of innocent men, women, and children, to obtain compliance in the name of their deity. As we will see, these are irrational, contradictory systems that place a deity before humanity, keeping people in bondage to a god-tyrant (Yahweh, God, and Allah) through the religious clerics (rabbi, popes, priests, imams, etc.) who act as interpreters of the deity's will. In Judaism, Christianity, and Islam, God is more important than human decency.

With respect to Middle Eastern traditions, there is another factor. Agricultural people usually have ties to nomadic, herding people. They evolve from a similar base, and early divisions of labor keep one group sedentary and the other—out of necessity, because of a lack of land—tending sheep, goats, and cattle. Nomadic people need specific goods available in the urban areas (metal tools, pottery, etc.) while the agriculturalists need products that are not grown or produced locally (leather, herbs, mushrooms, wool, cannabis, frankincense, henbane, myrrh, precious stones, etc.). There comes a time, however, when herding people run out of land or desire a different lifestyle, and they raid these city states, decimate the population, and take over. Beginning around 2400 BCE in the Middle East, we detect a different brand of polytheism—one that promotes a male deity who is at least co-equal with the mother-goddess, but who could also preside over all the others. Eventually, in the Western traditions, the male energy is placed on top and the female at the bottom of the celestial and social hierarchy.

Herding people worship what is everywhere—the sun, moon, stars, clouds, and wind—and have a patriarchal base because the male element predominates. Males are tending the flocks, actively protecting against predators, and defending territories; these are warrior people. Although polytheistic, the main deity is usually male. The hierarchy resembles the social hierarchy. Each group (hunter-gatherers, agriculturalists, and herding people) has different myths intimately connected to how they relate to the land and each other. Evolving out of the Middle East, with the collision of sedentary agricultural and nomadic herding people, we morph from a mother-goddess to a patriarchal emphasis. This patriarchal polytheistic emphasis eventually gave rise to the dualistic-monotheistic traditions, represented by Zoroastrianism, Judaism, Christianity, and Islam, with a matching political system and male ruler or king at the top—as above, below. These systems are based upon a male, authoritarian figure who accepts nothing less than complete submission—as does the king, pope, mullah, priest, or other religious cleric. Monotheism means an accentuation of the male energy, not that there is only one god.

Review

Hunter-gatherers tend to worship direct ancestors of a generation or so back and spiritual ancestors who go back much further. Why ancestors? Well, at one time they were gods; they picked us up, carried us around, taught us valuable things, and then went to another place. Humans miss the passing of close relatives, but also pay respect to ancestors of many generations back—the ancestors of the ancestors. There are evil spirits—the ancestors forgotten—and the good spirits, or those more recently departed, all of whom manifest themselves in the form of wind, storm, drought, illness, health, fertility, and in more personal characteristics. Ancestors are often traced back to other animal forms—for example, the big cats (the leopard and lion), the hunting dog, fox, wolf, wolverine, or crow, which represent an interesting connection to modern concepts of evolution. Population pressures and other environmental factors force these groups to periodically split, either through mutual agreement or stress and strife. And, whether peaceful or violent, this enters into the culture's mythic storyline, a trail built, maintained, and altered over the millennium.

Some of these hunter-gatherers become herding-nomadic people, while others learn to alter the growing pattern of plants (and animals) and remain more or less sedentary. Herding-nomadic people take what is in front of them, just as do their sheep, goats, horses, and cattle; agricultural people take what they produce from the land. The psychology of the herding-nomadic people is very different from that of farmers; anyone can pick a fruit or harvest grain, but not everyone can kill a bull or another human being.

Sedentary agriculturalists feed more people per acre than herding people, and thus populations tend to concentrate in specific geographical areas usually connected to immediate water sources. Increased population demands a different governing body, because strife and conflict can undermine the cooperation necessary between specialists and strangers. To avoid chaos and mayhem, explicit rules and regulations are created, usually sent by a deity (Shamash, Yahweh), a third, more powerful person with whom no one can argue, along with a mythical charter making legitimate who should lead and why people should follow.

Shamans of old become the priest-kings, who interpret the super-natural forces and the will of the gods and then transfer this to the body politic—as above, below, "Thy will (will of the god) be done on earth as it is in heaven." (Matthew 6:10). These priest-kings were intelligent people with a desire to stay in power; they had many secrets. They knew how to predict the positions of the stars and planets and commune with the gods. By accurately predicting celestial activity, they gained credibility and power. If Brophy (2002) is correct in his analysis of the Nabta Playa, a megalithic calendar circle located one hundred km west of Abu Simbel in southern Egypt and dated to 6–5000 BCE, knowledge for predicting celestial alignment emerged more than twenty-five KYA. In any event, the priest kings developed mythical charters that gave them the right to rule, as ordained by deities in charge of such matters. If "as above, below," then a ruler necessarily needs a great deal of support staff to help run all this; temple bureaucracies emerge and writing is invented to keep track of taxes levied to pay for upkeep of rulers and bureaucracies.

Nomadic-herding people feature a male deity on top with lesser deities below but, unlike the sedentary agriculturalists, their power structure is represented by councils and not impersonal bureaucrats.

The religious traditions existing in the world today can be seen as developing or evolving from ancestor and nature worship, with little need for social control mechanisms beyond daily face-to-face contact, to abstract and formalized systems with councils or bureaucracies. Once a system is built it takes on a life of its own; it becomes an entity, some-thing seemingly quite tangible (this is what a corporation is). Because there are priests and kings, this is "proof" that the constructed deities to whom they point (deities in the heavens or underworld) must also be tangible and real.

Few people in the Western world believe that there is an all-powerful male deity, with white beard and terrible disposition, who created all we experience. In the past this was considered historical truth, with a starting point of creation October 23, 4004 BCE. Fundamental Christians maintain this as historical fact. Traditions that direct our primal urges do not change rapidly. Nonetheless, in the Western world the image of this deity, or energy, has gone from faith and tradition, to challenge, change, and a story better suited to our time and technology. The story has become less personal and in some cases much more abstract and marvelously detailed, with interrelated correlations and mathematical computations. These are normal changes in the interpretation of the mystery of life and death, as new technologies and freedom of thought open to more and more possibilities.

Science and Religion

Within the Western scientific paradigm, any phenomenon has to be repeatable, verifiable, and quantifiable before accepted as fact. The social sciences (anthropology in this case) teeter on the edge of science, feeding back information to the sciences (math, physics, genetics, etc.) for verification or explanation. Virgin births, people coming back from the dead, people communing with extra-somatic (outside the body) spirits, and miracles are not repeatable, verifiable, and quantifiable. It is not that these experiences do not happen, but the *onus of proof lies on the shoulders of those who make such claims.* This is a problem: if you have enough power, you can turn this 180 degrees and lay the "prove that it didn't happen" at the feet of science. So, in these Western traditions (Judaism, Christianity, Islam) any claim can be made as fact, and anyone who disagrees is being insensitive and has to prove these supernatural things did not happen. Supernatural claims lie at the edge of the social sciences and in the Land of the Unknown. One has to take on faith some pretty outrageous, absurd, and preposterous events depicted in the Bible and Qur'an.

Fundamentalists, seeing a discoloration below the eyes of a statue of the Virgin Mary, prostrate themselves before God. The scientist, on the other hand, looks above the image and notices the pigeons on the roof. Monotheistic traditions are not systems wrapped around critical thinking; when read as historical fact, they are systems of ignorance and worse. They stifle thought and critical thinking, and in their place substitute faith and absolute submission to a deity. This is the same methodology of magicians and charlatans using slight of word and slight of hand. Anthropologists, psychologists, and historians have explained supernatural beliefs as emerging within contexts of emotional and social needs, and the necessity to organize life and death with a story. This organization becomes politicized and wrapped around power over people and resources, and, in order to sustain the status quo, these traditions resort to fear, threat, deception, and violence. So, we are on a ledge from which we can go up and attain that which we desire (peace, prosperity, and a platform to the stars), or we can jump into the abyss and continue wrangling over the will of an imaginary deity, the number of angels that can fit on the head of a pin, and who can legitimately interpret God's will. In today's world, this is absolutely absurd.

As a young child, I would catch fireflies with my brother and sister. This meant staying up until dark, patiently sitting and waiting for the first wee lights of the evening, and then going toward the illumination and capturing the lights in a jar. After catching several, the lid (with holes) was fit on top of the jar, and the jar set on the porch until morning. I remember being all excited the next morning, imagining I would see perhaps a sixty-watt Westinghouse light bulb or two in the jar. Instead, there were two or three brown bugs and no light. Perhaps the wrong bugs flew into the jar as we were putting on the lid, so stuck was I to my belief. So we would try again the next night—same result. Finally father revealed to us that fireflies have special glands that produce cold, chemical light—illumination of a different sort. Without understanding cause and effect, we can find ourselves in the dark looking at fireflies and telling ourselves stories. We have been doing this for thousands of years and will continue to do so, because this is part of what humans do as a means of organizing experiences and selling these interpretations to others. Our stories tell us about the physical world, relationships between people, and the nature of the supernatural world, or what I refer to as "spiritual taphonomy" (see Rush 2007). When these stories are fractured and out of step with an enlightened world, they are dangerous, for fractured "truth" can only be sold through intimidation and violence.

Storytelling

Storytelling is as old as our species. Stories are constructed to emphasize special aspects of our lives, including birth, how one should relate to deities, nature, strangers, and the living, and certainly death. The original stories were orally transmitted and would, one might suppose, stay in tune with technology, cultural stressors, and so on. Some authors suggest that stories or myths can be transmitted orally over the generations with little or no change, especially if the stories are sung as were the Psalms of the Old Testament and the Qur'an (Pelikan 2005). It is highly unlikely, however, that no changes would creep in, especially with the occurrence of political, economic, and socially significant events (and, of course, senility on the part of the storyteller).

With the advent of writing, these stories were transcribed on walls, clay tablets, papyrus, leather, and linen, which tend to freeze their content. Because there were few scribes and still fewer literate people, changes could be made to stories, myths, and mythical charters as time went on and when new circumstances presented themselves. Sacred literature could keep up and reflect prevailing beliefs and technology. Judaism, Christianity, and Islam, however, are experiencing one of the down sides of written language. When there are only a few hand-copied manuscripts in existence, scribes can control the content of recopied documents. Papyrus and other types of media, such as leaves and animal hides, wear out and have to be recopied over and over. But we make mistakes, and the simple change in the ending of a word could push the meaning of the thought in a totally different direction.

The point is that with only a few books available and few scribes to copy them, current situations would be added in and obsolete ones removed. When this is the case, the documents can keep up with and refer to prevailing conditions, situations, new ideas, or interpretations within the realm of spiritual taphonomy. We see this in the Yemeni parchments—fragments from 1,000 worn-out pages that were recopied and then discarded, found in what is called a "paper grave" while workers were repairing the Great Mosque at Sana'a, Yemen (Lester, 2002, 108). comments:

> Some of the parchment pages in the Yemeni hoard seemed to date back to the seventh and eighth centuries CE, or Islam's first two centuries—they were fragments, in other words, of perhaps the oldest Korans in existence. What's more, some of these fragments reveal small but intriguing aberrations from the standard Koranic text. Such aberrations, though not surprising to textual historians, are troublingly at odds with the orthodox Muslim belief that the Koran as it has reached us today is quite simply the perfect, timeless, and unchanging Word of God.

As more and more copies of sacred texts are made available they become geographically dispersed, leading to regional developments around the needs of each individual community. Thus we have the different inflections in the Gnostic texts, as opposed to what was elected into the New Testament. Success can have some unexpected consequences. With many copies it is next to impossible to alter the "divine word," without at the same time revealing religion's true character—that is, a construction and reflection of the king or priest, at a particular time period, and his power over people, which, in itself, is not good or bad, right or wrong.

As with the Yemeni parchments, it took a court order and political pressure before the Dead Sea Scrolls were released to scholars and the general public after they were found and translated. Why did we have to go to so much trouble to obtain the Dead Sea Scrolls? For one reason, these are probably scrolls originally housed in the temple complex at Jerusalem and removed (or re-copied) by those who are now referred to as the Essenes (worshippers of Esau) when they broke from the Maccabees (meaning "Extinguishers") sometime in the second century BCE. The Dead Sea Scrolls tell us about the original Jesus (Esau) and his message to the world (see Chapter Three), and they also show how the Essenes edited at least parts of the original texts.

The primary place, then, to uncover the Failed God, the fractured god, is with the instruction manuals associated with the gods in question and the social matrix surrounding their construction. These manuals tell us about the nature of these deities, life and death, "proper" behavior toward self and others, and so on. But obviously these writings were not intended for the average person; the average person had never seen a book, let alone read one. Some of these texts represent intellectual philosophies, legends, and poetry designed for discussion among the elite, or as stories originally told around the campfire or for more exotic uses. The Book of Job, for example, would be a wonderful story to tell an advancing religions cleric, after which the cleric would be tested as to meaning; this same procedure of story interpretation is used in Christian colleges today and is certainly standard procedure in getting a PhD or for initiation in Buddhist monasteries. Job had to make a choice—feel sorry for himself and continue to deny his circumstances, or cave into the reality that some mighty bad things can happen to some mighty nice people. Although Job places God before humanity by humbling himself (he gets failing grades for that), the other side is that kings and supernatural forces can do what they want. You are powerless in the face of kings and the forces of nature; accept life as it is and get on with living.

Some of these Biblical texts were constructed for political and economic purposes and certainly not for connecting the *individual* to the divine, or where the individual has a conversation with or, at the very least, identity with God, "I and the Father are One." These stories are the backbone around which the mythical charter is structured. In short, the backbone represents the purpose of the stories, and that is to maintain an identity; this is a long-term plan. This "maintaining tribal identity" story is recast from older stories, with guiding elements to justify the development, implementation, and continuance of a political entity for the purpose of restricting power and decision making to a few, and, at the same time, to limit access to status and wealth. These systems promote poverty, social and physical malaise, and the misuse of power.

As a clinical anthropologist, I am concerned with health issues and not simply content to watch the world go by, take notes, and sell them to my colleagues. I am interested in why people do what they do. In other words, what inspired the storytelling that justifies a rule or belief about the universe? I am also interested in what they believe and the outcome of their decisions. Many decisions, through the dictates of the king, were made for people, and some have followed us into the twenty-first century. Humans are a small-group animal; that is our biology. The philosophy/sociology that best matches this biology is self-responsibility and personal involvement in the group decision process.

A basic rule of information theory is that when diametrically opposed belief systems collide they will generate a third system. In the process, this system will dispose of that which does not fit—that which promotes social entropy or a decline in social health. On the other hand, this third system will maintain that which promotes negative entropy or the reduction of stress and the maintenance of social order. Maintaining a position of negative entropy requires understanding both the universe and ourselves as social animals, and this will not come about on a prayer rug in the mosque or on benches in the churches and temples. The mythic base line for modern stories will eventually involve a morality based on the self-responsible individual who can survive in densely populated, amalgamated worlds of endless technology and possibilities, and at the same time be a decent human being. This will be difficult for many people in diverse parts of the world, and so I challenge the media, the motion picture industry, and so on to mythologize in that direction. We need a different set of problems rather than that of political intrigue and killing each other. This is really getting old—4,000 years is enough.

Returning to storytelling, there is another category of story, or "cycle" story, told at certain times of the year, perhaps to celebrate ancestors or simply to entertain. Anyone who regularly attends church will know the type of sermon to be delivered, depending on the time of year or some current event. This is probably how some of the cycle stories altered, as the storyteller would comment in some way on a current social situation. Not all the tales in the Bible will be told in church; there is editing on the part of the minister. In a time period when most Westerners are literate, the clergy rely on the fact that the average churchgoer does not read the Bible or only reads selected parts.

Religion and Morality

Many people equate religion with morality or good deeds, but morality does not come from religion; rather, it comes from our biology, our group nature. Morality springs from social necessity or the need to cooperate in small groups; it does not begin with religion, and certainly not monotheism. Research has shown that children develop a moral sense long before indoctrinated into any religious tradition (see Scupin 2005, 60). Monotheistic traditions (Judaism, Christianity, and Islam) are responsible for some of the most horrendous cruelty to humanity, including the murder and torture of hundreds of thousands of innocent people. Imparting morality is not a prime consideration in these traditions. God comes first and doing things in His name has little to do with morality, but a great deal to do with maintaining the status quo. This is politics. The probability of abandoning the god myth is not likely to happen soon in many parts of the world, because it represents a useful metaphor in which a small group of people can control many others (these days with machine guns, bombs, and poisons, and the threat of arrest and torture). The god myth will evaporate when we more vigorously educate in rational, self-responsible behavior, beginning at a young age, and reinforce that behavior through our stories—our cinema, television, and print. Before we can uncover Failed God and the nature of the deities involved, we need a modern story of "what" we are (our biology) and then, from a social perspective, "who" we are.

Our Kind

What is the nature of humankind and our relationship to the universe? There are many powerful communities on this planet with differing opinions. These different interpretations create oppositions that are both beneficial and harmful. Beneficial in the sense that some interpretations move people toward more creative ways of conceptualizing the universe, and harmful in that members of other traditions actively, and often with powerful government backing, deceive, censor information, threaten, tax, terrorize, marginalize, and murder nonbelievers. What kind of a deity would condone such action? That would be a demon.

What can we say about *what* we are from a scientific standpoint? This is a bold question because our definitions are biased in the direction of our intent. If our intent is to enslave people, then we invent an all-knowing deity who created us out of clay and who rules with an iron fist. If our intent is scientific, we recognize our animal biology evolving over many millions of years and how that biology pushed culture into existence. Evolution, I need to emphasize, is an identifiable *process,* not a theory. God is a theory; God, as conceptualized in the three Western traditions, can only be accepted as theory, on faith. As the reader will see, early contributors to Christianity could not find tangible evidence that the God on earth (Jesus) existed, and thus forged and otherwise constructed data to fit a political agenda. The need to fabricate and construct documents underlines a realization by these priest-poets that Jesus was not a biological or historical fact. The Knight Templars, who conducted perhaps the first serious archaeological studies in Jerusalem, apparently couldn't find evidence either, as their major reference points appear to be Mary Madeleine and John the Baptist, who might have been real people.

Physical anthropologists are scientists who apply scientific methods, instruments, and techniques from diverse fields (genetics, biology, human anatomy, comparative anatomy, physics, mathematics, and computer science) when defining "what" we are. Anthropologists do not always agree and the disagreements center on interpretation. Science, then, is not truth; it is a process of discovery. So, what is there to discover? In a phrase, laws of the natural world, rather than accepting a deity who created all in a matter of days. Finding God through science makes a great deal more sense than simply accepting His existence on faith and praying in a church, temple, or mosque for this entity to pay attention to your animal nature (health, progeny, and wealth).

In order to uncover these laws, several principles must be applied. First, there has to be a separation of natural from supernatural phenomena. In order to do this, the scientist has to identify the laws and regularity of nature (where and when earthquakes appear, lightning, etc.), which include observable or measurable cause and effect ("when I do this [cause], this [effect] always happens"), both physical and mechanical. Second is the development of tools, or logical argument and mathematics and their systematic use. "We all know Jesus was a historical fact, now let's prove it" is an assumption that, if never questioned, will direct the path of research and often exclude material that disagrees with the original assumption. Along with this there has to be rational criticism and debate, and a general climate that tolerates skepticism. There is absolutely no way that monotheists can rationally or scientifically debate God as conceptualized in the Bible and Qur'an, and as my father told me years ago, "When you argue with a fool you become one yourself."

Third, there has to be demonstration and proof by empirical observation and research in order to extend the base of knowledge. Fourth, and evolving out of the above principles, science has to be self-correcting. When errors are detected or conclusions are faulty, they demand reconsideration, and old beliefs need to be replaced with better, more appropriate stories. This, however, is next to impossible unless there is freedom of speech, freedom of debate, and incentives to explore.

Any system, government, discipline, or field of study that does not allow lively debate and free expression, or that censors other traditions and the beliefs and behaviors of others, is a closed system. Closed systems, like theocracies and despotic political systems, must guard themselves against information generated in systems of free enterprise. Free enterprise means competition, and competition generates new ideas contrary to the old—competition and evolution can be seen as synonymous in that sense. New ideas are corrupting, and to hear or even stand close to someone with a different perspective would result in a spiritual disease. Judaism, Christianity, and Islam are closed systems; closed systems exclude and persecute those of other traditions. Why is that? Well, if you can't capture the market place on "truth," then your system goes no further. It possibly dies out or at least has to go through dramatic changes.

Western biomedicine shares many characteristics of monotheistic traditions, including suppressing competing medial systems using the threat of punishment, all done to maximize profits. Western biomedicine, however, is trapped within scientific methodology and, although still a monopoly and more interested in illness maintenance, is giving way to more traditional approaches to health. Don't get me wrong. We need the standardization, research, and number crunching, although it is at the expense of health care. To have credibility, Western biomedicine has to at least talk about prevention, and in doing so we are beginning to hear about the importance of nutrition, toxicity (most people die of malnutrition and cellular toxicity), and exercise. The spokespeople for the AMA and contiguous organizations are beginning to admit that you can't get the nutrients needed out of fruits and vegetables (they have been genetically altered for shape, color, and taste) and thus supplemental vitamins and minerals are necessary. It then becomes a question of arguing over how much. On the other side, the AMA, through the efforts of the FDA and certain senators, has attempted to make vitamins, minerals, and dietary fiber into prescription drugs, after they told us for decades these supplements were unnecessary. It is difficult to avoid politics. If everyone took a high quality vitamin/mineral supplement twice a day, with sufficient pure water (one ounce for every two pounds of body weight), with about forty grams of extra dietary fiber, along with regular, moderate exercise and/or meditation on a daily basis, doctor's visits would be cut in half. Along with this, if people stopped smoking, avoided dairy products and meat laced with hormones, ate whole foods, avoided prescription drugs, and cut alcohol consumption to a couple of drinks a day, this would likewise cut catastrophic illness in half. A nation full of physically healthy people would be an economic disaster for the medical community because there is no money in health; the money rolls in with illness maintenance (see Rush 1996).

New ideas and hard data enter the social sciences (anthropology, history, sociology) on a week-to-week basis. Textbooks gradually catch up and reflect these changes. Don't misunderstand me—I'm not saying we know what truth is, but if there is such a thing it is more likely to be found in an atmosphere of free speech and rational debate. Alterations in our view of the tangible world help us build the better mousetrap. What science does is help us understand the world so that we can better cope with the adversities that present themselves. If we have dominion over the land and sea, then we need to understand the laws so that we can take better care of that which supports us.

The laws of nature discovered over the past 100,000 years or so are wrapped around the processes of evolution and allow us to estimate the age of the universe—between nine and sixteen billion years depending on the scientific data you choose to look at. That represents a wide margin of error, but it is certainly a far cry from 4004 BCE. If I chose not to believe that the observable universe is at least nine billion years old, the cosmologists and physicists won't drag me out of the classroom and shoot me in the head. There was a time when openly critiquing the date of 4004 BCE could get you ostracized from the community. Remember what happened to Galileo when he publicly stated that the earth was not the center of the universe? Remember the Scopes Monkey trial? We are separated from Scopes by only a few years; this type of information suppression and manipulation (deception) for political ends has a long season. Look what happened to Allegro when he suggested that the *Amanita muscaria* mushroom was part of cult ritual in Judaism and Christianity. "You mean Jesus was a mushroom? And all this time I thought he was a savior!" Make note of the evolutionary processes as we take a long, long trip.

In the Beginning . . .

The prevailing "scientific" creation story, the Big Bang, is just that—a story. More recently it appears that it might be the "Big Bangs" theory. Although backed by mathematics, detected background radiation, and optical observations, we can only guess at what came before or why there was a Big Bang (or Big Bangs). Perhaps a singularity did explode. Perhaps two parallel universes (*p*-Branes) bumped into one another, a suggestion that comes from theoretical physics (String Theory). A Brane is not a place exactly but a mathematical possibility of extended space. Imagine, if you will, rippling tubes flowing through, around, inside, and so on in every point of direction. In the *p*-Brane theory, two of these ripples collide at one point or perhaps at several points, releasing a tremendous amount of energy. The "place" in which we live evolved out of that energy and seems to exist as a separate universe among others. In any event, the prevailing story goes like this:

Once upon a time there was this singularity in space, but there was no space because space can only exist if there is something to occupy it. This singularity was quite small by comparison, anywhere from a point, to the size of a box of stick matches, to perhaps a mile across, or maybe even the size of our moon. Within this singularity there existed everything and nothing at the same time, all the energy and anti-energy of a potential universe. I would say that it contained that which precedes energy—a thought perhaps, or that which precedes a thought. This is speculation but we are not stuck with the story; we can change it without arresting or killing our colleagues who harbor different opinions.

For some unexplained reason, this singularity exploded and a tremendous amount of energy was created and released, waves of energy that moved further and further apart. This is very similar to the Gnostic myth, where the First Principal for some reason emits a hypostasis (a burst of energy), which eventually becomes the spiritual and physical worlds. During the first micro-seconds of this explosion all the rules of the universe were created (gravity, etc.), perhaps for the purpose of controlling and directing the energy, although in another Big Bang a different set of rules might apply. The ancient Egyptians had a similar story.

As the waves of energy spread out from a cosmic center like ripples on a pond, numerous conversions occurred during cooling—or energy loss (entropy) or re-absorption—as the energy had to go somewhere, for it can only go back into itself if specific criteria are met. This cooling led first to vapor and, eventually, over the course of billions of years, to solid matter, just as steam condenses to water which then freezes into ice. This solid matter clumped together to form smaller black holes, singularities fashioned out of the same rules as the original, but with much less energy potential. These black holes are more unstable than the parent and, like little children bursting with energy, they spit it forth and breathe it back in similar fashion, as Brahman in the Hindu tradition. Brahman comes from the Sanskrit root *bri*, which means to breathe or expand. This energy, as it moved further and further away from its birthing place, cooled and became vapor, eventually forming stars. Because of gravitational and other forces planets eventually form, as matter is attracted to other clumps of matter. Our sun was created in such a fashion, as the story goes, lying as it does in one of the arms of our Milky Way galaxy, with planets forming many billions of years later. How do we know this? There are laws of physics, laws about heat and pressure, and gravitational and radiation principles that are predictable and subject to mathematical investigation and practical implementation—we have split the atom, gone to the moon, and sent probes into deep space. If our explanations about the universe were faulty, these triumphs could not possibly have taken place. I have talked to fundamentalists who believe that the moonwalks were done locally in a motion picture studio. It certainly takes a great deal of faith to believe such things; it takes just as much faith to be an atheist.

The age of the earth, the third planet from the sun, is between four and five billion years old and, again, physicists can mathematically demonstrate how the sun, earth, and planets were formed (gravitational attraction, etc.). The scientific position of earth's creation and dynamic nature may not be totally correct, but it is self-correcting. As new information becomes available, old models are discarded or corrected. The Big Bang as a starting point is currently being rethought, as this is an evolving story with a secular history attached.

From dating techniques (potassium/argon and uranium 235), we know when life (anaerobic and aerobic bacteria) was established on earth (three and a half Billion Years Ago during the pre-Cambrian), either through the seeding by comets or independent invention. Multicellular animals show up around two and a half BYA, and by a half BYA the sea floors are covered with life. This is supported by tangible data—thousands of fossils, the artifacts of a time past. Artifacts—and their tangibility—are so important that the religious community (especially in the Christian tradition) has collected bones, and so on, from real people, as well as constructed or invented others (see Chapter Three) to bolster their case.

In the Cambrian (570–510 MYA), there is a proliferation of species and the beginnings of colonization, or the clumping together of individuals or their remains. Colonization creates microenvironments or niches for species to exploit. Individuals not fit enough to survive in the open environment can thrive in the microenvironments. In the Ordovician (510–439 MYA), we note the emergence of the chordates (having a backbone), the phylum to which we are related. We also note the development of predator species, which begin another type of selective process. Up to a certain time period during the pre-Cambrian, life involved consuming inorganic and organic molecules to survive and generate more life. But eventually life begins to eat life and this leads to rapid natural selection; these are the monsters in our dreams. Trilobites, for example, are now better at detecting predators and hiding, have

harder exoskeletons, and stand a greater chance of surviving and passing on their genetic codes. Those species that cannot avoid the predators, those that cannot adapt, get eaten and die out. Humans, 500
million years later, became the ultimate predator, and that is probably
why there is only one true biped left on the planet (although that could
certainly end very quickly). Moreover, we have eliminated most of the
other predators (although we still battle bacteria, viruses, etc.), and
have turned to killing each other, not for food (at least not for many
hundreds of years, except in special cases), but for something more
abstract, for example, in the name of Allah, God, and Yahweh. In these
cases the myth or story has become more important than humanity
itself; monotheistic myths define humanity in a closed, preset manner,
which does not allow humanity to think past prevailing ideas and define
itself in a modern world. Science thinks past prevailing ideas and has
greatly extended our view of possibilities in a relatively short period of
time; science is pretty spiritual stuff.

In the Silurian (439–408 MYA), we encounter the real reef builders
and more extensive colonies, with new niches for species to exploit.
These reefs also change ocean currents, the "weather of the ocean" so
to speak, creating selective pressures of another type. Some plants and
animals like warm water, some cold, and some prefer a moderate temperature; thus temperature qualifies as a niche, a place. Vascular plants
make the transition to land—a new world to exploit. Imagine, if you
will, a shallow body of water full of plants waving in the current. Most
of these kelp-like plants don't store water and have flexible structures
so they can bend in the current. They have air pods that perhaps sta-
bilize them, and direct them to the surface and the sun from which
they receive their energy, converted through photosynthesis. Some of
their brothers and sisters, however, are different; they are mutants.
Their structures are sturdier and they store water perhaps initially in
pods, which weigh the plant down and selects for stiffer cellular con-
figurations. Chromosomes are conservative structures. The genes positioned on them enhance survival, and the alteration in one gene can have
profound effects on the whole organism. Mutations, or mistakes occur-

ring in the base pairs that make up a gene, are most usually lethal. Some of these mutations, however, are neutral or at least not disadvantageous in their current environment. These, as far as we can tell, are accidental. Perhaps some supreme being is in a workshop changing the base pairs once in a while out of boredom, just to see what will happen, in which case God is a scientist, involved in the process of evolution. In any case, what you can count on is that all is impermanent and everything will change. Due to an earthquake or simply the gradual spreading the ocean floor (plate tectonics), our shallow body of water becomes surrounded by land and gradually dries up. Those plants that have sturdy structures, that can store water, and that can protect themselves from radiation will survive. The plants did not crawl out of the ocean and put down roots on land. It was a lucky role of the dice, an accident. There does not seem to be a purpose to this and appears, instead, to be a matter of what works. Life has taken on many, many different forms during its 3.9 billion year history. We are only one of those possibilities, and in a million years or so we will be unrecognizable. This could be even more rapid when the medical community begins altering our genes and creating new purposeful mutations rather than waiting for them to happen. Science fiction writers have discussed these possibilities for decades and now they are about to happen, with the consequences totally unpredictable. As we will see, the energy responsible for evolution could care less if we manipulate genes or not—it is the outcome that's important.

In the Devonian (408–362 MYA), we encounter jawless fish that tell us a great deal about what structures of the head and neck evolved into parts of the inner ear and movable jaw. Lowland forests are widespread. How do we know this? We have the fossils.

In the Carboniferous (362–290 MYA), there is the transition from marine to non-marine or land dwelling animal species. Because of plate tectonics (movement of the continents), the geological features of the earth are changing; mountain ranges are pushed up, changing weather patterns, and shallow inland seas are drying up. Many species that previously occupied these seas are dying out. Mother Nature gives and takes away. Mother Nature pollutes and kills on an unimaginable scale.

In the Permian (290–245 MYA), we encounter higher elevations that more dramatically affect weather and climate, along with the presence of giant primitive reptiles.

In the Mesozoic (245–65 MYA), we encounter the oldest known birds, species that occupy still other niches, and the selective pressures contained within. Mammals (with hair, differentiated teeth, and live births) also emerge at this time (we are classified as mammals). Pangaea (the great continent) begins to break up (200 MYA), once again altering the geography, ocean currents, and weather patterns, as well as isolating species.

At the Cretaceous/Tertiary boundary, or the beginning of the Cenozoic (65 MYA), a catastrophic event occurred. Although there had been many such events in the past, this catastrophe was special. An extraterrestrial object, a meteor some seven to ten miles across, struck the Yucatan Peninsula traveling thousands of miles per hour. When it hit, millions of tons of molten material were catapulted into the atmosphere, falling to earth thousands of miles away. Most plant and animal species were incinerated in the holocaust that followed. One group of animals that disappeared, made famous in the movie *Jurassic Park,* was the dinosaurs (did God consider the dinosaurs evil and wicked?). This event created an information vacuum (information loss) or a diversity of ecological niches waiting to be filled. Numerous animals living underground escaped the holocaust, including the mammals and our protoprimate and primate ancestors. Catastrophic events leading to mass extinctions occur on the average of every sixty-five and 120 million years; keep that in mind as the end of the Aztec Fifth Era, December 23, 2012, approaches.

Our early mammal ancestors who escaped this holocaust resemble modern day rats and shrews. Physical anthropologists have been able to compare traits on the bones and teeth (morphological characteristics—eye orbits, claws, nails, dental characteristics, etc.) with more recent species and their changes over time. Again, there are gaps in our knowledge, but what we see evolving over the past sixty-five million years is an animal who goes from walking on four feet, to a biped (at least six MYA—for example, *Orrorin tugenensis*) living in small groups and, eventually (around two MYA), to a creature that is very human like— *Homo erectus*. Although not the first toolmaker, the tool this species manufactures (the Acheulean hand axe) suggests a creature with a brain capable of magical thinking (see Rush 1996, 2005). *Homo erectus,* from the neck down, with only minor differences (i.e., the cervical vertebra are somewhat smaller), is essentially human. With a brain displacement of between 800 and 1250 c.c., we are approaching modern brain size of between 1450 and 1550 c.c. The pelvis of *Homo erectus* shows they had a birthing pattern similar to us, that is, giving birth to totally dependent infants that need almost constant supervision for many months after birth. We know that *Homo erectus,* probably following predators that provided food through partially consumed kills, migrated into Europe by 1.8 MYA, and regionally developed there into Neanderthal by around 200 KYA (Thousand Years Ago). *Homo erectus* was also in China by at least one MYA and was regionally developing as well. *Homo erectus* even went into the islands of Java and east of Java (Flories, for example), and likewise regionally developed.

By 130 KYA, *Homo erectus* remaining in Africa had regionally developed into modern humans who, during various waves of migration out of Africa between 125 to fifty to forty KYA, interbreed with regionally developing *Homo erectus* groups in the Near East, China, and eventually (around thirty-five KYA) encountered Neanderthals in Western Europe. There is evidence of interbreeding, but Neanderthals as a distinct group were eventually displaced, perhaps violently or perhaps through the introduction of viruses and bacteria, which would have been devastating to these small, isolated groups over time (see Rush 1996). It has been suggested that their culture and technology could not keep up with rapid changes in weather patterns. I personally prefer the disease model, as there is no evidence that they were mentally not up to the task of adapting to changing environmental conditions. At any rate, after twenty-nine to twenty-seven KYA, after a long, long trip, modern humans with a chin are a single species and the only true biped primate—or so we thought. It now appears that *Homo erectus* groups hung on until about thirty KYA in Java, and the *Homo erectus* in Flores died out as recently as thirteen-twelve KYA.

With an open system, we can accommodate new data and perhaps reformulate our storyline. The message is that *Homo erectus* did regionally develop in various areas of the world and was probably fully capable of interbreeding with modern humans during different encounters in shared territories. This genetic mingling is clearly the case in modern Asian and North American Indian populations with shovel-shaped incisors (teeth are very conservative traits). *Homo erectus* had shovel-shaped incisors, but that trait is not at all common in European, African, and modern Middle Eastern populations.

There were many bipeds similar to us in many areas of the world by 130 KYA, but at this moment it appears that we are the only one left (with Sesquash, Bigfoot, and Yeti, of course, being possible exceptions). Think deeply into that—nature disposes of that which cannot adapt, just as culture relegates antiquated belief systems to museums and books in libraries where they collect dust.

Volumes of scientific data support the above story, although we can argue about specific details. The scientific data, collected over a long span of time, uncovered a set of rules operating in this universe. One of those rules states that nothing stays the same; all is impermanent, both physical and social. From plate tectonics to mutations in viruses, from political structures to religious belief, systems evolve and become new systems that incorporate or build on features of the old—*or they go extinct!* Those systems that don't keep up die out. Now, there may be a deity or energy that created the rules and set this universe in motion, but our biggest problem is realizing that we *are* this energy, and that this energy, or the deity who created it, is not separate from us. There are rules in operation or we would not have the experiences we do, and the energy or deity that constructed these rules is likewise constrained by them. In other words, the deity cannot arbitrarily change the rules at a whim. Fundamentalists might argue, however, that the deity can do what He wants, as if the universe runs according to Roadrunner physics. "God does not play dice with the universe." (Albert Einstein).

Magic and Religion

Magic and religion have been defined in a multitude of manners and dimensions, but no matter what definition we use, it does not incorporate the scientific method outlined above. Asad (1993, 29) states:

> My argument is that there cannot be a universal definition of religion, not only because its constituent elements and relationships are historically specific, but because that definition is itself the historical product of discursive process.

I think that Asad is correct in the larger picture, but there are core elements we can talk about that religion must contain and so a platform definition is possible. For my purposes I will define magic as a methodology to manipulate the rules of nature for some personal or group purpose. Prayer can be seen as a form of personal magic or an attempt to influence the will of the deity, just as a child will beg his parents to stay up late to watch a particular TV program, or when someone wishes on a star to win the lottery. These are actually forms of ancestor worship and animism, respectively.

In order to avoid the problems as critically analyzed by Asad (1993), I will conceptualize Western religions, specifically Judaism, Christianity, and Islam, as political systems instead of religions. A religion is a system designed to bind the *individual,* through rite and ritual, to the deity through *identity* and *communication with* the deity, as well as perhaps *becoming* the deity ("I and the Father are one"). This is the "old time religion" and not status, politics, and money. Once these ancient traditions were used to control and subordinate the individual to a priest, ruler, or king, they became political systems and ceased to be religions. Religion was essentially made illegal for the common person. As reported in the *New Advent Catholic Encyclopedia* (Volume XII, 1911):

> A . . . likely derivation, one that suits the idea of religion in
> its simple beginning, is that given by Lactantius in his
> "Divine Institutes," IV, xxviii. He derives religion from reli-
> gare (to bind): "We are tied to God and bound to Him [*reli-
> gati*] by the bond of piety . . ."

We are indeed bound (linked) to God or that energy that informs
all, but in my definition of religion that bond of piety does not include
slavery. You are not devoted to a god in the same way as being a slave
to the god, as is the case with the gods in Judaism, Christianity, and
Islam. You *identify* with, talk to, or become the god. Religion, as I'm
defining it, is a personal experience with the energy that informs all,
an ecstatic experience that touches where you came from and where
you will return; in popular religion, these are the esoteric rites of religious clerics at the highest level. The lower levels of clergy and the
congregation are denied these experiences and are instead treated to the
exoteric rites, that is, the sacramental wine and/or wafer in some traditions, while in others (e.g., Islam) you get to symbolically act out
your slavery to Allah, Yahweh, or God and their earthly representatives
(imam, priest, bishop, pope, king) by bowing in front of a wall, bowing
one's head in church, kissing the pope's ring, or prostrating yourself on
a prayer mat five times a day. As we will see, there is very little of the
"true" religious experience (the esoteric rites) in the world today. Most
people consider Judaism, Christianity, and Islam religious systems only
because this is what scholars inappropriately call them. These are political systems pure and simple. The Founding Fathers of the United
States understood the pain and suffering promoted by these systems
when they had political power, and that is why there has to be a separation of church and state. When these traditions attempt to influence public policy and opinion, they are simply acting as political
systems. Currently the Islamic community is attempting to pass laws
that would make it illegal to say anything critical about the alleged
historicity of Islam and its legal arbitrariness (there goes free speech!),
and the Christian community, in another act of censorship, is attempt-

ing to delete evolution from high school textbooks. There is great insecurity and fear in these irrational traditions, and for good reason.

These systems claim to be historical fact, and as such they are boxed within the discipline of history and are subject to criticism based on historical evidence. Belief in God only requires faith; there is no proof that God, as conceptualized in the Bible and the Qur'an, exists. There is no proof that prayers, donations, human/animal/vegetable sacrifices, self-flagellation, or circumcision can attract the attention of this deity or energy. There is no evidence that this energy can be bribed, cajoled, coerced, or otherwise convinced to do your bidding. The energy that informs all is not a "being" or "entity" paying attention in a special manner to you or me, let along a chosen people. Some people believe, however, that there are signs of prayers being answered, heaven-sent signs, and miracles, with statues weeping blood (the statue of the Virgin Mary at the Vietnamese Catholic Martyrs Church in Sacramento, California, is one of the latest examples). Miracles happen with equal frequency as disasters. The baby pulled alive from the rubble of an apartment complex leveled by an earthquake six days earlier is considered a miracle of prayers answered, but when the child living in the apartment next door dies, the prayers have apparently gone unanswered. This is indeed very impersonal and arbitrary. The real miracle, however, was the earthquake, for without it, no miracles could follow. Constructed or manufactured miracles are nothing less than deception. The ancient Egyptians and Greeks had mechanical statutes that spoke, moved arms, and dispensed liquids. I wonder if churches get catalogues in the mail advertising crying and moaning statues, discreetly sold and delivered in a brown wrapper.

Shadows on church walls or windows become Gestalt images encouraged by the clergy to resemble the Virgin Mary or Jesus; it's good for business. Even when the phenomenon is revealed to be from natural causes, a certain number of true believers hang on and imagine the emperor is wearing new clothes. I have yet to read or hear any serious scientist say that these imaginings (weeping statues, shadows on walls, dead people coming back to life) are phenomena attributable to a deity.

The energy that informs all is as impersonal as impersonal can be. The signs of God or the energy that informs all are not restricted to occasional miracles, including shadows on the wall. Just look around. Look into your child's eyes, for that is the miracle. You are the creator; you are God.

In our explanation of who we are biologically, we are constrained by our language. Our model, be this scientifically driven or carried along by religion and faith, will nonetheless be biased by each respective point of view. Scientists (outside of parapsychologists) do not intentionally look for a spiritual world complete with ghosts, angels, gods, and demons (spiritual taphonomy). Scientists are driven by the need to know, and of course by the money that funds the research and ultimate tangible rewards. Driven by the need to know could be considered pretty spiritual stuff, for certainly the Bible and the Qur'an were written by people who told us "what" and "who" we were through the lens of their science. These books are expressions of knowledge and wonder by particular peoples during specific slices of time. These books represent *sacred* history (stories constructed around myth and legend) rather than *secular* history (constructed around interpretations of archaeological data, inscriptions, and written records). The former is poetry and not self-correcting in the face of new data (it has no need to be when read as myth or poetry), while the latter is continually updated as new information is revealed. Fundamental Christians and Muslims would never invent a light bulb. They would never invent an automobile, the telephone, or television. They would never invent a rocket to go to the moon. Why not? In order to invent this technology, you have to question your beliefs and assumptions. I overheard one gentleman says, "If God wanted us to go to the moon, he would have made us in the shape of rockets." One of his buddies responded, "Yes, of course. And every time you fart, you end up on the moon!"

One of the basic cosmic laws set in place since the beginning of time is evolution, or motion, movement, change, and impermanence. The Bible and Qur'an are statements of change and evolution, for the earth and the cosmos were not created in an instant but emerged on a day-to-day basis. In fact, Adam evolves from clay (with the help of the deity, of course) either before (Genesis 2) or after the other animals were brought into existence (Genesis 1). There is a bit of scientific truth here (depending on the before or after interpretations), but much of the creation story in Genesis (a composite of Egyptians and Mesopotamian myths) needs revision or clarification if considered as fact; it is simply out of touch with our knowledge of the universe as it stands today (see Rush 2007).

Myth

This book is about myth and mythology, with myth being the stories themselves and mythology being the study of myth *and* the construction of other stories (meta-myths) by anthropologists, historians, and others to understand or explain the purpose or meanings of the primary stories/poetry. There are numerous templates we can place over mythic symbols and we can make comparisons between cultures. These templates include symbolism, structuralism, cultural materialism, cultural criticism, Freudian interpretations, Jungian interpretations, and so on. We have to be cautious of the interpretations that come from these models. The symbolists, for example, represent a variant of Freud but cooked in a different oven. Looking for latent meaning leads in two directions: 1) the use of symbols to uncover brain functioning; and 2) a constructed meaning, by the anthropologist, biblical scholar, historian, and so on, which may not correspond to the meanings assigned by the members of the specific culture. How could they? They are latent. Marvin Harris (1980) suggests that pigs became a taboo animal among the Hebrews because they were simply not cost effective to keep and eat. The problem with this is that the other Canaanite tribes taking up residence in the same area do not have such restrictions, and certainly this would not apply to the Arab tribes in the Arabian Peninsula. Putting the big red "X" across the pig may have had some competition-for-scarce-resources benefits, but the taboo more than likely originates with a story from Egypt that predates the restriction by at least 1,000 years.

Remember that the Hebrews lived in the delta region of Egypt for hundreds of years and would have known the Egyptian storylines. They also wanted that connection to royalty in their mythical charter and thus selectively borrowed from Egypt and other contiguous cultural groups. Here is, I think, a better story about the poor pig.

A stranger is defined as anyone not of your tribe. Strangers mean trouble because you cannot predict their actions; again, they belong to another tribe—they represent a "them" who can be dehumanized into "its," and all "its" are fair game—"Kill it!" Jesus understood this very well, for through "love thy enemy" he raised the status of everyone from enemy to that of a recognizable human being and hopefully a "thou," a God just like you. In the ancient Egyptian tradition, Seth, the evil brother of Osiris (see Rush 2007), eventually becomes associated with strangers or invaders and by design is metaphorical of life's obstacles. This mythic association most certainly existed prior to 1500 BCE. Seth is also identified with the boar or pig—because of its power, ferocity, cleverness, and ability to create chaos in the gardens—and this appears to be where the Hebrews (and eventually the Islamites) obtained their myth of impurity for this animal. We read in the *Book of the Dead of Ani*, Chapter 112 (Faulkner 1994, 114):

> It so happened that Re said to Horus: 'Let me see your eye since this has happened to it.' He looked at it and said: 'Look at that black stroke with your hand covering up the sound eye which is there.' Horus looked at that stroke and said: 'Behold, I am seeing it as altogether white.' And that is how the oryx came into being. And Re said: 'Look again at yonder black pig.' And Horus looked at this pig, and Horus cried out because of the condition of his injured eye, saying: 'Behold, my eye is like that of the first wound which Seth inflicted on my eye,' and Horus fainted before him. Then Re said: 'Put him on his bed until he is well.' It so happened that Seth had transformed himself into a black pig and had projected a wound into his eye, and Re said: 'The pig is

detestable to Horus.' 'We wish he were well,' said the gods. That is how the detestation of the pig came about for Horus' sake. [This last sentence is translated in Prichard 1969, 10, as, "That is how the pig became an abomination to the gods, as well as their followers, for Horus' sake."]

So which is it? Pig as a problem of competition for scarce resources, or pig as symbolic of life's obstacles and evil in the world? I prefer the second because this is how the Egyptians configured the pig and we are talking metaphor. Moreover, the Hebrews were separating themselves from the other Canaanite tribes, and food restriction doesn't allow you to "break bread" with others not of your tribe least you contract a spiritual disease.

I'm also interested in the meaning intended for the audience, the average person during the time these stories were woven together, just as there is an audience for the story I'm telling. All the intellectual discussions about what the different stories mean is not as important as getting into the head of the common person, the one to whom the message supposedly was directed, but unless we have a time machine this will always be problematical. We have enough difficulty trying to understand ourselves in our own culture, let alone someone who existed 2,000 years ago. If Giovannoli (2000) is correct (and I believe he is), these stories in a general sense direct our emotions and energies; they direct our beliefs about the world before us, and they tell us how to behave toward that world. Moreover, these stories are best understood in the context in which they were told—to people who were very superstitious in a period of great social turmoil.

The sacred texts connected to Judaism, Christianity, and Islam, we are instructed, are layered and they represent many things. Is that layering really there or is it evident because modern people with diverse biases invent it? An intelligent deity would have understood this and revealed His world and laws in a less than ambiguous fashion. Knowing the frailty and stupidity of humans (seeing He created them), He could not realistically trust the message to one or even a handful of people. That is not how an intelligent deity would handle this. We exist in a different social context than people living 2,500 years ago; we recognize the irrational and illogical nature of the picture presented. And because we experience our world in a very different way, it is difficult to grasp what appear to be inconsistencies, brutality, deceptions, and so on in these documents. Some traditions, however, forbid any critical thinking regarding sacred literature. From a fundamentalist point of view, you are not encouraged to think critically about events and miracles. Conversations with deities must be believed, and sacred spaces (churches, mosques, temples) must be attended and maintained. Those who break away from the dogma are branded apostates or heretics and are often shunned, tortured, and/or murdered in the name of religious truth (see Warraq 2003; Gabriel 2004). The release of the movie *The Da Vinci Code* (May 2006), brought forth attempts by the Catholic Church, fundamentalist protestants, and others to cut certain parts from the movie because they challenge basic foundations of Christianity, both indirectly and directly. This qualifies as politics. For example, *The Da Vinci Code* (Brown 2003) contains references and analogies that twist the accepted story. Sara, the supposed daughter of Mary Magdalene and Jesus, is analogous to Sara, wife of Abraham. Thus we see a replay of a royal bloodline (Sangrail) but it is the *female* bloodline where the god, Jesus, unites with Mary Magdalene, a human, and reunites god with the humanity he created in the form of a woman, Sara. This is a good story—a better story, in my opinion, than the current favorite—but it is also heresy and unlikely to be true.

More directly, *The Da Vinci Code* challenges one of the basic constructs of Christianity—Jesus died on the cross, arose from the dead, and ascended to heaven sperm and all. If this is not the case, then he didn't die for our sins and lives on through a daughter, Sara. A child continuing the bloodline after the god dies is a replay of the Osiris cycle (see Rush 2007). However, both *The Da Vinci Code* and the New Testament are based on the premise that there was a man by the name of Jesus who lived and died during the suggested time span (5 BCE to 33 CE). I will consider the evidence for Jesus in Chapter Three.

Obviously, these ancient stories in the Bible were intended to impart some message to the flock, to direct emotions and our animal nature, or else they would have been abandoned as falsehoods a long time ago. Many intelligent people suspend the rational mind when it comes to accepting these stories. The question is, "Why?" A recent publication suggests that there is a "God gene" (Hamer 2004), or a DNA sequence that codes for life's continuance physically, through sex and reproduction, and spiritually, through an ability to imagine something beyond, and faith or hope in the correctness of our imagination. Faith and hope, then, are part of our neural wiring. Without hope and faith in a future—here on earth or in another place at death—we see only toil and trouble in our lives; "life sucks," to paraphrase the Buddha. All life is sorrowful, then you die, at which point you become some other creature's food. This is disquieting to most, and thus hope or faith motivates us to look around the next corner instead of giving up—there is a will to life. Hamer's position is much like Pandora's Box. Zeus decides to punish mankind for not honoring him properly, and so with the help of other gods he fashions a beautiful lady named Pandora, equips her with insatiable curiosity, and hands her a jar or box which, of course, she is not supposed to open (like Adam and Eve and Judas, she is given an assignment). She is presented to Epimetheus (which means "afterthought"), the brother of Prometheus, who, as you remember, stole fire and gave it to humans. Prometheus placed humanity first and the gods second. Prometheus (meaning "forethought") warns him about accepting gifts from Zeus. Here is the exact conversation, with Prometheus chained to a rock.

> **EPIMETHEUS:** "Hey, man. All he wants you to do is apologize for giving fire to the humans ..."
> **PROMETHEUS:** "I care less than nothing for Zeus. Let him do what he damn well pleases!"
> **EPIMETHEUS:** "But I understand that he has a gift for me, a beautiful woman. They were talking about her in the baths

this morning, so just say you're sorry and let's be done with this. He'll let you go!"

PROMETHEUS: "He has a gift, you say? Well, he's a real ego-centric prick, Epimetheus! Zeus is a fool. I know what he has planned. Do not accept her."

But the warning goes unheeded or we wouldn't have much of a story. Pandora, once she's among humans, can't help herself. She opens the jar and out pours all life's miseries—disease, greed, anger, murder, and so on. Pandora, however, manages to put the lid on the jar before hope escaped. As has been said many times before, there is a will to life, all life, for once it gets started, like a parasite it grows to fill all possible space. Fortunately, life eats life, and a balance is maintained; keep that in mind the next time you look into the night sky.

Undoubtedly we are programmed for hope. The interest lies in the stories we wrap around this hope and then how the stories are used to direct thought and physical energies. I think it very difficult to place ourselves in the shoes, sandals, or thinking mode of these ancient people, and if that isn't thorny enough, there are those who assume there are higher levels of meaning or even a secret code contained within the Bible (see Drosnin 1998; Ingermanson 1999). Once again there is no proof that the intent of the writers of the Bible was to code information about future events in such an esoteric manner, nor would they have had the means to do so. If there is coding, we have to question the intelligence of a deity and his, her, or its inability to code in a manner understandable through the centuries. But there is a deeper problem. One would have to invent a computer and mathematical program or code to unmask the original code that predicted the future. This would require thinking outside the bounds of accepted dogma maintained by those in power who want to stay in power (again, remember Galileo). Had there not been a Protestant reformation, there would be no computer. Let's go deeper.

Future events are easy to predict—going to work tomorrow, what you will have for dinner, the likelihood that someone will be voted out of the senate. Prediction and prophecy are the same in that there is an expectation. Prophecy, however, predicts significant social and/or geological events, but prophecy cannot predict what it will exactly be or when it will exactly happen. The avenue around this is to predict in a cryptic manner, with symbols especially chosen to make a special point or two. Once an event occurs, the symbolists can read a prophecy to fit the moment. You will not encounter, "At precisely 12:22 p.m. Pacific time, on December 19, 2011, Joe Blow is going to jump off the Golden Gate Bridge," and then make it public. "Why not?" you ask. The answer is simple. If we could predict the future outside of everyday expectations, the future could be manipulated. "What is wrong with that?" you ask. There is nothing wrong with it, but can you imagine the outcome if everyone was changing or altering non-existent future events they don't like? Nothing could possibly take place because the conditions for its appearance have been altered. Also, the future is only a possibility and that possibility is based on time, which equals change. Just as nothing around you stays the same, neither do you or the conditions for a future event. Moreover, the further you move out from your life space mentally or physically, the less and less control you have—control equals predictability and expectations.

Merging Religion and State

Beliefs in supernatural beings, ancestor worship, shamanism, and religion are never separate from the social systems that spawn them. When we reach the level of state-type organization, beginning around 3000 BCE, we see the supernatural used to purposefully and intentionally control people for social projects; the gods were a personal experience. Eventually this was abused and used in an emotionally and physically oppressive manner, wherein the individual and god are separated and the only contact is through worship, just as one bowed down to the king. What we see in the vast majority of cases of the "true believer" today is indoctrination at an early age and the threat of punishment if he or she resorts to critical thinking or questioning of beliefs. Hope, therefore, is not the main reason many people maintain that Abraham, Moses, and Muhammad spoke to God or his representative, or that Jesus, son of God, was crucified for our sins, arose from death, and ascended to heaven. Christian and Muslim children are routinely told that nonbelievers go to hell (a real geographical place in the minds of fundamentalists) and are dealt with in some pretty gruesome ways. The Muslims, for example, bury their dead deep enough so that the individual can sit up and be interrogated by a couple of thuggish angels (Munkar and Nakir), and if he or she is not sufficiently indoctrinated in Islam the individual is severely beaten.

People believe these stories are true not out of hope, but out of fear. Instilling fear in young children is nothing less than emotional abuse and certainly does not lead to a more compassionate or peaceful humanity. This type of indoctrination is called enculturation, and any psychologist will tell you that those early "truths" are very difficult to erase. This emotional and physical abuse is accepted in the name of God; this type of abuse is fully acceptable in our culture and many others. If I, as a professor of anthropology, threatened students with hellfire and damnation if they didn't believe in evolution, I would probably be brought up on charges of emotional abuse and fired, or at the very least be considered insane. This indoctrination early in life is absolutely necessary if the belief in the respective gods, hell, eternal punishment, and heaven are to be accepted and maintained by these traditions. Very few people would believe such nonsense if this indoctrination in the supernatural occurred later in life, especially in the light of modern science. Critics and free thinkers now and in the past have had less direct access to the mass media as a medium for expressing contrary views. Again, this is politics. Suppressing information and overstating or fabricating aspects of one's tradition is pure politics.

When parents force a religious tradition on a child, this is not freedom of religion. Everyone living in the United States under the Constitution enjoys freedom of religion, and this applies to our children as well. Certain elements of the religious community have conceptualized the fetus as a living human being. Abortion, then, becomes murder. Using the same standard, an infant is a human being and should have the same protective rights as an adult, that is, freedom of religion (or freedom from religion). Using our technological and information base, it is doubtful that anyone over the age of twelve, and not indoctrinated early in life, would believe that the Bible and Qur'an represent historical truth, any more than they would believe that Mickey Mouse is a real person, that a supernatural agency gave golden tablets to Joseph Smith, or that Wiley Coyote does a great deal of business with the ACME rocket company. Early indoctrination and the use of violence (emotional and physical) to maintain a myth out of touch with current social circumstances clearly indicates an immense insecurity about the validity of the beliefs (and practices) in question. Scientists do not have to threaten people with hellfire and damnation if they choose not to believe two and two is four, the existence of a force we call gravity, or the presence of a Black Hole at the center of each and every galaxy. No one is forced to believe in evolution. On the other hand, it has become unpopular to burn people at the stake in modern Western society, so symbolic violence comes into play. As an example, in the mid-1980s some enterprising people created the Darwin sticker to compete with the Christian fish sticker, a symbol, by the way, that originally stood for the penis of Osiris, sacred flesh consumed by a fish (see Rush 2007). Popes and bishops wear the fish (or a fish head) as a crown. It is called a miter but is actually symbolic of the penis of Osiris representing fertility, which gives the term "dickhead" a new reference point. I have difficulty seeing the pope as a representation of fertility. Instead, history shows that popes represent poverty, suffering, and death. This is amplified by the revelation of the Vatican-Hitler deal, where Adolph wanted some Vatican treasures. So why didn't he just send a few boys to the Vatican or have brave Mussolini send in some Italian troops? They cut a deal that was good for both. Here is the actual conversation of this deal:

POPE: Thank you for taking time from your busy schedule of burning Jews, who sold out our God, Jesus Christ our Lord—Dio benedict!!!, down the drain!

ADOLPH: So you zay that you have zhem on the premises? Ya? And zay are zin good condition? Ya? Because our museum is very par-tic-u-lar, you know. We have our methods of finding out the truth. Ya? And of course we are the bad guys, and bad guys can do anything zay want. Ya?

POPE: Oh, yes, there can be no mistake. They are here and they are authentic, Dio benedict!! Would you like to take a look?

ADOLPH: Ya! Ya! Bring zem here! Ya! Ya! Magnificent. They . . . they look so new . . .

POPE: As you recall, he only wore them from Pilate's place to Calvary—very little wear. You are fortunate!

ADOLPH: Ya! Ya !

POPE: But this comes with an ensemble, a little extra but worth it. You will have something that everyone will admire, forever and ever, Dio benedict!!

ADOLPH: Vhat do you mean, a little extra?

POPE: Here it is—the actual underwear that Jesus wore the day of his crucifixion. Well, up to the point of his crucifixion. It might have been the morning of . . . No matter, they are in perfect shape. Take a look. Nice. Egyptian cotton, last a lifetime or two . . .

ADOLPH: I didn't know zha people wore underwear in zose days . . .

POPE: Well, that's why this is so rare—it is one of a kind! You have to admit that Jesus was a trendsetter!

ADOLPH: Are you sure you aren't Jewish?

So, Adolph got some sandals and underwear, which the pope stored for him, in exchange for Adolph not storming the Vatican. It was bad enough that he was taking London back to the Stone Age, but if he assaulted Vatican City he could add pissed off Catholics to a list of problems, like all of Italy and many places and people far, far away. The reader has to appreciate how powerful symbols are.

Getting back to the Darwin sticker, shortly after this appeared on the backside of cars and trucks, the Christian community responded with the Christian fish swallowing Darwin, and the letters "TRUTH" written on the Christian fish. This is symbolic violence. I've asked fundamentalists about this and they say, "It's only a joke." But when asked if we should have a Darwin fish eating the Christian fish, I am told that would be showing "insensitivity and disrespect to Christianity." Recently I have seen the Darwin fish, representing TRUTH, eating the Christian fish (MYTH); this is called a "cold war." Fundamentalists are like gang members—they want everyone to respect them but have no respect for the beliefs and practices of others.

The Da Vinci Code, in a similar manner as the Darwin sticker, struck a cord on the religious harp. Why? Because the old story has been cast into doubt, even if momentarily, but *The Da Vinci Code* allows the story to change without losing its central character, Jesus. The story appeals to the female reader or moviegoer because she no longer feels excluded. Many men are beginning to realize that gentleness is stress reducing and more likely to lead to cooperative behavior (not to mention better sex) not motivated by fear. Jesus (not Christianity) is simply a better role model then Moses, Muhammad, or Brigham Young; the latter are role models for tyrants and despots.

These ancient myths, spun from our experience of the world for many thousands of years, were likewise connected to an innate need to organize the world around predictable events. The only way we can successfully have any sense of control over our experiences is through an understanding of cause and *predictable* effect. Our newer story (evolution) requires faith, but it is self-correcting—we have faith that situations change, beliefs change, and our knowledge base increases. This new story has actually been in place since recorded history (ancient Egypt, for example) and must date back millennia before that. In the Egyptian tradition there is the concept of evolution; there are what appear to be references to genetics, as well as other sophisticated symbols that say life has gone through stages (see Scranton 2006) from our animal nature (Thoth as a baboon) to intellect (Thoth with a head of an ibis representing knowledge). With monotheism the evolution position became unpopular for over 1,700 years and, even at that, when scientists (naturalists) began to uncover the process of evolution there was no social forum. The Christian camp had a monopoly on truth, even after Darwin published *On the Origin of Species* in 1859. It took time for the scientific position to get into the popular press. Why? Because of censorship, intimidation, threats of loss of employment, and so on; again, this is politics. We have a liberal press in the United States and most European countries, and people have exposure to vast varieties of technology, ideas, art forms, philosophies, temptations, and so on. But the censorship strategy is still alive and well in fundamental monotheism. With this, the average person is in a bind: On the one hand, he or she would like to believe that there is an all loving, kind god in the heavens, but on the other hand there is another story, backed by science, which shows that much of the storyline of the Bible and the Qur'an is absurd. The scientific community is simply telling a more believable story, complete with mathematics, technology, and verifiable artifacts/relics. Our technology has advanced geometrically over the past century and the medical community hints at immortality by altering our genetic code. Although this is an old story found in many traditions, new stories of cloning and stem cell research promise a new heaven and a new earth, without having to experience the other side.

The old Sumerian epic of Gilgamesh (2700 BCE) and the priest Adapa (2000 BCE) are stories of hopelessness and sum up major themes in the development of gods. The gods are representations of who we want to be; we want power and control of our world, and, of course, to live forever. Gilgamesh (an early rendition of Heracles), a king of Uruk, was conceived of a mortal man, but his mother is a goddess named Ninsuna ("Queen of the Wild Cow"); she is also an interpreter of dreams. Our hero Gilgamesh is an immoral king, a womanizer, and through numerous complaints by concerned humans, the gods determine he needs to be put in his place. So they introduce him to a wild man, Enkidu, someone his equal in strength. They wrestle, become friends, Gilgamesh gets him laid (after which Enkidu is shuned by the animals he used to romp with), and they subdue the monster Huwawa. Gilgamesh decides to let the monster go but Enkidu kills it. The goddess Inanna gets pissed off and kills Enkidu. Gilgamesh, in his sorrow at the death of his friend, searches for the herb of immortality (death sucks), and is told by one of the first Noahs (Ut-napishti) that it resides in the briny deep. Gilgamesh dives down, retrieves the herbs, makes it back to shore, sets the herb down while he washes off the salt, and a snake eats the herb! Immortality is only reserved for the gods—whole gods (not half- or three-quarter gods) and snakes (they shed their skins and are reborn).

The story of Adapa gives us some psychological comfort and a message to monotheists. Adapa, who resides in Eridu near the Persian Gulf on the west bank of the Euphrates, is a priest who worships a patron god by the name of Ea, a subterranean, fresh-water god who brings wisdom to humankind. Ea is the forerunner to Oannes and later John the Baptist.

Adapa is fishing one day and the south wind comes up and turns his boat over. Adapa is then bobbing in the water and the fish are laughing at him. So he curses the south wind: "God damn you!" he roars, in a fashion similar to Jeremiah Wright, and the wind stops blowing. Without the south wind, no rain falls for watering crops or cooling the air; the crops dry up, ushering in global warming. This is the first recorded incident of global warming being caused by a human—a priest no less!

The head god, Anu (which translates as "above" or perhaps "god above") is not all that enamored with humans and does lots of nasty things—he is the one who unleashed the bloodsucking, oversexed, baby-killing monster Lamashtu on humanity, who is represented by Lilith, the reputed first wife of Adam. In any event, one day, while planning his next practical joke, Anu focuses his attention on the city of Eridu and notices that nothing is growing. So he asks around, "Did someone mess with the drip system? You know that I just had it installed and we have to give it a chance. Perhaps there is an electrical short somewhere, because it is all drying up! I won't have anyone to torment!" In stepped one of Anu's court administrators.

"No, no, your most highness. We were just coming over to tell you about this priest, Adapa, and the south wind you sent down overturned his boat, as it was supposed to do—it was as you so ordered. But he, your royal highness (bowing very, very low), he said, and I'm only repeating what he said ..."

"Well, spit it out man, I don't have all millennium!"

"He said, 'God damn you,' and we are sure that he wasn't praying that you would construct a dam across the river."

"Why, that little prick! He can't take a joke? Well, get him up here! I'll fix his priestly ass, and get Ea on the phone as well!" (Chuckle, chuckle, rubbing his hands together with a sinister look in his eye.)

Adapa is sent for but he confers with his patron deity first. Ea tells him from firsthand knowledge (Anu and Ea had a lengthy cellphone conversation) that Anu is going to kill him in a most gruesome way. So Ea gives Adapa three directives. First, when he gets to the gates of heaven, Adapa must praise the gate guards.

"Like they have never been praised before and maybe, just maybe, they will go back and sing praises to Anu. He will yell at you a little bit, and threaten and taunt you with remarks; for example, saying you have testicles smaller than those of an ant. And always, always, bow in this place, just as you would to the king.

"The second thing you need to do is humbly walk before Anu. Do not shiver or shake—your resolve is that, if you have done wrong, then you get what you deserve. No snivelling and crying, as people will lose respect for you. And forget all that new psychology stuff, where it's alright for men to cry. No, it is not. You can cry and snivvle before you go and after you get back, but not in front of Anu.

"Third, when you enter the room, there will be food and drink on the table. There will also be anointing oil and a shroud. The food and drink are poisoned; if you drink or eat you will surely die. Instead, take off your clothes, anoint yourself with oil, and put on the shroud. Then you will be safe and he won't kill you."

With the advice in mind, priest Adapa travels to heaven and encounters the pearly gates guarded by Dumuzi (Lord of the Underworld who represents the life and death return cycle—Tammuz in Hebrew) and Gestinanna (a vegetation goddess, sister of Dumuzi, a bookkeeper in the underworld, also called Gizzida). He praises these gods like they have never been praised, bows sincerely, and tells them wonderful things about themselves. The gods look at each other, and giggle a lot, for such sincere praise was hard to come by in this place. And thus they bring Adapa to Anu. Anu looks down at Adapa from his throne as an entomologist would look at an insect, at which point Dumuzi and Gestinanna look at each other, giggle, lean down, and whisper in Anu's ear. His facial gestures go from sinister to rather neutral, and at the same time he sits up on his throne.

"Well, what do you have to say for yourself?" asked Anu.

"I did wrong and am resolved to receive any punishment you render, oh powerful Anu, the most high of the gods," replied Adapa.

Receiving such praise, Anu motioned for Adapa to eat and drink. Adapa looked cautiously at the food, and then walked to the shroud and anointing oil, removed his clothes, applied the oil, and slipped on the shroud. With that Anu began to laugh in the manner of Jaba the Hut.

"Ho, ho, ho. I knew Ea couldn't keep his mouth shut, always getting in my way and helping you earthlings," said Anu. "I tested your trust of me, and had you trusted me and eaten the manna and drunk the elixir of life, I could have bestowed the gift of life on humankind. But nooooo, you had to listen to Ea. But of course he is your patron, and what is the point of a patron god if you don't take his advice? So I'll tell ya what I'm going to do. I'm going to give you wisdom and the license to heal; only priests will have this, so take some of this manna and spread it around to the other priests—no commoner is to have this, do you understand?"

"Yes, your royal highness."

"Alright, then be gone," said Anu. "I don't have all millennium to bestow favors. That's pretty catchy, 'Make my millennium." I can use that when Yahweh shows up.'"

So wisdom is bestowed and immortality denied, but Western bio-medicine, through wisdom, might just bring us immortality of a sort. Surgical repair of the body, organ cloning, DNA manipulation, and computerized prostheses are wonderful metaphors stimulating hope for and faith in continued life in the here and now. This hope lies behind the same sentiment as the Israelites: "If you don't get it here, you won't get it anywhere."

Entertaining Insanity

The Bible and Qur'an are considered by many to represent historical fact and accurate statements from real prophets who had real conversations with God. How would a psychologist or psychiatrist diagnose the behavior of someone claiming to have conversations with God? (See *Diagnostic and Statistical Manual of Mental Disorders* or *DSM-IV*, 1994.) Would a psychologist right away assume that this is a prophet who has actual conversations with supernatural agencies? Might the psychiatrist assume some chemical imbalance or illness brought on the auditory and/or visual hallucinations? Perhaps these prophets were on drugs, or perhaps they were just plain nuts? Or just maybe, originally, these were stories told round the campfire and on special occasions to entertain and inform and not to be accepted as truth? If you are a Jungian, archetypes would be your way out. In other words, these stories represent vivid dreams, perhaps, chunked together with deep structural symbols neatly tucked away in an archaic library in the human brain. Take your choice. For the scientist, however, supernatural cause is out, and I personally don't take archetypes very seriously.

These works were most certainly written for other religious clerics, as the average person was illiterate. If these works were primarily constructed for other religious clerics to interpret, then much contained between the pages is of little or no relevance to the average person. Religious clerics edit and censure the sacred texts, and with this we simply have philosophical and pseudo-historical discussions between intellectuals. If, on the other hand, their content was primarily directed at the average person, then these works are 2,000 years out of touch, and when the Bible and Qur'an are read as historical fact, morality and spirituality are left behind as well. Morality obviously meant something different 2,000 years ago. The social circumstances and stress factors that pushed these documents into existence will be discussed in Chapters Two through Four. I will have more to say about psychopathology as well in the following chapters.

In the Beginning There Was El, Innana, Baal . . .

Judaism and Christianity historically share the same emphasis on a patriarchal deity, and some scholars say this is the Western Semitic god, El. El was characterized as a bull or bull-calf, a symbol of strength. Scholars also state that El is the son of El'eb (god of the father), a much older god. This being the case, I suspect that there have been many generations of El, who is probably connected to pre-agricultural times. It would appear that as we go back in time El is linked to specific adjectives, such as strong, to be in front of, chief, leader, and *manna* (van der Toorn et al. 1999, 274), and depicted as old with gray hair and a beard, and, of course, with great wisdom (van der Toorn et al. 1999, 275). El's ancient connection to manna is of interest, as well as his helping/kindness attributes. When the word manna is encountered, it almost always is in reference to some magical power, that is, a mind-altering substance. This is not surprising, as it was encountered in the story of Adapa and Anu, and will be encountered time and time again.

The mythic theme of a god being the son of a god is ancient and probably mirrors the transfer of the power of kingship from father to son. It is also used to establish genealogical time depth for a mythical charter. In other words, your true identity and legacy is reflected in generations, as this adds legitimacy to one's claim to rule, land ownership, and so on.

In any event, Yahweh or Jehovah eventually displaced El. Yahweh is the god also taken on by the Christians and the name becomes *Deus* (Greek) or God, the "bright shining one." Later on El shares many characteristics with the storm/war and vegetation god Baal, suggesting competition between the two. The Gnostics saw Yahweh as Ialdabaoth, a morally corrupt and evil deity, a conclusion that many reach after reading the Old Testament as well as the Qur'an, and by observing today's world events.

For the Hebrews, El, Ali, Eli, Elu, Elyon (derived from the Hebrew verb "ala," meaning "to ascend"—see van der Toorn 1999, 293), or Elohim ('El 'olam), have been used in referring to this entity. Eventually this deity becomes Yahweh, with the Masoretic form being Jehovah, a composite of Yahweh and Adoni ("my Lord"—see Chapter Two). As the Hebrews broke away from the other Canaanites tribes there was an ideological war, with Baal and the mother-goddess Astoreth eventually discredited (demonized) and replaced.

Allah, the deity of Islam, is not derived from El. During the construction of Islam, beginning around 700 CE, those inventing this system turned the deity associated with Muhammad and the other Arabian tribes from the moon god of war, al Liah (il Liah, Hilal, Hiliah), to the god of Judaism, once they uncovered special, mythical charter information. These mythical connections come by way of Ishmael, the first son of Abraham through Hagar. And God said (Genesis 17:20): "And as for Ishmael, I have heard thee: Behold, I have blessed him, and will make him fruitful, and will multiply him exceedingly; twelve princes shall he beget, and I will make him a great nation." According to the Bible, Hagar finds an Egyptian wife for Ishmael (Genesis 21:21) and thus the twelve princes, as far as can be determined, are genetically Egyptian and Hebrew. This, at least initially, *excludes* all the Arab tribes from any connection to Abraham. This is part of the storyline that was ignored by the Islamic poets.

Al Liah was, in pre-Islamic times, only one of many gods and goddesses in a pantheon. In fact, al Liah has three daughters. Al Lat is the female form of al Liah, associated with Astarte, and is considered a domestic goddess similar to Nephthys of the Egyptian tradition. Al-

Uzza was a goddess connected to the tribe of Ghatafan, the patron goddess of Mecca, youngest of the three daughters, and she is identified with Venus as the morning star; her name means "the mighty one." She is also said to reside in a tree similar to the acacia. The third daughter is Manat ("fate"). She is a goddess of the tribes of Huzail and Khaza'ah and associated with shrines between Mecca and Medina. She is the ancient Arabian goddess of fate and destiny, and is personified as the evening star (also the planet Venus). But just as there are wars between kings, there are wars in heaven with gods and goddesses fading in and out of favor.

In each case (Judaism, Christianity, and Islam), the deity evolved to fit the needs of rulers and religious clerics, but there are differences in how this god is conceptualized. God in the Christian tradition is given a less stressed and angry disposition, and when made corporeal in the form of Jesus, becomes a kind, gentle, philosopher-healer. The gods of both Judaism (Yahweh) and Islam (al Liah) are exclusive to a people (a patron deity), have a nasty disposition, and will accept nothing less than total submission. Early on, the god of Abraham is approachable in human form (e.g., Genesis 18); that same god is seen as a plant god (Exodus 3:1–6; see Chapter Two), haze, or smoke by Moses (Exodus 19:9, 33:7–11), and the god of Muhammad only communicates through third persons (Gabriel, Shaytan, etc.). Al Liah has never been seen in any form, although he is imagined as having a very, very large knee (sort of like the knees of the Colossi of Memnon—Amenhotep III—on the west bank of Thebes), close to which sit all the Muslims who have martyred themselves in his name.

Ritual Sex and Judaism, Christianity, and Islam

For fundamentalists, Jews, and Christians, sex (nature) is presented as evil and demonic and should only be used for procreation. As the Israelites were breaking away from the other Canaanites tribes in order to maintain a tribal identity as a special people, they had to demonize the spiritual sex connected to the mother-goddess cults of the other

Canaanite tribes. Sperm should not be indiscriminately spread around. Women (who represent nature) were construed as evil, the human body became nasty and evil, male masturbation became a crime punishable by death (onanism, Genesis 38: 8–10), and of course using sex and drugs as a means of approaching the divine was restricted to the Aaronic priesthood. Pain and suffering were the methods remaining for approaching the godhead (see Rush 2005).

Drugs and ritual sex, however, were never completely abandoned. Thanks to St. Paul, the creator of Christianity, ritual sex (especially homosexual contacts) maintained itself, and we see this today with the numerous priests who have seduced alter boys and other members of the congregation. The news media play this out as simply casual sex by deranged priests, but it goes deeper then that. Homosexual ritual-spiritual sex was available to the individual in the Canaanite mother-goddess cults. This was not done recreationally (in most cases) but as a means to commune with the gods. Catholic priests are simply continuing the older tradition, and although they are to take a vow of celibacy, this can be overridden if the act is for spiritual purposes; a few "Hail Marys" and "Our Fathers" and you're off the hook. The Catholic Church has known about and, for the most part, condoned this behavior for almost two thousand years, beginning with Paul and continuing from there. The writings of Marquis de Sade (see Gillette 1967), a deranged nobleman, are not simply fabrications, but represent, at least in part, the actual behavior of priests. During the sexual act the priest is contemplating or communing with God, with the victim simply a means to an end. There is nothing right or wrong about ritual sex; the problem lies in the hypocrisy connected with the act for systems that condemn the behavior. Monotheistic traditions, if nothing else, preach a brand of hypocrisy that even puts politicians to shame.

Protestant ministers, especially evangelists, have frequently been accused of inappropriate sex with parishioners or church staff members, but the purpose of the sex, in many cases, has been to commune with God—this is how it is presented to the victim.

For Mormons, ritual sex is clearly revealed in the use of special clothing (patterned after the Jewish tradition) with appropriate openings in the garments to allow sex, but also maintain the husband's connection with God and not one's wife. God is more important than one's wife and we should not be surprised. Women are seen as mere containers, for it is only through God that women conceive and bring fourth life. Misogyny (hatred of women by men) is a central feature of fundamental monotheism.

Recently (April 16, 2008) a polygamous fundamentalist Mormon cult (FLDS) in Eldorado, Texas, was raided by child welfare officials because of accusations of child abuse (read this as, "emotionally disturbed men of advanced years having sex with/marrying underage girls"). During their investigation, authorities found a bed in the temple used for the purposes of ritual sex, most likely with young virgin girls although it probably went way beyond that. Although polygamy was supposedly outlawed in 1890, it is justified in this tradition on the grounds of "religious freedom," numerous polygamous marriages in the Old Testament, and the precedent set by Joseph Smith, the founder of this aberrant tradition, who was obsessed with sex (and alcohol). This should not come as a surprise—fundamentalist Judaism, Christianity, and Islam are an appeal to our animal nature. Although the Mormon establishment disavows any connection to the FLDS cult, they are directly responsible for perpetuating irrational thinking and consequent behavior. Young people indoctrinated at an early age and secluded from the larger society and contemporary reference points simply do what they are told. Mormonism is not a democracy, and slavery is alive and well in this and all fundamentalist traditions; men rule and women are to know their place.

Warren Jeffs, the grand patriarch of this cult, was arrested in August 2006 for numerous counts of incest and rape. Again, these fundamentalist traditions have little to do with a spiritual quest and everything to do with controlling the minds and bodies of unsuspecting, naive people. This is politics.

In the Islamic tradition, ritual sex is a male prerogative and usually reserved for high level religious clerics. Women are feared for having magical abilities. This is one reason that women are forced to wear clothing from the tops of their heads to the tips of their toes—"women give men erections." This, of course, represents emotional irresponsibility and consequent behavioral irresponsibility, but a woman's "magical" abilities represent a great deal of power that can be used to commune with the deity through sex. An unexpected consequence of hiding the magical female body is that wearing so much clothing, with little exposure to the sun (and the conversion of cholesterol under the skin to vitamin D), leads to high levels of health problems (osteoporosis, diabetes, and cancer) among Muslim women.

In Islam the underlying message of martyrdom, sitting next to the large knee of Allah, and receiving seventy-two virgins, is a celestial representation of ritual sex. Most see this as only an appeal to the male's animal nature but it goes much deeper. Many of the women sold into slavery in Saudi Arabia are used for these purposes, not by the masses, but by the upper level religious clerics (and rulers). The moon god cult is the primary focal point or motive behind this type of sex, and probably evolved from the worship or dedication to al Liah's (Allah's) three daughters.

Ritual sex is a time-honored activity practiced by many of the Gnostic sects, Masons, Satanists, Wicca, and is a feature of the Arthurian legends (see von Strassburg 1982); it is an act of love and love is God. Notre Dame de Paris, Chartres, and other cathedrals designed by the Knight Templars are a representation of the mother-goddess, with her head stuck in the ground and her open legs pointed to heaven. By simply entering these cathedrals, patrons are engaging ritual sex in the abstract.

Creation vs. Evolution

We are told that the Bible and the Qur'an are the revealed and divine words of God, the God of Abraham. If they are the revealed words, then the players would have to be real, identifiable figures in secular history. These works also would necessarily have to be perfect in every way—the moon, the stars, the sun in the sky. Mistakes in these works, however, would invalidate and remove them from secular history.

The deity connected to these traditions would understand the workings of everything, all the mathematical, mechanical, and genetic needs, and all that occurs at the atomic and sub-atomic levels. Even a god has to work within a set of rules in order for us to have the experiences we do of the tangible world. That power and wisdom, one would assume, should be expressed right down to every chosen letter in the Bible and Qur'an. There would be no mathematical mistakes, no scientific mistakes, no errors in geography, no mistakes as to when things happened, right down to the consistency of events (people, places). If we assume less, then this deity is not all-powerful. Some writers have suggested that inconsistencies are there because of scribal errors or errors in transcription over time. If that is the case, then we cannot just assume that the inconsistencies are scribal error; perhaps the rest is scribal error as well. The Dead Sea Scrolls have shown that some statements in the Old Testament, for example, cannot be attributed to scribal error. The errors are blatant, and it would be difficult to believe that the poets or authors of these documents thought they would stand the test of time as secular history, unless, of course, they never thought that the average person would ever be literate. Let's take a brief look at the Bible and consider some of these inaccuracies and their possible meaning (also see Chapters Two, Three, and Four). Keep in mind that there are similar problems in the Qur'an as it is, for the most part, a direct borrowing of stories from the Bible.

> Genesis 1: In the beginning God created the heaven and the earth. And the earth was without form, and void; and darkness was upon the face of the deep. And the Spirit of God moved upon the face of the waters.

This part of the creation story is quite old, did not originate with the Hebrews, and has it roots in Sumerian and Egyptian creation stories.

The creativity of the Old Testament lies in the ability of the priest-poets to rework the tale for their own special needs, and that is to have a god *with a purpose* looking after a special people. It has even been suggested that the creation story (and Genesis in general) was the last to be included in the first five books (Torah) as a means of tying the other books together. After Genesis 1:2 we begin to see problems that the ancients either weren't aware of, or the deity is not all-knowing (although we can "spin" the tale somewhat and find similarities to modern cosmologies).

In Genesis 1:3, "God said, let there be light: and there was light. God saw that the light was good, and he separated the light from the darkness. God called the light day and the darkness he called night. And there was evening, and there was morning—the first day." If this was historical fact, then we have a hint of the Big Bang. There is nothing yet created that can produce light, nor is there anything to reflect or obscure light, so let's give the deity a hand and postulate that there must have been a big, super large explosion. Separating the day and night is simply creating reference points, that is, gaseous matter coalescing into suns with darkness beyond, and with those hosting planets, like our solar system, we eventually experience day and night. This reasoning or detailed understanding was, however, not in the science of the day.

Now, the next few lines are a little out of sequence in terms of what we know about the developmental stages of the universe and, more specifically, life on this planet. But there is an evolving process going on; it didn't happen overnight and a previous stage must be reached before the next stage can happen. But the poets presented *their* scientific view at that time (see Chapter Two). An all-knowing deity, however, would have included a little more detail, unless, of course, He thought his creations were not smart enough to figure it out, although we were created in His image and at least reasonably intelligent. So what is this? Is this the word of God, or ink from the poet's pen describing the universe as they knew it in their time frame?

We have to assume that the energy that informs all is intelligent above and beyond anything we can imagine. With that assumption, we can say that the "errors" we encounter must represent something else.

The words in the Bible and Qur'an are divine in the sense that they come from our ability to reason, think about life, and overcome obstacles. What is communicated is an ancient conception of history and evolution. This is now considered metaphysical or sacred science (spiritual taphonomy), and the "divine words" represent a metaphor for the intelligence of human kind.

The Old Testament was not written for the masses but represents a mythical charter that justified land ownership and special privileges. It was written for a chosen few, for the express purpose of separating themselves from others, creating mythic references and associated rituals that would set them apart from the surrounding tribes. It also acted as a rulebook for proper behavior, as communicated by the teachers or rabbis (a celestial instruction manual); again, basically designed to isolate the Israelites from others. The rules and rituals were forced upon the people under threat of punishment from God, who uses kings and generals to enact His will. Judaism is clearly a political system, as all rules and rituals are designed to control the individual for the purpose of building a nation. It is not about an ecstatic experience connecting the individual to the godhead, except for special people; this separation of esoteric and exoteric rites began sometime after 560 BCE, not 1000 BCE as suggested by some scholars. This is not a system that promotes spirituality for the individual. One problem we encounter with monotheism is that, once it is labeled as "religion," most fail to understand that these are political systems, with reference to a deity simply adding credibility through an assumed powerful "third person." This has been standard operating procedure for over 5,000 years. There is absolutely nothing spiritual in fundamental Judaism, Christianity, and Islam, for to be spiritual the tradition must connect the individual to the deity in ways that go beyond praying for health, wealth, and progeny. Popular religion does not promote spirituality, because this could eliminate the need for temple, church, mosque, and the religious cleric. Spiritual experiences belong to the individual, and if you don't bring spirituality and God into the temple, church, or mosque, you won't find it or Him there.

The Old Testament contains two creation stories. The first, Genesis 1, has a scientific ring to it, while the second story (Genesis 2) is poetry and politics. Genesis 1 is a statement of science, and as such it represents a process in which one action leads to a higher order or more complex development. Strictly speaking, then, the creation (that which was created by the deity) is *evolution,* or a process of unending change and alteration. Looked at this way, modern day creationists were the first evolutionists; they simply misunderstood the nature of creation. Again, however, there are many inexcusable errors in the Bible and the Qur'an (see McKinsey 1995) if these works are the divine word of God. Some of these errors will be discussed in Chapters Two through Four.

Reason and Belief

A cat has an innate reasoning ability that is certainly similar to ours, but its awareness of the environment is quite different. We attribute our reasoning ability to a massive cerebral cortex and storage capacity, along with linguistic ability. But let's not feel sorry for the cat, for it intuitively understands calculus and physics or it would never be able to leap, jump, and catch its prey. It must know the chemistry of digestion and elimination or it would not be able to obtain the energy necessary to sustain its life. But that inner knowledge, the knowledge of the universe, is unavailable to its moment-to-moment consciousness. In other words, a cat will apprehensively watch an object like a ball mysteriously roll across the floor without legs or the appropriate smell of a living thing. As far as we know, a cat cannot convert its inner wisdom to an accurate explanation as to why the ball seems to move on its own power. Children at a young age are in a similar position. That is to say, they are not at a level of awareness that allows them to understand the "powers" (cause and effect) behind the physical world (Newtonian mechanics), let alone quantum mechanics. Myth comes to the aid of the child, and the only difference between the childhood and adult stories is that the latter are usually much more complex. Through storytelling, the child can learn that god or angels (energy and mass for an adult) move the ball across the floor, thunder is a deity rolling boulders around in heaven (discharge of electrons for adults), and so on. In Western culture, children learn quaint explanations for all sorts of things, such as the moon being made out of green cheese, Santa Claus bringing presents, the Easter Bunny placing candy eggs all over the place, and the tooth fairy giving a payout for the milk teeth we lose. Stories for children are usually wrapped in language and explanation that fit their emotional development. By the time the individual is six or seven years of age, these stories are brought into doubt as children detect their inconsistencies, learn the more subtle nonverbal messages of parents and others when such stories are discussed, and have older brothers and sisters "bust" the stories. For an individual after a certain age to continue to believe in a tangible Santa Claus who lives at the North Pole—with a bunch of elves constructing all this stuff for Santa to distribute all over the world within a few hours—surely evokes ridicule. Christmas is one of those times when all the adults are in on the deception but realize it—this deception, this lie, is considered acceptable. At the same time, adults (just like children) get caught up in the magic of it all, even with the intense materialism and capitalism surrounding this pagan holiday. It is mass cultural fun; people are even nicer to each other for a few days out of the year.

Some stories, however, are encouraged, and disbelief could, and still does, result in ridicule, torture, and/or death in some traditions. Also, like many cults (this pejorative term has been converted to "spiritual psychology" by some), once you become a member it is nearly impossible to leave, let alone think critically about the beliefs and practices. This is the case in many Protestant groups, who engage in shunning and turning other family members and friends against the individual who questions or abandons the faith, a common practice of the Seventh Day Adventists, Mormons, Jehovah's Witnesses, and other fundamentalist sects. Scientologists use similar tactics and likewise collect personal files on members, which are stored away in a secret place. One has to wonder about this practice of Scientology, its purpose, and the ultimate disposition of the files.

In cases of shunning, the individual experiences social death, which almost always leads to depression and occasional suicides (see Rush 1999; in my own private practice I have worked with many such individuals). Shunning and destroying families in the name of God is immoral at best, and certainly has nothing to do with the message Jesus brought to the world. This is likewise the case in Islam. In Islam apostasy, or leaving the tradition, can result in torture and death (see Chapter Four).

In the development of Judaism, according to the Bible, the rulers treated those who strayed from the cosmic laws quite harshly. This is a typical tactic in modern cults, where individuals are isolated from non-members and critical thinking is discouraged, while fear of physical punishment and rape, accompanied by massive amounts of emotional abuse, are standard operating procedures for obtaining compliance (see Perlmutter 2004).

Judaism, Christianity, and Islam claim to be the moral watchdogs of society, but at the same time they are soaked in blood. These systems have been around for a long, long time, and if they acted as moral lessons we would be living in a world of peace. There will be no peace on earth until there is a reconciliation of myths (the myths we live by), a movement away from thinking the Bible and Qur'an are the factual word of God, and a re-emergence of a curiosity about the mystery of life. We need to take the best out of these sacred writings, and the wisdom of other traditions as well, and establish a "truth" we can all live with and which will evolve to meet our social needs.

Judaism, Christianity, and Islam are not systems built from honest mistakes but systems built out of deception, lies, and fabrications. The deceptive foundations and additions have a time depth of over twenty-five hundred years. Because these foundations and additions are used to control behavior, those in charge (the religious clerics) are precisely those who have the greatest vested interest in maintaining the deception. Fundamentalism requires a male superiority, a suppression of female rights (women have to be suppressed because they have too much power), and censuring any information detrimental to the established hierarchy, a hierarchy acting through the "will of God." These traditions, however, have encountered several problems that will ultimately render them obsolete, with the first a world market economy which brings with it new ideas and freedom of choice, and second, the discovery of energy sources that will make oil virtually obsolete accept in the manufacture of certain plastics and other chemicals. The world will be a very different place in twenty years and unrecognizable in one hundred; the myths constructed 2,000 years ago will either adapt or die.

At the core of Judaism, Christianity, and Islam is not love, kindness, and understanding but judgment, violence, terror, and submission. There is nothing spiritual about worshipping a god any more than it is spiritual to bow down to the king or kiss the pope's ring. In all fairness, out of these traditions have emerged wonderful art forms (cathedrals, mosques, etc.), much of which, however, is simply a means of displaying the wealth and power of the religious clerics. Any spiritual ideals are overshadowed by the central theme of control by threat of violence, now and in the hereafter. One should not, once again, confuse morality with religion, as these are two entirely different issues.

Many of the players in the Old and New Testaments have become household icons in a manner similar to Mickey Mouse and Wiley Coyote. But you and I know that Mickey and Wiley are cartoon characters; they are metaphors. As we will see, Abraham was not the founding father of Judaism, and Moses, Jesus, and Muhammad are not who they have been presented to be. They are metaphors and represent the social times and the energy of the people during a time long past. There is nothing new in this book; scholars have known the historical facts regarding the construction of the Old and New Testaments, as well as the Qur'an, for many, many centuries, but most of the information has been ignored or suppressed by scholars and main-line media out of political correctness or fear of reprisal. Some may take offense to what I write, but I am not writing to be offensive. Instead, I am presenting a problem—these traditions, legitimized by their fabricated sacred writings and time depth, were purposely constructed to enslave the minds and bodies of men, women, and children, by force if necessary. When political and quasi-religious traditions are designed to terrorize, control, and impoverish, they no longer serve the good of humanity (see Kimball 2002; Juergensmeyer 2003). Instead, these traditions serve to destroy the human spirit, remove hope, and justify anything in the name of Failed God.

Emotional Responsibility and Self-Responsible Behavior

Many people believe that others, situations, or books give them emotions. This is not how the brain works. What people give you is information to which you attach a meaning, and then attach an emotion for storage and retrieval. Emotions are internally generated (see Rush 1999). Yes, it is predictable that people will upset themselves or get angry when dealing with certain information. However, there is too much personal irresponsibility in the world, and much of that stems from believing that others give you feelings. This comes from the fact that our language creates a reality. Our beliefs about how the world works can only come from our symbolic abilities—that is, our language, both written and spoken, including the agreed upon mathematical symbols. The language-creating-reality argument (Whorf-Sapir hypothesis—see Whorf 1964; Sapir 1966) certainly has it critics, but I have interviewed speakers of many languages over the years (English, French, German, Italian, Russian, Arabic, Mandarin, etc.) and I've yet to come across a language in which speakers consistently take responsibility for their emotions. It is a defense or rationale for behavior. If a person believes someone or something has made him angry or offended him, then he or she believes in the right to retaliate—often violently. This may be the lingering result of attributing all one's actions to the will of a deity. If there is a disease of language (as suggested by philologist Fredrick Max Muller, 1879–1910), emotional irresponsibility is surely that because it removes personal responsibility for any act.

Moreover, self-responsible behavior, or taking responsibility for one's acts rather than blaming them on others, can only come by way of emotional responsibility. Self-responsible behavior also includes critical thinking about the stories told about gods and goddesses, as well as critical thinking about the right for special people (religious clerics) to tell us what to think and how to behave. Self-responsible behavior and critical thinking are not welcome in Christianity and Islam but are an absolute necessity in a modern world.

Freedom of Religion

Fundamentalists, as well as less conservative religious groups and pro-life extremists, have attempted to overturn Roe vs. Wade by insisting that a fetus is a human being and thus entitled to all the rights of the Constitution of the United States and the Bill of Rights. Abortion is murder, according to these groups, and this has led to picketing and firebombing of abortion clinics, as well as the assassination of doctors performing abortions (see Perlmutter 2004). You can see how sacred life is to these groups!

I agree that a fetus is a human being—it is certainly not a cat, dog, bird, or tree. But let's take this a step further. An infant, at least, falls into the same category as a human being and most certainly should enjoy the same rights as an adult—including the right to legal representation and freedom of (or from) religion. Freedom of religion means that the individual has the right to select the philosophy of his or her choice. But there is no freedom for many children—Jewish, Christian, Islamic—because the parents force them to go to church, temple, or mosque, and in the fundamental condition they are forced to believe in a specific manner under threat of punishment (if not now, in the hereafter). So, if we truly desire to protect the right of the fetus, infant, and child, freedom of religion should be left to the child. Filling the child's mind with beliefs about powerful gods, prophets who communicate with gods, nature being corrupt, going to hell if you misbehave or don't accept Jesus or Allah as your savior, and so on, lead to confusion and sometimes psychosis later in life, when these beliefs are brought into doubt by more reasonable information coming through the scientific method outlined earlier.

Fundamentalist parents and clergy attempt to prevent the input of more reasonable information through censorship of outside sources, but this is becoming more and more difficult. We speak of mental health in this country, and one has to wonder how much neurotic and psychotic behavior manifests as the direct result of this early indoctrination in utter nonsense. If the young adult chooses to take up one of these traditions at the age of twelve, then he or she is certainly free to do so. Compulsory religious indoctrination, because the parents wish it so, may be a violation of individual rights, at least in the United States. With emotional responsibility, self-responsibility, and freedom of religion in mind, as well as factoring in the use of mind-altering substances, let's take a closer look at Judaism and Failed God.

CHAPTER TWO

Judaism

Adam was walking around the Garden of Eden, naming animals and smelling rose petals, when God approached and said, "I have some good news and some bad news." His voice rolled on the horizon. "Which would you like to hear first?"

Adam looked around, looked at the face in the sky, and replied, "Tell me the good news first."

God paused for a moment and then spoke: "I'm going to give you a penis and a brain. From the first you will derive great pleasure, and from the second you will acquire great intellect."

Adam stood shocked, not quite grasping the situation, but at the same time assuming that getting things was good. "Cool, man! Bitchin'! Awesome! But, but ... what's the bad news?"

God paused again, realizing that sometimes things go wrong in the workshop. "Well," God began, "I'm only going to give you enough blood supply to work one at a time." (A very old joke, possibly Irish, Catholic, or Jewish, but definitely not Islamic.)

Introduction

Who is responsible for history? In other words, is it the result of human causation, with wars and global warming caused by humans? Or is history the act of supernatural powers, with God creating wars and global warming to punish sinful people? Did Bin Laden act through the will of Allah, or is he simply a psychopath with all kinds of sexual hang-ups (sublimated into rockets, guns, bullets, explosives, etc.), recruiting naive and needy people to start a war, and excusing this in the name of God? Or is it a little of both? Who is responsible for history is an important question (see Albrektson 1967), as it helps to explain cause and effect and justify the acts of individuals and governments. That is to say, if humans cause war, then we can possibly fix this problem or at least limit its occurrence. If, on the other hand, war is God's will, then war can never be appreciated for what it is, and at the same time, God's will removes self-responsibility from any act. Anyone believing that God is responsible for all acts, regardless of the morality of the act or behavior, is simply functioning as an instrument of God. The reader can appreciate how popes, ayatollahs, and other religious clerics abuse this belief, by applying cosmic laws in an arbitrary fashion.

In the development of Judaism, Christianity, and Islam, the mythical charters of legitimacy are always attributed to acts of God, that is, the will of Yahweh, God, or Allah. Humans, as mentioned above, are only instruments. Without such attribution, those in power are more easily challenged. If all events are attributed to God, then loss in war or death of loved ones can be directed away from human causation. I have yet to attend a funeral where someone didn't say, "God's will." Of course, this is a form of psychological protection as well. All is attributed to God.

When wars or laws (Hammurabi's Code or the Ten Commandments) come in the name of a deity, they cannot be argued with. This is a third-person approach in which all acts—good or evil—are attributed to third party sources, in this case, the gods. Personal responsibility and accountability, sorely lacking in most world cultures, stem from this ancient belief that someone else—deity or human—tells you what to do and you follow orders. This lack of self-responsibility and placing the blame on others will be illustrated time and again in this chapter and Chapters Three and Four. Without emotional and personal responsibility, we encounter the suicide bombers, the rapists and child molesters, corrupt politicians, and others who believe that someone or something caused them to speak and/or act; these people blame all their failings on the actions of others, both natural and supernatural.

Definitions and Mythical Charter Building

The words Hebrew, Israelite, and Jew compress about 2,600 years of history. Hebrew refers to a language spoken by one of the Canaanite tribes inhabiting what was called Israel and Judah. This is the geographic area of Israel and Palestine today; thus we have the reference to Israelites, as in Jacob come Israel through his twelve sons (we don't hear much about the lineage of his daughter, Dinah). This would also be the land of Canaan so often referenced in the Bible. The Israelites spoke Hebrew, and because they are associated with the geography of Judah they are called Jews. These name changes are important because they represent stages in their separation from the other Canaanite tribes.

Throughout recorded history, credibility for ruling status has often depended on the depth of one's relationship to important ancestors (real or mythical) and/or connections to the king and court. The Hebrew Bible (The Old Testament), and the ideology and culture it created through fear, faith, and devotion, represent a mythical charter for land ownership and special privileges, just as a father would grant favors to an obedient or favorite son (or sons). The Jews see themselves as related to the mythic patriarch Abraham (see Rosenberg 2006), who had a special relationship with his tribe's patron god. But they also make connections to important people, for example, the Pharaoh in Egypt. The Israelites characterized themselves as a nation of priests. The meaning of this is subtle; priests in both Egypt and Babylon were accorded a high status—who wants to start at the bottom? You can't be Pharaoh and it is possible under the right circumstances to become a king, but priest is nice. Being a priest or rabbi, however, brings with it a higher level of commitment than does a non-priest. The status of priest is a method of separating oneself from the "lower levels" of society. But with this status is also a greater likelihood of not straying from the fold and maintaining an identity of a people or tribe. As with Egyptian and Babylonian priests literacy was very useful; although not all Israelites were literate, they seem to have had a higher literacy rate than the other tribe around them.

In ancient Egypt sons of the pharaoh and priests were usually circumcised, which, to the ancient Egyptians, meant immortality, for just as the snake sheds its skin and is reborn, circumcision symbolically represents rebirth. The Hebrews, however, changed this from an individual's rebirth to the birth of a nation. Symbolically, however, circumcision is a mark of royalty that is very useful when building mythical charters, and this was only one of many symbols and ritual performance borrowed from the Egyptians.

We must also assume that the Old Testament was put together with a futuristic purpose in mind. Scholars and theologians typically center on specific passages, but when looked at in total one sees an emphasis and re-emphasis on the necessity of following the cosmic rules as the means of obtaining the Promised Land. But this also included interpreting the past with prophesies regarding short (Joseph) and long-term (Ezekiel, Daniel) events. The purpose of the Old Testament is to substantiate or give proof (mythical charter) in order to legitimize special privileges and land ownership.

A mythical charter is a story, or compilation of myth, legend, and fact, designed to confer legitimacy for an individual, family, or group to rule, occupy a territory, or have access to special economic, political, spiritual or supernatural privilege and rewards. This is where we all want to be, that is, on top and in good standing with our favorite deity. One feature of the mythical charter is time depth and genealogy, and the other is connection to royalty.

Recording a genealogy for a mythical charter requires more than listing names. If people are to buy the story, the names must be made real through a story of their exploits. These exploits may place particular individuals in a bad light but also lend credibility to the story's authenticity, for to err is human. But the episodes telling of the bad side—incest, rape, murder, war, and prostitution—are equally correct, because this is the way things were in those times (and still are). A modern reading of the Old Testament might see Abraham's behavior of lying and selling his wife into prostitution as reprehensible at best. Then there is all the violence and slavery, as well as discrimination and hate toward outsiders (the Canaanites and the Hittites). This is the way things were—past tense, but certainly not the way things can be. Fundamentalists are trying to use these archaic models of life and the accompanying myths in today's world, but they are too fractured to fit. Why are the Jews so despised, especially by the Muslim community, who attempted to emulate the Jewish tradition almost word for word? First, the Jewish mythical charter clearly states that they are the chosen people and that God favors them, and because of this they should be granted special privileges and land holding. Everyone else in the world is secondary and is worthy only of the leftovers, the scraps; coming in contact with outsiders can result in a spiritual disease.

The Muslims, on the other hand, see themselves when they look into the Jewish mirror, for they too believe they are special in their mythical charter building and morally superior to everyone else. Why? This is because Ishmael, the son born to Abraham and Hagar, was born first. This is called primogenitor, or rights of the firstborn. Everyone else is less than a dog, and when the opportunity is right the dogs should be converted or killed. This type of thinking generates a great deal of fear and hate on both sides. The Jews and the Muslims cannot possibly be worshipping the same god.

Violence, slavery, and every other human rights issue in our own time were common practice for the Hebrews. These stories tell about past attitudes and behaviors that, although still in play in many areas of the world, do not fit; they are fractured and the shards are cutting humanity to pieces. However, these stories, written in the fashion of a historical novel, might also be telling us in a general sense that violence, rape, indiscriminate sexual activity, and *not* having a common goal lead to the destruction of the group's memory of itself. As one's genes move further and further out from a group without boundaries, the more watered down the memory of who is who, and potential rights and obligations (political and economic linkages) are lost. You become one of the masses now having to deal with networks of strangers. Looked at from our vantage point, these stories of mayhem instruct us on how exclusivity and favoritism divide people; we see this in both the treatment of insiders and outsiders. The Hebrew condemnation of the mother-goddess and the consequent view of women are not popular in a modern Western setting, but are still adhered to in many areas of the world, especially in the Middle East where these systems were invented.

The Bible, Qur'an, and associated apocrypha and hadith respectively, are mythical charters. And of course the various scholarly interpretations and apologies clearly show that they are constructions designed to give exclusive political, economic, territorial, and/or spiritual legitimacy to specific groups, that is, Jews, Christians, and Islamites. The New Testament does not make null and void what came before, but it does come with a new message. That new message, once the corruptions added by Paul and the rest of the Christian continuers are removed, is that you don't need to be micro-managed by rules. Simply be a decent human being, treat others the way you want to be treated, and you go to God's place; you don't need a priest or a church to accomplish this. Jesus' continuers have created something Jesus never intended. All those who accept human decency as a way of life will go to the Father/Mother; the priest is not the gatekeeper, nor is the church the portal. If there was any message from Jesus, the "Good News" is that you, the individual, are the gatekeeper and portal. Christian groups corrupted the message each in their own peculiar way, with some leading us right back to the wrathful god of the Old Testament (Catholics, Mormons, Jehovah's Witnesses, Seventh Day Adventists, and many others).

The conquest religion of Islam, which might be seen as a tribal revitalization movement, also takes us right back to the Old Testament. Islam (see Chapter Four) is stuck in the Dark Ages, with early indoctrination, censorship, and violence the only possible ways of maintaining recruits.

All three traditions (Judaism, Christianity, and Islam) have created charters and written documents giving special privileges to special groups, but Judaism produced the original that the latter traditions added onto and modified to fit their specific political ends.

El Who?

A quick review. Judaism and Christianity historically share the same emphasis on a patriarchal deity, and some scholars say this is the Western Semitic god, El. Islam, as we will see, does not initially share the same god but, instead, the pagan moon god of war, al Liah.

El was characterized as a bull or bull-calf. Some scholars also state that El is the son of El'eb (god of the father), a much older god. So the mythic theme of a god being the son of a god is quite common and mirrors the transfer of the power of kingship from father to son. Keep this in mind for Chapter Three.

Judaism in biblical times was made up of several sects. These include the Nazarenes, Pharisees, and Essenes (people living on the northwestern shore of the Dead Sea, notable for the caves in which the Dead Sea Scrolls were found). The Essenes, or followers of Esau, are dated to around 200 BCE; Esau is the Arabic word for Jesus and apparently the Essenes, who considered themselves a family, were very strict in following Jewish law. Many of the ideas about tribal identity and the chosen few must be very ancient indeed and common to herding, nomadic people, because these ideas justify a mythic tradition geared to one day finding a promised land to call their own (owning a piece of land is a spiritual ideal). For the Hebrews it was "the land of milk and honey," actually a relatively small, geographical place. For Christianity and Islam, on the other hand, the goal is the world (see Chapter Four).

After approximately 560 BCE we can recognize three major geographical areas with large Hebrew populations. The first is Babylon, where the educated Hebrews, and some for manual labor, were exiled in 586 BCE. The second is Palestine, where the poorer and less educated remained. Many of the Muslims in Palestine today are descendants of this original Jewish settlement forcibly (at the point of a sword) converted to Islam in the seventh century CE. Today they kill each other in the name of what we are told is the same god, but they obviously worship two different demons. The third group was settled in the delta area of Egypt, with a smaller group at Elephantine in southern Egypt.

The name ascribed by the ancient Israelites to the deity of this tradition, Yahweh, was revealed to Moses on Mt. Sinai or Mt. Horeb as the Tetragrammaton, YHWH. There are two other names referring to this deity: Elohim, a name too sacred to utter, derived from El and meaning "upper tier" or highest level god, and Adoni or "my Lord." Adoni (or Adonai) is an interesting word. It is Hebrew and composed of "ai," which means my or mine, and "Adon" which is actually from the Egyptian Aten or sun disk. T is pronounced D, and E is pronounced O in Hebrew. Some biblical apologists play down this direct association to the sun disk, and even go so far as to say the Aten sun disk is not a reference to the sun, which is only partially correct. The Aten is a reference to the energy that informs all, but it is still a sun disk. The Aten is a personification of that which no one can talk about.

There is a plant god in ancient Egypt named Ukhikh (u-he-keh), a word related to the verb ukeb, meaning "to shine." Is Yahweh (Y-H-W-H) possibly derived from Ukhikh? Switching Egyptian with Hebrew consonants makes an interesting fit.

The Old Testament is considered the old covenant with God. It begins with a creation story that fits our Western idea of a construct with a master craftsman who creates everything through thought and word. The first creation story (Genesis 1:1–28) is closely aligned with the modern model of evolution. That is to say, the earth is formed, and then water forms, then plants, then sea creatures, then animals, and then man and woman ("He made them in His own image"). They are placed in that order because intellectually or intuitively it makes sense, suggesting that the author could not announce or construct one part of this creation story without some precedent:

God→Earth→Water→Plants→Sea Life→Land Animals→Adam and Eve→Trouble in Paradise.

Any one stage is dependent on the previous. You can't have water without planet Earth; you can't have life without water, and so on. Isn't that evolution?

In the original story (Genesis 1:26–27), Adam (whose name has been given several translations, including clay, earth, man) and Eve (Hebrew is *Havva* or *Hayya*, meaning "living" or "animal") are created at the same time, and created "in His own image." Under these conditions God must be androgynous, both male and female (or mineral and animal, or inorganic and organic). Assuming that "His" image means male is similar to assuming that *la luna* really means a female moon in French. In Genesis 1:26–28 we read:

And God said, Let us make man in our image, after our likeness: and let them have dominion over the fish of the sea,
and over the fowl of the air, and over the cattle, and over all
the earth, and over every creeping animal that creepeth upon
the earth.

So God created man in his [own] image, in the image of
God created he him; male and female created he them.
And God blessed them, and God said to them, be fruitful,
and multiply, and replenish the earth, and subdue it: and
have dominion over the fish of the sea, and over the fowl of
the air, and over every living animal that moveth upon the
earth.

There is the philosophical possibility that the wording "after our
likeness," with an emphasis on "our," clearly indicates that the deity
speaking is only part of a larger entity who is both male and female, a
singularity which manifests itself in the tangible world as male or female,
the ultimate polarity in the field of time. Many scholars simply say these
are angels or this is a reference to the polytheistic tradition. Not so.
This idea of an androgynous god is found in the Egyptian tradition,
whose earthly manifestation was Akhenaten (Amenhotep IV), the heretic
pharaoh, portrayed as androgynous. This solves the chicken and egg
argument of which came first, male or female. Thus male and female are
the temporal stand-ins, the duality for a deity that is everything and
nothing at the same time—a singularity, that original black hole. This
god or energy is Atman (Brahman) in the Hindu, Amun in Egypt, and
Aten in Judaism.

But this leads to an interesting problem. If we were made in God's
image, then why are we told that the body is nasty and evil? If God
is a singularity, there cannot possibly be a judgment as to the manifestation of this entity as evil or bad. That is an insult to the deity!
As all comes from this deity, then nothing can be good or bad, right
or wrong; it just is. It is only through culture that we invent good and
bad, right and wrong, and attempt to separate our animal nature from

our intellect. In our lives we have the choice to pay attention to our animal nature, or arise above this and make our way to the stars from which we ultimately came. Judaism, Christianity, and Islam, rather than being spiritually directed, maintain an emphasis on paying attention to our animal nature. Spirituality has nothing to do with politics, economics, the clothes you wear, the food you eat, how you should have sex or with whom, or censoring information. Spirituality has nothing to do with shunning, physical or emotional abuse, or murder.

In any case, in the later version of creation (Genesis 2:1–25), just a few paragraphs later and obviously written by a different hand, we read something significantly different. The earth and stars are formed, then the deity had some idea about plants, but none had sprouted, so he created a mist or rain "which watered the face of the earth." And what would be the point of grass or fields, and so on, if there wasn't someone to manage the farm? So he scooped up some clay, breathed into the clay's nostrils (as any good shepherd would do if he wants to create a faithful "flock"), and man was created. Next he creates a garden, the Garden of Eden, and puts man in there to groom the bushes. So God creates all the animals, birds in the sky, all the beasties, big and small, and gives Adam two directives: "Don't eat the fruit of the tree of good and evil least you 'die'," and, "Give all the animals a name, and don't screw it up!"

This is a stern god and sometimes not very gentle to His children. Although some scholars see this as God giving man a task to encourage responsibility, I don't buy it. How can you develop responsible behavior if someone is always telling you what to do and what not to do? Who wants to take any initiative if there is a fear of supernatural reprisal; you do what you are told. There is no personal choice in this and certainly no self-responsibility. He wants to see if Adam will follow orders, as should any good servant or slave. But a good point is made in naming the animals, because naming and categorizing creates a separation between humans and animals, and that is absolutely necessary if our animal nature is to be suppressed, or at least controlled and directed by culture. Through classification we separate ourselves from all other animals and plants, and by doing so we begin a process of "knowing thy self" and everything is nature. This may be a directive for humans to classify, explore, and understand *everything*. In order to name the animals, they would have to be able to distinguish one animal from another, one plant from another, and this would extend to all paired opposites. This is the initiation of a consciousness designed for exploration, questioning, and comparing. In a word, to name requires studying that which you name, and this suggests a scientific approach— if you are going to get it right. The fundamentalists missed this, along with the concept of evolution, and instead became fixated on God.

This second creation story in Genesis does not make any scientific sense, whereas the first story does. Only as poetry would its draftsman have considered the second story true. What the poetry may be urging, besides men being on top, is to classify your world—you will make many mistakes and poor judgments, things will be tough, but with a little luck and God on your side, you will succeed. The second story is to direct emotions, while the first directs our logical mind (prose). There are many interpretations offered for the two creation stories; for example, the first story is about Adam's first wife, Lilith. But that is a cover-up. There are two stories because there are supposed to be. The first is their science—and it is pretty close, in a general sense, to our modern story—and it is there to show the reader that the writer is not dumb and stupid. In my opinion, there has to be a connecting story between these two creations (but no matter, as this is myth).

The second story is there to make a point, through dramatization, about a male god and male power. This is a clear message about dominion over the world and a change in the social structure, or moving away from the mother-goddess cults and onto the road of exclusivity. This required that woman be subservient to men in myth and in fact. Thus Eve is constructed around or from Adam's rib. I still have lab students wondering why the male skeleton has all the ribs! In that way, if you secure the cooperation of the man, then you have also secured the cooperation of his wife (and perhaps sisters or even mother). Eve is created from Adam's rib, an image suggesting that women are the property of men from which they came. A modern interpretation of this would be cloning, but then Eve would be a man and the story wouldn't work well in the Hebrew tradition.

In Genesis 2:25, "The man and his wife were both naked, and they felt no shame." Shame is encountered when they become something other than animals tending a garden, thanks to Eve and the snake. They eat from the tree of good and evil (probably referring to a mind-altering substance—not figs, as suggested in a recent documentary) and experience their world in a very different manner. The message here has nothing to do with nakedness; it has to do with controlling one's animal nature symbolized by the genitals, which stand for "all" of our animal nature—such as killing, trying to mount everyone you meet, pissing on your walls at home, being a bully, not sharing food, and so on. There is nothing wrong with genitals any more than there is something wrong with your heart, eyes, or right hand. The message is, "Follow instructions from those in power."

Following instructions from higher powers, such as parents, tribal leaders, or kings, is not a new idea, but in Genesis it is designed to show what happens when people don't obey. Disobedience results in deviance from the king's plans, with possible conflict as a consequence. In today's Western world, one *should* rebel against authority, especially if it is corrupt. For over thirty-five years I have asked students, "How many of you like being told what to do by those in authority?" I have yet to see anyone's hand go up. In the Middle East to this day, you do what you are told by someone in authority, and when you do not, you get into serious trouble. This is not to say that anyone likes being told what to do, but without freedom of speech and individual rights you keep your mouth shut. After all, Adam and Eve were thrown into the street (the first part of the Jewish exile story) and abandoned by their parent(s), at least initially, just to see how things would evolve. Adam and Eve got off easy, I suppose, because God didn't have others to stone them to death. Remember God is like the king, pope, or imam—they never do anything and instead delegate by divine decree.

Some scholars see Adam and Eve as a source of genealogical purity because these original progenitors are brother and sister, leading to social purity but also racism (see Leach 1976). In the first human creation story Adam and Eve are made at once, and to do this God had to use two different molds; in this case they aren't brother and sister but more like two different species. Women, in fact, are treated like a different species. After all, there are different sets of biological rules for women, just like there is a separate set of rules for children and household pets. Remember, the Bible does not say in the first story that Adam and Eve were made sequentially. Moreover, we have to assume that God is doing this in his workshop and, because he is separate from his creations, He is not using His sperm. Therefore the zygotes created by Adam and Eve (Cain, Able, and Seth) could not be called inbreeding because the donors cannot be clones or brother and sister. Adam and Eve didn't have any daughters of which I am aware, and this creates another problem. Cain, as you recall, was banished to the Land of Nod, "east of Eden." There were people there, thus the "mark of Cain" so no one would bother him. Where did these people come from? There must have been another creation right down the street, and Cain and Seth need women if they are to "be fruitful and multiply."

It is impossible, then, to locate the original egg and sperm donors. This is a problem with structuralism and the issue of incest; if you don't have some idea as to why certain symbols were chosen, or if you read too much between the lines, you end up with another myth, a story about latent hidden meanings, and Freudian stories of incest and bestial sex. This is complicated even more by the fact that there is that second creation story. In the second story Eve comes from Adam's rib, which good Freudians believe is symbolic of the penis. But even here she wouldn't be his sister or his twin—she would be him, Adam; she is a clone and of the same structure and worth. So Adam is having sex with himself and in the process creating the human generations. God creates but is not part of His own creation—this shows the immense separation of God from his creation, just as we see the immense separation of the ruler and subject. This is pure political poetry. This is the same story as the Egyptian *Atum* (Adam in Hebrew, perhaps?), who masturbates the world into existence with his right hand, which represents the female principle. We encounter the same issue of perhaps reading too much into the story with Abraham and Sarah (see below). I find it simply very difficult to read these stories literally, which necessarily forces one to imagine that which may not be there, which was edited out, or which was not intended. But, of course, that is a problem inherent in the nature of symbols, especially as they morph through time.

Eve is also seen as a temptress, the active principle, for she tempted Adam, the first case of emotional irresponsibility on Adam's part. Adam had to make the choice to follow her lead (a leftover from the mother-goddess cults perhaps?). In the Middle Eastern rendition, Eve, as the mother-goddess, is demonized because "she seduces"; this is emotional irresponsibility, for if the male caves into temptation, that is *his* choice. Muslim men to this day believe that women give them erections. This misunderstanding as to where emotions originate has led to the pervasive fear men have for women in the Middle East. She (nature) is considered the original evil in Judaism and that evil is symbolized as a snake. But think about this for a moment. What is being said is that evil (not following instructions) brings forth human consciousness and life, which can be beautiful or horrible. If Eve had followed the deity's instructions, there would be no beauty or horror; there would be nothing to grumble about. There would be no churches, cars, computers, C4, AK-47s, trauma medicine, politics, ice cream, beer, *American Idol*—nothing. Casting woman as evil is a literary device to take the story to another level. Eve is the chosen one, the most important element in the story, because she represents life.

In the West, on the other hand, many women applaud Eve and see her as perhaps the first feminist, or a woman who defies male domination as symbolized by the male deity. In some renditions of the story, Adam's first wife was not Eve but Lilith. When she demanded equality (she wanted to be on top once in a while) he said, "No deal," and she issued him a definitive hand gesture, left, and took up residence at the bottom of the Red Sea. Well, poor Adam was heartbroken and went sniveling back to Big Daddy, who sent some angels with an offer she couldn't refuse. She refused it, so God said that one hundred of her demon children would be destroyed each day. Lilith fights back. She seduces men in their sleep (nocturnal emissions), produces many more demon children then can possibly be destroyed, and then strangles human infants in their sleep! You see, she is still one up on God. She who illuminates humanity becomes demonized. Eve represents nature and nature thus becomes corrupt and evil. In the first creation story we see the mother-goddess on equal par with the male god, and then there is a social shift (Israelites exiled to Babylon?) and her role is diminished. Another purpose is to distance themselves from other Canaanite tribes.

Eve is the real hero in the Bible; she is the first sacrifice to a new order. Through her choice—a choice to grow up, a choice in favor of humanity over the obedience to a god (this is the story of Prometheus)— she met her symbolic death through rejection by the deity (see Rush 1999 for an explanation of how rejection equals death). Again, we also see in this story God giving Adam and Eve an assignment because He *had* to get them out of the Garden of Eden. Why? Because Eve would have wanted to redecorate the place, change it in some way, and Adam would have few opportunities to get into trouble. Without change and adversity (evolution), nothing happens. Beside, if Adam and Eve stayed in the Garden we would not have much of a story. We need to have compassion for Eve, for she symbolizes the base of our family tree dating back at least six million years. Moreover, if Genesis is approached with a full mind, the reader will realize that, as unscientific as it is in some parts, the central idea of evolution—change and adversity—is written on every page. When fundamentalists deny this, they deny a major theme in their own sacred literature. Remember: God created evolution and it is evolution that led to all you experience.

Adam was instructed to name all the animals by the deity and that included Eve, thus her association with "animal." These two stories of Eve's creation offer an interesting inconsistency, at least to us. So, besides understanding the first story as prose and the second as poetry, what else can be said? Would this have been seen as an inconsistency to the ancients? Perhaps there were two prevailing views at one time, that is, the older mother-goddess tradition, in which both male and female elements are necessary for life, and the more recent, patriarchal story, where the male is the major player. The latter is a political statement. The second story suggests the beginning process of dismantling the mother-goddess cults and removal of the female energy from the creation of the universe. In this second story, which seems to have taken precedence over the first in the popular mind, women are an adjunct or appendage, and women have been on the bottom ever since.

Most readers are familiar with the story. Eve can't follow instructions, eats the "fruit" (read this as mushroom—see Rush 2005 for a rendition of the tree of good and evil) that brings her to consciousness, figures that would be good for Adam as well, and both are eventually cast from the garden lest they eat of the tree of immortality, become gods, and sink back into the singularity. This is myth and it allows for evolution, history, or the starting point for a larger story—that of a wandering tribe of people and their need to maintain an identity and call some land their own. Eve was given an assignment, for if she had not eaten of the fruit there would be no humanity and no story to tell. Adam and Eve are cast from the garden (the first exile), and their way back to the "promised land" or "the land of milk and honey" is by following the rules of God. The rules of God, by the way, are the natural laws of the universe enmeshed in the laws of mathematics and physics, *not* the rules invented by priest-kings (what you should wear, eat, how often you should pray, who to hang out with, etc.). When you learn math and physics, for example, you are learning the rules of God. My grandfather was a Fundamentalist Christian, a school superintendent, and a mathematician. He had a very brutal teaching style, and although I didn't learn math well under his tutelage, he did suggest that learning math would bring me closer to God.

"God" referred to in Exodus, Yahweh again, is the patriarchal, patron god of Abraham's tribe, one of several Semitic tribes that had invaded the Tigris/Euphrates area around 2400 BCE. Semitic is a term referring to people speaking one of several languages originating in the Arabian Desert. The first Semitic king in the area of Nippur, Sargon I or Sargon of Agade (2370 BCE), has a mythic beginning similar to Moses. While the Israelites were in exile in Babylon, they would have encountered the following, very interesting story:

> Sargon am I, the mighty king, Monarch of Agade.... My
> mother was of lowly birth, my father I knew not, the brother
> of my father is a mountain dweller, and my city, Azupiranu,
> lies on the banks of the Euphrates.
> My lowly mother conceived and bore me in secrecy;
> placed me in a basket of rushes, sealed it with bitumen, and
> set me in the river, which, however, did not engulf me. The
> river bore me up. And it carried me to Akku, the irrigator,
> who took me from the river, raised me as his son, and made
> of me a gardener: and while I was a gardener, the goddess
> Ishtar loved me. Then I ruled the kingdom. (From Campbell
> 1991, 73.)

I'll come back to the above story when I discuss the Egyptian pharaoh Akhenaten.

In any event, Yahweh or Jehovah is the god also taken on by the Christians, and the name becomes *Deus* in Greek (or Dios in Spanish and Italian) or God in common parlance. Yahweh shares many characteristics with the storm/war and vegetation god Baal of the Canaanites. But in each case (Judaism and Christianity), the deity evolved to fit the needs of rulers and religious clerics. There are differences in how this god is conceptualized, so different in fact that they might be seen as two different entities or species. We can note that the name for the mother-goddess—from Innana to Astarte to Astoreth, and so on—changes over time and in specific geographies, but her general behavioral characteristics remain the same. She is the goddess of sex and war (life and death). By comparison, the god of post-exile Judaism is exclusive to a people, has a nasty temper, and will accept nothing less than submission. When we go from Judaism to Christianity, the deity is given a less stressed and angry disposition.

The god of Abraham is approachable in human form. He "walks in the cool of the evening," but Moses only sees that same god as a plant god or pillar of smoke. Now, the scholars might be able to see connections in the names of this shared deity through El, but these are not the same god. How can a deity be mean-spirited, overbearing, insecure, self-centered, vindictive, and insensitive for 1,400 years and then, almost in the blink of an eye, become the gentle hippie Jesus? (*Diagnostic and Statistical Manual of Mental Disorders, DSM-IV*, Axis: 296.89 manic-depressive psychosis perhaps?) Did the god evolve, are there psychological problems, or is He sadistically playing with us like a cat does a mouse? The god of the Jews and the god of the Christians are two separate entities. Again, scholars can apply any name they desire to this deity, but it doesn't mean that the god of the Jews is the god of the Christians. Christians, in the same manner as Islam a few hundred years later, claim a connection to the god of the Jews, but this is for political purposes only.

A major problem that surfaces has to do with how we define religion. Again, my definition is as follows: Religion refers to one individual's experience with the energy that informs all. This is through identity with the deity (not a separation from the deity—you *are* that energy that informs all), communication with the deity (direct communication with the deity—two-way conversation), or perhaps becoming the deity (you take on the characteristics of the god). Although no outside help is required, these were the original goals often encountered in group settings through initiations, where the individual is guided through mythic images and rituals all under the influence of mind-altering substances. The above definition precludes popular Judaism, Christianity, and Islam as religions. True religion was displaced in many areas of the world with the coming of monotheism sporting a male god, who creates but who is not part of the creation. Thus there is no identity with the god, for only special people are allowed to communicate with God, and anyone claiming to have conversations with the deity will usually be discredited by religious clerics, other parishioners, or the courts. To claim you are god is a major heresy, especially in Christianity and Islam, and deserves, if not the death penalty, perhaps time in a mental hospital. So that we do not get confused with political systems, true religion was suppressed and withheld from the masses (the esoteric rites) a long time ago. Judaism, Christianity, and Islam are political and economic systems masquerading as religions.

Each of the Western traditions comes with sacred scriptures considered historical fact by fundamentalists and others, and with a set of instructions for social living, moral lessons, land ownership, kinship, redemption, war, male-female relations, and so on; this is politics. The sacred scriptures are the Old Testament (Hebrew/Jew—a reference to a people and a place, that is, local-political), New Testament (Christian—non-specific membership, non-geographical, world-political), and Qur'an (Islamic—non-specific membership, non-geographical, world-political). There are also the "auxiliary scriptures" or other sources that help us understand who and why these scriptures were assembled, and many of their original sources. For the Old Testament there is the Talmud and associated literature, and for the New Testament there are *apocrypha* (meaning secret and not approved for public reading), or, in a word, writings not *voted* into the Bible and most dangerous to read. In the Islamic tradition there are *hadith* (plural, *ahadith*) or sayings attributed to Muhammad, with some considered authentic and others not, a ploy raising the possibility of legitimate hadith because of the existence of fakes (see Chapter Four).

All three traditions have put forth claims brought into serious doubt. The scriptures, which are supposed to be the revealed word of God, are full of inconsistencies, and there seems to be little historical basis for most of the events and people depicted in these works. For example, Jericho is a real place, a city occupied for about 10,000 years. However, this does not mean that events portrayed in the Bible are historical fact. Joshua (another name for Jesus) is said to have leveled the town blowing trumpets, but the time frame given in the Bible for this event does not match the archaeological data. Earthquakes have destroyed the city many times.

History, Legend, and Myth

History can be defined as the study of people, places, events, and dates. History is always subject to reinterpretation when new information emerges. History, because it outlines a people's past, tends to be political if nothing else; winners write history from their perspective (embellishment), while losers cover theirs up. For example, the history of World War II is structured very differently in Germany and Japan from that presented in the United States or Britain, and as far as the history lessons in Iran go, there was no Holocaust or burning of Jews in Germany during World War II, and no homosexuals live in Iran. And just as Sargon (above) created his own mythic history/charter, so do modern presidents (Bill and Hillary Clinton are current examples) by suppressing that which detracts and emphasizing that which enhances their exploits. All is as it should be; this is what people do. The Queen of England recently did the same thing by preventing a documentary on Diana from being aired.

Historians in an open society, however, do attempt to uncover the reliable data and develop general agreement that such and such happened or that such and such person really did exist within some time threshold; there is too much criticism to do otherwise. The reason for the general agreement is that there are written and visual records that can be more or less reliably corroborated (taxes, census tracts, king's lists, stained glass, mosaics, etc.) along with physical evidence (archaeological data). I find it incredibly interesting that we know so little about some of the most famous "people" on the face of the planet, and that mind-altering substances have been almost completely absent from historical discussions. If these substances were not important they would not be coded in the Bible, and certainly any reference would be absent from stained glass and mosaics in cathedrals. So why do scholars ignore the coding and obvious references?

With respect to people mentioned in the Bible and Qur'an, what we do know comes from myth (*sacred* history) and legend. Legends are often about real people who, through their own rendering or the renderings of others over a long, long period of time, are magnified over and above their real worth and accomplishments. The Bible, like all historical novels, always interjects names of real places and people to enhance authenticity. Although there may be some tangible, factual elements indirectly related to the storyline, for example the existence of Jericho and its destruction, this does not mean that someone by the name of Joshua had anything to do with it. There is a place called Happy Valley, California, but I don't suspect that I will find Mickey, Donald, and Goofy there, climbing bean stalks and slaying a giant named Willy.

In 586 BCE, the Israelites living in the area of Palestine were conquered by the Akkadians and exiled to Babylon. It is in this environment that they acquired and rewrote for their own purposes many of the Old Testament stories (Garden of Eden, Noah's Ark, Moses, David, Solomon, etc.). Sometime between 560–539 BCE, Cyrus (a Persian thug) conquered the Akkadians and told the Israelites to go home. This, by the way, is another "let my people go" story, and combined with Adam and Eve and the story of Akhenaten (told below) we get the legendary tale of Exodus. Shortly after 560 BCE, the Israelites abandoned polytheism and adopted monotheism. This is reflected in 1 Samuel 7:4 (written after 560 BCE): "So the Israelites put away their Baals and Astoreths and worshiped the Lord only." This is most probably the time when rather harsh rules were created to maintain group identity, using God or Yahweh as a third-person power source delivering specific rules of conduct with the ultimate goal of separating from the Canaanites. If you are going to change the rules, the "exodus" from Babylon to Israel around 560 BCE would have been the perfect time to tighten up and get your act together. During chaos and upheaval people often look for direction and direction they got, mostly in the negative, through incantations of exclusion. "Thou shalt not" extended into all aspects of a person's life and certainly to the worship of other deities. This also meant suppressing certain types of ritual sex—both hetero and homo-sexual—and ritual drug use (cannabis and other substances—at least for the masses) common to the mother-goddess cults.

For an unsettled people, a place to call home would be of paramount importance. Moreover, a decision to turn toward monotheism needed a starting point, and with this starting point came the construction of a mythical charter incorporating five main cornerstones of the Jewish tradition. The first is a genealogy of blood relationships with a lengthy time depth. Second is the connection to royalty through ancient Egypt. The third is a "promised land" provided by a deity if certain rules are followed; fourth, the commencement of monotheism. And fifth and last is the construction of a book containing mythic frames, legitimiz-ing the previous four—"So it is written, so it shall be." At about the same time, the Greeks were separating supernatural from natural phe-nomena and creating science. To accept the Old Testament as fact, sto-ries had to be wrapped around geographical locations and certain personality types, who make the story come to life and read as history (and thus as "scientific"). In the time period representing the creation of the Old Testament (560–530 BCE), people were controlled by leg-islation invented by the rich and powerful and kept in place through threats of violence. This is exactly what we see in the Bible and Qur'an, and enacted in many areas of the world today. The reader must also appreciate that most people during biblical times, and until quite recently, were illiterate; they could neither read nor write. Just as the Egyptians had sacred writing the Israelites had the same, and by placing the sto-ries within a sacred context in order to appeal to the superstitions of the day, the stories become real and "truth." Words, paragraphs, and stories written on paper are placed outside of you and they can reach the next generation, and the next, and so on. The original knowledge of the fabrication of the Old Testament is lost and several generations later what is written becomes fact. Although most of us take writing for granted, the Israelites, in a fashion similar to the ancient Egyptians, saw writing as magical—words came to life, they bring people to action. The ancient Hebrews might, indeed, have believed that if they wrote something down it would become true through magic. Even today there is a belief that, if a scholar writes something, it must be true or at least worthwhile, especially if he or she can claim some connection to specific universities. Truth, then, gets linked to a personality or group. But just as our daily news reporting reflects mainly opinion and political agenda, so too does the writing of university historians. When it comes to our current reporting of daily events called "news," the closest statements of truth are the results on the sports page. The recording of history has changed little since the conception of writing. Regardless of what is written, it tells us a great deal about the people and social circumstances of the people who wrote it.

For the Israelites at this time period (560 BCE), these stories offered hope, a metaphorical fresh start, and direction. Time marches on, and these stories of hope are presented as fact. The priest-poets either believed as true what they were transcribing from generation to generation, or they knew these stories as possible truths or legends. But they also understood the power of symbols, especially after a very long relationship with the Egyptians. The priests, particularly those living in the delta, would have known the names of kings going back to and even before their first sojourn in Egypt. They would have paid attention to the political situation and been fascinated with the Egyptian civilization; they more than likely would have had friends among the elite. To expect less is naïve at best. The priest-poets knew the pharaohs but did not name them. This indicates a purposefully constructed story with the intent of forging a history difficult to verify.

Genesis and Evolution

I briefly discussed "Intelligent Design" in Chapter One and the conclusion that it is simply another word for creationism, or the belief that a god, a craftsman with a terrible temper, created the tangible universe. Because the scientific community cannot explain certain phenomena for reasons of complexity or gaps in our knowledge, supporters of the "Intelligent Design" position jump to the conclusion that there has to be a creator being in a laboratory somewhere in the sky. This creator being, this male god, this craftsman, did not do this creating all at once. There is a progression or evolution—God's creation occurred over a period of six days. The deity simply could not create humans first, for there are precedents to everything. We can take this literally or as metaphorical of something else.

Many scholars and scientists see the impossibility of the universe being created literally in six days. And, of course, others argue that a day in the life of a god could be a billion years or so, but if we come to this conclusion how should be treat the word "day" throughout the Bible? The problem is that if you read this as fact you never get down to the intended meaning, which is usually the simplest meaning or common denominator. During discussions of meaning, authors invent new myths, write books about them, and present them as possibilities. In my opinion, we have to take the meaning of the creation story to the lowest common denominator: 1) things take time; 2) one thing precedes another thing; and 3) God, or the energy that informs all, created the process of evolution. This energy left us evidence of our climb from bacteria to bipeds—there are hundreds of thousands of fossils. They are clues we are assigned to follow, clues that will lead us to that energy. Just as Eve and Judas are given assignments, so are we. To deny evolution is to deny God. Now, God doesn't micromanage the process of *what* to create or how it *should* evolve. Instead, it is an issue of what works, and you cannot know this without cutting the apron strings and allowing creation to do its thing. Only a stupid God would preset every living thing or behavior, for He could never experience variety; He would be bored to tears! So He flicks a switch and "ga-boom"—energy is in motion. The deity did not create humans or any other living or inorganic thing. God created evolution, and there is nothing special in any part of it; it is what it is, without judgment of good or bad, right or wrong. No intelligent deity would spend its time micromanaging people any more than He would micromanage a flea. Monotheists must believe that God micromanages fleas, mosquitoes, raccoons, and worms, for if He micromanages humans exclusively, then all other living things must have free will. This is absurd.

Although I am not sure how this is accomplished, the creationists and intelligent design people work with a closed system of non-change, but draw their conclusions from a text that explicitly says that evolution and change are the rules of life. The text reads (Genesis 1:1–2): "In the beginning God created the heavens and the earth. Now the earth was formless and empty." The text does not read: "In the beginning God created everything at once, BANG—sun, moon, stars, sky, clouds, cats, people, turnips, and roses!" We have a progression, an evolution, and scholars like to show this progression over six days. This is in contrast to the Hindu tradition, which sees creation as an never-ending cycle wherein history is unimportant, for whatever has happened has happened a billion times before; all is impermanent, all is illusion. In the Jewish tradition, however, change is seen as unique, directional, specific to a people, and leading to some inevitable outcome—a plan (see Albrektson 1967). Genesis thus stands as a treatise on creation through evolution, and a nomadic tribal group evolving into special people with a land grant bestowed by Yahweh.

Even if one does read Genesis as myth, one problem is that the myth is fractured and out of touch with the world as it is. Not only is it not in accord with our scientific knowledge, it is not in accord with political possibilities. Genesis is a looking back at what was. By contrast, science looks forward to what could or might be.

The universe and everything in it came along as a sequence of events conditioned by the rules of evolution, all part of the energy that informs all. As mentioned in Chapter One, there is a purpose for these stories. On the one hand, they indicate that the priest-poets understood something about evolution, that one thing progresses in complexity from one stage to another (from Abraham to the Nation of Israel). On the other hand, they realized that the second creation is a political statement of male superiority (Yahweh) and female submission (mother-goddess). This is also a sacred history lesson and a lesson in genealogy. These were important to the Israelites, for without this progression they could not build a mythical charter with time depth or have a story of who they are and from whence they came; they would have no identity.

Clearly, nearly everything written in both the Old and New Testaments has ancient precedents found in the myths of many cultures in the Middle East (see Thompson 2005 for a comprehensive review). Let me present some examples. Genesis 6:9 begins with the flood story; there probably was a great flood and it may have flooded the margins of the continents, but it did not flood the world. This was possibly caused by an earthquake, or global warming resulting from a slight tilt in the earth's axis, with melting ice sheets raising sea levels around 350 feet between 9000 BCE and 5600 BCE. In any event, billions of gallons of water came into the Mediterranean basin, flooding vast areas and drowning thousands of people. A portal to the Black Sea (originally a fresh water lake) gave way with the rising water, turning it into salt water and drowning the settlements on the shore. There was flooding into the Tigris-Euphrates river settlements closest to the Persian Gulf and along the coast of the Arabian Peninsula, as well as on the Indian continent, and there is evidence of costal floods in Australia and the Americas.

The memory of water pouring over mountaintops and obliterating everything in sight would have stayed in the folklore through story telling and elaboration over time. Eventually it was written down in cuneiform as part of the Epic of Gilgamesh, and was encountered by the Hebrews when they were exiled to Babylon in 586 BCE; this comes down to us as the Noah story in Genesis. The flood was a natural event and not an act of a wrathful god against sinful people. In fact, the original flood story in Gilgamesh had to do with the *capriciousness and personal problems of deities* and not the sinful acts of humans. In the Old Testament this is turned upside down, for now the deity is perfect and it is humans who are out of line. This wrath against humans in the Old Testament was also added to maintain fear of the deity and instill the new laws (among other reasons). When we look around the world today, some suggest that we are in need of another flood (perhaps the prophetic global warming will take care of this for us). Apocalyptic politicians (see Chapter Five) and the liberal news media are a replay of Genesis 6: 5–7:

And GOD saw that the wickedness of man [was] great in the earth, and [that] every imagination of the thoughts of his heart [was] only evil continually.

And the LORD repented that he had made man on the earth, and it grieved him at his heart.

And the LORD said, I will destroy man whom I have created, from the face of the earth, both man and beast, and the creeping animal, and the fowls of the air; for I repent that I have made them.

This is pure and simple infanticide and cruelty to animals; you don't like your children because they won't behave, so you kill them, just as real parents, by law, can have unruly children stoned to death (see Chapter Three). There is a great deal of psychopathic behavior in the Bible, which the psychiatric and psychological communities must agree with if their DSM-IV is as universal as they contend. We cannot just push this aside as one culture's idiosyncrasy and scream ethnocentrism when defining mental problems using the DSM-IV, for these events must have seemed unusual even for the people at that time (or they never would have written them down). Our ancient ancestors would not have spent their time writing down mundane stuff like, "Yesterday Fred's donkey took a dump in the road." Now, if the donkey could talk or fly, or if someone reports a strange dream, that's what gets written down. These prophets must have been seen as just as crazy then as now, but insanity was assigned a different cause (deities and demons) in those days. Disturbed communication patterns would have been recognized as such 2,500 years ago, just as they would be recognized today. *Assigning insanity to a different cause does not excuse it or allow it to continue.* Okay, people were superstitious in those days and believed that people talked with deities, deities helped humans win wars, drove them crazy, and so on. But that does not mean that it is appropriate to maintain such beliefs in the face of science and what we understand about our world today. Do fundamentalists still believe that the earth is the center of the solar system? Do they still think that God resides in a temple, church, or mosque? Do they still think a demon or angel possesses a feverish person hallucinating? Do they still think the universe was created 4004 BCE?

In any event, to accept the flood story in Genesis as fact takes an immense leap of faith. God tells Noah to build an ark and gather up two of every living animal (or seven of every "clean" animal) and place them in this craft, including fish, whales, porpoises, elephants, crabs, and spiders, along with all the animals from North and South America. (Did you know that Noah must have been the first person from the European-Middle Eastern area to visit the New World?) The boat or ark was 450 feet long, seventy-five feet in width, and forty-five feet high. This would have been impossible! Beside the animals, insects, and plants, where would you put the food and provisions for the crew? I recall my early years of Sunday school, when I was about ten years old and hearing the story of Noah. After the teacher read the story, one of my friends who lived on a dairy farm nearby asked a very embarrassing question: "If you had two of everything—all those animals, from all over the place—and you have Noah, his wife, and their sons, how would they ever be able to get rid of, ah (his voice trailed of), the poop?"

Well, that got little Arthur in trouble. But he knew something about poop. During the winter months they might have a measly thirty milking cows in the barn, and it was his job to help clean up the cow plops. Arthur knew about poop, but the remark from the teacher was telling in itself—"We don't question the scriptures!" So the story of Noah cannot represent fact. The flood is a literary device (some call it an archetype). It is a story about beginnings or starting over, of going from one place to another, a story of hope, perhaps, but it is also used to establish genealogical connections between the deity and His most favorite human in the whole wide universe, Noah. Further, the story is used as the basis for turning the Canaanite tribes and other strangers from human beings into targets, or "its." As I recall, the teacher skipped over the next part about Noah and his son Ham (Genesis 9:21–27).

The sons of Noah who came out of the ark were Shem, Ham and Japheth (*Ham was the father of Canaan*). These were the three sons of Noah, and from them came the people who were scattered over the earth. Noah, a man of the soil, proceeded to plant a vineyard. When he drank some of its wine he became drunk and lay uncovered inside his tent. Ham, *the father of Canaan,* saw his father's nakedness and told his two brothers outside. But Shen and Japheth took a garment and laid it upon both their shoulders; then they walked in backward and covered their father's nakedness, and their faces were turned the other way so that they would not see their father's nakedness.

When Noah awoke from his wine and found out what his youngest son had done to him, he said, "Cursed be Canaan! The lowest of slaves will he be to his brothers."
He also said, "Blessed be the Lord, the God of Shem! May Canaan be the slave of Shem.

May God extend the territory of Japheth; may Japheth live in the tents of Shem, and may Canaan be his slave."

I never heard anything about this episode in Sunday school, and its meaning will be discussed when addressing the origins of the Israelites. However, one line is especially important because it represents a turning away from nature and the idea that nature is corrupt. That is,

"Then they walked in backward and covered their father's nakedness, and their faces were turned the other way so that they would not see their father's nakedness." This represents an aversion to nature; to look at nature is corrupting. Why was this part of the story not told in Sunday school? Religious clerics often rely on the fact that most churchgoers do not read the Bible, and thus they can leave out (censor) that which does not fit their agenda.

In 1 Samuel 2:8 and Job 38, the wise priests tell us that the earth rests on pillars and has foundations. This is similar to the Greek god Atlas, upon whose shoulders rests the earth, or, in a similar fashion, the Egyptian Hathor in the form of a cow, whose four legs keep everything in place. Again, this story reflects their cosmology and cannot possibly be the revealed word of a supreme, intelligent deity. Genesis is not only about the evolution of the physical universe; it likewise has to reflect an evolution in thinking, knowledge, and wisdom. Genesis is a reference point for who we were and our relationship to the universe at that time in history (between 560 and 300 BCE).

The Patriarchs

Although Noah is not considered one of the Patriarchs of the Bible, he is the head of the Semitic genealogy so important in constructing a mythical charter. Noah is the base of the human tree, and Abraham is the starting point for the Hebrew lineage, as well as for the Christians (*before* Abraham circumcised himself), while Isaac is the granddaddy to the twelve tribes of Israel. Noah is the starting point that tells what came before (complete with a god who likes a special person), and it is through him and his children that we repopulate the world. Noah is credited with originating grape vineyards for wine production and he is the "righteous man" whom God saves (along with his wife and sons and their wives) as seed to start anew. His three sons, Shem, Ham, and Japheth, represent the three races of the world.

As quoted above, Ham does something very, very nasty to Noah while he lies in a drunken stupor. Ham probably had anal sex with Noah as a sign of domination, or perhaps this was a ritual, spiritual act (homosexual-ritual sex), as was common in the mother-goddess cults at the time. Moreover, this ban against male homosexuality in particular, was, more than likely, borrowed from the ancient Egyptians. One of the Forty-Two Judgment Deities (see Rush 2007: 100, and Gate Card Six), Face Behind Me, seems to judge acts of pedophilia, and there is Wememty, a snake god who judges homosexual behavior. Because women were accorded a great deal of freedom in ancient Egypt, at least according to the current interpretation, they possibly saw male homosexual behavior as odd or unusual; there is no judge of lesbian or heterosexual behavior.

Back to Ham. His other name is Canaan, and here we begin the justification for discrimination against the Canaanites; this is the "sins of the father (Ham) will be visited on the sons" belief. So, whatever Ham did, his lineage will pay for it—forever! Ham's behavior and Noah's curses symbolically represent the Hebrews splitting away from their Canaanite roots, and a more violent, judgmental, and guilt-ridden movement toward exclusivity, righteousness, perfection, and so on. Moreover, if taken literally, this begins the shunning, persecution, cursing, and murder of Canaanites, and essentially everyone else. At the very least, the design is to keep members away from "strangers," lest they share some sperm and thereby water down the tribe or contract a spiritual disease. So in Genesis we have a clear statement of racism, slavery, discrimination, and eugenics—Holy Scripture allows such practices if read literally. Now remember that we have to think in black and white. In other words, either the Bible is the revealed word of God and unalterable, or it is a collection of legends and myths for political reasons. Also keep in mind that Muslim poets plagiarized much of the story in the Old Testament, including people, places, and events, as they created their own mythical charter (see Chapter Four). Thus, if the story does not stand up as historical fact in the Bible, it fairs no better in the Qur'an.

Abraham: The Founding Father

The basic axis around which the Hebrew poets hung the stories of the Old Testament is the idea of a place called home, or a special geography in which to settle once and for all. But they had to leave one place, in duress of course, and go to this "promised land." This appears to be a common storyline among the Arab peoples of 2,500 years ago and is the storyline in Palestine today. The cultural complex surrounding the Hebrew people (and Semitic people in general) was one of being always on the move herding sheep, goats, and eventually camels (1500 BCE). As we progress from the mid-Third Millennium BCE to around the time when the Israelites are exiled to Babylon (586 BCE), available land is shrinking and these herding people become more and more dependent on towns and urban areas for comfort and basic necessities. Geography (usable land) and population growth collide, along with differing mythic frames of reference, basically polytheistic with both male and female emphasis, but highly compatible from a religious perspective.

Beginning around 800 BCE, we encounter Zoroastrianism, a patriarchal, dualistic system, but which can be considered monotheistic in that the male energy is accentuated, with the female energy minor or nonexistent. In this tradition, clearly developed to inform rulers about how they should rule lest they go to hell, there is a good male god, Ahura Mazda, and he is pitted against his evil twin, Angra Mainyu. With some reworking of their own traditions as well as those collected in Babylon, along with ideas from Zoroastrianism and Buddhism layered between abundant knowledge of the ancient Egyptian tradition (and most certainly the heretic Pharaoh Akhenaten), Jewish monotheism is born between 560 and 530 BCE.

Prior to this time, the two systems of polytheism and monotheism were commingled, with the monotheism coming in mainly from Egypt and the polytheism already in place. The Bible instructs in the evolution from polytheism to monotheism and it involves two main push factors. The first involves identity and maintaining a genetic line of descent, while the second was quite mystical. The priest poets concoct a tale that they will not get the land and special privileges unless they maintain the Covenant and worship Yahweh only; they were desperate and made a pact with a god (a demon), a supernatural being who demands absolute submission. They came to this sometime during their twenty-eight years of exile in Babylon. The very young, those born in Babylon, and their parents would have spoken of the land that was taken from them, and that one day they would come out of their exile and return to their "promised land," "the land of milk and honey." I'm sure that this was a constant conversation for around twenty-eight years, when one day Cyrus shows up and tells them, "Go home. But stay in touch and don't forget to send the bagels!" This is the first part of the Exodus story, poetically reflected in Adam and Eve initially expelled from the garden because they couldn't follow instructions. The second part comes from Egypt.

A major component of the Jewish mythic charter is Abraham. Abraham is seen as the founding father through his covenant with Yahweh, an agreement that states that Abraham would submit and worship Yahweh exclusively, in exchange for a land grant to bring forth the nation of Israel. This land grant extends from "the river of Egypt to the great river of the Euphrates—the land of the Kenites, Kenizzites, Kadmonites, Hittites, Penizzites, Rephaites, Amorites, Canaanites, Girgashites and Jebusites." (Genesis 15:18–21) God, of course, warns Abraham his descendants will be strangers and enslaved for four hundred years, but God will fix it up so that they will be free and, in the process, acquire great possessions. As a mark of this commitment, Abraham circumcised himself (a custom borrowed from the Egyptians) at the age of ninety-nine, for it is from his loins that a great nation would materialize. The issue of "to circumcise or not to circumcise" was a "sore" issue in the early construction of Christianity. St. Paul apparently liked foreskins so much that, with mental gymnastics that would put any politician to shame, he convinced the clerics that it was unnecessary, that their founding father was Abraham *before* he was circumcised.

In any case, who was Abraham? He is supposed to have lived sometime around 1800 BCE, but there is absolutely no historical visibility for Abraham outside of the Hebrew stories. There are no written documents (cuneiform script, etc.) undisputedly of that time period discussing Abraham and his exploits; there are no cuneiform tax records, no storyline, no nothing. Scholars attempting to trace these stories a century ago saw a problem in identifying his birthplace—either Ur in southern Mesopotamia, as referenced in the Bible, or Haran in northern Mesopotamia. One of my students brought back a blurred picture (taken from a Humvee moving up the Euphrates River and heading for Baghdad) of Abraham's mud-brick house. I also have been able to identify the exact place where Willy the Giant, slain by the mighty heroes Mickey, Donald, and Goofy, hit the ground. It was a short ways away from Happy Valley, California. Should Abraham, like our triplet heroes, be considered a legend or a real person? Abraham is obviously a construction for the main purpose of genealogical depth. But that is not enough. You have to pad this with storyline, often contradictory, to show him as a real person "who did all these despicable things, and we apologize for him and those wicked, wicked ways. But he was our kin, so what can you do?" When trying to establish the character, the exploits cannot be rosy, smiley, and happy, or you won't have much of a story and no one will believe it.

The Abraham Mystery

What was the significance of his name change from Abram to Abraham and his wife's name from Sarai to Sarah? Why did he and Sarai really go to Egypt? What is the significance of Abraham stating that his wife was his sister, when he could have said this in such a way as to avoid confusion as to sister, as opposed to "daughter of his father, though not of my mother"? (Genesis 20:12) Why was Sarah given a maidservant when she left Egypt? Is Abraham the founding father of both Judaism and Islam? Like detectives, we have to follow instincts, notes from other scholars, and come at this from a number of angles in an attempt to follow the logic of the priest-poets.

According to the Bible, Abram's time period is around 1800 BCE. This is around 1,300 years before the Israelites begin to bring their history together into what today is called the Old Testament. There are claims that written material existed before 586 BCE, but I will leave that to the integrity of the biblical scholars. In any case, the name Abram means "the Father (or God) is exalted." When building a mythical character of this nature (a story that justifies one's legitimacy without tangible proof or credible corroboration) the founding father is of primary importance, because he is responsible for establishing communication between the deity/deities (the code) and acting as a role model for the basic beliefs and ritual (creed) that are subject to elaboration as social circumstances dictate. You are unlikely to hear about Fred the Depressed, Sam the Dumb, Chris the Puny, or Eustis the Unusual. No, the name has to represent the ideal as seen by these ancient storytellers, that is, "exalted." Abram is also what we could call a shaman-like individual who acts as a conduit between the spiritual realm and the living. Keep in mind that Abram's god was his family cult god, and this family deity would be around him all the time. I'm sure that he had his methods of contacting this deity, probably a telephone in the shape of a mushroom or cannabis bud.

The story of Abram is pieced together as a historical narrative, and within the narrative there are literary devices for moving the story along, drawing attention to significant persons, events, and symbols, and leading the reader or audience to some conclusion. Of course, this is myth, so magical help is at hand to assist the hero on his journey. For example, Ur is not such a fun place, there isn't much happening there, but it is there in name to add two facets of the story—antiquity of the mythic genealogy, and that Abram, the man from Ur, has roots on the Euphrates and perhaps some land claim to that area, even if it is only the fact that he was born there.

Abram marries (sleeps with, has sex with) his "sister" Sarai, leaves Ur, and travels north along the Euphrates to Haran where they settle. But then Abram hears the words of God telling him to leave Haran and "go to the land I will show you." (Genesis 12:1) Under the guiding and protecting hand of God, Abram and Sarai (and Lot) travel to "the great tree of Moreh at Shechem" in Canaan. Here is where God tells Abram that this is the land he will give to his descendents. Abram builds an altar, then moves on toward the hills east of Bethel and pitches his tent, with Bethel on the west and Ai on the east. There he likewise built an altar to the Lord and called on His name. Then Abram set out and continued toward the Negev. (Genesis 12:8) So around 1800 BCE, Abram's patron deity (*his* tribal/household deity) hands over a large hunk of land just because God, as would be the case with any king or pharaoh, can do what he likes. Of course delusions of grandeur help the story along, combined with mind-altering drugs, the conduit to Yahweh. Also keep in mind that Genesis was probably written last in order to tie the following four books of the Bible together. Back to Abram.

A severe famine hits, obviously caused by God, and Abram and Sarai go to Egypt where there is plenty of food. Remember that the god of the Hebrews must have a plan, a future outlined for a special people, and you don't get this inflection in the surrounding traditions. But Egypt also offers an opportunity for common folk to make connections with powerful people, in particular, the pharaoh. The name of the pharaoh connected to this time period is never mentioned, although we are given the names of kings in other lands. This is definitely, without doubt, a purposeful omission. Why? Because this is myth and not history, and to give names to the pharaohs would let Bastet out of the bag, so to speak, and there wouldn't be much of a story. Egypt is important for another reason—it provides a later bridge to Moses and royalty. There are two connected stories as to the origins of the Jewish people: one through Pharaoh and Sarah (her new name) and one through Abraham and Sarah.

At this juncture we encounter an interesting and curious story that puts Abram in a bad light and thus is of ultimate significance in understanding the history of the Jewish people. Sarai is very beautiful (we are not informed of this earlier), and once in Egypt Abram fears that people would kill him and take his wife. Why did he not fear this all along? Paranoia from smoking too much pot? So, he pawns her off as his biological sister. Now, Abram does marry his "sister," but she is not his biological sister through the same mother—she is a half-sister. Some scholars have interpreted this as taboo in light of the fact that Sarai is barren (see Leach 1969). But I don't think that is the intended symbolism. Abram is married to his sister as a parallel to the brother-sister mythic marriage of Isis and Osiris, and to the pharaoh being married to his sister in some cases. This connection to Egypt and the Pharaoh is extremely important and so we would expect to encounter these bits and pieces of symbolism.

The Pharaoh hears of Sarai's beauty, takes her into his palace, gives Abram "sheep, cattle, male and female donkeys, menservants and maidservants, and camels." (Genesis 12:16) I don't think camels were domesticated in 1800 BCE. If this is to be taken literally, then Abram, through the lens of Western culture, is a pimp. Wealth (deserved through special privileges) is another aspect of the Hebrew mythical charter, and that initial wealth is based on deception and prostituting his wife (he later pawns her off on Abimelech, King of Gerar, once again as his sister). "But the Lord inflicted serious diseases on Pharaoh and his household because of Abram's wife Sarai." (Genesis 12:17) What? Did I read this correctly? God inflicts diseases on Pharaoh and his household because Abram lied and misrepresented Sarai? If this is read literally, Abram is rewarded for his deception (institutionalized lying?). The wording is curious here, that is, "because of Abram's wife Sarai" and not because of Abram. Seen from our standpoint, *Sarai* is the victim. She is forced into prostitution because Abram is a coward. Abram gains considerable wealth in the transaction, but there seems to be an extra point being made. Not only does Sarai become Pharaoh's concubine, she also becomes his *wife* by sleeping with him, and it would seem that having sex with her is connected to the first plague associated with the Hebrew presence in Egypt. According to Bennett and McQueen (2001:52), it was venereal disease that Abram and Sarai were sharing with others in Egypt and the Middle East, but as Abram and Sarai are mythic characters, this is sheer speculation. With the plague, Pharaoh asks Abram to fess up, which he does, and Pharaoh tells him and Sarai to leave with all Abram had acquired. Pharaoh, in another sense, has been taught a lesson. Pharaoh's lust is a plague on the land—uncontrolled, it leads to bad results. But there is another message here. In short, don't fuck with the Hebrews because their god, the real McCoy, will beat you up, because those with power have their favorites, right or wrong.

Abram is now a person with possessions. Sarai, we are told, is barren, but we cannot be sure that it is Sarai who is barren, and this, I believe, is important. It represents, at least on one level, a further usurping of the female's magical ability to bring forth life, as was the central message of the mother-goddess cults. What is being said is that fertility and fecundity are God's will and the female is reduced to the level of a container with no special status, a further carving away of the mother-goddess. Perhaps it is Abram who cannot impregnate, but we do not hear about impotent males.

In any event, Sarai has an Egyptian maidservant. Because it is *her* maidservant, we cannot assume Abram gave her to Sarai. This maidservant, Hagar, is given *by Sarai* to Abram as a concubine to continue his bloodline. Apparently he had no maidservants of his own, or maybe, just maybe, the message is that life comes through the permission of the female. After all, it is Sarai who makes the suggestion.

If we want to read this as a history lesson, then there are some important points to consider. First, Hagar was probably given to Sarai by Pharaoh. Why would he do this? Well, the only reason Pharaoh would do so is if Sarai was with Pharaoh's child! So we have a possible connection of Sarai and the Pharaoh, and Abram and Hagar. Let me digress for a moment.

The Hebrews are attempting to establish their legitimacy as an important people with a place to call their own. Certainly one way to accomplish this was to marry well or connect one's self to a royal lineage in some fashion. More than likely, the early construction of the Israelites' mythical charter was intended to develop legitimacy by forging a blood relationship with Egyptian royalty. They were drawn to the Egyptians, and the Egyptians were certainly not Canaanites or Hittites. Historically, the Hebrews and other Semitic groups came into Egypt "peacefully as merchants, or took service as cooks, brewers, seamstresses, vine-dressers and the like" (Aldred 1988, 117) during the Middle Kingdom (2036–1668 BCE). But after the Hyksos invasion and conquest, the attitude toward Asiatics (Middle Easterners) in general soured, not that they necessarily were oppressive and brutal toward the Egyptians, but because they were foreigners and little could be done about it until Kamose, the last ruler of the Seventeenth Dynasty. He challenged the Hyksos Pharaohs in the north, and then under the reign of Ahmoses (which begins the Eighteenth Dynasty), the Hyksos were removed from the landscape. During the time the Hyksos occupied Egypt there would have been intermarriages with royalty. and this leads us to a very interesting story involving Yuya, Commander of the Chariotry, part of which is outlined below.

Back to Abram and his sojourn in Egypt. In connecting Sarai to

Pharaoh, Pharaoh (a god on earth, a stand-in for Horus, the son of the sun god Re) becomes the "loins" through which a great nation would be born and *not* Abram. This relationship destroys their genealogical connections and they would become lost in the Egyptian world; they wanted their own identity, although happy to borrow bits and pieces from all points of the compass. Not only that, the Egyptians left a great deal of written history and this would be troublesome if people wanted to research their claim. So it is best to stick with an unknown (Abram), who can only be imagined but never truthfully identified (we can identify most of the pharaohs). To illustrate the problem, if Sarai was with child, Pharaoh would have given her a maidservant (Hagar, in this case). Now, if Pharaoh impregnated her and she gives birth to a child of Pharaoh, this places more importance on the female line than the male. Royalty comes through Sarai by way of Pharaoh and not the loins of Abraham, and this forces them into a *matrilineal* position if they chose to trace their identity through Sarai. With this they would also lose special status with El or Yahweh. Again, the poets realized that a connection with pharaoh would eliminate Abram as a genealogical connection, so a revision had to take place. What is also interesting is the name change given to Sarai by God (Genesis 17:15), that is Sarah, which translates as "princess," the very status she would merit as one of the Pharaoh's concubines, not as Abram's wife.

Moreover, the Israelites were cutting away all connections to other traditions—the mother-goddess cults and some Egyptian symbolism—but they still needed a connection to royalty and this comes through Moses. In other words, at this juncture of storytelling the authors have two possibilities in terms of genealogical connection—one through Abram and one through pharaoh.

In Genesis 20:1–5, Abraham (God changes Abram to Abraham—"father of a multitude of nations"—in Genesis 17:5) prostitutes his wife (pimps her as his sister again) with Abimelech, King of Gerar, and through his deception obtains sheep, cattle, and male and female slaves. This is twice in a row; this is habit formation. So, deception pays off, especially with strangers. This is sort of like spiritual extortion, a protection racket, if you will. I think most people agree that this type of behavior—pimping one's wife—is reprehensible at best and enhances social stress, and those who behave like this lack integrity and personal responsibility. It was not considered appropriate then any more than it would be appropriate today. We also can appreciate the treatment of women during that time period, for Sarah, his wife, is mere chattel to be traded for whatever suits Abraham's fancy. On the other hand, there are important women in the Old Testament, perhaps suggesting ambivalence toward the female energy. After all, women were certainly important in Egypt.

When people compose stories of heroes and their adventures, they usually have some outline or at least an ultimate goal. Genesis, for example, was probably a late addition to the books that followed and constructed as an introduction to Exodus, Leviticus, Numbers, and so on. Deuteronomy was also a late compilation, making the rules more uniform. The goal was to build a credible story of group membership and land ownership sanctioned by God. Kings during this time period were considered stewards or overseers of that which still belongs to God. The exception was Egypt, where pharaoh was the son of the Sun and qualified as a god on earth. It is a matter of connecting the dots, from the establishment of God as fact, the king as God's representative, with the populace bowing down to the king, and by analogy, God as an extension of the male principle with women bowing down to men. Humans are servants to this deity, and the best servants get the best of what God can provide, that is, wealth, slaves, property, and so on. Keep in mind that slavery and prostitution would have been common fare during this time period, although I'm not sure that it was customary to pimp one's wife.

After leaving Egypt, the story shifts to Abraham and Sarah's concern that he will not have sons through her. Remember, she may have had a son through pharaoh, but we have no storyline about such an outcome. In any event, Sarah suggests that Abraham take Hagar, the maidservant given to her by pharaoh, as his concubine. He does so and through Hagar he begets Ishmael, which translates as "God listens" or

"God has heard." Sarah becomes jealous in time and tells Abraham to drive both Hagar and Ishmael into the desert. Poor Abraham—you are damned if you do and damned if you don't. Sarah (female element) is, once again, the active principle. God then says he will take care of them both, that a nation will spring from Ishmael, and then states that Sarah will have a child. Both laugh, and the child born is Isaac, which means "laughter." At this stage the emphasis is shifted from pharaoh to Abraham, who begets Isaac at age ninety-nine while Sarah is a few years younger. Although not impossible, the average life expectancy during 1800 BCE is certainly not much more than thirty or thirty-five for men and somewhat younger for women. Why was Abraham pitched as "ancient"? This has several possible meanings—one of which is that God can do what he wants, another is that people whom God favors live long lives, and, of course, with age comes wisdom. In other words, you can't start a nation without wisdom and special help from your supernatural friends. Thus Abraham represents the wisdom of the ages, and with this knowledge a nation is inevitable. I will have more to say about Ishmael in Chapter Four. Let me emphasize that there is no historical visibility for Abraham, Sarah, Ishmael, Hagar, or Isaac, except that invented by the priest-poets.

Isaac

The Gnostics (various Christian sects developing in the first through the fourth centuries CE) saw the god of the Old Testament as confused, morally corrupt, and certainly demonic; they called him Ialdabaoth, which translates into something like "disorder bringer," as well as suggesting that this is the first entity to do so. Certainly most of the activities attributed to Abraham, Isaac, Jacob, and others, sanctioned by Yahweh, break all the Commandments. There is a repeated theme of lying, cheating, stealing, murder/torture, adultery, and so on, all permitted and apparently sanctioned by Yahweh. God also helps by bringing plagues and famine. As mentioned, my impression is that the stories about Abraham and the other patriarchs were originally morality stories borrowed and handed down through the generations and these stories were then incorporated into the Old Testament as building blocks or frameworks for their mystical charter, which included special privileges and land ownership. If the Old Testament is read as historical fact, we see a tradition that is based on those beliefs, attitudes, and behaviors that destroy trust and group cooperation. Turned around, these stories tell us exactly what *not* to do. But for the Gnostics, they took this literally. Why? Because, in their minds, this is what *rulers* (supernatural or otherwise) do—they cheat, steal, lie, murder, and rape, and, for the Gnostics, Ialdabaoth was responsible for all the evil in the world. For the Gnostics, the Ten Commandments were given to Moses to enslave humans.

The Gnostics pointed to a different code—the "First Principle" or that which is everything and nothing at the same instant, much the same as Brahman in Hinduism and Amun (the hidden one) in Egypt. For the Gnostics, "The trouble with Yahweh is that he thinks he's God." In other words, this energy (First Principle) did not create Ialdabaoth, as that could only come from female energy (although that ultimately comes from the First Principle), in the form of Wisdom or Sophia. Much the same as Eve in the Old Testament, Sophia is burdened with creating all the evil in the world by creating Ialdabaoth (Yahweh). The Gnostics trace their lineage back to Seth, the third son of Adam and Eve, and their job is to gather up all the energy first dispersed by Sophia when she created Ialdabaoth, and then by Ialdabaoth, who created everything in the universe we experience. When this energy is collected, they will return it to the First Principle, "I and the Father are One." Or perhaps this is a reference to matter that collapses in on itself and becomes a Black Hole, representing a pulsating universe in a fashion similar to the Hindu tradition.

Back to Isaac. As mentioned above, Isaac's original father might have been Pharaoh, but this presents many problems as to lineage and depth of lineage. On the one hand, such a story could provide a connection to royal lineage and land ownership, but on the other hand, the Egyptians kept lots of records—carved in stone, in many cases, which could overturn their claims. The lineage depth of their mythical charter also allows competition with the oldest of the old for land. There is a lot to be said for proving that you settled a place first, like staking a claim either through the Pharaoh-Sarah or Abraham-Sarah connection.

Isaac, as you recall, was involved in a famous non-event, where Abraham is instructed by Yahweh to bind Isaac and sacrifice him. Abraham willingly complies, but at the last minute an angel ("angel of the Lord") or perhaps God Himself stays his hand and a lamb is sacrificed instead. There is a similar story, invented by the Muslims, of Abraham's binding of Ishmael that takes place in Mecca, which was a non-place in the time frame given for Abraham. What is the message? Is God really above humanity? Does God really come first and is thus more important than human decency? I tend to side with the Gnostics in their depiction of Yahweh as demonic.

Isaac marries Rebekah (which means to tie up or secure as in a home—"my pad") and they have twin sons, Esau and Jacob. In her womb the boys "jostled each other," and when Rebekah asks why this is happening, the Lord quickly stops everything he is doing, cleans the clay from the potters wheel, and tells her a long-ass story, a prophecy from the mouth of God—the twins will represent two nations and the older will bow down to the younger (this is also the theme in the Joseph story below). Now, when a prophecy comes from God, you best follow along or get into serious trouble. Esau is born first, making him the oldest, but he "was red, and his whole body was a hairy garment." (Genesis 25:24–25) What does this mean? There are several interpretations. Perhaps, as the story was unfolding, there was a future plan—a conflict, a war perhaps—from the descendents of the brothers. This might simply be a reflection of tribal rivalry, often between relatives, distant as they might be. The interpretation most favored is that Esau represents nature and is seen as corrupt. Esau has an imperfection, like one might find on a goat, or this might be analogous to the evil brother, Seth, in the Egyptian tradition, who was characterized as having red hair. The lineage of Abraham cannot contain imperfections, at least at the biological level (eugenics conceivably?). This is brought out because

Jacob has a strong ally in his mother, a representation of life (and perhaps wisdom?), while Isaac is more interested in Esau's ability to hunt. It is up to Rebekah, who also represents nature, to change the rules, that is to say, nature controlling itself or herself for the good of humanity. Esau is fine, he is great, but we have to move past nature, so here is the myth building. We have to secure the aid of nature/Rebecca (learn her secrets) if we are going to accentuate humanity over our authentic selves, our animal nature. This is what her name implies—to secure an understandably uneasy partnership with nature in order to correct nature. The first thing we have to correct is ourselves, through the separation of our animal nature from our ability to explore and understand—the ability to be wise and rational. This is a play on the Cain and Able story but more complex. I'm not sure what the ancients would want us, in the twenty-first century, to read into this story, but it also involves trickery and conniving instigated by the mother, Rebekah, a wicked woman who does what she does because God told her it would happen. Read through the eyes of 2,500 years ago, this event could indicate that trickery and conniving, deception and deceit, represent wisdom or being clever. Or maybe it is what women are good at. At the very least Rebekah is following an assignment, thus justifying her behavior; she played her "God said it was alright" card.

Another possibility is that God has a plan, and the plan is for Jacob to get the blessing because He simply chooses Jacob, much the same as He chooses the Hebrews/Israelites as His chosen people. But, again, this episode may also be another statement against nature and our slavery to biology. Esau represents nature, which has to be overcome. I hope the reader can appreciate how easy it is to create an endless variety of comment on biblical matters, or myth layered on myth.

In any case, it sets the scene for knowing that Esau will be treated differently than Jacob; in a sense, Esau (another spelling for the Arabic word Jesus) is a *stranger* and that just might be the subtle point of it all. Again, Isaac likes Esau because he is a good hunter and Isaac loves meat (nature) and would probably just sit around all day eating lamb chops and licking his fingers. Rebekah represents the active principle and a necessary player to move the story along. You cannot have change without deception, crisis, or conflict (an evolutionary process), and just like the snake that tempts Eve, Rebekah tempts Jacob. This, again, places women in an ambiguous position; this is certainly a statement of power. Esau, cast as different, an *outsider,* loses his birthright through trickery and deception, a deep trench traveling the length of the Old and New Testaments. To further indicate his outsider status we read, "When Esau was forty years old he married Judith daughter of Beeri the Hittite, and also Basemath Daughter of Elon the Hittite. They were the source of grief to Isaac and Rebekah." (Genesis 26:34) Not only would it have been terrible for Esau to marry a Canaanite (the Israelites were also Canaanites), but the Hittites were not Semitic people! They were Indo-Europeans, from the steppe area of Eastern Europe, who raided into the central area of what is now Turkey around 2300 BCE, although their history does not begin until 1700 BCE. These were nomadic people and thugs, and they came equipped with a male dominant, polytheistic tradition and ritual sex. They probably cussed a great deal, liked to fight, and used a plethora of mind-altering plants in ritual settings overseen by a shaman-like individual wearing a leopard skin. They also spoke Indo-European language dialects amalgamated with the languages they bumped into—you cannot get more alien than that. Isaac must have been more than pissed and a spiritual disease was inevitable. Back to Isaac and more of Esau shortly.

Isaac is almost a mirror of his father, Abraham. In Genesis 26:1, we encounter another "famine in the land." This time, Isaac is told by the deity *not* to go to Egypt, a piece of real estate will become his property and that of his descendants, and their numbers will multiply. "So Isaac stayed in Gerar," and once again there is this fear that "the men of that place" will think his wife Rebekah so beautiful and desirable that he will be killed. So, he pawns her off as his sister. Sound familiar? The king who comes for her is Abimelech, king of the Philistines! Is this the same king with whom Abraham swapped sex for possessions? In any case, Abimelech one day notices Isaac being just a little too friendly with Rebekah and realizes that she is *not* his sister and instead his wife, and confronts him. Isaac gives the lamebrain excuse that he was fearful that the men of that place would desire her and kill him. Well, obviously the men of that place were not lusting after Rebekah, for after being there "a long time" no one seems to have been interested in her at all. This comes out in almost all translations of Genesis, when Abimelech says, "One of the men *might* well have slept with your wife, and you would have brought guilt upon us." (Genesis 26:10) Should we simply accept the words, Isaac's lame excuse, and leave it at that? Should we simply assume that outsiders (non-Israelites) should be fearful of despoiling Isaac's property (his wife), lest Yahweh launch a plague as he did against the Egyptians? I think we need to go deeper. Obviously, the Philistines have some cultural integrity, that is, adultery is not a good thing because it invites conflict. Adultery is frowned upon in our own day and age for that very same reason, although that does not mean the behavior is uncommon—take note of some prominent politicians and evangelists. Abraham and Isaac resemble tricksters who go about creating unrest but promoting change; Murphy has become the trickster in our own time.

But I think there is another message here: It is perfectly okay to deceive strangers and deception pays off. Abimelech tells his people, "Anyone who molests this man or his wife shall surely be put to death." (Genesis 26:11) Abimelech is a powerful man, and with this order allows Isaac to plant crops wherever he wants and to raise and pasture his sheep/goats throughout the land. Is this out of guilt? Or perhaps there is the memory of what happened to Pharaoh after he slept with Sarai ("God will get you")? This seems to be implied in the story. At any rate, Isaac becomes very wealthy, so much so that "the Philistines envied him" and he is told to "move on" by Abimelech. Notice that Abraham and Isaac are not portrayed as common people. They go right to the head of the class with private meetings with the king (Pharaoh, in the case of Abraham) and so on. (Genesis 26:26–30) This implies that the Hebrews are important people, and this is acknowledged by kings and commoners alike; you cannot present the story in any other way.

Read literally, you see Isaac as a man who is less than honorable, considers women objects or chattel, and can avow or disavow his connection to them. This could symbolize a shutting off and turning away from one's animal instincts but at the least a distancing from nature. Also keep in mind that many of these stories were originally told around the hearth and they are about legendary people. Perhaps the deception, murder, and so on were seen as humorous in some renditions, and as a serious message in others, just as we see humor in the absurd antics of politicians and movie stars. There is likewise a great sense of humor that issues from this tradition, not found in the Old Testament, and it would be hard to believe that these stories originally had no punch lines (see Telushkin 2002, 17).

In my opinion, the saga presented in the Old Testament is by and large about a shift in thinking that corresponds with the development of urban centers, diverse tribes entering that political geography, but at the same time attempting to maintain tribal identity. One value I see in the Old Testament is that it invites us to question our values and behaviors. The outrageous behavior of Yahweh and other main players in this story is telling us exactly what the Greek myths tell us: If you act outrageously (lie, cheat, steal, sleep with your secretary, etc.), then people lose respect for you. Many people dislike the Jews because their mythical charter states that they are the chosen few and better than everyone else. If people claim to be better than everyone else on the planet, claim to have the truth, and so on, those on the other side will cast them in a negative light. This is one of the messages in the story of Joseph reported below, where he has a dream and reveals to his brothers that they will bow down to him. This is not simply a mechanism to get Joseph from one geographical place to another. Joseph suffers from the all too common affliction of telling the people the truth before they are ready to hear it. This is the same as the Buddha saying, "Enlighten others only when they are ready." The story says that, when you claim superiority, such pronouncements separate you from others; this breeds resentments. This is a reflection of our small-group nature. This is "Us" vs. "Them," and in this condition you can pretty much do what you want to strangers (as did Abraham). And this is precisely the condition in which Esau finds himself with his brother Jacob.

Jacob

We continue along a path, the path of deception and taking advantage of others, which these stories either condone or condemn depending on interpretation. It is also important to understand that the storylines and mythic frames connected to the tribal groups existing in the Syrian-Arabian desert at that time (1800–1700 BCE) would have been different from that of the time period when the Old Testament was compiled. In fact, they would have been two different cultures. The language spoken in 1800 BCE would have been different in 560 BCE. We only have to look at the changes that have occurred in English over the past 1,000 years. For anyone who doubts this, read the prelude to *The Canterbury Tales* in Old English and see if you can understand it. This is called linguistic drift, resulting from random changes in sound units, with new words entering the vocabulary and old words altering in meaning. The first books of the Old Testament were compiled sometime after 560 BCE, and the stories represent an interpretation of the older stories, orally transmitted for the most part. Oral transmission has a tendency to keep up with prevailing political and social issues. Simply put, the stories and their references at 1700 BCE, when the Hebrews were wandering about, would have been very different in 560 BCE. Thus, all the stories in the Old Testament must reflect attitudes and behaviors from around 600–300 BCE. The impression the Jewish scholars have given us is that there is a cultural continuity over a time period of about 1,000 years! Even the ancient Egyptians could not manage that; the Egyptian culture of 2500 BCE is not the same culture at 1500 BCE or 500 BCE. This causes many problems in translating Egyptian texts.

Continuing with this theme, the attitude toward women would have been very different in 1700 BCE when compared to 600 BCE. By comparison, look at the attitude toward women in the United States one hundred years ago and then consider Europe 1,000 years ago. In 1700

BCE women would have been chattel, pure and simple, for these wandering tribes and the storyline would have centered on male energy guiding the flock *and not giving land grants.* The story changes when they become weary of wandering and realize the potential of these urban areas. Urban-agricultural areas offer a different psychology and lifestyle, with different comforts and certainly goods and services; these geographies can be addictive and desired. It is easy to get genetically lost in an urban setting because it is much more difficult to control male sperm. The best of both possible worlds is a land where a tribal group can build their own city populated only by their tribe, and the rest of the world can go to hell.

In any case, the female energy is very important in the urban-agricultural setting of 600 BCE, and to get the "boys back on the farm after they've experienced gay Paris," in order to return to the "good old days" of tribal superiority and thus male superiority, the mother-goddess had to be carved away. The female energy, in fact, is considered the "abomination" (1 Kings 11:5). In 2 Kings 23:13 we read,

> And the high places that [were] before Jerusalem, which
> [were] on the right hand of the mount of corruption, which
> Solomon the king of Israel had built for *Ashtoreth the abom-*
> *ination* of the Zidonians, and for Chemosh the abomination
> of the Moabites, and for Milcom the abomination of the
> children of Ammon, did the king defile. (Emphasis added)

Male-dominated monotheistic traditions could be seen as a statement of resentment at being enslaved to our biology, but in the Hebrew tradition it is more about exclusivity, of breaking away and separating from the other Canaanite tribes, just as the Hebrews were separate as a wandering tribe. So the Hebrews were simply continuing on their same nomadic path, but in an urban setting. Unintentionally, perhaps, the female energy is undervalued in the process; but there does appear to be ambivalence, as mentioned earlier, which I think is a reflection of the old and new attitudes toward the female energy and perhaps their connection to Egypt. Remember that it is the female principle that took the risk of actively participating in nature, trying new things, and breaking away from the authority of nature played by God, rather than passively receiving and accepting it as would a bird, tree, cockroach, or Adam. It is my solid opinion that much of what is in the Old Testament was originally "what not to do" stories designed to control one's animal nature.

Back to Jacob. The story is set for Jacob through the elimination of his brother, Esau. The elimination of political rivals—even brothers— is an old story. Jacob has twelve children (and thus he sires the twelve tribes of Israel) by various wives, with the last two (Joseph and Benjamin) born of Rachel, who dies giving birth to Benjamin. The Israelites most surely invented the soap opera. In passing, the name Rachel means "ewe" or sheep, but a beautiful sheep of course.

Twelve is referenced numerous times in the Old and New Testaments and this cannot simply be coincidence. Twelve is a reference to sign of the Zodiac, thus the reference is to the sun and the sun god, who went by many names in the Middle East (including Egypt). The sun god was seen as universal in the Middle East, and it was the heretic Pharaoh Akhenaten (discussed in detail below) who closed the temples in Egypt and, by royal decree, stated that the only god of worship was the Aten or sun disk. This was a type of oppressive monotheism, as seen in the world today. Aten, as mentioned earlier, becomes Adon or Adoni (my lord—a synonym for Yahweh) in the Hebrew tradition.

The story of Jacob is short but involved. Esau has a grudge against Jacob and, from our perspective, rightly so. In fact, if the authors didn't see Jacob's behavior as reprehensible, Jacob would not have feared Esau or felt guilt about his behavior; it would not have been mentioned. Jacob is certainly aware of this since it was his choice to usurp Esau's position of inheritance, although he still played the "mother said it was alright" card. Esau, however, is a little more forgiving than Jacob had imagined. I think that many of the original renditions of biblical heroes came with paired opposites, one illustrating what not to do (animal nature), and the other our more human side—let it go and get on with life.

Jacob leaves Beersheba and heads for Haran, but on the way he stops for a rest and has a dream, in which he saw a stairway resting on the earth,

> with its top reaching to heaven, and the angels of God were ascending and descending on it. Above it stood the Lord, and he said: 'I am the Lord, the God of your father Abraham and the God of Isaac. I will give you and your descendants the land on which you are lying. Your descendants will be like the dust on the earth, and you will be spread out to the west and to the east, to the north and to the south. All peoples on earth will be blessed through you and your offspring. I am with you and will watch over you wherever you go, and I will bring you back to this land. I will not leave you until I have done what I have promised you.' When Jacob awoke from his sleep, he thought, 'Surely the Lord is in this place, and I was not aware of it.' He was afraid and said, 'How awesome is this place! This is none other than the house of God; this is the gate of heaven.' (Genesis 28:10–17)

Here we have a reiteration of the promise to Abraham, that is, land ownership and special privileges, along with deception and fraud with respect to treatment of his brother. The ladder symbolism was directly borrowed from the Egyptian tradition (see Rush 2007), where a ladder is needed to climb up to the different gates of the underworld. In Genesis 29, Jacob is treated to deception in return (what goes around, comes around?). He makes a deal with Laban, his mother's brother, for the hand of his daughter, Rachel. The promise was that he (Jacob) would work for seven years, after which he would marry Rachel. Well, time marches on and when it came time to complete the bargain, Laban instead substituted Leah, the oldest daughter. Culturally, the younger daughter, Rachel, cannot marry before her older sister, so that part is understood. However, Laban still did not keep his word—even to a close relative, and, instead, Jacob is obliged to work for another seven years to obtain Rachel (seven plus seven equals fourteen, half the cycle of the moon, or more myth making?). Is this dishonesty, or should Jacob have understood the cultural rules? But there is more, much more. Looked at from our perspective, women are the subjects of men and have little or no control over their lives. As in Islam, they are merely "cows." Again, this is the old tradition, and since that time Judaism and Christianity have gone through reform—many of these sentiments are not in play today in most Christian and Jewish groups.

Jacob engages in other deceptions that make him rich and is deceived in return. His daughter is raped, and the sons avenge this act by means of deception and then killing every male in town. Jacob disperses the brothers, wrestles with God (symbolic of the Hebrew's wrestling with their faith and morals), and finally we come to Joseph, the eleventh son born to Jacob, Rachel's firstborn.

Joseph, Meaning "Doubler"

As mentioned, Jacob, a son of Isaac (whose name was changed by God to Israel, which represents the twelve tribes), had two sons by Rachel, Joseph and Benjamin. Let us not forget that Jacob also had a daughter, Dinah. Her mother is Leah, and Dinah is Leah's seventh child and Jacob's eleventh (seven/eleven). Dinah is important in that her rape is a vehicle for dispersing the tribes; Joseph is disgusted with how the brothers took revenge and tells them to go their separate ways. This also serves as another example of male vs. female importance—Dinah does not bring forth a tribe. What this means is that this is a patrilineal culture, and the relatives on the mother's side are much less important in terms of identity. This is precisely why the Jews could not trace Isaac through Sarah and Pharaoh.

Joseph is important for three reasons. First, he interprets dreams, and it is through this vehicle that he is moved from Canaan to Egypt. Second, through dream interpretation he "saves the world" and is made pharaoh's "Double," or vizier of Egypt. And third, this story, as I outline below, represents a possible genetic connection of the Hebrews to Egyptian royalty. This is questionable, however, because the Egyptians saw the Hebrews as foreigners, and although there were arranged marriages between outside states (daughters or slaves given to Pharaoh by kings of other countries), for political purposes the only way a foreign king would enter royalty was by conquest. Egyptian commoners, however, could obtain high status in the court.

Dreams in Biblical times, just as today in the Middle East, were considered prophetic (see Miller 1994; Sviri 1999; Szpakowska 2003). Sviri (1999, 252) comments:

> "The veridical dream is one forty-sixth of prophecy," states an Islamic tradition attributed to the Prophet Muhammad. This statement implies that while prophecy has ceased, Muhammad being the Seal of the Prophets, messages of divine origin can still be communicated through dreams, albeit on a *smaller scale* than prophecy. (Emphasis added)

What "smaller scale" means is that Allah will never speak to another human again, except for perhaps small talk. The dream being "one forty-sixth of prophecy" is similar to the Jewish position that, "A dream is one-sixtieth of prophecy" (see Bialik and Ravnitzky 1992, 790), both fractions relating to astronomical calculations.

Szpakowska (2003, 123), referring to ancient Egypt, states: "From earliest times the Egyptians exhibited a desire to contact those in the far world through various means. The nature of archaeological record likely reveals only a fraction of these, and while it is biased towards the elite of society, enough remains to suggest that eventually dreams provided an effective means for direct communication between this world and the divine."

Referring to Gregory of Nyssa (fourth century CE), Miller writes,

> Gregory recites briefly the dreams of the butler and the baker familiar from the Biblical story of Joseph (Gen. 40.1–9).

Both butler and baker had dreams, each seeing himself and performing his usual duties; Gregory explains that these "images were imprinted on the part of the soul that has fore-sight ... and enabled the dreamers to have prophetic powers for a time." What Gregory does not say directly is that both of these dreamers were baffled by their dreams; in their case, the prophetic power lay in the dreams but was not evident to the dreamers themselves. Discerning the meaning of these dreams was the province of Joseph. ... It becomes clear that the existence of such heroic biblical dreamers and dream-interpreters as Daniel and Joseph has presented something of a problem for Gregory's view of dreams. Would Scripture allow "fantastic nonsense"? No, says Gregory, and he saves the biblical text from *hallucination* by appealing to yet another kind of dream, one that is neither biologically induced nor enigmatically obscure. Gregory says that Daniel, Joseph, and other Biblical dreamers were "taught by divine power" about things to come, *with no "turbidity" clouding their sense-perception.* [Emphasis added]

In short, dreams from the biblical texts originate outside the dreamer and are divine in origin, with the terms "hallucination" and "turbidity" perhaps an attempt to remove mind-altering substances from the formula. Gregory would not have made a point of this unless it was common knowledge, at least among priests, that mind-altering substances were connected to dream behavior and prophecy. This is a weak attempt to cover up the real origin of these dreams and prophecies, that is, by way of mind-altering substances.

Special people have lots of dreams, but dreams are important because they are the conduit between this geography and that other, sacred space (heaven or hell) and associated personnel. Shortly after 9/11, the news media ran several videotapes of the thug Bin Laden, one of which showed him sitting around several friends or perhaps relatives, with one reporting a dream where she saw a large blue bird fly into a building. Baffled by the dream, she now understood its significance—the airplanes used in 9/11.

Joseph, as you will recall, was his father's favorite son. As the story goes, Joseph reports a dream: "We were binding sheaves of grain out in the field when suddenly my sheaf rose and stood upright, while your sheaves gathered around mine and bowed to it." (Genesis 37: 6) The brothers, who were already jealous of Joseph because he was their father's favorite, decide to kill him, but instead sell him into slavery. He is taken to Egypt (delta area) where he is sold to Potiphar (one of pharaoh's officials—he is the Captain of the Guards). Potiphar's wife attempts to seduce Joseph, and when he refuses her advances she tells her husband that Joseph tried to seduce her; Joseph is then put in jail. While in jail he interprets the dreams of pharaoh's cupbearer and baker, revealing that in three days the cupbearer will go free, while the baker will hang. The interpretations prove correct, and as the cupbearer is leaving jail Joseph says, "Remember me." But, of course, the cupbearer forgets. All is not lost, however. Two years later pharaoh has two dreams he cannot interpret, nor can the temple priests, which have to do with seven lean, ugly cows consuming seven fat cows, and seven shriveled heads of grain consuming seven fat heads of grain. The cupbearer remembers Joseph, he is sent for, and Joseph correctly interprets the dream, that is, there will be seven bountiful years and seven years of famine. Let me pause for a moment. There is no evidence of such dream interpretation in the Egyptian records, and one would think that an event of such magnitude would be recorded.

To continue, because Joseph correctly interprets the dream, tells pharaoh to stockpile grain, and saves Egypt from disaster, pharaoh makes him his "double" or vizier of Egypt (Genesis 39–41). There is a similar story in the Book of Daniel. This is a wonderful story, perhaps my favorite because I am fascinated with dreams (see Rush 2007). More importantly, we begin to see an almost direct borrowing from a historically factual situation that has two paths leading away from it.

First, this may simply be more of the mythical charter (hedging their bets, so to speak), designed to accomplish what the story of

Abraham and Sarah could not initially do without losing lineage depth. That is to say, it bridges the mythical gap to Egyptian royalty. Second, an Asiatic who fits the description of Joseph may have married into Egyptian royalty, but this does not mean that he was Hebrew, or that the story of Joseph being sold into slavery by his brother, as reported in the Bible, is true and factual (see Aldred 1988, 96, 117). As I mentioned earlier, it is unlikely but not impossible that a foreign, full-blooded Asiatic male married into royalty during the beginning of the New Kingdom, after the Hyksos had been driven from the landscape. It would be difficult enough for a commoner to marry into royalty, let alone a despised foreigner.

Joseph and Yuya

Joseph may be patterned on a man named Yuya, who fathered a daughter (Tiye), who married a pharaoh (Amenhotep III). This pharaoh must have loved this woman to the very core of his soul; she must have been really, really, really special. She seems to be somewhat of an outsider or possibly not a full-blooded Egyptian, and pharaoh made her his Great Wife, either concurrently with Sitamen, another Great Wife (perhaps his sister), or on her own. This was bound to create lots and lots of problems, rivalries, murder—lots of stress in the palace! Amenhotep III had a dilemma over two wives, their children, and who would take over when Papa Pharaoh passed into the netherworld; this may be the basis of the story of Solomon's dilemma over the two women claiming to be a child's biological mother. In any event, Amenhotep III and Tiye produced Amenhotep IV, or Akhenaten, the heretic pharaoh.

Let's look at Joseph more closely. He saves the Egyptian civilization and becomes Pharaoh's double, or vizier (*mshna*) of Egypt. There is no evidence of a man named Joseph connected in some important way to a pharaoh in Egypt. But there is a tomb, found in 1905, (Valley of the Kings—KV-46) belonging to a man named Yuya (and his wife Tiuyu or Tuya), which parallels part of the story in Genesis. Yuya was Commander of the Chariotry to both Tuthmosis IV (1413–1405 BCE) and Amenhotep III (1405–1367 BCE). He was not a slave assigned a high position in pharaoh's employ. The word for his title in Hebrew is mshna, which means *to double*. In Yuya's tomb is inscribed, "Whom the king has made his double." Keep in mind that the Old Testament is a mythical charter and not history. One of the problems noticed by biblical scholars is that of attempting to put exact dates to events—the Bible is not a history lesson and attempting to exactly match up people with events and some sort of timeline is silly.

In the biblical account of Joseph, pharaoh also gave Joseph an Egyptian name, *Zaphnathpaaneah*. Now, Joseph and Yuya are composite names: *Yu* and *seph* for Joseph, and *Yu* and *ya* for Yuya. Zaphnathpaaneah written with Egyptian phonemes is S ph-ntr-iwf-'nh. The first part of this is *Seph*, which is not a Hebrew name. Now, when you combine *Yu*, the first part of the vizier's name, and *seph*, you have Joseph. This is too much of a coincidence to be ignored (see Gadala 1999).

Pharaoh gives Joseph a wife and her name is Asenath; Yuya's wife's name was Tuya. Asenath may have simply been a made up name by the biblical scholars because it's a man's world, or it might be her birth name—only mother knows your real name, as this prevents evil magic from being worked against you. A-se-*nath* is derived from Zaph-*nath*-paa-neah, and probably means something like "devoted to the goddess Neith"; she is a very special goddess (see Rush 2007, 292). In any case, Yuya and Tuya have a daughter named Tiye who marries Amenhotep III. Let's make a connection.

Amenhotep III may be the template for Solomon of the Bible. There are so many similarities between them that there has to be some connection. They were both involved in building bureaucracies, monuments, and sites of fortifications, as well as taxation. Also, there is no evidence that Solomon, or David for that matter, ever commanded a large kingdom with hundreds of thousands of soldiers. What I see in this is a very insecure people in search of a role model and they found that in Egypt. Both Amenhotep III and Solomon were said to be wise, and the story about Solomon determining the biological mother of a child, by judging the child be torn in half and half given to each, is the same story as Amenhotep having to make a choice as to who should be the Great Wife, Sitamen or Tiye. He is the one who is really torn apart.

Now, Queen Mother Tiye is in trouble here, because if Yuya is part Asiatic, she is not one-hundred percent Egyptian, her bloodline is questionable, and thus not as close as Sitamen to royalty. The Egyptians looked down on the Hebrews just as the Hebrews looked down on the Hittites, other Canaanite tribes, and everyone else. Remember that the Hyksos came into and ruled Egypt in the Fifteenth Dynasty, inhabiting, for the most part, Lower Egypt. Beginning perhaps with Taa II (1555 BCE), but certainly with Kamose (around 1545–1539 BCE), the Hyksos were challenged and eventually forced from Egypt by Amose (1539–1514 BCE), which begins the Eighteenth Dynasty. Joseph or Yuya may be connected to those original Hyksos invasions.

Be that as it may, Tiye and Amenhotep have a son, and Sitamen has sons. The killing of the first born as a punishment in the Bible (Exodus 13:14–16) might represent the killing of only one child, that is, the son of Amenhotep III and Tiye, or Amenhotep IV or Akhenaten. Tiye seems to already have lost one or two children (Nebetiah and Beketaten); they are noted in the records one moment and gone the next. As I said, there is stress in the palace.

Akhenaten and Moses

To protect her son, Tiye sends Amenhotep IV by water to her relations at nearby Goshen, but we can't be sure they are Egyptian or Asiatic relatives. Combined with the Sargon the Great story noted earlier, this event may represent a real occurrence, but the composite story in the Bible is a much better prelude for a hero myth of Moses which means "son."

It was Amenhotep IV or Akhenaten, the heretic pharaoh, who closed down the Amun priesthood at Thebes, built his own palace at Amarna, and dictated that the only god worshiped would be the Aten or sun disk. Recall what I said earlier about the Aten and the word Adon

(Lord) as a synonym for Yahweh. Although monotheism was an old story in ancient Egypt, Akhenaten is credited with being the first repressive monotheist, in a fashion similar to the biblical Moses, Paul, and, more recently, Muhammad, the various popes, Brigham Young, Ayatollah Khomeini—there is a long, long list.

Akhenaten lived at Thebes for several years until he was probably told to leave by the very powerful priests of Amun-Re; thus his move to Amarna (another Exodus?). He reigned from 1352–1336 BCE and then disappeared. He may have simply died. But there are suggestions he might have felt threatened in Amarna and perhaps attempted to cement some alliances with different groups, such as the Shasu to the east and Nubians to the South, and may have been a ruler or general in the Land of Cush (modern day Sudan), at least for a short time after the end of his reign in Egypt. This is an interesting story but verification is not possible at this time.

There is no evidence of anyone named Moses or any such Exodus connected to a person by that name. This would have been a gigantic event and recorded in Egyptian texts. The Bible suggests that Moses left Egypt with 600,000 men, not including women and children. Altogether, that would be at least one million people; there probably weren't one million people living in all of Egypt at that time. So, like other stories in the Bible (for example, Noah, David, Solomon, Sampson, and so on) there is a storyline, borrowed from the Babylonians and Egyptians, and then tailor-made and hand sewn to fit a purpose, plan, or political agenda. Remember that a central theme in the Old Testament is that a deity has a plan for his chosen people. But the other central themes are time depth and connections to royalty. Many biblical scholars believe that Moses actually wrote much of Exodus, and their timeframe for Moses is around 1440 BCE. Are there really documents in the hand of Moses that can be accurately dated to 1440 BCE? If verifiable documents do not exist and if the stories are more recent, perhaps dating to between 560–520 BCE, we cannot assume a continuity of thought, people, places, and dates. It is obvious that important parts are missing from most of these stories—people and places that would have been written down if these stories represented history. Why, for example, aren't the pharaohs named? My personal opinion is that the story of the Exodus is a composite story written sometime between 560 and 530 BCE. The story is patterned after some individual(s), with a storyline reworked for their needs. It makes a great deal more sense to assume this reworking because of what we know about Akhenaten.

Akhenaten's tomb was found at Amarna but it had been looted. Royal tombs took years to complete and his tomb at Amarna was not completed; Akhenaten's body had long since been removed, if it ever was interred there. However, there are suggestions from scholars that he was driven from Amarna, went to the Sinai, and hung out with the Hebrew tribes (Shasu) for "forty" years. His journey to the Sinai may have been to forge a link with the Shasu, develop a big enough army, storm back into Egypt, and retake his rightful place as Pharaoh.

After he died or left Amarna, a pharaoh by the name of Smenkhkare took over for a year or so—some scholars suggest that this might have been Akhenaten's beautiful wife, Nefertiti, or perhaps an older son of Akhenaten, a co-regent. Akhenaten and either Nefertiti, or a second wife, Kiya, had another son, however, and his name was Tutankhamun. (I wonder if the boy king, King Tutankhamun, has any Hebrew genetic markers that might clarify this possibility.) His original name was Tutankh*aten*, but once Akhenaten was out of the picture his name was changed to Tutankh*amun*, he left Amarna, and took up residence at Thebes. He restored the Theban priesthood and worship of the many gods and goddesses in an attempt to restore the old ways (see Chapter Three). His wife's name, originally Ankhsen*aten*, was likewise changed to Ankhsen*amun*. King Tut, as he is more popularly known, was most probably murdered by Aya, his chief advisor, who also became Pharaoh by marrying Tut's wife, Ankhsenamun. There are several possibilities as to why Tut was murdered, one of which is that Aya, although a commoner but certainly not a foreigner, was not of royal lineage, and the only way he could become Pharaoh is by marriage to someone who was of royal lineage, that is, Tut's wife. But I think there is perhaps another reason. Tut's father, Akhenaten, had unleashed a spiritual plague on the landscape and all was despair. Pharaohs are powerful people, sons tend to follow in their father's footsteps, and it would be in the best interests of the Egyptian priesthood and the Egyptian people to not endure such terror again. The ancient Egyptians understood that people are different and they have different spiritual, emotional, and physical needs. The gods and goddesses represented hope in their many guises, and appealing to the gods and goddesses could be considered a form of psychotherapy (see Rush 2007). These people had spiritual experiences with their deities of a nature only rarely encountered in popular religion today.

After Akhenaten disappeared several other pharaohs briefly ruled, that is, Smenkhkare (1331–1332 BCE), Tutankhamun (1332–1322 BCE), Aya (1323–1319 BCE), Horemheb (1319–1292 BCE), and Rameses I (1292–1290 BCE). Some have speculated (see Gadala 1999) that during the later part of the reign of Aya or during the reign of Horemheb, Akhenaten returned to Egypt to reclaim his birthright. He presents his staff or scepter to the powers that be (which would have a cobra head, fashioned out of solid brass or even gold) and he passes many tests. Some priest did agree that he was the legitimate Pharaoh, but others realistically calculated the upheaval if he were reinstated. Akhenaten can't get anywhere with this; there is too much hostility. His temple complex was still inhabited by a few hangers-on, there were monuments in Thebes with his name on them, and the stability of Egypt was threatened. So he once again gets out of Dodge. He may have recruited Hebrews living in the delta (six, sixty, or perhaps several hundred—not 600,000!) whom he leads back to the Sinai, and with their help he reunites with the Shasu, a term referring to the Israelites in Egyptian records (see Aldred 1988, 122). Now understand this: Akhenaten would have considered himself the "chosen person," the legitimate Pharaoh as sanctified by the gods. He was a god on earth. This is perhaps how he convinced the people to leave the delta, as well as persuaded the Shasu that they were His, Akhenaten's (God's), chosen people. But they have one big problem—land to call their own. So Akhenaten tells these people that a certain plot of land is theirs, because

He, Pharaoh, a god on earth, says so. As Pharaoh he would have been exposed to all the esoteric rites, especially those using mind-altering substances—our mythic hero Moses certainly knew these rites. Akhenaten was a god on earth who could bequeath land or anything else he desired; he was still the son of the Sun. The mind-altering substances were probably used to contact the deity for advice or simply for third-person credibility.

Akhenaten's goal (as was Moses' in the Bible) was to push into the territory of the Canaanites and occupy their land. But he made a fatal error—he incurred the wrath of Horemheb, who was also a god on earth, possibly over water rights. Feeling the Shasu could be a threat, Horemheb pro-acts, goes to the Sinai, and kills Moses/Akhenaten. Akhenaten, because he was Pharaoh, is brought back to Egypt, perhaps entombed for a short time at Amarna, but more likely buried in the Valley of the Kings with other royal mummies removed from the Royal Tombs at Amarna. The tomb at Amarna was then desecrated, with cartouches removed. According to Egyptologists, the mummies removed from Amarna were placed in tomb KV-55 (Valley of the Kings), but then that tomb was vandalized, probably by royal order, to wipe out Akhenaten's name (see Aldred 1988). To avoid the possibility that members of Akhenaten's family would challenge Pharaoh, they altered their history by attempting to erase any reference whatsoever to Akhenaten, but they did not totally succeed. Again, it is the winners who write or rewrite history.

Obviously the story of Moses in the Bible is myth, but it might just be wrapped around a real person, with Moses/Akhenaten connected to the House of Pharaoh. The Moses story makes a powerful connection to royalty; Yuya may have been non-Egyptian, and famines may have plagued the land as they did in the Old Kingdom. Shaw and Nicholson (1995, 96–97) make an interesting statement about famine:

> That famines took place during the Old Kingdom is not in
> doubt, and the surviving visual evidence includes several
> fragments of relief from the walls of the 5th Dynasty cause-

way of the pyramid complex of Unas (2375–2345 B.C.) at
Saqqara. These reliefs depict numerous emaciated figures,
their ribcages clearly visible, seated on the ground and
apparently weak from hunger. It has been argued by some
scholars, partly on the basis of these reliefs, that the Old
Kingdom (2686–2181 B.C.) ended largely because of pro-
longed drought and increasing desertification. The 'autobio-
graphical' inscriptions in the tomb of the provincial governor
Ankhtifi (c.2100 B.C.), at El-Mo'Alla, describe how he saved
his people from 'dying on the sandbank of hell' . . .

The biblical story of Joseph may itself have taken place during the
Second Intermediate Period (1650–1550 BCE), and it has been suggested that it was a Hyksos king of Egypt whom Joseph saved from the
effects of famine. Famines were not new, and when a famine ended,
Pharaoh (or a Hebrew, in the case of Joseph) wanted to take credit for
it.

Yuya's Egyptian marriage brought forth Tye, who married Amenhotep
III, and they produced Amenhotep IV or Akhenaten. The story would
not have worked with Sarah and Pharaoh through Isaac, as it then is
simply a story of ancient Egypt, and the Hebrew connection would
slowly and surely melt away and finally disappear into the fabric of
Egyptian history. But with Moses we have it both ways, that is, time
depth to Abraham through Joseph, and the royalty connection to *per-
aa*, House of Pharaoh.

Which story do you like better? I like the Akhenaten, a.k.a. Moses,
better because it is easy to see the dynamics of what was possibly happening politically and socially in history, in both the Egyptian and
Hebrew worlds. When you are building a mythical charter you need a
story that a people can believe in, the bits and pieces of which were
heard as legends told around the campfire. Surely the story of Moses is
an old tale of a wandering people who leave one place in search of
another. This is what wandering people do and one should not be surprised. If they were fishing people, they would have a different story

regarding that geography. There are obstacles to overcome, magical help shows up in the nick of time, and once in this other place, "the land of milk and honey," they won't have to wander anymore, forever. This is an important theme in science fiction today. If this story is to appeal to the masses, it cannot be beyond their understanding of key points; it has to make sense to them. Scholars can argue about who wrote what and various meanings, but this is a story of hope—life (nature) sucks, but things will work out and God is on our side. These stories are very old and what the Hebrews did was to connect elements of the story to royalty, and to do this you change the names of the characters, locations, and obstacles to overcome. These stories entertained and acted as a method of social control, of what to do and not do. They were parables no different than those turned by Jesus. They eventually became codified as fact—they had nothing else to rely on for their history or sense of connectedness with past days and the ancestors who lived them. These stories, several thousands of years old, connected them with their past, the forces of nature, and each other, and there is a history of sorts here. People write about their desires, behavioral outcomes, and the outcomes of others. These stories tell us how people were in those days; they tell us about the social and psychological problems that emerge when diverse people collide on finite amounts of land with limited resources. They tell us of self-centered rulers, they tell us that life is misery, and they speak to our animal nature. They also tell us what to avoid, but only if you put humanity, rather than God, first. If there is a secret code in the Bible, it is, "Put humanity first and God second." Why is this? Well, when we put humanity first we can cooperate, solve problems, and live very, very well as we explore the universe. Not a great deal of cheery stuff in the Bible. God comes first and we hear about murder, death, threats, and judgments—all of our baser stuff. We are told that if we follow the rules and submit to the deity, the door will open to heaven, that "land of milk and honey." In other words, if you are good, Big Daddy will give you some candy. This means micro-management and no sense of self-responsibility. Putting God first absolves one of personal responsibility for anything you do.

Scholars have recognized another level of symbolism generated in all of the biblical stories and sacred history. Jacob wrestling with God, for example, tells us of a consciousness, a realization that we wrestle with ourselves. Should we obey our animal nature or the god within? Perhaps this is simply a struggle between your self-responsible potential and your basic animal nature, your Ialdabaoth. Or maybe the message is that you give up the imagined God outside of you and utilize that godly quality within to become a self-responsible, decent human being.

Hallucinogens and Religion

One of the first books I read to suggest mind-altering substances were connected to the Western traditions (Judaism, Christianity, and Islam) was Field's work, *Search for Security* (1960). This was an academic publication that didn't receive any play in the media. Field, a psychiatrist, suggested that most of the mountains in the Sinai Desert are covered with oil shale and frequent lightning strikes can ignite this type of rock, giving off gases—nitrous oxide being one of them—that would seem to glow. She suggested that Moses, when on the mountain during lightning strikes, could have experienced the deity after inhaling this gas. Field also suggested that this might be the same gas the oracle at Delphi inhaled while meditating over fissures in the earth's crust. Again, her work was not widely publicized and few people were exposed to this possibility.

Next came Schonfield's very popular book, *The Passover Plot*; this appeared as a mass market paperback in 1965. Jesus, according to Schonfield, might have been drugged and may not have died on the cross but some time later. *The Passover Plot* created quite a stir, but was overshadowed a few years later by John Allegro's *The Sacred Mushroom and the Cross* (1970). I remember a cartoon from the *Toronto Star* that showed a matronly lady with a frying pan in her hand standing next to a priest seated at the dinner table, with the comment, "How do you expect to have your hallucination if you don't eat your mushrooms!" No one threatened or attempted to kill the cartoonist or boycott the newspaper, unlike the threats and murders perpetrated by the Muslim community in Europe over cartoons of Muhammad, teddy bears, and stage plays (see Chapter Four). Although Allegro's book was readily available, even in paperback at one time, the message never really crossed into mainstream thinking. Why? Because of political correctness on the part of historians and biblical scholars; Allegro cast doubt on their interpretations of the Bible. Allegro's message is that mushrooms (and other mind-altering substances) were, for the Hebrews and Christians, the conduits to God. Since the late 1980s numerous books, by both academic and popular writers, have entered the mainstream, claiming hallucinogenic plant use by personalities in the Bible and Qur'an, but they have been publicly denied by religious clerics. The Christian community treats any new information, any suggestions or research that detracts from the constructed dogma, with intense anger. The issue of drug use for communing with gods is treated with a great deal of hostility because it suggests that the whole thing is nothing but one large communal psychosis engaged in by the religious clerics (obviously very disturbed people by modern psychiatric standards). Popes, priests, ministers, and imams encourage their members to have faith in *their* psychosis, to believe that what they tell you is true—"There is a god with a beard who lives in the sky. There are special people who die and then came back to life. Those who accept Jesus or Allah go to Heaven." This is to be accepted as historical fact with a threat attached— "Believe it or go to Hell" (or worse!). Psychiatry came out of shamanism and the priesthood; the first psychiatrists were those brave people who began to question the experiences of others and establish norms, or what is considered appropriate at a particular time among a particular people (see Chapter Five).

In a recent publication (Ruck et al. 2001—also see Bennett and McQueen 2001; Irvin and Rutajit 2006; Irvin 2008), the authors look at Greek myth and the Bible for symbols relating to mushrooms, or other mind-altering substances. Many of the Greek myths, no doubt, were generated during plant-induced, mind-altered experiences, wherein the story refers to the substance (mushroom, ergot fungus, wine) and the substance generates the story. Mystery cults would have used references to the gods during their cult rituals, and these stories might have been told during altered states, thus creating a bond with a particular deity or the god's behavioral characteristics.

Some detractors emphatically state that the mushrooms and so-called "references" to other mind-altering substances are the products of vivid imaginations. But I think there are enough written and visual references, and certainly a history and prehistory of drugs and religion, which go way beyond "vivid imaginations." Shamans and priests have used mind-altering substances for thousands upon thousands of years to commune with the supernatural world. Are we to assume they suddenly gave up these magical plants and the real god, with a capital G, stepped up and began talking to special humans? That is simply beyond reason. It makes sense that mystery religions and secret societies would keep quiet about their anointing oils and elixirs, but references to substances end up in the stories, sometimes referred to as the Golden Fleece (the cap of *Amanita muscaria*), Avalon (golden apple, also a reference to this mushroom), manna, bread, and so on. Knowing what we know about the use of these very powerful "mind-blowing" substances all over the world, and their use in magical-religious traditions, let's look more closely at certain behaviors and imagery in the Bible.

To this point, all the major male players in our story had conversations with or visions of God, or some other angel, spirit, demon, or deity. Are these merely stories of heroes with magical helpers, as expressed by Campbell (1949), or is there something else being said? The connection between religious/spiritual experiences and specific plant and fungus species was made hundred of thousands of years ago. Our ancient ancestors frequently came across cannabis, datura species, opium poppy, and mushrooms of various types, consumed them, and experienced alterations of awareness or consciousness. We know that shamans all over the world use mind-altering substances to commune with the gods for diagnostic and healing purposes, and usually both the patient and the shaman, with other group members present, consumed the substance. The Hindus used a substance called *soma* to commune with the gods, which may have been *Amanita muscaria,* or a mixture of several substances including datura and cannabis. *Amanita muscaria* does not grow in the Indus Valley and probably was obtained from the Indo-Europeans (Aryans) through longstanding trade relationships. The Indo-Europeans raided into Persia, Turkey, Greece, and Germany, and undoubtedly introduced new substances to the people they conquered. Once again, I find it difficult to believe that these substances were used for thousands of years for magical religious purposes, and then one day the cult practitioners stopped because a real god revealed himself.

The Zoroastrian (800–600 BCE to present) tradition clearly communed with Ahura Mazda using the same substance (*haoma*) as the Hindus, and it would be reasonable to believe that most, if not all, the religious traditions in the Middle East and Egypt were connected to one or more prescribed mind-altering substances or brews used in rites and rituals. These people literally thought that gods resided in plants or that the plant was a conduit to god. For example, not only is soma a plant or brew, it is also a god in the Hindu tradition. Moses encounters the God Plant—"the burning bush that did not burn"—on Mt. Sinai. Remember that this is not recreational use of these substances; this was serious business and the shaman or priest used these substances in prescribed ritual settings. These people were very superstitious; bad trips might suggest neglect of the ancestors. In my opinion, we only have four choices regarding voices from God:

- He actually spoke to or through special humans
- Special people simply have vivid imaginations and a knack for storytelling
- These special humans were on drugs
- Or these special people (Abraham, Jacob, Moses, etc.) were psychotic

Take your choice.

Around 600 BCE the Greeks established a scientific method in which, to understand the universe, it was not good enough to assume that the cause was a god or deity; it was necessary to separate natural events from supernatural beliefs. The central rite in the Mediterranean mystery cults, by and large, involved an initiation with cosmic forces through the use of one hallucinogenic substance or another. This must have been a profound experience, but it led in two directions. One was to the energy that informs all, and second, these rites, in all probability, had something to do with actually fostering this separation between the natural and supernatural realms. This is because these experiences can promote insights into cause and effect that do not require a deity or supernatural cause. The Eleusinian mysteries represent a case in point. A major ceremony, led up to with "lesser" rites, involved consuming some sort of barley wine that was complete, scholars believe, with the parasitic ergot fungus *Claviceps paspali*. This fungus manufactures ergotamine bonded to lysergic acid amides, the next best thing to LSD. These mystery cults may not have been available to everyone but certainly many of the important Greek philosophers took part. We must assume that there was a reluctance to attribute a god to the experience by some. At a certain point, however, perhaps during alchemic experimentation in the Middle Ages (or even before), it was realized that there were substances or chemicals in plants that gave rise to the extraordinary sights and sounds expressed as experiences with gods, and that they were not necessarily a conduit to the godhead. Also by this time, and probably for 1,000 years or more, these magical substances were excluded from the masses and, instead, became part of the esoteric rites of the high level religious clerics. The use of these substances, then, is suppressed, their purpose becomes less and less common knowledge, and finally they are lost to the masses. They are coded, however, in art forms (for example, drawings of the alchemists—see Heinrich 2002), in cathedral mosaics (St. Mark's Basilica—see Chapter Three and Rush 2005), literature (see Ruck et al. 2001), and modern art forms (see Rush 2005). Let's go back and consider the possibility that special people had conversations with God. The first and most obvious answer, and the one touted as fact, was that Noah, the patriarchs, and prophets were *actually* communicating with an external deity or deities. This communication came about in a number of ways.

Dreaming, for example, has been considered a possible conduit to the gods for thousands of years in the Middle East. In fact, dreams act as powerful events, indicating one's connection to that extra somatic "other." The belief in contact with dead ancestors is as old as humanity (see Jaynes 1990). Abraham could hear the voice of God in his waking state and Jacob encountered the deity in dreams. Moses encounters God in the form of a burning bush ("that did not burn") on the mountain near Midian (of the Midianites), and asks, "Who are you?" Yahweh replies, *Ehyeh asber ehyeh,* or "I am who I am," or "I shall be what I shall be," or "He who brings into existence whatever exists." Moses experiences this version of God in a much different way than did Abraham. Yahweh and Abraham were friends—Yahweh was someone he could talk to, and this was because Yahweh was his household, patron deity; the deity was always at his side. This is a different type of "Judaism" than what came later for the masses. The deity Moses encounters, however, is aloof and demands total submission. This is the next stage of Judaism. This god is not always just hanging around with little to do, and when you desire contact an "internet connection" must be established. This is a definite shift away from the individual experience of the deity—the common experience for all as in the mother-goddess cults—to one of contact through special people, with special and secret methods of contact, with the added element of danger. The channel of communication between human and spirit world was to have the spirit "descend" upon you, and this is accomplished through a potion (oral consumption in the form of "bread") or inhaling the spirit in the form of smoke. The plant, then, is not simply a literary device; rather, this is how our ancient ancestors communed with God. The plant is the conduit, and it is through its consumption (a sacrifice?) that you establish a direct circuit to the godhead and God, or one of His assistance will speak to you. Plants as a conduit to the spirit world are not unique in myth (see Ruck et al. 2001).

The second part of this is that the biblical poets must have had some direct experience with the "plant" Moses encountered on Mt. Sinai. More likely this is a mushroom (*Amanita muscaria*) and not a plant. A freshly dried *Amanita* cap placed on the ground does, indeed, resemble a burning coal. I have on numerous occasions placed a cap of this mushroom on the ground in a conspicuous place when students and staff come to my herb garden tours. There is always amazement at how the mushroom cap resembles a burning coal "that does not burn," especially when prompted to "see the plant glowing as a coal on the ground." Ptah and Osiris in the Egyptian tradition (see Rush 2007) are wrapped as mummies and resemble the stalk of a mushroom. I am certain the Hebrews were familiar with this mushroom because the ancient Egyptians obviously were aware of this and other mind-altering substances, and the Catholic artisans coded its existence and importance in their mosaics and stained glass.

The Hebrew word *messiah* ("anointed one") comes from the ancient Egyptian word *MeSSeh,* which references the king and the oil containing crocodile fat that is poured over his head during the coronation process. The word messiah in Greek is Christ. Anointing people with oil is a common occurrence in both the Old and New Testaments. Why a crocodile and crocodile fat?

The crocodile (*Sobek*) represented fertility and the flooding of the Nile but it also symbolized royal power. In the New Kingdom (the time period of Moses) the crocodile is connected to the sun god Re, and in this case represents the primordial or creator god coming, as the reptile does, out of the depths of the murky Nile. Thus, the anointing was symbolic of this creative/generative property. The messiah, then, is a representation of creation or new beginning, and the Jews prophesied that a messiah would come along, in the near future, and bring a new order to the world. But anointing has another function; it brings one in direct contact with the gods. Anointing was not simply oil dabbed or poured over the body; it contained mind-altering substances.

Moreover the recipe for making this anointing oil was given to Moses by God (Exodus 30:22–33):

> Take thou also thee principal spices, of pure myrrh five hundred [shekels], and of sweet cinnamon half as much, [even] two hundred and fifty [shekels], and of sweet calamus two hundred and fifty [shekels],

And of cassia five hundred [shekels], after the shekel of
the sanctuary, and of olive oil a hin:
And thou shalt make it an oil of holy ointment, an ointment
compounded after the art of the apothecary: it shall be a
holy anointing oil.

And thou shalt anoint the tabernacle of the congregation
with it, and the ark of the testimony,

And the table and all its vessels, and the candlestick and
its vessels, and the altar of incense,

And the altar of burnt-offering with all its vessels, and the
laver and its foot.

And thou shalt sanctify them, that they may be most holy:
whatever toucheth them shall be holy.

And thou shalt anoint Aaron and his sons, and consecrate
them, that [they] may minister to me in the priest's office.
And thou shalt speak to the children of Israel, saying,
This shall be a holy anointing oil to me, throughout your
generations.

Upon man's flesh shall it not be poured, neither shall ye
make [any other] like it, after the composition of it: it [is]
holy, [and] it shall be holy to you.

Whoever compoundeth [any] like it, or whoever putteth
[any] of it upon a stranger, shall even be cut off from his
people.

In my opinion, this recipe is probably of Egyptian origin and not
the original recipe for several reasons. There is a curious substance,
"calamus," mentioned in the formula. In the *Revised Standard Bible*
it is called "aromatic cane," in *Young's Bible*, "spice-cane," in *Darby's
Bible*, "sweet myrtle," and in the *New Jerusalem with Apocrypha*,
"scented reed." Obviously the identity of this plant is open to question
and its original reference appears to have been altered from the Hebrew,
no doubt to cover up the real nature of the anointing oil. The word
"calamus" does refer to a plant (*Acorns calamus*). The ancient Egyptians

used this in perfumes, and it does contain chemicals that can alter physiology and which may be mind-altering in large doses. Calamus, however, could be a corruption of the Hebrew *qneeh-bosem* or *q'aneh-bosm*, and in modern Hebrew *kanabos*, which is cannabis or marijuana. Many scholars agree, but not all. It has a lot to do with what you think the constituents *should* be, that is, some sort of polish or oily incense to make the place smell nice, or perhaps something more exotic. I would put my shekels on the latter.

There are different species of calamus. The Cree chewed the one that grows native to Northern Canada for its medicinal value. At any rate, it is reported to be hallucinogenic. The above ingredient list is undoubtedly just one of many recipes for these oils, and I suspect the ingredients depended on their availability. According to scriptures, the Hebrews coated just about everything with them. Here is the catch. These oils were proprietary, and it is highly unlikely that the real recipe would have been written down and handed around in this fashion, saying, "Here is the holy mixture; don't make these oils." These oils were probably assembled around a main ingredient that might be more or less available all year round. And that main ingredient would have to be transdermal, or at least something in the mixture that would act as a carrying agent for absorption. THC soaked in heated olive oil (120–140 degrees Fahrenheit can be accomplished by leaving the oil out in the hot sun) for a week or so is transdermal under normal conditions, but not in sufficient quantities for any kind of mind-blowing trip unless one takes a bath in it. Heating and filtering the oil is not mentioned in the formula outlined in Exodus.

Calamus root contains high levels of alpha- and beta-asarone, which share some structural similarities to mescaline. So, I would not want to rule out calamus root. Again, are alpha- and beta-asarone absorbable through the skin? Yes, but only in small amounts and you don't experience auditory or visual hallucinations. It is better absorbed through a mucus membrane, but there is no suggestion of absorbing it through a nasal cavity, by ingestion, or via enema. Again, I do not think it wise to believe that the recipe as presented in Exodus is genuine. I just don't think such a proprietary item would be made available to everyone. They did use these oils, and if I were preparing such a mixture here is what it would contain.

First, there is a central ingredient around which I would make this oil, a chemical that would, without doubt, penetrate the skin (transdermal). Here are my choices for the Middle Eastern and Egyptian world: *Datura metel* native to Afghanistan and Pakistan, *Atropa belladonna* (belladonna) native to Europe, North Africa, and Asia, but my favorite choice is *Hyoscyamus niger* or *H. muticus,* henbane. The word hyoscyamus is from the Greek hys+*kyamos,* meaning "swinebean" because of the seed pods it produces—it looks like a bean stuck in a very small tulip, and it's called swine because it stinks. So we have several possibilities for the main ingredient in the anointing oil—calamus, qneeh-bosem or q'aneh-bosm, and in modern Hebrew, kanabos, and now hys+kyamos. So, which is it? It was probably hys+kyamos or henbane. The plant is available in the Middle East, Europe, North Africa, and Asia; it is quite available and very popular. It is one of the components of Witches' Ointment and Witches' Brew, or pilsenkraut, a drink that was outlawed around 1780 CE by the clergy in Germany because only special people ordained to engage in such practices were sanctioned to travel to God's house. Henbane was replaced with hops, which is a sedative.

The myrrh, sweet cinnamon, and cassia are there for odor control and perhaps to prevent the oil from becoming rancid, and the olive oil is simply there to make the other ingredients coat whatever was anointed. But there is another part to this; you can add cannabis to the brew and double the effect, or at least change the effect of the henbane alone. The hallucinogen in henbane is scopolamine, which is also carried on the space shuttle in transdermal patches for motion sickness.

The use of drugs to commune with God or gods is a time honored practice, and it would be naïve to think the patriarchs and prophets were really communicating with God and didn't need "supplements." But of course, as the statement in Exodus reveals, these substances were eventually removed from the congregation and used in esoteric rites for the elite. This is exposed in the following passage (Exodus 30:30–33):

And thou shalt anoint Aaron and his sons, and consecrate them, that [they] may minister to me in the priest's office.

And thou shalt speak to the children of Israel, saying, This shall be a holy anointing oil to me, throughout your generations.

Upon man's flesh shall it not be poured, neither shall ye make [any other] like it, after the composition of it: it [is] holy, [and] it shall be holy to you.

Whoever compoundeth [any] like it, or whoever putteth [any] of it upon a stranger, shall even be cut off from his people.

Although this is a somewhat ambiguous statement, the fact that Yahweh gives Moses the recipe indicates that Moses is to make more but only for the Aaronic priesthood. This, then, is the third instituted drug law in the world, the first being the Hindu's outlawing of soma for the masses and the second Zoroaster's outlawing of haoma (again, except for the priesthood). Jesus, however, brought it back in style.

But there is also a different type of anointing oil, a "perfume" (Genesis 30: 34–38):

Take to thee sweet spices, stacte, and onycha, and galbanum; [these] sweet spices with pure frankincense: of each shall there be a like [weight]:

And thou shalt make it a perfume, a confection after the art of the apothecary, tempered together, pure [and] holy:

And thou shalt beat [some] of it very small, and put of it before the testimony in the tabernacle of the congregation, where I will meet with thee: it shall be to you most holy:

And [as for] the perfume which thou shalt make, ye shall not make to yourselves according to its composition: it shall be to thee holy for the LORD.

Whoever shall make the like to that, to smell thereto, shall even be cut off from his people.

This mixture may represent the anointing oil for the exoteric rites of the congregation. There are two mixtures and they both cannot simply be for enhancing the smell of the temple. I tested these mixtures and found that calamus roots did nothing, that cannabis does have a minor tranquilizing effect, but the most dramatic effect was with the use of henbane, belladonna, or datura. As these contain solanaceous compounds (transdermal), they have easy access to the capillaries under the skin, then into the blood stream, and into the brain. In my opinion, the mixture in Exodus is not the anointing oil but a fabrication of the poets to cover up their secret rites. There is nothing special about the recipe given in Exodus. Certainly it could be used as a kind of polish and fragrance for the Ark and Tabernacle, so why would it be forbidden to all but the Aaronic priesthood? (Exodus 30:30) And why are there two recipes?

Although there are oil recipes in Egyptian medical texts, there are no formulas for such anointing oils among the ancient Egyptians, although there is much that they never wrote down, or which perhaps lies undiscovered in a tomb or forgotten in a museum. They were aware of hemp for making rope or cords, but according to Manniche (1989, 82–83) there is no evidence that they used cannabis as a mind-altering substance, but, of course, they never gave us the formula for embalming a human, although they did for the Apis Bull. The absence of evidence only means we don't know and that we should continue to ask questions. I'm sure there were many formulas for anointing oils, perhaps for specific purposes or favorites at a particular temple complex. These would have been proprietary, guarded, and held in secret. I think it would be naïve to think that the Hebrews and ancient Egyptians were ignorant of the properties of cannabis and other mind-altering plants. Oil was poured onto the mummy of King Tut, but as of this date that oil has not been analyzed for content. This would be a simple procedure.

Some plant substances have always been trade goods because they simply don't grow everywhere; this didn't just happen one day with drug lords in Columbia and then spread out from there. In my opinion, mind-altering plants have been part of religion, magic, and the rituals that support them for a few hundred thousand years, and it certainly started much earlier than 50,000 years ago.

As an aside, the part I like is how the Hebrew priests feather their own nests, for there is a requirement that people pay for their services (Exodus 30:11–16) within the context of these anointing oils. This is, no doubt, where Paul received his revelation to charge parishioners for the services of a priest (see Chapter Three).

> And the LORD spoke to Moses, saying,
>
> When thou takest the sum of the children of Israel after their number, then shall they give every man a ransom for his soul to the LORD, when thou numberest them: that there may be no plague among them, when [thou] numberest them.
>
> This they shall give, every one that passeth among them that are numbered, half a shekel, after the shekel of the sanctuary: (a shekel [is] twenty gerahs:) a half shekel [shall be] the offering of the LORD.
>
> Every one that passeth among them that are numbered from twenty years old and above, shall give an offering to the LORD.
>
> The rich shall not give more, and the poor shall not give less than half a shekel, when [they] give an offering to the LORD to make an atonement for your souls.
>
> And thou shalt take the atonement-money of the children of Israel, and shalt appoint it for the service of the tabernacle of the congregation; that it may be a memorial to the children of Israel before the LORD, to make an atonement for your souls.

One part is of interest because it amounts to celestial extortion ("then shall they give every man a ransom for his soul to the LORD"). This may be where the Catholic Church got the idea of people paying for salvation, which, in part, led to the protest by Martin Luther. But this is a clear statement that God holds humanity hostage, and release is obtained by paying a ransom. This has nothing to do with religion and is a clear statement of politics and economics. Moreover, why does God need money? You would think He could pay for his own temple upkeep and personnel. After all, He is smart; He can make gold and diamonds!

But anointing oils are only part of the picture, for Moses also encountered the deity as a bush that would not burn (Exodus 3:1–5):

> Now Moses kept the flock of Jethro his father-in-law, the priest of Midian: and he led the flock to the backside of the desert, and came to the mountain of God, [even] to Horeb.
>
> And the angel of the LORD appeared to him in a flame of fire out of the midst of a bush: and he looked, and behold, the bush burned with fire, and the bush [was] not consumed.
>
> And Moses said, I will now turn aside, and see this great sight, why the bush is not burnt.
>
> And when the LORD saw that he turned aside to see, God called to him out of the midst of the bush, and said, Moses, Moses. And he said, Here [am] I.
>
> And he said, Approach not hither: put off thy shoes from thy feet, for the place on which thou standest [is] holy ground.

The substance in this case is probably *Amanita muscaria* (see Ruck et al. 2000; Bennett and McQueen 2001; Heinrich 2002). But there is more. Moses encounters this chameleon deity as a column of smoke (Exodus 33:7–11).

> And Moses took the tabernacle, and pitched it without the camp far from the camp, and called it the Tabernacle of the congregation. And it came to pass, [that] every one who sought the LORD, went out to the tabernacle of the congregation, which [was] without the camp.

And it came to pass when Moses went out to the tabernacle, [that] all the people rose, and stood every man at his tent-door, and looked after Moses, until he had gone into the tabernacle.

And it came to pass, as Moses entered into the tabernacle, the cloudy pillar descended, and stood [at] the door of the tabernacle, and [the LORD] talked with Moses.

And all the people saw the cloudy pillar stand [at] the tabernacle door: and all the people rose and worshiped, every man [in] his tent-door.

And the LORD spoke to Moses face to face, as a man speaketh to his friend. And he turned again into the camp; but his servant Joshua the son of Nun, a young man, departed not out of the tabernacle.

There are many ways of interpreting this, one of which is that God has many forms, with smoke being just one of them. Keep in mind that the ancients believed that deities resided in plants, trees, rocks, mountains, and, in this case, smoke; this is called *animism*. A modern rendition of this, of course, is that Moses is "hot boxing" in a tent. Without paraphernalia (cigarette papers, pipes, etc.), one method of obtaining the THC in cannabis was to burn the plant in a closed area. Today we might consider this wasteful because drug laws keep the costs artificially high.

Getting back to Moses, the tent, and his assistant "Joshua the son of Nun," why did Joshua not leave the tent? Possibly this was to make sure that the tent didn't burn down or to keep away others least they see the origins of the smoke. But they were all probably consuming the smoke, so the "origin" of the deity was not a problem. Therefore, we must look for another meaning and that is with the word "Nun." Joshua the Son of Nun implies that Nun is a family (sur) name. According to biblical sources, Joshua was of the tribe of Ephraim. But it might also refer to a geographical place as well. Nun (or num) could also stand for a direction (southwest), the number fourteen, or perhaps it simply means a mystery. The word occurs in Psalms 119: 105, and was borrowed by the Islamic poets and found in the Qur'an at the beginning of Surah 68; it is also found in Rush 2007, 287. Its meaning is obscure at best. The word is not found in the New Testament. Nun in the Egyptian tradition was the primal abyss out of which all life emerged. The context of Moses "hot boxing" in a tent (Exodus 33: 11) is the first reference to Joshua as "the Son of Nun." In Numbers 13: 8, we read that Oshea is the son of Nun, and in Numbers 13: 16 Moses calls Oshea, Jehoshua (or Joshua). In Deuteronomy 32: 44, the spelling of Joshua is Hoshea. Regardless of the spelling, Joshua is always referred to as the son of Nun. Why is this? Is there another Joshua or is there a message imbedded in the name? The literal meaning of Joshua is "salvation," and if Nun refers to the primal abyss out of which all things come and into which all things return (sort of like a "black hole"), then Joshua Son of Nun means salvation or a new beginning. Ritual repetition (the multitude of references in the Old Testament to Joshua Son of Nun) is designed to get the attention of the deity, and the fact that Joshua was of the tribe of Ephraim (one of the most war mongering tribes) suggests that a "new heaven, new earth" (salvation) would come about violently. Further, if Nun is a reference to the number fourteen, this points to the Osirian cycle, with Osiris torn into fourteen pieces by his evil brother Seth, and the mid-phase of the moon (new moon). So, in my opinion, the imbedded message is that a violent overthrow would lead the Hebrews to that "land of milk and honey," a new heaven and a new earth. This, I believe, is what Akhenaten had in mind. The message is very similar in the Islamic tradition where through "struggle" (jihad), the non-Muslim governments will be overthrown and, with everyone now Muslim (or dead), the world would be at peace (see Chapter Four).

One final comment: The word *cloud* in Hebrew is *anan* (*Ayin, nun*) but also can mean enchanter, soothsayer, or sorcerer. So perhaps son of Nun means son of the cloud, with the cloud representing the deity, so Joshua is also the son of God. This possibility will be discussed in Chapter Three.

Yahweh is related to the verb "to be," which means to exist or "be actively present in." Thus, from linguistic studies, Yahweh is one of many names for a primary pagan god known to all ancient Semitic peoples before the birth of monotheism. The tribe of Levi, to which Moses belonged, knew the word and that it could be shortened as a sacred invocation—Yo! or Yah! or Yahoo!—like a mantra. What is likewise of interest is that Moses' mother Jochebed (or Yokheved) is derived from Yahweh, suggesting that there was a more ancient matriarchal association with God's name.

Moses' trip to Mt. Sinai and his conversations with the God-Plant date to around 1400 BCE. Monotheism, however, did not take hold for the Israelites until their exile in Babylon in the sixth century BCE. It is also noteworthy that once their capital city of Jerusalem was destroyed (between 586–539 BCE) they suppressed their interest in polytheism. Such extreme stress forced into existence a monotheism, passed on to Christians, which was ancient and lurked within their polytheistic tradition, a tradition that began in Egypt within the time frame for our mythic hero Moses. I will also mention that it is around this same time period that Siddhartha Gautama (566–486 BCE) founded Buddhism just a few hundred miles to the east.

Cecil B. DeMille Got It Wrong

The pharaohs are not named in the Bible, which to some scholars is important because they name other people and places with great detail. So, why are they not named? It is difficult to believe that they were ignorant of these very important people, traveling in and out of Egypt as they did generation after generation. I'm sure, as is the case with people today, they did a lot of name dropping. The pharaoh often referred to in the Bible regarding the Hebrews as slaves in Egypt is Ramesses II or Ramesses the Great—Ra-Moses, or Ra is born or Son of Re, whose dates are 1290–1224 BCE. It is unlikely that Ramses II is the pharaoh connected to anything like the Exodus for if he was, he would have been drowned in the Red Sea; we have his mummy. Moreover, Ramesses II was immensely powerful and it is unlikely he would have allowed Moses to turn his kingdom upside down with plagues and other disasters. The bottom line is that this is sacred not secular history and the storyline can be anything the poets can imagine. I think that Cecil B. DeMille's admirers need to rewrite the script if this was originally presented as some sort of history lesson, although it was and is a cinematic pleaser.

Exodus is perhaps the cornerstone to the Hebrew faith. The story of Exodus is a story of liberation and outlines the birth of Israel, the formation of a holy and exclusive community, and the guiding of the chosen few to a "promised land," so that the Israelites are no longer aimlessly wandering, "lost in the desert." Many symbols and rituals were directly borrowed from the Egyptians. The Ark of the Covenant, for example, was reportedly carried by the Jews, in which they stashed their god (some say the Ten Commandments, others say mushrooms or cannabis); this is the relic sought after in the movie *Raiders of the Lost Ark*. The ark was borrowed from the Egyptian tradition of placing the god Amun, during the Opet festival, on a ceremonial barque (barge or boat), and carrying it in a procession through the streets for all to see. The Ark as portrayed in some Bibles is certainly a composite image put together from biblical descriptions. However, this is a completely Egyptian image, with Isis and her outstretched wings on top of the Ark and the symbols for Osiris (Djed pillar) and the Isis knot, a protective amulet, embossed on the sides.

We can see, then, that the Old Testament is not a history lesson and instead represents a mythical charter for a chosen people, one that fractures as history but can be read poetically. Read literally, the Old Testament condones violence, murder, lying, cheating, stealing, and revenge, and therefore can neither stand as a system of morality nor as a religions tradition. Instead, as the Gnostics realized long ago, Judaism has little to do with religion and more to do with politics controlled by a deity who is certainly more demonic than angelic, and has a terrible relationship with his sons and daughters—that is probably why Yokheved left Yahweh and now resides with Lilith at the bottom of the Red Sea.

The Bible Code and Prophecy

One of the most recent attributes of the Bible is that it is an elaborate code of immense prophetic value. The ancient cultures all had what we interpret as codes, or references to things outside the knowledge or understanding of the casual reader. Much of the coding, however, is simply our inability to understand its meaning (see Singh 1999); "coding" may be an illusion caused by time and mythic layering.

Getting back to the Bible, some in the academic community, using a computer program, believe they have been able to identify a code imbedded in the Bible that reveals future events (see Drosnin 1998), while others (see Ingermanson 1999) see this as bogus. The idea of coding should not be totally dismissed, as can be pointed out with respect to the use of mind-altering substances to commune with the deity. But finding "mysterious codes of prophecy" is often, again, a product of Biblical misinterpretation. In other words, it is difficult for scholars to agree on the meaning(s) of the Story of Job. There are many problems with the alleged "Bible Code," and although I am not a mathematician, computer programmer, or software engineer, I have to rely on reasonable explanations for why the alleged Bible Code does not exist. To begin, I can't find evidence that the Hebrews told their people not to think, but were instead told to strictly follow the laws in the Old Testament, especially Numbers and Deuteronomy. Under these strict circumstances, novel information contradicting their laws and beliefs would not enter the system. The deity demanded a strict adherence to the laws. If this is really what the deity wanted—although we could say this was reverse psychology, knowing that His chosen people could never strictly follow the rules—then what would be the purpose of a "secret Bible Code" if no one is going to be able to invent a means (computer, cipher algorithms, etc.) for detecting it? Moreover, if you are going to offer prophecy or prediction of future events, then why place it "between the lines" so to speak?

But there is a more important issue. I cannot accurately predict the day or time of an event, or the people involved in it, unless I have advanced notice of the variables in play at the moment. I can predict the candidates for the next presidential election and who will win, but that is because I have a great deal of information at my disposal. The weather is a good example. Because we possess technology that can number-crunch numerous variables, we can predict accurate temperatures, cloud cover, storms, and so on, for up to two weeks. But as we go further and further into the future we end up with more and more possibilities, and prediction becomes more and more problematical. Evolution is about what works or simply happenstance, and under these conditions the future cannot possibly already exist. If the future is already worked out in absolute detail, then no matter what we do it has all been preordained! Moreover, if whatever you do is already preordained, then you cannot be held accountable for any act because it was never a choice—the act or behavior was assigned.

Finally, the prophets in the Old Testament, for the most part, predicted what *already* happened, and predictions were really designed to suggest possibilities if people did not mend their ways. Also, these prophets (as well as latter day prophets such as Nostradamus and Edger Casey) made predictions that were quite vague and, as with any story, subject to various interpretations depending on need or intent. Except for Casey, the others lived in fairly small worlds, and as situations change and governments come and go the predictions are more and more likely to fit some situation. It also helps to have lots of predictions about lots of things.

But there is also another side to this. If I predict that a tyrannical leader in some country will be driven from power, and then add to this some strange names, colors, or icons—the more the better—eventually this will happen. Tyrants are always deposed or die. If, on the other hand, I predict that a specific leader will be assassinated on such and such a day and at such and such a place (unless I have foreknowledge of the plot), it won't happen. Why? Because that type of specificity can only be created after the event has occurred. I realize this is absurd, but if the future was already determined there would be absolutely no purpose for evolution. So, within this logic, it doesn't make any difference what you do because you have already done it! So that I don't fall off the edge with this, we appear to live in a universe where predictions can only be general in nature and never specific without foreknowledge of variables. This is why we can see that the predictions in the Bible involve: 1) predictions of events during biblical times, and 2) predictions made only after the fact. We can predict that novel information would have great difficulty entering the minds of people strictly adhering to the Old and New Testaments. There would be no automobiles to alter the landscape, no computers, no electricity, no motion pictures, TV, cell phones, or rockets to the moon and beyond—nothing.

The statements of Nostradamus or those of Edger Casey are ambiguous and can point in any direction, depending on how you desire to use their statements. The Bible Code cannot predict future events. Using history you can develop probabilities, but that is not prophecy. Darwin, as an example, "prophesied" that our ancient hominid ancestors would be found in Africa, but was this prediction sent by God or is this simply a logical deduction from evidence at hand? Perhaps we should refer to Darwin as "Prophet Darwin."

Daniel's prophecies in the Bible, resulting from an interpretation of dreams, are a good case in point, and any careful reader will recognize that they are a play on the dream interpretations of Joseph (Genesis). There is the dream that King Nebuchadnezzar cannot interpret. Daniel interprets the dream, but unlike Joseph who saves the day, it spells doom and gloom for the King in a similar manner as Joseph foretells the future of the baker—doom and gloom. According to biblical scholars, the Book of Daniel was written around 530–520 BCE, making Daniel's predictions a discussion of a past event, as Nebuchadnezzar was dethroned by Cyrus the Great between 560–639 BCE. Some interpreters stretch this into our time by making a connection with the overthrow of Saddam Hussein in 2003, which shows how eager some scholars, ministers, priests, and other religious clerics are to read into the Bible what is not there or ever intended to be there. They grasp at straws, hoping beyond hope of finding some truth to this God and Jesus story. Prophecy for the Old Testament poets was a way to explain past or current events, with a prediction about the near future. Daniel could easily prophesize the downfall of Nebuchadnezzar; he had lots of historical examples and it was only a matter of time. But this prophecy was only written after the fact, so it is like news reporting what happened today, yesterday, or last week.

Prophecies can be self-fulfilling; that is to say, if you tell people that something will or is going to happen enough times and they begin to believe it, the event can materialize. Psychologists have written extensively about this phenomenon. This is not to say that if people are told and believe that global warming is a fact, it then becomes self-fulfilling and the world is destroyed. I am talking more about people's behavior and how public opinion pushes or conditions the possibility of social events around them. For example, the liberal democrats have taken a vocal and defeatist attitude toward the war in Iraq. How has this influenced public opinion? What would have been the outcome if they were in full support of the war (like they were originally)? The Republicans, on the other side, have made their own predictions about the consequences of pulling out of Iraq and the terror threat the world faces. Only history will tell, depending on who writes it. I have more to say about apocalyptic politicians in Chapter Five.

Prophecy also moves the story along because it directs the actors in the play—it points them in a direction. That is to say, the prophecy says that the world is coming to an end, so how do you want to prepare for this? The best way to prepare is to get our genes off the planet; our manifest dynasty is to explore the universe and the deity is leaving all kinds of clues to follow. This deity wants to be known, but this energy cannot be known if hampered by Bogus Deus.

Prophecy is that which issues from prophets (shamans), those celestial brokers or middle-men/women who act as conduits between the spiritual world and the living. They are proactive in terms of saving Egypt (Joseph), and they signal gloom and doom (Daniel, Revelation). Zachariah, through divine presence of course (Gabriel or Gabriella), brings tidings of the birth of John the Baptist (Luke 1:5–14), a central figure in the Christian myth. Prophecy is a method of alerting those in authority (or you and I) to obstacles, and because the message comes from God through a respected cleric in the neighborhood, it must be believed. In fact, prophecy was perhaps the only method of public forum in oppressive societies without free speech.

Let's now turn to Christianity and an analysis of why it has little to do with a mythic hero by the name of Jesus.

CHAPTER THREE

Christianity

Paul says (1 Corinthians 15:14), "And if Christ has not been raised, our preaching is useless as is our faith. More than that, we are then found to be false witnesses about God that he raised Christ from the dead."

Once upon a time ... there was a man named John who belonged to a Jewish mystery sect called the Essenes (200 BCE–100 CE), followers of Esau, which is Arabic for Jesus or Joshua, the very same Joshua, Son of Nun, who faithfully guarded Moses' tent after conversations with God. Joshua, as the story goes, is actually none other than King Tutankhamun, a god on earth, the son of another god on earth, Akhenaten, the earthly representation of the Aten (sun disk). Esau or Jesus, then, is the Son of the Sun.

During one of John's meditative sojourns into the desert, he had a drug-induced revelation. There were core beliefs in the Essenes' tradition of which everyone should be made aware. First, the world is going to end unless people become self-responsible and stop their sinning. Second, you do not need a whole bunch of rules and regulations; you simply need to be a decent person to avoid sinning. And third, messages must be delivered without threat, and to help matters along, John would introduce apostles to the sacred sacrament that would connect the individual to the godhead and justify being a decent person. This was the mystery, the connection to God's house and the secrets within, he revealed to the world.

John defected from the Essenes, came "out of the wilderness," and broke his oath of secrecy to the family. He is not too subtle about this, delivering his message standing on street corners, where women are washing clothes, and in public baths: "The world is coming to an end. Let me cleanse your soul in preparation for the second coming!" Who or what was the second coming? This would be Esau, or the boy King, a god on earth. To a select few (his disciples), he offered proof of the second coming through a guided drug experience, and in a very short period of time he had devoted converts, one of whom was Peter or Simon Peter.

John, unfortunately, attracted the eye of the authorities. The Essenes disowned John and plotted his permanent removal, but fate intervened. It seems that Herod the Tetrarch lost a battle with Aretas, the king of Arabia Petrea. He really got beat up and lost many men. John, on the other hand, was winning his battle with conversion and becoming just a little too popular. Some Jews (the Essenes) saw the destruction of Herod's army as a sign from God and mandate for the populace to rise up and overthrow the government. John was arrested. Here is the actual conversation at the time of the arrest:

Officer: "Are you John, a.k.a. John the Baptist?"

John: "Yes, I am. Are you and your well-armed men here for baptism?"

Officer: "No. Oh, no. I am here to arrest you for selling drugs!"

John: "But officer, I'm not selling drugs. I'm giving them away, no charge!"

Officer: "Tell that to the judge!"

John and the police are approached by a bystander and John is asked: "Are you the anointed one, the Christ, Esau?"

John replied, "No, he will be here, he is coming back. Have faith. Go break some bread with Peter."

As John is being dragged away, he yells out to Peter, "Keep up the good work. You know where I keep my stash, the 'bread.' And tell Mary I'll see her later."

Mary never saw John again, at least alive, for Herod had him murdered, his head cut off, and served up on a platter, a story circulated far and wide to discourage dissidents. (Author's rendition of the origins of what is called "Christianity.")

Introduction

"The world is suffering from four terrible diseases." All became silent, then the Buddha resumed. "It is the disease of *maya* (illusion of life), *avidya* (lack of critical, logical thinking), the fear that one's desires will not be met, and the fear that illumination will expose you for who and what you are. You are everything around you, and you are in everyone's heart and they in yours. And there *is* a cure for ignorance." (Author's rendition of the Buddha's Four Noble Truths.)

The Buddhist philosophy includes the idea of an intangible realm, Sukhavati, a lotus pond in the West. At death this realm is a possibility, especially with help from Amitabha, the Buddha of unending compassion who will help peel away the illusion of this world. Buddhists say no to life; all life is sorrowful. To overcome the steady supply of losses, disappointments, deaths, injury, poverty, and so on, you eliminate fear and desire. Moreover, there is an emphasis on meditative, inner states designed to shut out the world and seek peace within one's self—the god within. This represents the psychological counterpart to devoted Jainists, who use more physical means of reaching the same end. Here is the point: In these Eastern traditions you follow the rules and avoid attracting bad karma. Jesus, as we will see, was promoting the same idea but with a slightly different twist; you don't need a plethora of rules and regulations because rules and regulations separate people. Just as the caste system in Hinduism and following one's *dharma* separated you from other castes using different sets of rules, so the Hebrews created a set of rules that, if followed, separated them from all other groups. With Jesus, however, there is a different approach—abandon the rules that separate people and be a decent person. This is really all he had to say. This is a message that would fit all times, and when the time is right, it will return; this is the "Second Coming." The message was corrupted—St. John the Baptist knew this would happen; he tried to warn us (Matthew 7:14–20):

> Because straight is the gate, and narrow is the way, which leadeth unto life, and few there be that find it.

Beware of false prophets, which come to you in sheep's clothing, but inwardly they are ravening wolves.

Ye shall know them by their fruits. Do men gather grapes of thorns, or figs of thistles?

Even so every good tree bringeth forth good fruit; but a corrupt tree bringeth forth evil fruit.

A good tree cannot bring forth evil fruit, neither can a corrupt tree bring forth good fruit.

Every tree that bringeth not forth good fruit is hewn down, and cast into the fire.

Wherefore by their fruits ye shall know them. (Emphasis added)

This is a well-worn phrase meaning beware of people who claim to have the truth—Jesus is talking about spiritual truth; he is not talking politically, like look out for evil kings or school board members. "False prophets" is a clear reference to traditions that would enslave the mind with gods, demons, and ritual silliness. But then he extends into the political with "people are known by what they do, not what they say they do." You are what you do; you reap what you sow. As the reader will see, if there is such a thing as an anti-Christ, then Paul and the Catholic Church are it. Through the efforts of Paul and his continuers, they turned the simple message of Jesus into a political system designed to enslave and not enrich, to create misery, poverty, and violence, and not peace on earth.

The approach to conversion connected to Jesus was simple; it was different and Jesus didn't tell you what to think. But what helped to symbolically move this approach along was his ability to heal the body, the soul, and society, the one metaphorical of the others. The potential to alter society with the coming of the Jesus myth was quite high because people willingly involved themselves, and no one was forced to join. These simple strategies were perverted first by Paul and then his continuers, leading us back to lots and lots of rules and regulations. It led us back to being told what to do and what to think, to accept as fact a fabricated story of Jesus, and to abandon personal responsibility. Jesus, as the story goes, is crucified (sin atonement), comes back from the dead, and ascends to God's place (he went home) with a message, "I'll be back," which has to be accepted as fact on faith alone under the penalty of eternal damnation. Popes, bishops, and priests act as God's helpers ("moral" watchdogs) strictly enforcing the rules and regulations. And, of course, if you grow up in the system you just accept as fact what adults and religious clerics tell you. The Jews, however, lived in a "rebellious house." Why? Because under the religious vale was also a tradition of learning and seeking knowledge and this places the deity, his power, and his objectives under the microscope.

Once again, the message of Jesus is not burdened with all kinds of rules put in place to separate people. What Jesus had to say is in reality Judaism stripped for export. His message fits everyone. Moreover, you are not forced to join. From the start, however, let us not confuse the message of Jesus with Christianity, as they are two entirely different things.

Most Christians are not aware that there are many similarities between Buddhist doctrine, the character of Jesus, and the development of Christianity. Some scholars (see Mack 1995) see the Greeks, and especially the Cynics, as the major influence. The source of these doctrines, however, must have been shared far and wide, but were unfortunately corrupted by Paul and others over the past 2,000 years. There are two types of statements attributed to Jesus—those with the Buddhist (or Cynic) touch and those added by his continuers. These statements, in most cases, are incompatible. The original messages of the Jesus stories, that is, critical thinking and curiosity, were considered very dangerous to the development and continuation of the more recent Christ story. According to St. Augustine (late fourth/early fifth century AD—see Freeman 2002, vii):

> There is another form of temptation, even more fraught with
> danger. This is the disease of curiosity. . . . It is this which
> drives us to try and discover the secrets of nature, those

secrets which are beyond our understanding, which can avail
us nothing and which man should not wish to learn.

Augustine's statement should alert the reader to a central issue in
Christianity and Islam—do what you are told by religious clerics and
don't think too deeply into the matter, *or else!* You have faith only
because of threat of punishment if you refuse. This to me is celestial
extortion and the clerics representing these traditions should be ashamed.

The word faith, however, meant something very different to the early
John the Baptist/Jesus groups. Faithfully following the teachings did
not mean that you were to become dumb, stupid, and not question the
world as it is. John the Baptist or Jesus could not have been so influential, had this simply been a system of faith and disallowing the questioning of self and others, the power system, and other possibilities.
Unfortunately, the greatest fracture leading to the political monarchy
called Catholicism was the abandonment of questioning and "knowing
thyself" in exchange for blind faith, belief, and acceptance of what
those in authority (religious clerics) said was truth and how this truth
was to be ritually enacted.

Rejection and Social Control

As elaborated elsewhere (Rush 1996, 1999), humans fear rejection, for
rejection equals death. Our ancient ancestors survived as a group, not
as singulars wandering in the forest. To be cast out of one's group was
a death sentence—physically, socially, genetically, and perhaps spiritually, if you believe this form of awareness comes from outside the self
or through the ritual actions of others (religious clerics). Fear of rejection is part of our genetic make-up and it, along with food sharing, are
primal points around which cooperative group living revolves—not
religion. Acceptance and food sharing are prominent features of the
original Jesus movements. Talk about getting back to basics!

At our core is an animal who clings to life, copulates, and eats to
maintain or continue life, and who needs to feel included in the group

(acknowledgement). These represent chakras one, two, and three in the Kundalini Yogic tradition (see Rush 2005, 150–162). The popular self-help spiritual communities, on the other hand, believe that our animal nature is secondary to some imagined loving little child who gets corrupted by parents and culture. This is naive at best.

Our first acquaintance with rejection comes from parents and others tending us when young. You need a set of rules, and obtaining compliance is often accomplished through rejection. How we reject—physical abuse, verbal abuse, and so on—lays part of the foundation for how we interpret ourselves and the world around us. On the other hand, the complexity of this nature-nurture interplay does not allow the conclusion that one type of rejection leads to specific types of personalities or personality problems. We can say, however, that children treated respectfully respond differently to their world than those who are emotionally and physically brutalized or taught to hate others. This does not mean that a child should never be yelled at or spanked (as some politicians have concluded)—these are perfectly good communication tools. However, if these techniques are all that reside in your communication skills tool kit, then those are the tools you will use, and these are the tools the child will learn and probably use in raising his or her children (see Rush 1999). Without fear of rejection culture could not have emerged, because its primary intent is to keep people *in* the group conforming to group rules and combining brainpower for cooperative effort. Guilt and shame are absolutely necessary for group living. This primal fear of rejection, however, has been used and abused by religious clerics for thousands of years.

Humans have the capacity for reason—the ability to stand back from a problem, pull it apart, and come up with viable solutions. We are sophisticated animals and our nature is that of participant-observers and problem creators and solvers. When we stand back from specific problems, we see them through a lens polished and made "clear" by significant others, including religious clerics who claim to have the "truth." Millions and millions of people around the world today believe things as historical truth that could not possibly have happened all because of the fear of rejection (including shunning, physical abuse, torture, and death in some cases), of being outside of one's reference group (family, village, etc.). The systems that support these stories are terribly insecure in their beliefs or they would not have to resort to such tactics.

Rejection and shunning are entrenched in the Christian tradition. The early beginnings of the Catholic Church as we know it today were steeped in symbolic rejection through excommunication of different priests spreading alternative or Gnostic views. Assuming that he had some sort of power through a mythical charter (which included Rome as a resting place for Peter and Paul, a continuity with the Apostles, and tracing the earliest bishops back to Rome), Victor (189–198 CE— see Duffy 2001, 13–14) seems to have been the first to assume power in the Catholic tradition and excommunicate those with heretical ideas in an attempt to bring the stray sheep back to the correct pasture. Excommunication, a form of shunning, is a method of isolating, marginalizing, or removing from influence individuals and groups not abiding by the "truth" as constructed by those in power. Victor (and others before) realized that, in order for Christianity to survive as a recognizable entity, all the churches had to be on the same page with similar dress codes, timeframes, and, most of all, message from the pulpit. There had to be orthodoxy. All had to be in agreement as to how many angels could stand on the head of a pin. The goal was standardization, along with a central spiritual geography (Rome) and authority (bishop and/or pope) for formulating policy and settling theological matters. This is like modern day fast food restaurants; no matter which restaurant in a chain you choose, the menu is the same.

With respect to the Catholic Church, once this power was centralized in Rome, excommunication of wayward churches or priests was often accompanied with physical violence. Christianity, then, was steeped in politics from the onset. What kind of politics? The politics of "truth." The origins of Christianity, as put forth in this chapter, have little or nothing to do with someone by the name of Jesus, who, as the story goes, was born in Bethlehem (around 3 BCE), was crucified (around

30 CE), and ascended to heaven. Within the story, however, is a central platform for the emergence of Christianity; things are so bad (Roman oppression, starvation, sectarian strife, continual war) before, during, and after this time period that a new social order was necessary. The mythic hero Jesus is merely a personification, a violent cry, if you will, to establish a new world order, with Paul outlining and corrupting this "new heaven, new earth."

Origins

Christianity derives from the Greek word Christ, "the anointed one," which derives from the Hebrew *messiah,* which derives from the ancient Egyptian word *MeSSeh,* and refers to the crocodile, Sobek, and crocodile fat. As mentioned in Chapter Two, when the Egyptian pharaoh was crowned king he was anointed with crocodile fat, which was poured over his head (Gadalla 1999). According to some scholars (see Bennett and McQueen 2002), the Hebrew anointing oils were mixed with a mind-altering substance(s), possibly cannabis, mushrooms (*Psilocybe* species, *Amanita muscaria*), maybe mandrake, perhaps henbane or datura species; then again, there is also belladonna or combinations of the above. The Hebrews would have learned these recipes from the Egyptians. These substances allowed contact with the gods through very powerful mind-altered experiences. But they weren't for everyone, as the components were expensive and available to only a few. These rites amplified and confirmed beliefs and practices associated with entities that grab us and are referred to as "spirit." In Isaiah 32:15 we read, "Until the spirit shall be poured upon us from on high, and the wilderness shall be a fruitful field, and the fruitful field shall be counted for a forest."

The use of mind-altering drugs for obtaining spiritual experiences or communicating with deities is a time-honored practice going back thousands and thousands of years, deep into our prehistoric past (see Devereux 1997). Drug experiences are at the base of most of these traditions, including Hinduism, Buddhism, Zoroastrianism, Judaism (see

Chapter Two), Christianity, and Islam (see Chapter Four). To minimize or ignore the importance of these substances, as is the case with most modern scholars, is to paint only an incomplete picture (at best) as to why these stories were written and their impact on Western Civilization. The beginnings of what we call "Christianity," or celebration of the anointed one, were organized around these experiences, first with all group members (the Apostles) participating in the Eucharist, but, as the system developed, with the mind-altering substances restricted to the religious clerics (see Ruck et al. 2001).

Messiah

The word messiah first appears in the prophecies of Daniel (Daniel 9:25) and is probably the reference used by the author(s) of the Gospel of Mathew (Mathew 24:15). The Book of Daniel was possibly written between 530 and 520 BCE, after Cyrus captured Babylon and told the Hebrews to go home (see Chapter Two). This might be seen as liberation but not for all, especially those with political and economic ties and ambivalence about returning to Palestine.

Beginning around 2500 BCE and continuing to this day, the Middle East (modern day Israel, Palestine, Jordan, Syria, Saudi Arabia, Iraq, Iran, etc.) has gone through invasion after invasion, with a type of warfare and politics designed to destroy one form of organization and replace it with another, thus producing a melting pot of diverse peoples, languages, ideas, and, most important, creating intense social stress. Within all this the Hebrews usually didn't fare well militarily— it is difficult to attract allies when you promote yourself as a special people, better than all the rest. Out of this, especially between 300–100 BCE, there emerges a story of world destruction and starting over— Armageddon, apocalypse. The doom and gloom belief spawned what has been called "cult" development or groups with a different message breaking away from "mainstream" Judaism.

Christianity begins its origin myth utilizing the prophecies of Elisha, Elisa, Daniel, and so on. The belief was that an "anointed one" (Christ) would appear and liberate the oppressed, especially the true believer, or those special few abiding by specific rules. In order to sell the belief in the prophet or god-like abilities of a messiah, you need true believers to help Jesus spread the word; for this we need disciples (students), who, after indoctrination, become apostles—twelve apostles. Twelve, by the way, has the same symbolic value as the twelve tribes of Israel and is a reference to the sun god, the Aten or Adon(is) in Hebrew.

So, what would be the easiest method of "creating" a true believer? What would Jesus do? We know what Moses would do—he would threaten you with the wrath of Yahweh or perhaps have you murdered, just as Brigham Young did to some of his followers. But, what would the Prince of Peace do? He would hand you a joint and tell you stories: stories designed to alter attitudes toward self and relationships with kin and stranger alike, and stories that point toward those things that are truly spiritual or not involved in politics or economics. Jesus really doesn't tell you to do anything; it is a matter of how you interpret his stories and the perverse spin of the Christian clerics, especially Paul, who was obviously a very disturbed individual (not stupid, but emotionally disturbed).

Jesus (see Ruck, et al. 2001) is referred to as "The Drug Man," which doesn't mean he was a drug addict. What it does imply is that his disciples (and undoubtedly others) were indoctrinated into his teachings through mind-altering substances. This was a mystery cult that became a little too open. There was no threat or force involved in entering the cult. People seem to willingly join cults because they are attracted by the message and the personality of the leader, who is perhaps desperate or insane. So, there is a bit of "free will" in joining. Brainwashing, as we understand it today, is a way of persuading the individual under stress (perhaps using physical torture) or by an altered state of awareness, to retranslate beliefs about themselves, others, and the world in general (stress leads to altered states of awareness—see Rush 1999). A basic cornerstone in Judaism is fear of the deity; terrible things will happen (and often did) if you don't follow the rules. The methods used to instill the message and rules were fear, threats, and physical violence. This falls more closely into the category of brainwashing through emotional and physical abuse.

Jesus, on the other hand, had a different approach: "Here is what I have to say; take it for what it is worth." He also had a message that is modern even by today's standards. Jesus' message (and I'm separating Jesus from Christianity, as they are two entirely different things) is simple and points to critical thinking and self-responsibility. On top of this, his delivery combined two of the most potent methods for altering awareness, beliefs, and behaviors, methods far more effective than fear and violence *in the long term*—that is, gaining attention through storytelling and drugs. A very powerful, willingly engaged, mind-altered guided experience, through the use of cannabis, *Amanita muscaria,* belladonna, henbane, mandrake, and so on, is one of the quickest methods of producing "illumination," especially among ignorant people or those who believe that gods reside in plants and potions. I will return to drugs shortly.

Jesus Who?

The amount of ink used in telling, retelling, and discounting the existence of the mythic hero Jesus as portrayed in the Bible and the Gnostic texts would probably fill a small lake. As interpretation after interpretation appears, one would think that we are expanding our knowledge base. In fact, these interpretations become meta-myths (or myth about myth) and we end up interpreting the meta-myth as well.

I do not know if the Jesus of 3 BCE–30 CE discussed in the Gospels existed as a real person. He is more likely a constructed focal point for those seeking power, clever rascals who would manipulate the ignorant masses with fabricated stories complete with relics (nails from the cross, the cross itself, a shroud, a grail, etc.). Jesus, however, has absolutely no historical visibility. Peter, a person with some historical visibility and supposedly a close apostle of Jesus, only speaks through Paul and he says little.

Why is this, if Peter was right there when all these wonderful things were happening? Why is this, if he is considered the beginning point of popes and their power and authority? Peter was illiterate, and I think that it is very possible that Paul didn't like what Peter was saying. And what was Peter saying that Paul rejected? The story I'm going to tell has been told before; it is totally contrary to anything that Christianity stands for today, and that is why it is not taught alongside the Gospels. I believe that there is something called cultural integrity—the story needs to be told, understood, and appreciated so we can move on.

Peter, Paul, John, and Mary

What Peter told Paul was that Jesus was not here now, but he would show up "soon," a "second coming." It was John the Baptist who was spreading the news, baptizing and healing people *in the name of* Esau or Jesus, just as faith healers do today—they heal in the name of God or Jesus. The baptism of Jesus (Matthew 3:13–17) is really John baptizing himself, as it would be through him that the Christ would come. This you will recognize is the old third-person ploy, where healing or words of wisdom are attributed to others. John's philosophy was simple because he truly believed the world was coming to an end, and thus churches, priests, food restrictions, and clothing styles were unnecessary. And forget your possessions, for John believed that heaven came from decency toward one another and not personal possessions or wealth.

With Paul realizing that Jesus was not a real person, and that John the Baptist was the conduit through which Jesus spoke, we don't have much of a story. Remember that Paul used to persecute Christians, but I think that someone might have taken him on an unplanned drug trip, the Gnostics maybe, perhaps on the road to Damascus (Galatians1:16–24). After this he changed his position regarding followers of Jesus. So Peter is marginalized. What is even more revealing is that Paul never mentions John the Baptist, suggesting to some that the Baptist was not a historical person; perhaps Paul was not a real person. To top it off, Paul never met Jesus although they were supposedly contemporaries. So, here we have Paul, a pseudo-apostle in contact with Jesus through visions probably gained from plant substances. This is strange, unusual stuff, but we can make some sense out of it when we factor in mind-altering substances. As Vermes comments:

> Knowing that he could not designate himself an apostle along traditional lines, he emphasized instead that he had been directly chosen by the will of God (1 Cor. 1:1; 2 Cor. 1:1; Gal. 1:1), or through a supernatural vision: "Am I not an apostle? Have I not seen Jesus our Lord?" (1 Cor. 9:1); and later, "Last of all, as to one untimely born, [Christ] appeared also to me. For I am the least [i.e., most recent] of the apostles" (1 Cor. 15:8–9). This vision must allude to the revelation at Damascus, which according to Galatians 1:16 entailed an order to become an apostle to the Gentiles.

Paul, then, has visions and hears voices. Does this sound familiar? In order for Paul's message to be heard it has to come with authority, in this case Jesus, but at the same time he has to appear intelligent and more than a mere lunatic. The Book of Romans, assigned to the pen of Paul, is an interesting document sent to people in Rome, fellow monotheists, and followers of Esau. The Romans and Paul, no doubt, shared similar insane ideas or his writings would not have survived. Pretend for a moment that you are sitting quietly in your living room, watching chefs making clothes out of chocolate (there was such a cooking program) on your newly purchased HD TV, and the postman knocks at the door. You place that all important, previously recorded program on pause, open the door, and sign for an envelope. Opening the envelope you find about fifty handwritten pages, beginning with (Romans 1–16):

> Paul, a servant of Jesus Christ, called to be an apostle, separated unto the gospel of God,
>
> (Which he had promised afore by his prophets in the holy scriptures,)

Concerning his Son Jesus Christ our Lord, which was made
of the seed of David according to the flesh;

And declared to be the Son of God with power, according
to the spirit of holiness, by the resurrection from the dead:

By whom we have received grace and apostleship, for obedience to the faith among all nations, for his name:

Among whom are ye also the called of Jesus Christ:
To all that be in Rome, beloved of God, called to be saints:
Grace to you and peace from God our Father, and the Lord
Jesus Christ.

First, I thank my God through Jesus Christ for you all,
that your faith is spoken of throughout the whole world.

For God is my witness, whom I serve with my spirit in the
gospel of his Son, that without ceasing I make mention of
you always in my prayers;

Making request, if by any means now at length I might
have a prosperous journey by the will of God to come unto
you.

For I long to see you, that I may impart unto you some
spiritual gift, to the end ye may be established;

That is, that I may be comforted together with you by the
mutual faith both of you and me.

Now I would not have you ignorant, brethren, that often-
times I purposed to come unto you, (but was let hitherto,)
that I might have some fruit among you also, even as among
other Gentiles.

I am debtor both to the Greeks, and to the Barbarians;
both to the wise, and to the unwise.

So, as much as in me is, I am ready to preach the gospel to
you that are at Rome also.

Reading this in today's world, what would you make of this? How
would the folks in Rome have received this in 55 CE? During this time
period there were diverse groups branching off the work of John the
Baptist, or the Jesus cults, much like we have EST, Scientology, Heaven's

Gate, Dravidians, wicca, extraterrestrials, personal angels, vampire clubs, and so on in our own time popping up during times of intense social upheaval. Paul is representative of many paranoid schizophrenics who send all types of letters to senators, representatives, police chiefs, friends, relatives, on and on. His letters begin with praise for the receiver (or group), then you get his sophisticated ranting, and the letters end with praising the intelligence of the receiver; this is especially the case in Romans. His references to the Old Testament might be compared to impressing professors with line and verse from different scholars worthy of mention. I'm impressed (and also suspicious) that so many of these "rantings-in-ink" have survived (see also Corinthians 1, 2; Galatians; etc.), and I would not be the least surprised if others do exist. Imagine a man, an angry but educated tent-maker, who gets into drugs, talks to Jesus, and then becomes a true believer to the point of starting a uniform club, that is, organizing ideas that were already in play. The individuals to whom he wrote were floundering, no charismatic leader had come along, and Paul stepped up. The importance is the timing of the letters, with Paul outlining a philosophy and clarification of procedure in spite of Paul's recognizable insanity (then as well as now). This is what drugs can do to an unstable mind. Certain of the books in the New Testament attributed to Paul are problematical on many levels, like Deuteronomy and Hadith in the case of the Old Testament and the Qur'an, which were constructed (or portions added or subtracted) after Paul's time in order to clarify points made to Paul's original writings (see Mack 1995). In short, the individual churches to whom Paul wrote must have been promoting a similar brand of insanity.

I find the dates assigned to all the books in the New Testament suspect. Acts, for example, is mainly about Paul and I find it difficult to believe that Paul, a tent-maker, had the wherewithal to traverse the Mediterranean and Middle East as reported. It is unlikely that Paul had many friends, as this was a time of social unrest and poverty and his proselytizing would have been troublesome to the authorities, as suggested in Acts. His wanderings have to be considered legendary and not factual. Paul's mass mailings, without the use of copy machines and computers, also suggest that most of his time was spent writing (not proselytizing), with the ultimate goal of being listened to by someone, to have someone believe his story of communication with Jesus, and that his alignment of "truths" came from this third-person (Jesus) relationship.

After considering the pros and cons as to when any of the materials of the New Testament were written, the best that can be established is that the Gospels, Acts, Romans, and those chapters that follow: 1) were written between 55 and 170 CE; 2) none of the books are pristine and unaltered from an original; and 3) the early dating for the Gospels, Acts, and so on comes from biased priests and intellectuals, past and present, who want to believe in the existence of Jesus and his mythic storyline. They would forge and otherwise invent *all* the New Testament to fit their agenda. If there is such a thing as cultural insanity, Christianity is it.

Because of his positioned advocacy for a Christian church, most believed Paul's story of visions of Jesus, or at least we don't hear people contradicting it. Why? Because the people to whom he was writing were also using substances to commune with the supernatural world and they could not very well contradict Paul for what they themselves were doing. So, Paul is having visions. Are we to assume he is communing with Jesus, or is he merely psychotic or on mind-altering drugs?

Again, cultures all over the world have included mind-altering substances in their mystical rites and rituals. We see this first with shamans, who then become full-time priests, who then reserve access to the gods for themselves. Gradually the use of mind-altering substances shrinks to a special few. Among the other Canaanite tribes we see a gradual movement into mystery cults, once again maintaining a proprietary right to the sacraments simply by keeping them secret. This is why I believe that the recipe for the anointing oils used among the Hebrews is a fake (see Chapter Two). Notice that there are two recipes, one for the anointing oil and one for the perfume. Some of these oils, then, were not simply to place an odor on alters, incense burners, and the sons of Aaron. Exodus 30 represents the beginning of the end of communal anointing and consumption of the god. The date for this was probably between 560–530 BCE. The common people were left to rely on wine and beer, and of course entertainment once the Romans showed up with their pizzas and crucifixes. Anointing oils came into Christianity with many rules and restrictions as to their use (see Dudley and Rowell 1993). There are also many variations in these oils but once again mind-altering components are not mentioned. It seems that the oil gets it magical punch after being blessed by some high order religious cleric! Do these priests and bishops really believe that by waving their hand over oil they impart some magical healing power to it? Is that all that's required? Ordaining individuals to perform magical acts is an age-old practice first mentioned in the story of Adapa and Anu (see Chapter One).

Christianity is wrapped in glorious detail but it seems that the detail is dependent on the historicity of Jesus. Is it really necessary for Jesus to be a real person, or is it his message that really counts? For the Catholic Church, Jesus has to be a real person who passes on his power/mission to Peter, who then passes it on to the next, and then the next, pope after pope after pope, all of whom are infallible in word and deed. This is a social genealogy tracing back to a person who probably smoked pot with John the Baptist, a.k.a. Jesus. This justifies a Vatican, popes, priests, the whole shebang. I can hear Peter laughing and crying at the same time. Jesus is a metaphor about something very important, and it really does not matter if he was a real person. Fundamental Jews, Christians, and Muslims get hung up on the deity and miss the message.

Jesus has been confused with historical fact. No self respecting Buddhist would ever say that the stories and legends surrounding Gautama Siddhartha (Buddha) are historical fact. The stories of the Buddha represent a philosophy of living and dying, as are the stories about Jesus. The basic message behind the symbol of Jesus is that God is inside you, and you don't need a church or a priest; just be a decent human being. This is really all any reasonable supreme deity wants as well. Being a decent person in the eyes of Jesus did not include instructions from religious clerics, nor did it include a bunch of rules and rituals, and it certainly didn't involve going to church or temple and paying a priest. The message is *not* Jesus but what he *represents*, that is, know thyself, self-responsibility, and having compassion for others.

The historical connection to Jesus may relate to the Essenes, or followers of Esau (the Arabic word for Jesus and also Joshua). Some scholars, however, have suggested that Esau is none other than King Tutankhamun. The Essenes were prominent between 200 BCE and 100 CE and very strict adherents to Judaic law and an apocalyptic outlook. Specific statements attributed to Jesus, however, are a 180–degree turnabout from adherence to Jewish law. John the Baptist was a teacher or priest who may have defected from the Essenes, a secret sect, and stripped it for export by removing economics and politics but maintaining the secret sacrament, or that which made the deity tangible. When you know the secret you no longer need a priest or church. Jesus is symbolic, an invention of the Essenes, birthed into the world through John the Baptist. The message has to do with what unites and divides people and how to identify with, communicate with, and become the energy that informs all. For if you take away all the rules and regulations that serve to divide people, what is left must be universal and representative of all that unites us. I believe that this is exactly what John the Baptist did. Here is a wonderful story, and one that is much more likely than the common Christ story.

Once upon a time there was a man named John who was a teacher or leader among a secret Jewish sect called the Essenes. Essenes were followers of Esau or Jesus or Joshua Son of Nun. Some scholars also think that Joshua is King Tut, the son who attempted to carry on the teachings of the Father, Amenhotep IV or Akhenaten, the probable Moses of Exodus.

Somewhere around 27 to 28 CE, our hero John became disillusioned with the strict, secret teachings of the Essenes and went into the wilderness to think things over. When he reemerged he had a boon to give the world, a personal experience with God along with some good news—

well, sort of. He began preaching the end of the world, preparation for this event through a spiritual experience with mind-altering substances, and basic rules for social living. His relatives and other Essenes were not happy with this because he had broken an oath of secrecy, and this might be the basis of the hostility "Jesus" expresses toward family members in Matthew, Mark, and Luke. Fanatics like Paul and the Baptist alienate many, many people and especially family members (guilt through association). The Essenes were a "family."

John the Baptist began anointing people with special oils, handing out mushrooms (manna, bread, cake) or whatever the Essenes used (anointing oils for sure, *Amanita muscaria*, etc.), and guiding their experience. In that experience he was dramatically changing the way they saw the world. There *are* other possibilities, and these possibilities happen when we get along with each other. "Love thy neighbor regardless, but don't lust after his or her mate," "Do unto others," and so on. He also learned that not everyone needs to receive the message so dramatically—not everyone has to partake of the holy sacrament. You need twelve good men to symbolize the sun's rays fanning out and telling people the good news—and the bad news. So you are selective. You can't stand on a street corner and hand out mushrooms and pot, but you can attract people with a message, especially if there is fascination or entertainment value. Street performers attract a great deal of attention, and John the Baptist was an unrivaled street performer of a bygone day. He became a super-salesman, selling a new way of living and offering to a chosen few an opportunity to touch the energy that informs all. He was simply the messenger who came to announce the messiah and referred to "Jesus" as a third person who *will show up, in the near future,* and "anoint you with fire" (Matthew 3:11–17):

> I indeed baptize you with water to repentance: *but he that cometh after me* is mightier than I, whose shoes I am not worthy to bear: he shall baptize you with the Holy Spirit, and [with] fire:
> Whose fan [is] in his hand, and he will thoroughly cleanse

his floor, and gather his wheat into the granary; but he will burn the chaff with unquenchable fire. (Emphasis added)

Again, John was very successful with his messianic movement; in fact, too successful. People are having hallucinations, releasing demons, feeling hope, somatic complaints disappear, people "see" for the first time, and so on. Out of jealousy and/or malice, someone or a group (Essenes perhaps) brought what was going on to the attention of the authorities. The Baptist was arrested for a series of disruptive events, but was murdered because of his potential to agitate the public and challenge the politic. The Bible tells another story, but it is carefully constructed so as to reveal the exact identity of Jesus. In Matthew 14:1–14 we read:

At that time Herod the Tetrarch heard of the fame of Jesus,
And said to his servants, *This is John the Baptist; he hath risen from the dead*; and therefore mighty works do show forth themselves in him.
For Herod had laid hold on John, and bound him, and put [him] in prison for the sake of Herodias, his brother Philip's wife.
For John had said to him, It is not lawful for thee to have her.
And when he would have put him to death, he feared the multitude, because they counted him as a prophet.
But when Herod's birthday was kept, the daughter of Herodias danced before them, and pleased Herod.
Upon which he promised with an oath to give her whatever she would ask.
And she, being before instructed by her mother, said, Give me here the head of John the Baptist in a dish.
And the king was sorry: nevertheless for the sake of the oath, and of them
who sat with him at table, he commanded [it] to be given [her].

And he sent, and beheaded John in the prison.

And his head was brought in a dish, and given to the damsel: and she brought [it] to her mother.

And his disciples came, and took up the body, and buried it, and went and told Jesus.

When Jesus heard [of it], he departed thence in a boat, into a desert place apart: and when the people had heard [of it], they followed him on foot out of the cities.

And Jesus went forth, and saw a great multitude, and was moved with compassion towards them, and he healed their sick.

This is closer to the historical story (John the Baptist is Jesus), so close, in fact, that in the Gospel of John, Jesus and John become antagonists; John the Baptist is pushed aside symbolically and morphs into Jesus. Ironically, John the Evangelist, mythic author of the Gospel of John and also, some say, Revelation, becomes associated with John the Baptist in Medieval art (see Hamburger 2002, 65–82). In this art John the Baptist is seen as the practical, nuts and bolts half of the team. He tells of the coming of Jesus, prepares all who care with baptism, first with a cleansing, and then a revelation or connection to the godhead via a mind-altering substance. This substance becomes associated with the sacrificial lamb, Christ. Christ, then, is inside of you—that is the big secret. Of course, you have to consume his body first (the sacrificial lamb, the mushroom, the manna, the bread).

John the Evangelist, on the other hand, writes it all down, that is, sets it to *poetry*. This amounts to the magician priest and his poet interpreter. John the Baptist is to John the Evangelist as Peter is to St. Paul.

When people tell stories they are grounded in the events around them. We can appreciate how the Israelites constructed a story around the historical events of Akhenaten, and it is quite possible that John the Baptist continued the memory of this god-king through his son, also a god-king, King Tutankhamun, a.k.a. Joshua, a.k.a. Esau, a.k.a. Jesus. Our mythic hero Jesus, however, comes with a universal message.

The Invisible Man

Evidence that someone by the name of Jesus was connected to the Christian death and resurrection story in the New Testament is hard to come by; Jesus has no historical visibility. In fact, the early Christian poets, when constructing the story of origins, encountered the same dilemma.

Let me pause for a moment. If Jesus is a mythic hero, then nothing attributed to him can be historical or factual; the parables, for example, were gathered from numerous sources for the purpose of, again, constructing a mythical charter. When I read a book, fiction or nonfiction, I don't get hung up on the author; it is the message the author brings to the world. It really doesn't make any difference if Jesus or any of the players in the Old and New Testaments were real historical characters; it is the *message* that's important. Worshipping the messenger is absurd.

But the question remains, was there a real Jesus? Again, I can find no reliable evidence for the existence of a magical person by the name of Jesus who lived in Palestine from 3 BCE–30 CE. The Gospels are of little use, as they were written many decades after the alleged death of Jesus and they may not have been written as history lessons in the first place. Paul, whose statements and actions appear in Acts, 1 and 2 Corinthians, Galatians, Philippians, 1 Thessalonians, and so on, was probably a real person (some say he is a replay of Saul), but he never met Jesus (although we are told he was a contemporary of Jesus) and relied on third party information, in a similar fashion as urban legends rely on third party testimonials. Paul, by the way, was never an apostle of anything except himself. Peter, a named apostle of Jesus, offers nothing. He is used by the creators of the biblical gospels to build a personality and create a mythical charter for future bishops and popes who have economic and political advantages. Peter, in fact, may have been the only apostle of Jesus a.k.a. John the Baptist. The Acts of the Apostles, attributed to Luke (the Gospel of Luke), were allegedly written sometime between 63–70 CE Although the author uses references to "we" in Acts, these stories are written in the third-person style so that no one can argue with the author. The authors of the Gospels and Acts were not reporters at the scene taking notes; they were playwrights making characters come alive. If there were such a large following with the twelve apostles, one would think that Paul, in the role of historian, would have more to say about not only the apostles, but other devotees. There are a number of apostles mentioned in Acts but they are doubtless constructions.

Now think about this: If Jesus (John the Baptist) was pulling away from the rules and structure of Judaism and creating a universal path for all to follow, he never would have suggested the construction of something called Catholicism or Christianity with all the rules, rituals, status distinctions (rich vs. poor), and conspicuous wealth of popes and bishops.

There is one short paragraph attributed to Josephus, the Jewish historian, who was born just a few years after the mythical crucifixion and ascension of Jesus took place. Here is the statement in *Jewish Antiquities,* Book 18, Chapter 3, Paragraph 3 (Josephus 1999, 590):

> Now there was about this time Jesus, a wise man, *if it be lawful to call him a man; for he was a doer of wonderful works, a teacher of such men as receive the truth with pleasure.* He drew over to him both many of the Jews and many of the Gentiles. He was [the] Christ. And when Pilate, at the suggestion of the principal men among us, had condemned him to the cross, those that loved him at the first did not forsake him; for he appeared to them alive again the third day, as the divine prophets had foretold these and ten thousand other wonderful things concerning him. And the tribe of Christians, so named from him, are not extinct at this day.* [Emphasis added—see below]

That's it—one paragraph! Josephus was a historian who would, one might assume, be quite impressed with someone who had magical powers and could do wonderful things, especially arise from the dead and ascend to heaven. Josephus was also a Jew, and for a Jew to call someone "the Christ," the anointed one, the savior, after spilling so little ink, is just a little bit too disingenuous. Not to mention the statement that he "appeared to them alive again the third day;" this deserves a little more elaboration. To incriminate the Jews with "at the suggestion of the principal men among us" is just too incredulous. To say "the tribe of Christians, so named from him, are not extinct at this day" implies he believes this person to be the Christ, the Messiah of the Jewish tradition—not likely. We thus have Jesus—who worked miracles, died, came back from the dead, and ascended to heaven, saying he would return—in one paragraph! These must have been very common events to deserve such little ink. Some authors have suggested that, although Josephus wrote about Jesus, parts of the paragraph were added at a later date by some "enthusiastic" Christian cleric. Let's replay Josephus and remove that which was claimed to be added, but still proving Jesus was a real person.

> Now there was about this time Jesus, a wise man. He drew over to him both many of the Jews and many of the Gentiles. And when Pilate had condemned him to the cross, those that loved him at the first did not forsake him.

The sympathetic positioning of words is unlikely, as I'm sure Josephus would have seen the Christians as a disruption to the social order. This, then, would eliminate:

> He drew over to him both many of the Jews and many of the Gentiles. And when Pilate had condemned him to the cross, those that loved him at the first did not forsake him.

Here is what we are left with:

> Now there was about this time Jesus, a wise man.

If this is what Josephus originally wrote, it tells us nothing. In fact, it is so commonplace that one would wonder why he would mention Jesus at all! Most scholars see the paragraph about Jesus attributed to Josephus as a forgery. Some authors, on the other hand, even in the face of logic, still claim that Josephus did write about Jesus—if only a few kind words! Vermes (2000, 277), for example, suggests that Josephus would never claim that Jesus was "the Christ." But then he goes on to affirm:

> The flat assertions, "He was the Christ" and that his resurrection on the third day fulfilled the predictions of the prophets are alien to Josephus and must have derived from a later Christian editor of the *Antiquities*. However, declaring the whole notice a forgery would amount to throwing out the baby with the bath water. Indeed, in recent years most of the experts, including myself, have adopted a middle course, accepting that part of the account is authentic.

Vermes (2000, 277) goes on to say:

> We must focus our attention on the two expressions by which Josephus characterizes Jesus "a wise man" (*sophos 'aner*) and a "performer of astonishing deeds" (*paradoxon ergon poietes*). Both phrases are complimentary in the terminology of Josephus: talking about Old Testament personalities, he applies "wise man" to King Solomon and the prophet Daniel, and "performer of astonishing deeds" to the miracle-working prophet Elisha.... So it would seem that, by describing Jesus with the help of those two basically positive phrases, "wise man" and "performer of astonishing deeds," Josephus succeeded in formulating a detached judgment about him.

Vermes' last sentence is interesting: "So it would seem that, by describing Jesus with the help of those two basically positive phrases, 'wise man' and 'performer of astonishing deeds,' Josephus succeeded in formulating a detached judgment about him." How is that detached, and how in the world does that prove Jesus was a real person? Whoever forged this paragraph would have read Josephus and looked for other places to insert words to give credibility to the existence of Jesus. He would have read about Solomon and borrowed the words; he would have read about Elisha and found those accolades fitting. It seems reasonable to me if *any part* of this tiny, itsy bitsy paragraph was added in, that does indeed invalidate the whole thing, just as it would if being offered as testimony in a court of law. Moreover, because there was no baby in the first place, we don't have to worry about how we dispose of the bath water.

The final fracture in this paragraph attributed to Josephus is that "the passage is not found in any early copies of Josephus. It does not appear until *The Ecclesiastical History of Eusebius* came onto the scene in AD 320." (McKinsey 1995, 102) This forgery in Josephus' work, and probably the statement about James as well as many others, occurred sometime around 320 CE, and is probably the work of Eusebius of Caesarea, the bishop who wrote *Ecclesiastical History*. In another work of his, *Praeparatio Evangelica,* he makes a very self-condemning statement: "I have repeated whatever may rebound to the glory, and suppressed all that could tend to the disgrace, of our religion." (McKinsey 1995, 102) In short, what Eusebius did was to obliterate priceless historical documents and forge others. His *Ecclesiastical History* is considered a "landmark in Christian history" by the authors of *Merriam Webster's Encyclopedia of World History* (see Doniger 1999). With Eusebius' statement above, that is, "I have repeated whatever may rebound to the glory, and suppressed all that could tend to the disgrace, of our religion," one has to wonder about anything written in *Ecclesiastical History*. In my opinion it represents, again, part of the mythical charter validating the construction of what we call Christianity through multiple sources. This is outright fraud, purposefully and shamelessly perpetrated.

Josephus (1999, 594–595), however, did write about John the Baptist, and the story is set within a war between Aretas, the king of the Arabia Petrea, and Herod. Herod lost and thought this was a sign from God. John the Baptist was gathering a large following and he considered this a problem if the populous became agitated. So John the Baptist was murdered (decapitated?); this is the real "crucifixion" in the Bible. John the Baptist, then, is connected to a historical event and it is the Baptist, not Jesus, who had a large following and was a political threat. Keep in mind that in those days overthrowing a government usually meant getting a large crowd and beating up the guards. Yes, the military can be called in, but you can never be sure if they will take your side or if some general will use the ruckus to gain power for himself. Even today with modern weapons, crowd control is tricky business. An unruly crown could call for the resignation of government officials, or, at the very least, create a lot of grief.

During the early part of the Current Era there were numerous pagan (polytheistic) groups and monotheistic offshoots of Judaism. Paganism tends to be inclusive; pagan groups can see their deities in the beliefs of others. Caesar, in his *Gallic Wars,* for example, saw the same gods in the Celtic traditions as were found in the Greco-Roman pantheon. Monotheism, however, presented a problem that we still experience today. Monotheists cannot and will not see their deity as having any connection at all with pagan traditions. They consider the gods of all other traditions demonic, exclude all others who do not belong, divide people, and, when given enough political power, violently eliminate non-believers. Let's use that as a backdrop to the marriage of one political system (Rome) with another (Christianity) and the reader can decide whether or not Christianity qualifies as a religion.

The pagan religions offered individual communing with the gods, with group rituals designed to bind together group members through shared membership. Pagan traditions offer the individual identity and communication with the deity, as well as the chance to become the deity in some cases. Monotheism offered a different formula. From the time of St. Paul until 320 CE, numerous groups formed around some of the statements attributed to Jesus, like love they neighbor, accept strangers, and do unto others, and this made a great deal of sense to most people. They were able to identify, communicate with, and become Jesus through the "sacrificial lamb" or mind-altering substances. Some groups, however, became political and changed the agenda from one of identity with the deity, to a relationship or *worship* of the deity. Using the distorted writings of Paul and others, these groups reverted back to Judaism, eliminating some of the rules (e.g., circumcision) and inventing new rituals. Storylines were invented; thus the Gospels, with the last Gospel of John designed to promote Jesus to the status of God. The dates for the construction of the Gospels are suspect because they were edited (for the most part) by true believers who desired to have these documents written close to the timeframe given for Jesus' death. For Mathew, the dates range from 50 to 80 CE, for Mark, 50–80 CE, for Luke, 59–80 CE, and for John, the last gospel, some time between 70 and 80 CE. These dates, however, are wrapped around educated guesswork. The first three Gospels were written around the same time by people probably known to one another, or perhaps there was one story (written by an unknown author called "Q"), a stage play, that was copied and evolved into what are now the Gospels.

Paul, whose dates are 10 CE to around 67 CE, certainly influenced the construction of the first three Gospels, but why are the first three Gospels so similar to one another? There are two possibilities. The first is that they represent three independent, perhaps first-hand renditions of the story of Jesus, which is what Christian clerics would like you to believe. This is unlikely, for as far as we know the first-hand witnesses, mainly the apostles, were illiterate. Second, the language in the Gospels is too similar to have been written down independently many years after the alleged events. These stories were probably edited and crafted from one story (Q—see Powelson and Riegert 1999, and Mack 1995 for their analysis), and constructed at the same time by several individuals who were known to one another many decades after the alleged events, altering statements slightly. However, one would realistically assume more differences in the statements than we find. In today's world, three different reporters covering the same news story never say exactly the same thing sentence for sentence, word for word, unless working off someone's notes (Q). If three separate individuals are telling the same story, religious clerics maintain, it must be true. To me, though, this is the downfall of these Gospels—they are too similar. The Gospel of John appears to have been written, as mentioned, to convert Jesus, a human, to Jesus the Son of God more in keeping with the Essenes, and this is where John the Baptist comes back into the picture and is pushed aside by Jesus. To have Jesus as the main player, John had to be marginalized and a path cleared for Jesus, the God without competition. After all, John was dead but Jesus lives on.

Time goes on and various groups continued to proselytize. Some groups followed the teachings of the Baptist/Jesus, which included the use of mind-altering substances (e.g., Gnostic sects), while others reverted back to Judaism with lots of rules and regulations, and with the esoteric rites restricted to the clergy. Those following the Baptist were more involved with the individual's identity with the deity, while the latter were more interested in worship of/slavery to the deity, and this led to continual conflict over truth and politics. Then we have to add the pagan groups with whom the monotheists were also in conflict. The social unrest and violence perpetrated by the "Christian" groups is well documented. We hear of poor Christians fed to lions and burned at the stake, but this was done not because they were Christians but because they were disruptive to the social order. Not bowing down to Caesar is the excuse later Christians give for the burnings and other circus acts; everyone bowed to authority. The pagan groups could care less what anyone believed and the Jews, as a special people, were not particularly interested in converting anyone. The Christian groups, especially those following the teachings of Paul, were involved in worship rather than identity with the deity, and were socially disruptive. This is a replay of how the Jews treated the polytheistic Canaanites when they turned to monotheism.

Time marches on and we come to Constantine (280–337 CE). Likewise, he could care less what deity anyone preferred, but the hostility and social unrest caused by these groups detracted from managing his kingdom. He had no love for the Christians going around proselytizing, picketing sacrifices, destroying religious sites, and telling all pagans they are wrong and monotheists have the truth. The Catholic Church came about as a political move by Constantine. He simply said, "You are either going to come over to my side and stop all this strife or else I will eliminate you." Well, those who had formed around the worship story of Jesus the Christ stepped forward. These were the followers of Paul and his continuers. With the granting of special privileges (tax exemptions), Christianity became a purely political organization. There is no evidence that Constantine especially liked Christians, but the poets had to create a story about Constantine seeing a cross during one of his battles and converting to Christianity on the spot. I don't buy the story, and the fact they had to invent one (believe me, he never saw a cross) suggests he never converted. On his deathbed the priests might have spoken for him, but Constantine wasn't stupid and he understood that the orthodox Christians should not get too much power. By converting to Christianity, Constantine would have diluted his power base and it is unlikely that he would have done such a thing. Constantine, let's not forget, was a ruthless thug, and out of guilt he might have converted on his deathbed just to hedge his bet.

Jesus and His Message

Just as there are several faces of Jesus (human, god, healer, teacher, etc.), there are several types of messages attributable to him. At least for me, we need to consider those statements that clearly resemble core elements of Buddhism and which were probably similar to the core messages of the Essenes, once the rules, regulations, and rituals are removed. These messages stand out, for they are common desires of most—that is, to be loved, cared for, treated fairly, and so on. It does not make any sense to risk life and limb to spread a unique message of peace, and that God is within each of us, thus eliminating the need for a church or priest, and then wrap it around the same old economic and political system with privileges of the few maintained through fear and violence. Once again, Jesus and what is called Christianity are two entirely different things. A close examination of statements attributed to Jesus will make this dichotomy quite clear.

As we saw in Chapter Two, our main source of information about Yahweh, the Jewish law, the patriarchs, and further myth building past the first five books of the Old Testament, comes from other books of the Old Testament, the Talmud, the Dead Sea Scrolls, and then meta-myths or stories explaining the original stories, through interpretations of the words and phrasing contained within these documents. In Chapter Two we also saw how the origin story of creation in Genesis 1 matched the science of the day (prose) and which is close to modern day ideas of progression or evolution; certainly the creation happening in six days is suspect. The second creation story reported in Genesis 2 is a poetic political statement, and it is the one that stuck in the cultural mind because of its patriarchal emphasis, reinforced over the centuries by the male agenda, and the place of women in a world dominated by men. The creation story was taken literally, you recall, until quite recent times, although there are still those who consider the myth as historical fact. Creation stories are common to most cultures, and correspond to their scientific knowledge of the world and universe around them during a specific slice of time.

I also showed how Eve got a bad rap while the Israelites were condemning the mother-goddess cults of the Canaanite tradition. In the process, nature becomes corrupt and women—who represent nature—end up on the bottom. However, there seems to be a great deal of ambiguity about women and their power—being able to seduce symbolizes a great deal of influence. I likewise pointed out that Deuteronomy was added later, the purpose of which was to harshly reinforce the laws and enslave the hearts and minds of a people through the fear of God's punishment. This fundamental position was a good fit during the time of the Herods and the political climate before and after the time of Jesus.

Judaism was synchronic with the Roman politic, that is, lots of rules and harsh punishment for those who break them—they policed their own and the authorities liked that, to a point. The message of Jesus, on the other hand, was not in synchronicity with Roman rules and regulations. Jesus was not the least bit interested in power or wealth; his message was be nice to people. This was something quite new because he didn't say, "Be nice to people *or else!*" Those types of statements were additions by people maintaining the old Jewish position that people were like sheep in need of a shepherd, "B-a-a-a-h"—a tradition that promotes followers, dependence, and a lack of personal responsibility.

Jesus as Hero Myth

Although hero myths deal with individuals, their social reference is quite profound, with the heroes in many ways representing the good, the brave, or the energy of the society within which they emerge (see Campbell 1949). There are several types of heroes. For example, there is the hero who dies, as does Jesus. And then there is the hero who slays the monster, catches the bad guy, or overcomes some personal or social problem or obstacle, be this a physical problem, a tyrannical ruler, or boss. We are all, in our own way, heroes. Through his or her efforts, energy (personal or social) is renewed and all is brought back into balance. This is the most popular type of hero, as portrayed in novels, movies/videos, and even cartoons. Walt Disney's *Mickey and the Beanstalk,* a popular cartoon short in the mid-1950s, is an excellent example of the hero story, the elements of which can be seen in more modern presentations. In *Mickey and the Beanstalk,* we have a hero triplet. In other words, Goofy represents the body waiting for instructions and Donald represents passion, usually anger and chaotic behaviors, that is often referred to as blind or unrestrained passion. Mickey clearly represents cool intellect and cleverness with language. Mickey is also a diplomat, but a person to be reckoned with when the chips are down.

The story begins with the birth of Mickey, Donald, and Goofy in a barn in Happy Valley, California; they are born in a manger on hay provided by the owner. They rapidly grow up, and before the owner dies of starvation he bequeaths his land and belongings to his faithful "sons." Walt Disney left this out of the original script in order to have enough time to elaborate other aspects of the story. This, by the way, is how the biblical poets, piece by piece, assembled the Old and New Testaments—they made them up. This was not accidental any more than the political myths created by modern news organizations. These poets understood the difference between myth as a political statement and real, historical events; unless, of course, they were using mind-altering plants in their interpretation process. Some authors (see Mack 1995) suggest that they didn't *know* the difference, and an explanation for this, which has been excluded from the analysis, is the use of magic mushrooms and other substances. They did not know the difference between "real real" and "drug-real." A god resides in a plant or mushroom/fungi, and when consumed you become one with the god ("I and the Father are one"). This is what they believed.

Keeping in mind the triplet (Mickey, Donald, and Goofy), our heroes are also facing starvation because a precious harp, female in form, was taken away by a Giant named Willy. The harp (cornucopia, Grail, lotus, rose) had the song of eternal life and whoever possessed her possessed its magical power. So, everything has dried up; by taking the harp the giant has initiated global warming, and Mickey, Donald, Goofy, and all of Happy Valley will soon die of starvation. Someone should tell Al Gore that it was all Willie's fault.

Our hero Mickey decides to take the cow (the "udder" failure) to town, sell it, and restock their pantry. Of course, you and I know that selling the cow and restocking the pantry does not solve the problem of bringing back social and natural vitality. Mickey, however, returns from town, not with groceries but with magic beans. He asks, "What will happen if you plant these beans in the light of the full moon?" Donald, with dashed hopes of filling his belly, responds, "Yeah, you get more beans!" He then goes ballistic and knocks the beans from Mickey's hand, and they roll into a knothole in the floor, which, from a Freudian perspective, looks surprisingly like a vagina, the female principle.

Dismayed and hungry, our heroes take to their beds and dream, no doubt helped along by whatever opium was left in Walt's pipe, while at the same time the beans sprout (the male principle) and lift the house and our heroes into the sky, wrapped in and around the tendrils of this gigantic beanstalk. The beanstalk represents a magical vehicle, provided by the person from whom Mickey initially traded the cow, for leaving the bounded space of Happy Valley, acquiring what is needed, and then returning, bringing the world back to proper balance (see Campbell 1949). The beanstalk is the night journey and a time of danger, as tendrils both protect and abandon, as they destroy symbols of comfort—the bed, the chair, the house itself—and move our heroes into danger's gaping maw. This is the underworld of the deep subconscious; this is The Twelve Gates and our animal nature symbolized by an erect phallus poking through the clouds and penetrating into another world of mystery and jeopardy.

Mickey, Goofy, and Donald, cleansed of all worldly concerns, emerge from the night journey and into the light. They realize this is another place, a magical place, where all things are possible, and instead of turning back they press on with hope, curiosity, and determination, the very things missing in Happy Valley. They see a castle in the distance and run toward it, overcoming obstacles on the way. They encounter large mushrooms (Walt knew his mushrooms), gigantic insects, and a huge footprint, which is a warning they have gone past the bounds of the known world and danger is all around.

All obstacles are overcome—they "cross the waters" of the moat to that other side, enter the castle (the jaws of death), and we find our heroes on top of a table covered with food from end to end. The food represents life or that which sustains the body, whereas the harp (the cornucopia, the Grail) is what brings forth life.

Our heroes discover the magic harp, and we are then introduced to Willy, "an amazing kinda guy," who eventually captures Mickey. Using his intellect and wit, Mickey buys time by convincing Willy that he can read palms and predict or prophesize how long someone will live. More importantly, he determines that Willy can change into all kinds of shapes! Mickey challenges Willy to change into a housefly, but Willy, who is dumb but not that dumb, changes into a pink bunny rabbit instead, and catches our three heroes with a fly swatter about to clout out his brains. He imprisons them but Mickey escapes.

Willy, in a sense, is like the European dragon, which represents greed and the monster or bully in all of us. In this case Willy likes to eat, and his abduction of the harp represents food hoarding, but of course Willy can use the food. Willy is a "somatic kinda guy." Again, he represents the monster *and* the creativity in all of us, or the ability to change. Willy, the monster within, has stolen our vitality, symbolized by the harp, just as tyrannical rules, popes, and imams steal the vitality of the people they are supposed to be looking out for.

The singing harp puts Willy to sleep. Mickey then steals the key, rescues Goofy, Donald, and the harp, and then hastens down the beanstalk with Willy in hot pursuit. Once back in Happy Valley, they cut the tie to the giant's world, kill the giant, return the harp, and bring the world back into balance.

The elements and process in this hero myth are as follows:

1) Hero or heroes in distress; some information has been removed from the system.
2) What is necessary is not available locally and magical help emerges to secure what is required. Magical help (beans) provides our heroes with the means of transport to some other place.
3) On the journey to that place obstacles are encountered; obstacles are overcome, some with magical help.
4) That which is necessary is located and other obstacles present themselves but are overcome.
5) Information is retrieved and returned to the starting point and all is brought back to balance.

Let's see how closely the life and time of Jesus fits this hero mold.

Once upon a time a child was born who was conceived from a union between the Virgin Mary and God, although as the Christ or Savior in the Jewish tradition there is the requirement that Jesus be from the house of David. But no matter, this is myth. Keep in mind that in Christianity (as well as Judaism and Islam) God is not part of his creation and thus having sex with God does not connect you to the house of David. So, to connect Jesus to the House of David, Mary hooks up with Joseph, a carpenter reported to be of the house of David, the thuggish mythic king of a bygone era. With this, in a similar manner as Abraham, Yahweh, and Pharaoh, a dual connection of depth of genealogy (house of David) and magical help (God and his favorite people again) is accomplished. This is really the same story of Abraham and Sarah, where Abraham is ninety-nine years old and God writes a prescription for Viagra or Horny Goat Weed, and bingo, Sara is with child. This is an act of God and not an act of nature.

In any event, Jesus is born in Bethlehem, Judea. The myth states that he was born in a manger because there was "no room at the inn." This "birth in a manger" places Jesus' arrival in the context of the common person and not kings and queens, an important reference point for attracting the masses. Recall that Mickey, Donald, and Goofy are common peasants. Jesus also rode into Jerusalem on a donkey, to once again appeal to the common folk. This is you and me, not a bunch of bureaucrats or princes and kings. The initial story of Jesus is about going beyond politics and money just like the story of *Mickey and the Beanstalk*.

While Jesus is still in the manger, the Magi visit him, perhaps a reference to priests of the Zoroastrian tradition (Persia). This is a curious incident, for the Magi come into town inquiring (Matthew 2:2–6):

> Where is he that is born king of the Jews? For we have seen
> his star in the east, and have come to worship him.
>   When Herod the king had heard [these things], he was
> troubled, and all Jerusalem with him.

> And when he had assembled all the chief priests and
> scribes of the people, he inquired of them where Christ
> should be born.
>
> And they said to him, In Bethlehem of Judea: for thus it is
> written by the prophet,
>
> And thou Bethlehem, [in] the land of Judah, art not the
> least among the princes of Judah: for out of thee shall come
> a Governor, that shall rule my people Israel.

No one would be foolish enough the ride into town and inquire about a new "governor of the people," especially to the powers that be. The Magi riding into town and questioning the whereabouts of Jesus is a lame story, because the Magi would have been undercutting the authority of Herod simply by making such a statement; Herod would have them arrested and disposed of. This is simply part of the mythical charter, that is, an initial recognition of a magical birth and acknowledgement, by people in far away places, and it sets the scene for who Jesus is and the politics surrounding anyone questioning authority. You can see how quickly this story moves from a message to the common people to divine rule *over* people. To get people's attention, and thus establish rules all should live by, the messenger (Jesus) has to have a *divine* message—a recognized mandate from heaven from someone more powerful than the temporal king.

Jesus is first moved to Egypt, discussed below, and then, around age three, he travels to and grows up in Nazareth, a mythical, non-existent place in his lifetime, and only created as a map reference sometime after 170 CE. The reference to Nazareth is mentioned in the Gospels and this suggests that these documents were either not written until after 170 CE, or they were reworked after that date from earlier versions. In any case, there is evidence that a village existed in pre-Christian times where Nazareth exists today, but there is no evidence that this village was called Nazareth. Mystical places are important in hero myths because they are geographies of energy, for this mystical place is adjacent to the Silk Road. All the towns along the Silk Road must have been magical, with different looking people and strange weapons, cargo, stories, beliefs, and practices. The Jewish merchants in this area of Galilee had to be more open and tolerant of many, many traditions. Jerusalem and Bethlehem, on the other hand, are different geographies south of the Silk Road, with more conservative practices of Jewish thought and where ritual behavior was very strict.

Back to Bethlehem and the Magi. Herod doesn't like the idea of possibly being challenged and says, "Bring the child to me so that I can also worship him." Joseph has a dream and is told to pack his bags and move Mary and Jesus to Egypt, where they stayed until Herod died. Why Egypt? Was it really because Herod had it in for Jesus or is this part of the storyline? Would Egypt really be a safe place to go? Even if Herod had no jurisdiction in Egypt, he knew who did, and either by currier, FedEx, or email, I'm sure he could get the authorities to arrest Joseph, Mary, and Baby Jesus. This sojourn in Egypt follows the initial storyline for Abraham and Joseph. Abraham was told to go there either in an attempt to connect to royalty or simply to pimp his wife and get a road stake (acquire wealth). Joseph went without choice but acquired, through his own efforts, a connection to royalty, prestige, and wealth. There is more to this Jesus-in-Egypt story edited out of the original storyline; there has to be. Egypt represents an important connecting point, first with Abraham, next with Joseph, then Moses—all connected to pharaoh, and then between Jesus and pharaoh. Let's take a side trip.

Some scholars suggest that the template for Jesus is actually King Tutankhamun, who ruled all of Egypt from 1334–1325 BCE, but certainly there are many models from which to choose. However, because the connection to Egypt and pharaoh was important in the story of Moses, so Jesus could benefit from that connection as well. But then we run into a similar problem as before—the connection to Egypt obliterates Jesus as a local, unique phenomenon. This is another wonderful story and it goes like this.

Essentially what we may have is some real Egyptian history tweaked to fit the mythical charter for the Jews. In other words, some scholars

(Gadalla 1999) see David, Solomon, Moses, and Jesus as having their Egyptian counterparts in the Pharaohs Tuthmosis III (David), Amenhotep III (Solomon), Amenhotep IV (Akhenaten/Moses), and Tutankhamun (Jesus). Backtracking to the Essenes, other scholars (Osman 2004) see them as remnant followers of Akhenaten a.k.a. Moses, and that Jesus was Joshua, son of Nun. These are not the popular opinions, not that many scholars don't silently hold similar ones (and there are many who do), but we live within a period of political correctness and many scholars say one thing and believe another. This, of course, amounts to a constructed lie. Remember that the Bible is poetry and it is unnecessary to match up timelines from the Bible (sacred history) to ancient Egypt (secular history). The poets purposely rearranged the dates to obscure the connections to ancient Egypt.

As a continuation of the discussion of Akhenaten/Moses (Chapter Two), Akhenaten closed the temples in Egypt and declared that only the Sun Disk, the Aten, could be worshiped. The priests at Thebes were not happy and Akhenaten felt threatened, so he moved north about 200 miles and builds what today we call Amarna. The priests are very powerful and again threaten Akhenaten; he either dies or leaves Amarna (the symbols still work either way) and flees to the Sinai in 1336 BCE (or thereabouts), and a pharaoh by the name of Semenkhkare rules for two years, more or less. Akhenaten's son, Tutankhamun, became pharaoh and ruled from 1334–1325 BCE. So here is the storyline.

Akhenaten was pharaoh and therefore a god on earth. Understand this—Akhenaten would have been considered a god on earth to all Egyptians and he established a type of strict, and at times apparently brutal form of monotheism. Tutankhamun, when he was old enough and especially when he became pharaoh, maintained his worship of the Aten. Although he changed his name from Tutankhaten to Tutankhamun for political reasons and opened the temples and restored the temple rituals, *he likewise maintained the worship of the Aten*. Do you see the problem? This is the original attempt at the coexistence of polytheism and monotheism, side by side, with monotheism having powerful political support, and it led to a society divided. This is exactly what you had when the Hebrews broke away from the other Canaanite tribes, and exactly the same thing that materializes when monotheistic traditions gain the upper hand politically—pain and suffering. Regardless of his concessions, King Tut had to go. His great uncle, Aye, murdered him. Why? As mentioned in Chapter Two, oppressive monotheism had divided the Egyptian people and they did not wish a replay.

The murder of Tut a.k.a. Joshua, son of Nun or Jesus, is the basic storyline handed down generation after generation and became the storyline of the Essenes, followers of Esau or Jesus. Tut will one day return, his "second coming," and restore the glory of the father, Akhenaten, also a god on earth. Or, they might have thought that Tut would have a son—after all Tut was a god on earth and he would return and reinstall the Aten, the Sun Disk (Adon in Hebrew). Tut and his father (Akhenaten) at death would have boarded the Sun Barque, and during the day traversed the heavens (Nut) as the Sun God, Re. At night, Re is swallowed by Nut, the Sky Goddess, dives into the primal abyss (the Nun), and traverses the Twelve Gates of the Underworld battling Apophis, the monster serpent, and then emerges from the primal abyss (the Nun), reborn through the vagina of the Sky Goddess Nut as the morning sun. The Sun/Son will return (see Rush 2007).

Remember that Akhenaten was a god on earth, Tut would have been the Son of God, and Tut himself would have been a god. So here we have Father and Son. The Aten is characterized as "all light," the same reference given to Horus, the Holy Spirit, the son of the god Osiris, the midnight sun, who is the night counterpart of Re. This is the Osiris Cycle represented as the Trinity in Catholicism.

In any case, this leads to an interesting possibility. When Tut became pharaoh he moved the royal court back to Thebes, but according to archaeologists it is unlikely that Amarna was abandoned all at once. Like any cult, those who gave up the most to move to Amarna in the first place would have had the most to lose by returning to Thebes—this is called cognitive dissonance (see Festinger 1956). There were from 20,000 to 50,000 people living at Amarna and certainly all did not leave at once (another part of the Exodus story?) but probably over a span of ten to twenty years. In fact, after Akhenaten died or left Amarna, the people who remained would have been isolated and marginalized, lest the rest of Egypt be re-infected with the spiritual disease called Aten worship or monotheism. Those who stayed the longest were those most committed, but at some point, possibly during the reign of Aye (1325–1321 BCE) or more probably during the reign of Horemheb (1321–1292 BCE), all remaining were evicted. Mummies were collected from their tombs and moved to the Valley of the Kings. The site was vandalized, specific names erased, and the site subsequently looted. Recall from Chapter Two that there is the possibility that Akhenaten returned to Thebes, perhaps during the reign of Horemheb, to reclaim his rightful place as pharaoh. After "forty years" (between ten and forty years) this would have been a great shock to the Theban priesthood, not to mention Horemheb, whom he knew from Amarna. If he did return it would have been perhaps a generation after his departure, but his memory was inscribed in the temples and tombs of Amarna and Thebes. To once and for all erase that memory, all still living in the city were driven out and the temple site cleared of Akhenaten's name—well, almost. Those driven away (a forced Exodus?) most likely fled north or east, with some eventually finding sanctuary with the Shasu in the Sinai. Cognitive dissonance in this case is another wording for hope and the belief in a return of their god (Akhenaten), the son of their god (Tutankhamun), and a return to their land of milk and honey (Amarna).

The temple sites at Amarna are like no other, depicting scenes of family life, with people "expressing excitement and even ecstasy in the presence of their rulers, and joy and pride in the awards that were bestowed upon them." (Aldred 1988, 18) The temple designs are also unique in being more open to the sun. What would promote such a radical departure from the Egyptian tradition, a departure no doubt initiated by Akhenaten's father, Amenhotep III? Akhenaten was obviously insane—excuse me, eccentric—and it is possible that mind-altering substances played a part. It is also quite possible that Akhenaten may have involved his loyal followers—not just the priests—in this holy sacrament, sealing their commitment. Those who stayed after Tut left for

Thebes may have promoted the message that the god-king, Tut, would return, and the Aten would reemerge as the focal point of worship—Akhenaten symbolized the Aten. Scholars tell me that there must have been a ceremony (this could not have been done in secret) after Tut "passed," and certainly there was the embalming, a process occurring over a period of seventy days. This would have taken place at Thebes, south of Amarna some two-hundred miles, and if Amarna and its inhabitants were marginalized, gossip and rumor would flow—remember that these people believed in their gods and supernatural events, the biology of hope takes over, and several stories could have circulated. One, of course, was that Tut was dead, but another story is that he would return, just as his father would return, to people's astonishment, several years later—from the east, not from the West, the land of the dead. *For the ancient Egyptians, gods also died and were reborn.*

An interesting aspect of Akhenaten's brand of monotheism is that the site of Amarna—the city, temples, and tombs—are all on the east bank of the Nile, whereas the other kings and queens of the New Kingdom were buried on the west bank (Deir el-Bahri, Valley of the Kings, etc.). How might one interpret this? It suggests that the living and the deceased are not separate, and there is a preparation for the return of the deceased symbolized by the Sun/Son. Amarna was a place of life, death, and resurrection, not in the sky barque—that was reserved for Akhenaten—but Amarna was their living ideal of the mythic Field of Reeds. This was the land of "milk and honey," the promised land of the faithful followers, until their leaders left and those remaining were evicted. The mythic goal is to get back to this wonderful place.

This is a good story but it has an interesting twist to it. If Akhenaten left and was gone from the scene during King Tut's reign, but then emerged after Tut was murdered, the son begets the father and they become one and the same (talk about the return of the dead!), but it does help to perhaps better understand the origin and symbolism of the Christian Trinity (Father, Son, and Holy Ghost). I love this story and it is probably closer to secular history.

Another point to consider is that Tut seems to have been hastily buried in a quickly prepared tomb (KV-62), but his original tomb, KV-23, was usurped by Aye. Why was Tut so hastily buried? Assuming that these people believed in their gods and their powers, to kill a pharaoh, the Son of the Sun God Re, would not automatically receive applause from the gods, especially the Aten. The gods have laws about this; killing was not necessarily a good thing, unless of course you are killing your enemies. I'm sure the priests of Amun-Re saw Akhenaten as an enemy of the gods. So Tut was quickly removed from view to possibly avoid the wrath of the Aten, unless the gods sanctioned it. Remember that Akhenaten closed the temples, which was an insult to the gods, and the sins of the fathers are passed to the sons. Tut's murder in all likelihood was a conspiracy involving priests communicating with gods and seeking direction. This would legitimize the act of removing an offense to the gods, and stop further sin from being passed to any sons Tut might sire. A hasty burial would also engender speculation, gossip, and rumor, just the stuff to generate some pretty wild storylines.

It is agreed among Egyptologists that the idea of resurrection meant heaven, the Field of Reeds, or some spiritual geography, but not the geography that you left behind at physical death. This, however, might have changed with Akhenaten. When Akhenaten left Amarna, there was a promise of, "I'll be back." When Tut suddenly left the scene—murdered—this belief may have been transferred and one day he would return, just as the newborn Sun returns from His cycle of birth and death. Remember that many people followed Akhenaten to Amarna—he had his own army. When he went to parts unknown (I believe that he was killed, probably by Horemheb, and brought back to Egypt), many stayed on as followers of the boy king, King Tut. Tut was murdered to halt the divisive form of monotheism installed by his father. And just as the sun rises in the east, this is where Akhenaten and Tutankhamun will emerge; this is why most Christians worship on Sunday, facing east.

A group of true believers hung onto the tradition that the boy king, King Tut, the Son of God and also a god himself, would return. Again, gods died and were reborn in this tradition. These "hangers-on" even-

tually left Egypt, living on the move with the Shasu and eventually settling in Canaan or Judea. The tradition stayed alive in the sect known
as the Essenes, a strict mystery cult. These were followers of Esau, or
Joshua, or Jesus, and when He comes back, He'll set things straight,
separate the wheat from the chaff, and there will be hell to pay! Many
times when a pharaoh came to power, he did so by beating up his opponents or immediately thereafter. The mythic storyline is pretty clear
even though this was not always followed in real life: if you follow the
cosmic laws, *ma'at,* the gate to the Field of Reeds will open for you.
The Essenes were very strict about following the rules, with many new
rules most certainly added to the cosmic list represented by the Judges
in the Hall of Judgment (see Rush 2007). There was a rule for every
little, itsy, bitsy thing that you do, and with each rule you symbolically
distance yourself from others who have their own set of rules to contend with. Esau became the modern Jesus, birthed through John the
Baptist one fine Christmas morning, in a manger no less. King Tut is
laughing and shaking his head. Back to Jesus.

Sometime around 28 CE, John the Baptist, an Essenite, comes out
of the closet and attempts to wash away the sins of men (ignorance)
through baptism. This is the connection of John the Baptist, who may
have been a real person, and the mythic figure of Oannes, who came out
of the Red Sea or Persian Gulf (John the Baptist came out of the wilderness) to give knowledge to mankind. In any event, John had wonderful things to say, but they were attached to a third person because John
came with no authority. So, his message had to be attributed to one
more powerful than himself—Esau, Jesus a.k.a. Joshua a.k.a. King Tut,
who promised us immortality simply by believing in his sacrifice to
remove sin and his second coming. Further, as Osman (2004, 43) states:

> John the Baptist was not, however, preparing the way
> for Jesus to be born, but for his Second Coming. . . . John
> represented the prophet of the end of time, the eschatological
> messenger of the Old Testament prophetic books.

This in all probability answers the question as to why the Knight Templars were not interested in Jesus and Mother Mary so much as John the Baptist and Mary Madeleine; the latter may have been real, tangible people.

Getting back to the Bible, although there is no information about Jesus' stay in Egypt, this sojourn most probably is an attempt to link with royalty. One of the reasons that we don't have much of a story about the Egyptian connection is that it could be too easily contradicted through record keeping during that time period. He appears to have five major "going-to-another-place" emphases in the story—from Bethlehem to Egypt, then to Nazareth (a non-place), then back to Jerusalem, and to "someplace," a wandering in the desert/wilderness perhaps, but with eventual return to Jerusalem on a donkey. Our heroes Mickey, Donald, and Goofy go to and come back from that "other place" in a straight line, but there are obstacles both conscious and subconscious. The path taken by Jesus is semicircular in a manner similar to that of Moses a.k.a. Akhenaten leaving Egypt and then returning. Unlike Moses, however, Jesus is a representation of, or someone in sympathy with, the common person (universalistic); Moses is a representation of a special group or God's chosen people (particularistic).

Jesus is not portrayed as a tyrant as was the case with Moses but, instead, more like a wise teacher, or almost exactly like Buddha. Remember that Buddha was also a teacher and not a ruler or conqueror as his father desired. The Jews were looking for a messiah who would liberate them from Roman oppression; they were looking for Muhammad. John the Baptist, on the other hand, did not come with an army. Instead, he stripped away all the rules and cosmic laws connected to the Essenes and came with a simple message: "Wash the sin from your hands and be a decent person, for the end is coming, and you want to be prepared and judged decent." John the Baptist was undoubtedly a rebel who realized that the common person had no access to mystery cults, and if your goal is to instill wisdom (Oannes again), the message has to fit everyone—not one special group. Back to the journey.

Jesus visits Jerusalem during the feast of the Passover when he was around age twelve ("when a boy becomes a man"), and impresses the rabbis with his knowledge and wisdom. This would have been between 7 and 10 CE. From 10 CE to around 28 CE, he wanders around (that's about eighteen years). Moses wandered for forty years but maybe Jesus was a quick learner, or perhaps he didn't have to contend with unruly subordinates worshiping a sacred cow every time he went to the mountain for a set of rules. Jesus, the Son of God, received preferential treatment and his ordeal was shortened. These eighteen years represent his night journey, and it might coincide with the time frame given above for Akhenaten leaving Amarna and returning during Horemheb's reign. This is a time of purification, cleansing your soul of all the crud and getting down to business as to what is really important in life. This extended period of cleansing was encapsulated and symbolized by his encounter with John the Baptist, "magical help" designed to sustain him during his temptations. This is the test to see if the cleansing is complete.

Another aside. John the Baptist, according to scholars (see Wilkinson 1888), is synonymous with the mythic superordinate powers of Ea and Oannes of a former time. Ea is a Babylonian, subterranean, freshwater god who imparts knowledge and wisdom. Oannes, an Akkadian variant of Ea, emerges from the Red Sea or Persian Gulf with a human head along with his reptilian head and imparts wisdom, but "cuts" himself off from humanity, perhaps representing the more graphic beheading of John the Baptist (if that is how he was dispatched). I have in my possession a photo taken at the Gruuthuse Museum, Bruges, Belgium, of a platter with a head on it. No one seemed to know whose head it was supposed to be, although I found that hard to believe. This was an interesting museum complete with guillotine and chopping block, and it was apparently a medical facility at one time. Torture and medicine— a poetic teaming of art forms. In any case, Christianity promoted much of the technology of torture in Europe, but torture, unfortunately, is a worldwide phenomenon adhered to by all nations of the world and justified under many truths. I was puzzled that no one knew whose head was rendered in clay on a large platter, but I believe that it was John the Baptist.

Baptism, the major activity of John, has nothing to do with brutalizing someone who chooses not to believe in your truth. Baptism is a cleansing ritual representing a new birth—giving up one's old ways, becoming a different person, or making a new start in a spiritual life. This is symbolic of cleansing away one's sins in preparation for revelation; you cannot have revelation without purification. I think it is well established that the ancient Egyptians, Hebrews, and Canaanites used anointing oils in their rituals, and there are strong suggestions that these oils would probably alter consciousness. Baptism might also be part of the anointing process, that is, *removing* the oil and the mind-altering substances contained within (see Bennett and McQueen 2001). Removing the oil would shut off the divine encounter with the gods. So there might have been two types of baptisms—a before, symbolizing cleansing of sins, and a cleansing after the fact, symbolically removing the old beliefs and replacing them with a new wisdom. There is always a termination ritual (see Rush 1996, 1999). Also keep in mind that not everyone would react the same way to anointing; some people have bad trips. A "baptism" in this case removes the evil and stops the experience, depending on your cultural lens.

After his encounter with the Baptist, Jesus is tempted by Satan; this is a test of character and a very different person emerges compared to Moses and Abraham. Mickey's tests come by way of the giant, Willy, with whom he is matching wits. Jesus is matching wits with Satan and refuses to submit as well. The message is quite clear: never submit to a god or a demon. Abraham and Moses (and Muhammad) appear to be instruments of a self-seeking, overbearing, insecure demon. Jesus, on the other hand, is on another path (*zodiakos*), not of physical conquest and identity for a special group, but a spiritual quest that anyone can join. Integrity is the word. Test of character is so important because Jesus, a new model, has to be set apart from the masses. In Matthew 4: 1–10 we read:

Then was Jesus led by the *Spirit* into the wilderness, to be tempted by the devil.

And when he had fasted forty days and forty nights, he was afterward hungry.
And when the tempter came to him, he said, If thou art the son of God, command that these stones be made bread.

But he answered and said, It is written, Man shall not live by bread alone, but by every word that proceedeth out of the mouth of God.

Then the devil taketh him up into the holy city, and setteth him on a pinnacle of the temple,

And saith to him, If thou art the son of God, cast thyself down, for it is written, He shall give his angels charge concerning thee: and in [their] hands they shall uphold thee, lest at any time thou dash thy foot against a stone.

Jesus said to him, It is written again, Thou shalt not tempt the Lord thy God.

Again, the devil taketh him up upon an exceeding high mountain, and showeth him all the kingdoms of the world, and the glory of them,

And saith to him, All these things will I give thee, if thou wilt fall down and worship me.

Then saith Jesus to him, Be gone, Satan: for it is written, Thou shalt worship the Lord thy God, and him only shalt thou serve. (Emphasis added)

Notice how Jesus ends up with the Devil; the Spirit takes him there. Can that Spirit be identified? I believe that its reference is well known to high-level religious clerics worldwide. In any case, his animal nature is being tested—not his spirituality. You want to serve your ability to reason (your Lord, your God) and have compassion, and not your animal instincts—those evil, nasty things inside that bring us to life. The instincts have to be controlled: "Give thy not into temptation." There is nothing really spiritual in the temptations themselves; his reaction to them represents reason, that Jesus can tell the difference between the tangible world and the spiritual. But they do clarify that Jesus is a man and not a divine being, for had he been a divine being his spiritual integrity would have been tested and spiritual integrity has nothing to do with food, injury, or power over people. Unless a person can control or suspend his or her animal nature, a spiritual life is unavailable. A spiritual life is one of connectedness to all that is and has nothing to do with politics and money. As Gandhi said, "There is more to life than clinging to it or having more of it." There is more to life than sex and filling our bellies, although sex and food are what make the spiritual life possible. Life is also more than money or status. The temptations, however, are exactly the same in symbolic value as the temptations of the Buddha, which in my rendition go something like this:

> While Buddha was meditating facing east under the Bo Tree, seeking inner illumination, he reached Chakra Six, Ajna or sight of perception; he was with the gods. They surrounded him, danced their dance, and the Buddha said silently as a mantra, "I am creating this; *Tat tvam asi*."
>
> With that the gods taunted Buddha—they tested him; he was motionless with his hand in the *varada mudra* position—he was without fear. The God of War, *Mara*, leapt forward with a weapon in each of his eight arms, "We will annihilate you!" Thousands and thousands of slings, arrows, molten wax, spears of every type and shape turned the landscape to darkness, but they fell as rose petals and lotus blossoms at Buddha's feet. He had no fear.
>
> Then the God of Love, *Kama*, stepped up with his two beautiful daughters, as lovely as lovely can be, and they danced for the Buddha like no one has been tempted before or since. The Buddha was motionless, with no desire. His hands in *dhyani mudra*, a light surrounded him, and in a moment of the mind-of-time the Bo Tree turned to a serpent, the *Naga Raja*, with an open hood offering wisdom, "All is

impermanent; all is illusion." The daughters turned to dust, which was gently borne on the wind, and in its place stood *Dharma,* the God of Social Duty, riding a large white Elephant. "You there, Prince! What are you doing out here? Don't you know there are pressing problems back at the palace! There is unrest in the streets, and this needs your attention. Get up, get up; do your dharma, your duty!"

Buddha touched the ground, *bhumisparsha,* the immovable spot. The elephant bowed, Dharma stepped back, and all turned to illumination just as the sun emerged on the horizon.

The first temptation of the Buddha is that of fear, or Chakra One, Muladhara, clinging to life. Jesus is tested with something less psychological, that is, preservation of the flesh should he jump off the mountain. The second temptation for the Buddha is sexual desire, or *Svadhishthana* (Chakra Two). Sex promotes life, just as the bread Jesus would morph from rocks.

Finally, Chakra Three is social duty (*Manipura*—"Jeweled City") or to do one's proper work. Buddha's proper work was to follow in daddy's footsteps and be a great ruler; Jesus was promised rule of all the lands he could see from the highest mountain. It may be a coincidence that the temptations are exactly the same, but when added to other points below a heavy Hindu/Buddhist influence is felt in the story of Jesus.

There is lack of clarity regarding the actual whereabouts of Jesus, from approximately age twelve to age thirty, and this is typical in this type of story. Jesus goes to the Temple in Jerusalem, he is wise, he asks questions, and because of his lack of experience in the world as it is, he is in a bind. His mind opens to the reality that very intelligent people will do irrational and inhuman things to each other. His psyche opened up and he fell in. How can a boy become a man and then do terrible things to others? Is that what "becoming a man" means? He went mad, and the only cure for the madness was to get off the psychiatric ward or become the chief psychiatrist. Now, it doesn't say this any-where in the literature I have examined, but it has to be there. Jesus did not express his wisdom to the rabbis in order to become one of them. He went to the Temple and the rabbis, and asked, "What ails you?" Or, "What's wrong with life, and how do we fix it?" This is the same storyline as in the Arthurian Grail King legend. Few rabbis had answers, so what Jesus was seeking could not be found locally. We have no information on those missing years beyond our own imaginations, but this keeps the story going, the speculation and consequent questions. Like Mickey, Donald, and Goofy, Jesus climbs the metaphorical beanstalk.

And like Buddha and Moses before him, the wandering is metaphor-ical of being lost and finding one's self (you cannot possibly find your-self unless you are lost), gaining knowledge and special tools, and planning one's actions. This eighteen-year time period was edited out and most likely contains the night journey that is possibly similar to the Egyptian Book of the Dead. But whatever the story, it's a "beanstalk" story.

From around 28 CE until his demise (30 CE), Jesus heals and casts out demons and attracts people with his messages, which, by the way, are not clearly delivered. He speaks in parables, leaving the interpre-tation to the audience, a clever method of instilling self-responsibility. His disciples have difficulty understanding his parables, which means he is forcing people to think and question. Thinking and questioning are the very strategies for appropriate social living and which are *forbidden,* especially in Christianity and Islam. Jesus does not communicate a mul-titude of rules, as found in the Jewish sects, suggesting that his teach-ings fit everyone and not a special group. If he is the Son of God, this is a real problem for the Jews because the God of Jesus (the same god of Abraham, Moses, David, etc.) *does not* have a special people—every-one is special. This represents a shift in thinking and resulting logical con-clusion: If one god created all, then it is all special and not for the benefit of any exclusive group. Should the Jews go along with this, realizing that their god lied to them and that they aren't special people after all, or should they hang on to the old story? You can see this starting out as a small crack in the matrix of their mythical charter and resulting in absolute fracture. You cannot have this both ways—either the Jews are special or everyone is special. Not only does the charter fracture but this can lead to neurosis and worse. I have personally watched fundamentalists go absolutely ballistic when presented with information from the scientific community. This overly defensive, violent reaction would be a red flag to a psychologist or psychiatrist, and certainly a threat to some, and out of fear a few politicians have suggested (Denmark passed a law along these lines) that presenting the religious community with information (and this can come in the form of cartoons) that contradicts their position is a form of "insensitivity." This is what happens when the irrational world gets the upper hand; there can only be acceptance of their psychosis and any debate is considered "insensitive."

In any event, the night journey, those eighteen years or so climbing the beanstalk, did not end when Jesus returned to Jerusalem. Just as Akhenaten might have come back to Egypt for a visit, so does Jesus. But, in both cases, they go with a promise of return. The journey is incomplete. Jesus found out "what ails you" and he knows how to fix the "dis-ease," but he is not successful in delivering the boon (love, compassion), the "good news," *so that it would stick*. Jesus found, because of our small-group nature, that it is much easier to sell people fear, hate, anger, and so on, anything that appeals to our animal nature (clinging to life, sex, status), and more difficult to appeal to love, compassion, understanding, self-responsibility, intelligence, and rational thinking. After all, look what the authorities did—mythic Jesus comes into town and says, "I'm God, and I love you," and they murdered him! Our divinity is there, but how do we bring it out and make it at least as important as our animal nature? So he went away a second time (Mickey, Donald, and Goofy only go up and back) to find out how to make it stick. I can see Jesus now, climbing that beanstalk, talking to the gurus, gods, and demons of a time past, not slaying giants. Jesus understood that our way out of this was symbolic; we have to change the storyline of who and what we are, and we will never accomplish this by creating rules that serve to separate and alienate, or by beating each other up. Back to the details.

Jesus returns to Jerusalem and disrupts the temple by overturning the moneychangers' tables and the tables of the sacrifices, birds, and such. This is synonymous with Mickey, Donald, and Goofy upsetting Willy's tranquility by showing up in his castle. Money exchanging was a common event in and around temples and synagogues, as was the sale of sacrificial animals, but money corrupts—the priesthood becomes very wealthy and thus influential. Willy is getting "fat" with all the food (vitality) issuing from the magic harp, "food" that should go back to the people. Most biblical scholars see this as a statement against the rulers and authority. But some, me included, understand Jesus' aberrant behavior as a symbolic distancing of spiritual matters from issues of money and politics. This is the "render under Caesar what is Caesar's and render unto God what is God's." If Jesus is doing anything, he is tearing down the ethnic rules wrapped in a very thin religious cloak that are designed to control a specific group of people. This was to be substituted with a new message, with common principles, guiding all human interaction: "Do unto others as you would have done to you." In order to do this you need to "know thyself" and "exorcise *your* demons," but also thank them for being there ("love thy enemy") and "love thy neighbor as thyself."

The major message Jesus delivered tore away the ethnic trappings and was so radical that he had to go. In my opinion the "turning over the tables" is a statement of the inappropriateness of money and politics connected to his idea of spirituality. Money and politics corrupt and have nothing to do with spirituality and being a decent human being. This is the message suppressed initially by Paul (the anti-Christ) and those who came after, that is, the bishops, popes, and other religious clerics, for obvious reasons—Christianity has *everything* to do with economics and politics and little to do with spirituality and decency. Yes, churches do a great deal of charitable work and are to be commended, but fundraising is big business in itself and it helps to enrich the church and support the bureaucracy. Christianity is the economic and political arm with Jesus on the letterhead. Lest there be any misunderstanding, there are lots of decent Christians; it is the institution I criticize, an institution that began with deception and corruption and maintains it each time the religious clerics open the doors and start the show. The original messages of Jesus (or John the Baptist) did not include a church and religious specialists. The "church" is everywhere and everyone is his or her own ministry or priest. Morality cannot be taught in the sense of going to church and having a minister or priest tell you what is right and wrong, good and bad, and then paying him (or her) for telling you what you already know. If you do not bring morality into the church, temple, or mosque, you won't find it there. Attending church and praying to God are not moral acts, nor is paying the religious cleric so that God will overlook your sins. History tells us a great deal about morality as administered by popes, priests, and other pretenders (for example see Wills 2000).

To continue, during and after his wanderings Jesus acquires the boon, the ability to heal society as symbolized by his ability to heal sick individuals. This also means he brought people *hope* by raising the "dead," which symbolically represents spiritual rebirth or "the bringing to life the dead mind so that one might see anew." But Jesus cannot do this alone, so he chooses witnesses or twelve disciples whose duties include: 1) spreading the word of a miracle worker and that they have witnessed or personally had spiritual and mystical (contact with the deity) experiences; 2) asking questions during gatherings so that his message can be delivered (sort of like an Amway meeting or political debates, with staged questions from the audience); and 3) functioning as an adjective or determinative emphasizing their symbolic connection to the zodiakos, the path, and twelve tribes of Israel (all the people of the world). Jesus is their messiah or Christ as well as the Sun God, in this case, the Son of the Sun.

Then we have the Last Supper that is a signal of departure, as this will be his last experience of this world—for now. He gives Judas an assignment, who, as his most loyal disciple, tells the authorities where to find this dangerous person "who dares to call himself God!" He is brought before thug Pilate and suggests that he is God, and this, or whatever reason, seals his fate. Remember that if Jesus is not executed, then there is no story to tell. Also, in order to have a good story there have to be obstacles and intrigue. Judas, for example, has several sides, two of which are: 1) the devoted servant who knew what was required if Jesus was to succeed in his teachings, and 2) that of traitor. The popular thinking is "Judas was a traitor" and that's probably where the biblical poets were going with this. Why? Well, if Jesus has a co-conspirator in his own death (the loving servant, Dr. Judas Kevorkian), then this is simply an act of assisted suicide and therefore does not qualify as a means of removing the sins of mankind. This has to be perceived as an event evolving out of evil social circumstances that manifests through our animal nature. This had to be portrayed as a most horrible act by the authorities (the Passion symbolizes the brutal Roman rule), rather than Jesus killing himself in a planned suicide. Jesus becomes a martyr, the sacrificial lamb. Judas, then, is characterized as a traitor or one not to be trusted in popular parlance, and his image was used to condemn the Jews for killing Jesus. But I read an interesting twist in all this. Both Luke (22:3) and John (13:2) state that Satan or the Devil made Judas betray Jesus. "The devil made me do it!" Why is that? Only someone possessed or tempted by Satan would betray the Lord, Jesus. Christianity does not promote self-responsible behavior.

Looked at through another lens, this is to illustrate the difference between Jesus and others—Jesus was not corrupted and Judas was. But no matter how we read this, Jesus had to die, or the story is left without a punch line, the boon for society (new wisdom), which is either with us today or available in the second coming. I believe that it is with us today, and like the Kingdom of God, it is right in front of us and we don't see it. How, then, do you get people to experience and appreciate heaven on earth? The answer is: He went away so we, who are gods like him, will figure it out. "Don't make me come back just to be nailed to a cross a second time. When I come back I want to experience a compassionate world."

Jesus also had to die in a horrible, humiliating manner, which adds shock value and a glimpse of what people endured during that time period and in some areas of the world today. He is issued a cross, drags it to the hill where it is stationed, he is nailed to it, then speared by a soldier, dies, is removed from the cross, and taken to a tomb for burial. Three days later (actually a day and one-half later—see McKinsey 1995, 307–308) he comes back from the dead, meets Mary Magdalene and others, and tells them not to say anything to anyone. He then ascends to heaven saying, "I'll be back." Arnold certainly got a lot of mileage out of that line as well.

Three is a magical number because it represents completion and the trinity. But why does Jesus cleave the prophecy by returning a day and one-half earlier? Is this just an error of the biblical poets or is there a special meaning here? More opportunity to layer myth!

There are many similarities between the story of Jesus and *Mickey and the Beanstalk:* 1) Heroes in both have humble beginnings; 2) there is a problem which cannot be solved locally; 3) the hero/heroes are transported to some other place; 4) there is a wandering or night journey; 5) obstacles or tests are encountered and overcome; 6) magical help is available; and 7) there is a return with the message (in the case of Jesus) or object (magic harp) designed to fix the world or bring the world back to a balanced state. Mickey, Donald, and Goofy accomplish their goal, and peace and prosperity is returned to Happy Valley. The same, however, cannot be said for Jesus, for his message was ignored in favor of a sin atoning savior and a return to an old system, a familiar system of rules and oppression. Had his message stood on its own and carried on as a message of compassion and self-responsibility without the economic and political trappings, this world might be a different place. Jesus is dubbed the founder of Christianity, which is part of the myth. Christianity was founded and based on a creed assembled after his alleged death. One of the main contributors was Paul; more about Paul later.

These hero myths give us moral lessons and point society in a direction. They give culture an "out" in times of crisis by suggesting that solving a problem may mean not obeying society's dictates; you have to think outside the box. We know of the mythic hero Jesus only through the eyes of interpreters, but as to a real person we run into serious difficulties. There is a tomb that some claim belongs to Jesus and Mary Magdalene (as reported on the History Channel in March 2007), but there are many problems with this discovery. If it is in fact the tomb of our mythic hero Jesus, then this causes great problems for those who believed that Jesus ascended to heaven bones and all, and this is especially troublesome if he and Mary had children. You can't have a god spreading his genes around (as Zeus did), and if this is the case, then we have gods all over the place and we are back to polytheism. Just think of how many gods could be produced in 2,000 years! This would certainly be troublesome to the Christians, especially the Catholic Church, because someone claiming to be God might be the real McCoy and not a heretic after all. You can see one reason why the Catholic Church went ballistic over *The Da Vinci Code*.

To fundamentalist Christians it makes a difference as to whether Jesus and his deeds are historical. Unable to intellectually touch the spiritual plane of these stories, they cling to a belief (usually out of threat and fear of eternal damnation) that there was a person by the name of Jesus, who was crucified on a cross, died, came back to life, dropped in to see a couple of his friends, and then went to heaven to reunite with his self or his Father (depending on your interpretation of the trinity). Most are not concerned in the least about his simple message to the world and instead get hung up on symbols originally designed as attention getters in the story, that is, powers of a magical being and all the other mystical parts. This all-powerful mystical being (God) gets the attention; God becomes more important than humanity.

One significant difference between *Mickey and the Beanstalk* and the life and times of Jesus is that Jesus dies and did not save the world, whereas Mickey, Donald, and Goofy return to Happy Valley and all is brought back into balance. Sin-atoning saviors, as is the case with Jesus, die. The symbolic value of this is the death of one age and the beginning of a new era. The movie *Armageddon*, starring Bruce Willis, likewise fits this type of hero who dies saving the world. The storyline is much the same. There is a problem (the world will be hit by a meteor), the problem can't be solved locally, he recruits "magical" help (his motley group of oilrig workers), they go into space, obstacles have to be overcome, and reluctantly Willis stays behind to detonate the bomb that will cleave the meteor so that it travels harmlessly past Earth. In this case his death does save the world. What we see is martyrdom deeply etched in patriarchal, male-centered traditions. Martyrdom, in fact, is one of the quickest ways to attract the attention of the deity and is considered *the* spiritual act in Christianity and Islam.

What Did Jesus Really Say?

In my opinion one of the more important messages attributed to our hero Jesus comes from Mathew 10:34: "Do not suppose that I have come to bring peace to the earth. I did not come to bring peace, but a sword. For I have come to turn . . ." Some have interpreted this as a statement of violence (the Christian "sword verse") toward others in a fashion similar to Surah 9:5 of the *Qur'an*. Most biblical scholars would agree that Jesus talked in riddles or parables because straight out logic usually does not work. By telling a story, you bypass the mental filters and force the listener to think about what is said. Some have suggested that the parables were incomprehensible to many of Jesus' followers (see Vermes 2000), but that is the point of a parable—it is something to think about and the receiver, who has been encouraged to think independently, determines the meaning of the message. The fact that the poets have the disciples ask for meaning suggests that what Jesus had to say was new and "deep." The parable above is stating, "What I (Jesus) have to offer, *a new way of living* (and you don't need a church or a priest), *will divide people.*" The words in italics are the symbolic worth of the sword. That is the meaning of his statement and not that he intends harm to anyone as in the Islamic sword verse. The agenda was a prompt for people to think and realize that there is a better way of treating one another, and when the time comes you need to prove, by thought and deed, your social worth. Parables will be interpreted to fit the moment. Jesus understood synagogues as economic and political institutions that have little to do with his agenda. He also felt that everyone should be a minister and priest, similar to the idea that Judaism is a community of priests. Spreading the word does not mean telling people how they should act. You spread the word by *being* a decent person; you are what you do, not by telling others how to do their lives. Proselytizing, going door to door for converts, would be contrary to anything Jesus stood for; he only spoke when people asked him questions. Can you imagine one of these Mormon proselytizers knocking on your door and when you open up he says, "Quick, ask me a question, so I can tell you a story!"

I am not going to retrace the footsteps of others in attempting to find the historic Jesus. Instead, I will provide examples that lead one to conclude that anyone by the name of Jesus—living between 3 BCE and 33 CE, whose birthday was on December 25, who stirred up trouble between the Jews (Pharisees and Sadducees), insulted King Herod by claiming to be the Son of God, and attracted disciples—came with a new message. He did not symbolically give his life in order for his continuers to create more of the same. That is to say, Jesus represents a tearing down of the economic and political institution called Judaism, and replacing this with self-responsibility and respect for others. He was not about reinventing the wheel or recreating an economic and political system like Judaism (Catholicism). This was not his purpose, or the purpose of the story. His message or purpose fractured the moment Catholicism was organized as a political and economic unit, with much of the absurd, drug-induced philosophy echoed in the writings of Paul, and it remains fractured to this day.

So, what can be attributed to Jesus that would be radically different from the practice of Judaism and yet have an internal consistency that Jews and non-Jews could follow?

Inclusiveness and Enemies

Neighbor (as in "love thy neighbor") in the Old Testament is not a reference to just any neighbor. Nowhere in the Old Testament does it say, "Love thy neighbor even if he is a Hittite, Canaanite, Persian, Akkadian, or Egyptian." In Leviticus 19:18 we read, "Thou shalt not avenge, nor bear any grudge against the children *of thy people,* but thou shalt love thy neighbor as thyself; I [am] the LORD." Many Christian groups claim that this is a reference to *all* neighbors, irrespective of their ethnic origins or religious preference, but this is not the case. For example, in Genesis 26:34–35, we read about Isaac's first born, Esau, who married two Hittite women, "who were a grief of mind to Isaac and Rebekah." The Hittites were neighbors but Isaac certainly did not love them.

"Love thy neighbor" is an exclusive reference to others in the *Jewish* community *and not a general statement that encompasses the world.* The Jews are, according to their myth, a "chosen people," and when we look at the behavior of Abraham, Moses, David, and others, they care little about anyone not born of a Jewish mother. Moreover, you can even take advantage of close kin (witness Jacob stealing the birthright of Esau) if you can get away with it. The statements attributed to Jesus in Matthew 5:43–45 are clearly *inclusive* rather than exclusive.

> Ye have heard that it hath been said, Thou shalt love thy neighbor, and hate thy enemy:
> But I say to you, Love your enemies, bless them that curse you, do good to them that hate you, and pray for them who despitefully use you, and persecute you;
> That ye may be the children of your Father who [is] in heaven: for he maketh his sun to rise on the evil and on the good, and sendeth rain on the just and on the unjust.

What Jesus is saying is that God does not distinguish between one group of people and another—all are treated alike. We are all "chosen people," we are all neighbors, and we deserve respect. The Jews, within this new philosophy, lose their preferential status.

"Love thy enemy" is another statement that does not jump out at me in the Old Testament. There are two types of enemy, that is, the enemy you kill (Exodus 15:6, Numbers 10:9, Deuteronomy 32:42; 33:27, 1 Samual 26:8, etc.) and then the enemy killing you (Exodus 15:9, Leviticus 26:25, Deuteronomy 28:57, 1 Kings 8:33, etc.). So what does "love thy enemy mean?" Recall that Jesus spoke in parables and what is probably being said, following the Buddhist sentiment, is that *YOU* are your own worst enemy. Those you see as your "enemy" are a mirror of you, and you should thank them for helping you "know thyself." Jesus also implied that there are enemies who *will* hurt you. In Luke 22:36 we read, "Then said he to them, But now he that hath a purse, let him take [it], and likewise [his] sack: and he that hath no sword, let him sell his garment, and buy one." Sword, in this context (see Gabriel 2004, 132), refers to a "dagger or short sword that travelers used for protection against robbers or wild animals." Combining the statements you cipher, "Love thy enemy, but don't be dumb and stupid!" The "love thy enemy" that issues from Jesus is a statement in contradiction to the exclusive Jewish community who perceived all others as enemies or potential enemies. Strangers are potential enemies; it is easy to convert a stranger into an "it," and "its," because they are less than human, can be cheated, lied to, and killed. In the militaries around the world a human being is a "target," just as is a tank, car, or bridge, and you can't get any more impersonal than that. A target, a piece of paper with circles drawn on it—why, a clay pigeon gets more respect than that! Enemies and strangers, in one sense, can be seen as synonymous, but, as Jesus implies, if you treat strangers with kindness then it is highly likely that they will see you in a different, more favorable light. But don't be dumb and stupid; carry a "sword," an edge, which equals healthy paranoia.

Rules to Live By—Relationship with Family

Family was certainly important for the Hebrew people. However, although important, there is some pretty outlandish treatment of family members. Sarah tells Abraham to drive his son (her stepson) and his concubine Hagar (her loyal maidservant) into the desert (Genesis

21:10). Jacob, at the urging of his mother (Genesis 27), deceives his father and usurps his brother Esau's heritage. Joseph's brothers (Genesis 37:18), after reporting his dream that he would rule over them, decide to kill him. Thanks to his brother Reuben the action was prevented, but he is then sold into slavery to a passing group of Ishmaelites for twenty pieces of silver (Judas is paid thirty pieces of silver for betraying Jesus—inflation or astronomical code?). Although the story is designed to get Joseph into Egypt, it also suggests the inner struggle we have with ourselves, that is, the enemy within—anger, jealousy, insecurity, and so on, and the impulse to approach the world on that level rather through reason and understanding. Daddy Jacob doesn't seem to be very helpful as a role model. Joseph was simply spoiled, blinded by his own self-importance, and he is about to be taught a lesson, but with a positive ending.

In Leviticus 19:3, a person is to *fear* his mother and father. Leviticus 20:9 states, "For every one that curseth his father or his mother, shall surely be put to death: he hath cursed his father or his mother; his blood [shall be] upon him." In Deuteronomy 5:16 we read, "Honor thy father and thy mother." So which is it, honor or fear your parents? No one really honors those they fear; these are mutually exclusive positions.

In Deuteronomy 21:18–21 we learn how to deal with unruly children:

> If a man shall have a stubborn and rebellious son, who will not obey the voice of his father, or the voice of his mother, and [who], when they have chastened him, will not hearken to them:
>
> Then shall his father and his mother lay hold on him, and bring him out to the elders of his city, and to the gate of his place;
>
> And they shall say to the elders of his city, This our son [is] stubborn and rebellious, he will not obey our voice; [he is] a glutton, and a drunkard.
>
> And all the men of his city shall stone him with stones, that he may die: so shalt thou remove evil from among you, and all Israel shall hear, and fear.

Jesus also said, "Honor thy mother and father" (Luke 18:20); he says nothing about fearing mommy and daddy. But he is also reported to have said (Matthew 10:37), "He that loveth father or mother more than me, is not worthy of me: and he that loveth son or daughter more than me, is not worthy of me." Jesus a.k.a. John the Baptist, through his contact with Gentiles, telling people to repent, "The world is coming to an end," and other of his behaviors, was an embarrassment and a betrayal to most of his family members (Essenes). This may be the reference point for frustration over family members interfering with this message to the world. But what I think is really being said is, "Don't follow the path of our fathers and mothers, sisters and brothers, a path of exclusivity. If you love that path, then you can't love my path because it is going to be a bumpy road and only those committed to self-responsibility and human decency need apply." But this also might be a statement that either he, Jesus, or He, God, comes first. I do not believe that he ever said or suggested such a thing, as this would represent a reversion to Judaism where God *does* come first and humanity second. Jesus was for humanity just as was Eve and Prometheus; Jesus was not for himself or God. Most Christians do not have a clue as to what Jesus originally stood for.

The above statement, however, is followed with, "And he that taketh not his cross, and followeth me, is not worthy of me." (Matthew 10:38) This, of course, is a suspect utterance, as Jesus had not been crucified at this point. Some might say that he was simply revealing future events, but nowhere does he suggest *how* he would die. Would the average person understand the metaphor "pick up your cross and follow me" before his crucifixion? I do not believe the Christian metaphorical rendition of the cross was available until many years after his mythic death, although some (see Mack 1995, 87) suggest it was. From his magical birth, statements about his healing abilities and his death at the hands of Pilate are all mythic statements. The storyline is one of hope and rebuilding the world, but not a world based on politics and money. The intended storyline was not about God or Jesus; it was about you and me and how we do our lives, not as slaves to God, but as citizens cooperating in spite of God and Nature.

Paul originally persecuted Christians but then "saw the light," never met Jesus or John the Baptist, and apparently had only minimal contact and conversations with Peter. These are calculated attempts to place himself (Paul) into the sandals of Jesus and increase his own illusory self-importance. As Freeman states (2003, 117), "Paul casts himself in a comparable role" as Jesus, that is, as an intermediary between humanity and God. In other words, Paul saw a way to elevate his own importance, suffering as he did from a severe inferiority complex. Paul even goes so far as to say that having faith in the death and resurrection of Jesus was sufficient to ensure salvation (Freeman 2003, 118). That is to say, simply believe and don't think too deeply.

Slavery

In the various editions of the Old Testament, servant and slave appear synonymous, but certainly a servant, in some cases, might be a freeman who has indentured him or herself to a particular household. Or the reference could mean being a slave to God, like a priest or monk. Slavery was common practice throughout the Middle East and Egypt for many thousands of years and still exists today as an accepted practice in the Muslim tradition (see Segal 2002 and Chapter Four of this work). Slavery for the Israelites was justified through "God's will," and, as time went on, a literal interpretation of the Old Testament. This interpretation allowed slavery to exist in this country as a time-honored institution until about 150 years ago. Slavery is a clear example of where a human being is reduced to the level of an "it." There are other meanings connected to the word slave, such as, for example, being a slave to our beliefs, emotions, or animal nature.

Interestingly enough, the word slave is mentioned only once in the New Testament, that is, in Revelation 18:13, but the reference is not something attributed to Jesus. I cannot find anything in the statements attributed to Jesus that suggest slavery was good, bad, or otherwise because that was not part of his message. Decent people do not enslave others. In the Pauline tradition, "Those who were slaves were to stay, for they would soon be freed by Christ. A Christian

freeman, on the other hand, should consider himself a slave of Christ."
(1 Corinthians 7:22) Paul was being politically correct and cautious.
Think about this for a moment: Jesus came with a simple message,
and enslaving people in any manner would not have been part of the
program unless he was building another offshoot of Judaism with
tons of rules and regulations.

One's Relationship to State and God

In the Jewish tradition, God and State are one and the same. The rules
and the laws (Leviticus, Numbers, and Deuteronomy) are cosmic laws.
These laws, however, are in place to keep the Hebrews separate from
other people, and because they come with such authority they must be
obeyed under penalty of death. There is a rule for everything—the food
you eat, when you can work, whom you should marry, with whom you
should have sex, and so on.

With Jesus, however, there is a clear separation of religion and State.
We read in Matthew 22:21, Mark 12:17, and Luke 20:25, "Render
therefore to Caesar, the things which are Caesar's; and to God, the
things that are God's." Another clear indication of this separation
occurred with the moneylenders in the temple (Matthew 21:12–13):

> And Jesus went into the temple of God, and cast out all them
> that sold and bought in the temple, and overthrew the tables
> of the money-changers, and the seats of them that sold
> doves.
> And said to them, It is written, My house shall be called
> the house of prayer, but ye have made it a den of thieves.

Freeman (2003, 101) offers an interpretation of this act:

> What Jesus meant to achieve by this provocative action has
> been endlessly debated. His gesture may have been a sym-
> bolic one, a recognition of the passing of the old order—and

the Temple with it—at the coming of "the new kingdom," but he may also have had a more overtly political aim of expressing popular disquiet with the ruling elite.

Freeman's first interpretation is perhaps closer to the point, that is, spirituality and being a decent human being are Jesus' primary concerns; money and politics corrupt the prime objective. Moreover, once you remove money and politics the temple is unnecessary. In Matthew 6:5–6, Jesus says:

> And when thou prayest, thou shalt not be as the hypocrites [are]: for they love to pray standing in the synagogues, and in the corners of the streets, that they may be seen by men. Verily, I say to you, they have their reward.
>
> But thou, when thou prayest, enter into thy closet, and when thou hast shut thy door, pray to thy Father who is in secret, and thy Father who seeth in secret, will reward thee openly.

So, you don't need a church; God is equally available in your closet, the attic, the woods—God is everywhere, and to assume that salvation requires going to church and paying a minister or priest is absurd! Although suggested in Luke, it was Paul who stated that ministers or priests should be paid for their services, a practice that comes in with the Jewish tradition. Vermes (2000, 72) states:

> Paul mentions as a second precept of Jesus transmitted by tradition the entitlement of the Christian preacher to be provided for by the faithful (cf. Luke 10:7): "The Lord commanded that those who proclaim the gospel should get their living by the gospel" (1 Corinthians 9:14).

Paul supported himself by making tents, probably because, at that time, there would be little money in preaching; it could even be dangerous. What he accomplished, however, is what we see today; people giving ten percent (or more) of their income (tithing) to the church to gain health, wealth, and progeny (paying the deity to pay attention to our animal nature). There is absolutely nothing spiritual in this at all (see Rush 2005, 155–156).

What Jesus is saying, again, is that you don't need a church and you don't need a priest. Paul and others corrupted the message and brought money and politics back into the picture—Jesus, if he was a real person, is rolling over in his grave! One's relationship with God is quite personal. Why is this? We read in John 6:56, "He that eateth my flesh, and drinketh my blood, dwelleth in me, and I in him." In the Gospel of Thomas (108) Jesus states, "He who will drink from My mouth will become like Me. I myself shall become he, and the things that are hidden will be revealed to him." This is the communion with Jesus/God through the mushroom; this is the conduit to the other side of you. What is also being said is, "Be like me, follow my example, and you are likewise God." If God is everywhere, He must be in you as well. This is pure Buddhism expressed in Sanskrit, *Tat tvam asi,* or "You are it"—you are that energy that informs all. This is not a Greek idea. Claiming that you are God, of course, is the great heresy in monotheistic traditions. Why? Because if God is in everything, including you, then you don't need a church or priest as a conduit—*you* are the conduit. These are the exact sentiments, along with the necessity of asking questions ("What ails you?"), encountered in *Parzival* by Wolfram Von Eschenbach around 1200 CE. By 1300 CE this type of "dangerous" thinking was squashed by the Catholic Church.

Food

Food restrictions are very important in the Jewish tradition (as they are in Islam). The importance of food restrictions is not because of health reasons, which is the modern interpretation for restrictions on pork, shellfish, and so on. The original reason for food restrictions in Judaism was to separate Israelites from everyone else—you cannot sit down and have a meal with others because eating together represents an important bond. "Breaking bread" with others means that you have a relationship and are no longer strangers, but the type of "bread" you break or consume points to another meaning discussed below.

For Jesus, on the other hand, food restrictions have nothing to do with a spiritual life and, in fact, he recognized that restrictions separate people. Eating together became a focal point in the early Jesus cults, but, as alluded to above, what you ate was not, initially, food in the common sense. In Matthew 6:25 Jesus states, "Therefore I say to you, Be not anxious for your life, what ye shall eat, or what ye shall drink; nor yet for your body, what ye shall put on. Is not the life more than food, and the body than raiment?" Hopefully the reader is getting the point that what Jesus had to offer was 180 degrees in opposition to what already existed, that is, Judaism with all it rules and regulation. What Jesus had to say was in total opposition to what Christianity became; Christianity is a retrofit of Judaism and a regression to a primitive mentality, the dark ages, a place where people need to be micromanaged and brutalized, mentally and physically, to save their souls from damnation.

Jesus would eat with apparently anyone. In Mark 2:16 we read, "And when the scribes and Pharisees saw him eating with publicans and sinners, they said to his disciples, How is it that he eateth and drinketh with publicans and sinners?" In Luke 5:30 we read the same: "But their scribes and Pharisees murmured against his disciples, saying, Why do ye eat and drink with publicans and sinners?" Eating with non-Jews could result in contracting a spiritual disease! Non-Jews are referred to as *goyeem*, the Gentiles. In Christianity, on the other hand, all non-Christians are considered potential Christians. For Jesus it was not a matter of being a Jew, pagan, atheist, or Osirian—it makes no difference. Just be decent to people, and decency does not include lying, cheating, stealing, murdering, raping, pillaging, censoring, and so on. You can see how both Christianity and Islam, as retrofits of the House of Judaism, perverted this.

Heaven

The Old Testament does not offer mythic themes of heaven and hell as did the Canaanites and others, for example, the Egyptians, from whom the Israelites borrowed much of their mythic storyline. It seems that the Israelites thought that, if you don't get what has been promised to you by God here and now, you are not going to get the "promised land" anywhere else. Certainly current Jewish thinking does accommodate a heaven and hell, which begins to crystallize in this tradition around 200 BCE with the belief that the world was coming to an end and there will be a judgment.

In the Buddhist tradition we encounter a heaven, Sukhavati, that great lotus pond in the West, but most Buddhists consider this more a psychological entity rather than a real, tangible place, and at death you better understand that all you experience is created in your mind. In Christianity heaven and hell are conceptualized as *real,* tangible geographies, and the only way to get to heaven or the House of God is by accepting Jesus as your savior. According to this position you can be a corrupt lawyer, politician, womanizer, murder, or rapist, but as long as you accept Jesus as your savior you're in. It is unlikely that Jesus would have said such a thing because he was more interested in decent behavior—now. My position is that Jesus' conception of heaven is closer to what is attributed to him in the Gospel of Thomas (113—see Cameron 1982, 37), which does not fit with the political and economic agenda of the Catholic Church:

> His disciples said to Him, "When will the Kingdom come?"
> [Jesus said,] "It will not come by waiting for it. It will not be a matter of saying 'Here it is' or 'There it is.' Rather, the Kingdom of the Father is spread out upon the earth, and men do not see it."

If you want to control with fear, then sell people heaven and hell as separate geographical places and invent ritual curses, or incantations, to sling at the appropriate moment. The current incantation is, "You're being insensitive to my religion." The present environment is not important; death in war gets you to heaven. Squandering resources is not important because this place (planet earth) isn't the real place. If you want people to be decent, however, then promise heaven as a by-product of decency *here and now,* and this would result in heaven on earth. This is the message that Jesus brought to the world, a message that was twisted and perverted by Paul and further pulled, stretched, and fractured by his continuers.

Apocalypse or the End of the World

The belief of a pending apocalypse shows up in the Jewish tradition some time in the second century BCE and was stressed in the writings of the Essenes. This idea is based on similar beliefs held by the ancient Egyptians and Hindus but with a big difference. For both the Hindu and Egyptian this was an individual or personal ending of existence, a personal apocalypse, and not a world event. For the Egyptians and Hindus death was expressed as an individual adventure (reincarnation for Hindu and resurrection in Egyptian), a reliving of one's life to, in a way, correct the mistakes (ignorance in Hindu and sin in the Egyptian). In the Zoroastrian tradition this also appears to be a personal journey. The story of Noah, however, changes this. The ending of life is global, but in a personal way, for God personally checked each person and found a few good people to tend the animals. This thinking evolves out of intense social stress and symbolically is a calling for a new heaven and earth, or an end to oppression and the beginning of a new social order; the Egyptians and Hindus were not suggesting a new world order. Jesus (or John the Baptist) would have certainly been aware of this philosophy, but taking into account what I stated earlier, a new heaven and earth would occur here and now if people would simply engage in healthy, helpful, and non-hurtful behaviors.

There are two positions within biblical literature as to where and when the Kingdom of God will show up. The first is when Jesus returns for the "second coming," which then prompts the end of the world.

Then there is the Thomas Gospel that states the Kingdom of God is right in front of us and we do not see it. The second is more in line with the predominant Jewish position that if you don't get it here (land and special privileges), you aren't going to get it anywhere. John was accommodating both geographies—the here and now and the hereafter. In other words, be decent here and you won't have to worry about the hereafter. I think it is easy to understand why the Christian poets opted for an imagined heaven or geography, some other place rather than the here and now. The "here and now" is horrible, and it is difficult to sell the idea of "heaven on earth" when people are being brutalized by both government officials and clergy. You have to tap into our ability to imagine.

When I read these passages I sense frustration, anger, and, except for a few statements attributed to Jesus, the helplessness of the here and now, but yet with a hope that the second coming is at hand. I think Jesus was attempting to teach self-responsibility—if you want things better, fix yourself, but love that enemy within because he has taught you what you do not like. This message will dawn on you, like the thief in the night, and steal your ignorance and trade it for illumination. Love those you can and have compassion for the rest, and then you and society begin to heal. You will begin to see and walk again in a straight path (zodiakos) to God's House. Following me and my teachings is all that is required. When you begin to see things the way they are, you will see heaven. It is right here—open your eyes! Seek and ye shall find, and where should you look? Look into your soul. Eat what you want, but be kind to your body, for although this is not about fleshy things, you need the body to transport your soul, your life's energy. But don't run afoul of the government; obey the laws and be a decent person. Spread the word. "Now, for you loyal followers, come over here, ask me questions, and we'll pass a joint or two around"—actually, they probably consumed cookies, bread, or even honey laced with cannabis. Interestingly, John the Baptist is also associated with honey (Matthew 3:4; Mark 1:6). Imagine this: Jesus has just arisen from the dead, and in Luke 24:37–43 we read:

But they were terrified and affrighted, and supposed that they had seen a spirit.

And he said to them, Why are ye troubled? and why do thoughts arise in your hearts?

Behold my hands and my feet, that it is I myself: handle me, and see; for a spirit hath not flesh and bones, as ye see me have.

And when he had thus spoken, he showed them [his] hands and [his] feet.

And while they yet believed not for joy, and wondered, he said to them, Have ye here anything for food?

And they gave him a piece of a broiled fish, and a honey-comb.

And he took [it], and ate before them.

This is a curious statement. A guy comes back from the dead, tells people not to be alarmed, displays his hands and feet, and then asks them, "What's for dinner?" And what do you suppose they have? I suspect the message here is that Jesus had a bad experience on mushrooms; he became very sick and people thought he was dead (this can occur with *Amanita muscaria*). Dead people on their way to heaven, and just passing through, do not need a box lunch. The fish stands for fertility (the penis of Osiris symbolized by the pope's or bishop's miter), and the honey or honeycomb represents the sun and illumination, or wisdom through the sacrament (cannabis, *Amanita muscaria*, henbane, etc.). *Amanita muscaria* is nasty tasting stuff, which honey tends to neutral-ize. Revelation 10:10 is instructive:

And the voice which I heard from heaven spoke to me again, and said, Go, [and] take the little book which is open in the hand of the angel which standeth upon the sea and upon the earth.

And I went to the angel, and said to him, Give me the little book. And he said to me, Take [it], and eat it, and it

244 | **Failed God**

shall make thy belly bitter, but it shall be in thy mouth sweet as honey.

And I took the little book out of the angel's hand, and ate it; and it was in my mouth sweet as honey: and as soon as I had eaten it my belly was bitter.

And he said to me, Thou must prophesy again before many peoples, and nations, and languages, and kings.

This, I believe, is the real Bible code—symbols connected to stories pointing to a spiritual experience with the energy that informs, and this experience comes by way of mind-altering substances, such as, in the above case, *Amanita muscaria*. The mushroom cap had been soaked in honey and it could, indeed, look like a book, scroll, or small loaf of bread. It would be sweet but "bitter" in the stomach—in other words it made him sick, a typical reaction after consumption of the mushroom and before the "spiritual connection" is established. This spiritual experience, a communing with God, was part of cult ritual for the priests but restricted from the masses. These ritual practices came back to public "consumption" through John the Baptist, but were then corrupted by Paul and his continuers.

There is another interesting episode in Acts 8:9–25. We have this magician or healer called Simon the Sorcerer who was probably a shamanic-type person, but he hadn't been initiated into the "real deal." After seeing Peter and John "place their hands" on the people of Samaria, Simon realizes that there was a secret that he could use on his own. Simon then attempts to buy "laying on of hands." "Laying on of hands" cannot simply mean touching someone, unless we are speaking metaphorically of being close to those in the know. In other words, because the original apostles were close to Jesus, the ability to heal was magically passed through them in a similar way to how Anu gave Adapa and other priests the concession on healing. It has become as simple as that for modern day evangelists, but the original meaning is more cryptic. It is more likely to mean to remove someone to some other place for some purpose (often punishment), and that purpose was initially to introduce them to the sacrament, the sacrificial lamb, *Amanita muscaria,* which can be a punishing experience. Conversations with God were not economically driven and Simon's offer to buy the secret was refused. This might be one method of separating the wheat from the chaff, or choosing between good converts and those committed to another agenda.

The Jesus Image

In order to have a hero story, there has to be visual imagery depicting his or her physical presence or characteristics. We certainly have one for Yahweh as drawn by Michelangelo, with gray beard, muscular Greek body, and a stern disposition. This is the image of Zeus. We have an image for Moses with a beard and long hair, usually with a staff and perhaps the Ten Commandments tucked under his arm. There is no representation for Muhammad because the image was already taken by Moses and they distanced themselves from that image, under penalty of death, by outlawing any image at all. The underlying message, however, is very subtle: there can be no image of someone who never existed. This was initially a way of poking fun at the Christians and Jews.

Mickey, Donald, and Goofy in *Mickey and the Beanstalk* are depicted in the peasant garb of medieval times. Our cultural hero Daniel Boone is dressed (as are others of his period) with buckskin clothes and a coonskin cap. For Jesus there are several themes, mainly concerned with facial characteristics and magical hair. He is portrayed as Semitic at one point on the scale, European (with blue eyes and golden brown hair!) at another point, and African at still another. There are also images that show him as almost effeminate, while others more rugged. One thing that seems to have remained the same is his long hair depicted as brown, golden brown, or black. Pauline Christology attempted to represent Jesus with short hair, and by example males should wear their hair short (the Greek and Roman style) while women should wear their hair long. "Doth not even nature itself teach you, that if a man hath long hair, it is a shame to him? But if a woman hath long hair, it is a glory to her: for [her] hair is given her for a covering." (1 Corinthians

11:14–15) This is one of many of Paul's misogynistic statements, which suggests two things. Either he thinks he is giving women a compliment for living in a man's world, or he really had a great deal of rage for women along with confusion about his own sexual identity. His writings point in both directions. In other words, Paul was on the extreme end of things. I would, in part, diagnose him with a Narcissistic Personality Disorder (Axis II: 301.81).

Paul's suggestion about the length of hair for Jesus seems to have been ignored by the early Christian continuers, and there is perhaps good reason for this. Jesus or Christ is the Sun God. He has his twelve apostles and his birthday is on the winter solstice (December 25), which means the rebirth of the sun, three days after it stands still— December 22. Worship is on Sunday (not Saturday as in Judaism and Seventh Day Adventists), and he is depicted with a sun halo, which is the sun disk or Aten (Adon in Hebrew) of Akhenaten, the heretic pharaoh. Then there is the hair. The hair likewise connects Jesus to Samson who, although not a god, was a sun-hero brought up as a *Nazarene* or member of a Jewish sect. They take vows to not drink wine, cut their hair, and avoid "corpse uncleanness" for a specified amount of time (usually thirty days). After completing the vow, the person brings offerings of wine, bread, meat, and oil to bribe or influence the deity to confer good health or whatever, the head is shaved, and the hair burnt in a fire. Symbolically you are assigning your power, your being, to God; you are a slave. Jesus was also called the Nazarene; he is always depicted with long hair. Samson (Judges 13–16), as you will recall, had incredible strength due to his long hair. Head hair represents spiritual energy, which emanates from the top of the head. Hair can be corrupting, especially when crawling with lice, and the only way to rid yourself was shave your head. You don't see many long-haired Egyptians unless they are wearing wigs. Samson, like Jesus, was also sacrificed (self-sacrificed) as a means of bringing order to the world through destruction, with Samson destroying the pagan temple and the rulers seated within, and Jesus "destroying" the temple by turning over the moneylender's tables, but also playing a part in the destruction of the world and the evil within at the end of days.

But there may be another reason for Paul's desire for men to have short hair, and that would be to separate them from women. Apparently Paul was a grotesque little man, terrified of women (perhaps because of their rejection of him) and a guilt-ridden homosexual. Bennett and McQueen (2001: Part 2, 175) comment:

> That an individual, such as Paul, could be capable of the
> extreme mental-gymnastics necessary to condemn others for
> an act that he himself is guilty of, is exemplified by the
> actions of the modern Roman Catholic priesthood, members
> of whom have been again and again exposed for the same
> homosexuality which they have so hypocritically preached
> against.

As discussed in Chapter One, many Catholic priests and clerics in Protestant sects use sex as a means of touching the divine, that is, ritual sex for the purpose of using sexual energies for spiritual purposes. Most researchers when discussing the subject of homosexuality miss this very important feature. This does not excuse predatory sexual behavior or the hypocrisy surrounding it. Ritual homosexual sex (and occasionally heterosexual behavior of Catholic priests) is a time-honored tradition going back to the mother-goddess cults and most certainly thousands of years before that. Ritual sex is not simply recent decadent behavior on the part of a few priests and other religious clerics. Again, this is a time-honored practice. The Old Testament bans homosexuality (see Leviticus 18:22; 20:13–14) because it is an "impure" act, but using sex for spiritual purposes is conceptualized or rationalized as a means to an end.

Christians, representing numerous sects or cults, certainly existed prior to 50 CE, but the reference to Christ reaches much deeper into the past. The idea of a messiah (or Christ in Greek), "the anointed one," came out of the Jewish tradition, but its origins appear to be Egyptian. There are several references in the Old Testament to a savior who would come along and liberate the Jews from political oppression and institute a new heaven and earth. The Jews were looking for someone like Muhammad because they knew this liberation would not be peaceful. Instead, they were treated to a man from the wilderness, John the Baptist, preaching apocalypse now. The different cults that assembled from this (Jesus, Christian, Gnostic) were usually at odds with one another over interpretations of their beliefs and rituals. For example, some Jesus and/or Gnostic sects shunned the world altogether, while others maintained much of the mother-goddess rituals of the Canaanites, such as ritual sex (hetero-and homosexual), use of cannabis and other drugs, and so on, but wrapped in a monotheistic and patriarchal framework rather than a mother-goddess one. Then there were those who broke all the Commandments lest they become slaves to a demon (sentiments that were more ideal than real). Some have conjectured that this is where modern day Satanists trace their lineage. This is a defiance of celestial authority, and not necessarily secular authority.

In any case, the "Anointed One," as discussed in Chapter Two, is an ancient reference to the anointing of pharaoh with liquefied crocodile fat (*MeSSeh*) possibly mixed with herbs (transdermal) that would be absorbed through the skin. This anointing was a communion with the sun god Re and the energy that informs all. Some have this experience when they meditate; some have this experience when they pray. Some can get there through pain, and for some sex is the avenue of choice. And then there are mind-altering substances that are a little more predictable in their effects. All the above avenues are used to touch the spiritual plane, but the most dramatic, controllable, and reliable are the drugs, an issue inexcusably neglected by many modern scholars.

Going back to the Essenes or followers of Esau, they would have had knowledge of Zoroastrianism, a tradition dating back at least to 600 BCE, and perhaps as far back as 800 BCE, and they borrowed many of their ideas. Zoroastrianism evolved out of Hinduism in the unstable political landscape a few hundred miles to the west of India, that is, Persia or modern day Iran. Several centuries later, Christians, as well as the Mohammedans of the sixth and seventh century CE, borrowed from both the Zoroastrians and Essenes. The ideas connected to Zoroastrianism were most probably encountered in Babylon where Nebuchadnezzar II in 586 B.C.E exiled the Israelites.

Zoroastrianism

Zoroastrianism can be seen as the first ethical religion. Hinduism, out of which this tradition emerged, is not particularly interested in right or wrong, or good against evil. In Hinduism the emphasis is on ignorance (*avidya*) and illumination (*moksha* or release). With Zoroastrianism we encounter a religion that not only pits good against evil but also has elimination of evil as an ultimate goal. The ancient Egyptians saw that good must always combat evil, but there was never an emphasis on eliminating evil as symbolized by *Apepi* or *Apophis* at the primordial level and *Seth* on the social. Why is this?

Well, if you remove all evil there is no reference point for good. Many years ago I was invited to speak to a Chaplin's parishioners at a military base in the Midwest. When I came to the part about good and evil, and said that the elimination of evil would remove a reference point for good, I thought I was going to get lynched! Many Christians hold the idea that evil is something that resides outside the individual and that one day evil will be vanquished. Jesus had a different message, the "good news"—evil resides in each of us and it is the individual's responsibility to clean up his or her "evil" before suggesting that others do likewise. Jesus would never suggest, imply, or desire dying for your sins, as the world has been informed. On the contrary, "Die to your own sins, for salvation is a personal thing not bestowed by others." We read in Matthew 7:1–5:

> Judge not, that ye be not judged.
>
> For with what judgment ye judge, ye shall be judged: and the measure which ye give, shall be measured to you again.
>
> And why beholdest thou the mote that is in thy brother's eye, but considerest not the beam that is in thy own eye?

Or how wilt thou say to thy brother, Let me pull out the mote out of thy eye; and behold, a beam [is] in thy own eye?

Thou hypocrite, first cast out the beam out of thy own eye; and then shalt thou see clearly to cast out the mote out of thy brother's eye.

Zoroastrianism differed from the Hindu tradition in other important ways. In Hinduism, *Tat tvam asi* means "You are it" or "You are God," you *are* the energy that informs all. In Zoroastrianism, on the other hand, you and God are two entirely different things, sort of an amalgam of Hinduism and the gods of ancient Greece. Except for the magi, you never join with the god; you are always subservient or the subject of the deity, just as you are subservient to the king and are his subject. The endless round of death and reincarnation, as found in Hinduism, is replaced with a more linear philosophy in Zoroastrianism that says that you are born, live, and then die. You get one shot at this life and after death you go to another geographical place, hell or heaven, depending on how you behaved during life. We also find in this tradition personal responsibility for behavior, which gets lost when these beliefs are borrowed into Judaism, Christianity, and Islam. This concept of personal responsibility, which is conjoined with individualism, probably came into Persia with the Indo-Europeans, who stormed into this area sometime after they came into the Indus Valley (modern day Pakistan). Individualism is not part of the Hindu philosophy; there is no word for individual in ancient Sanskrit.

Zoroastrianism, like Judaism and Islam, is a mirror of king and subjects. The king and community are subservient to the deity, the community members are subservient to the King (who interprets the will of the deity), and women are subservient to men (specifically, the husband). What social and/or environmental stress factors pushed such a tradition into existence? There are many reasons, but the major one is that India and the Hindu tradition did not have to contend with an invasion by foreign people with foreign beliefs and practices, as did the countries to the west. What we call Persia (Iran today) is open to invasion by both traders and, more importantly, nomadic people who force their traditions on others. This area of the world has experienced some sort of invasion or political disruption, on a continual basis, for approximately 4,500 years. This is still happening today.

What Zoroastrianism is saying is this: Bad things happen because people make bad things happen, and if you do bad things you will be judged in the hereafter. This is psychological protection which allows us to believe that bad people—bad rulers, politicians, neighbors, relatives, administrators or school board members, all "evil doers"—will one day get their comeuppance. There is evidence of torturing, dismembering, and raping of innocent subjects at the whim of rulers throughout this area of the world (and it continues today). Emotional survival in such an environment takes an act of imagination. This is also one of the first, if not the first religion to suggest that nature is corrupt, and is probably the origin of some of the angels and devils encountered in Judaism and Christianity.

Zoroastrianism was the religion of all of Persia (ancient Iran) before the unprovoked and forceful conversion to Mohammedanism or Islam, the religion of peace, during the late seventh, early eighth century (CE). Zoroaster, which is the Greek form of Zarathustra, founded it sometime after 1000 BCE. Nigosian (1993) gives a date of between the seventh and sixth centuries BCE. Scholars are not quite sure of the dates because many of the scriptures—the Avesta—were destroyed by the thug Alexander the Great in the fourth century BCE, with further losses occurring during the barbaric Mohammedan book burning of the seventh century CE. What remains of the present scriptures consists of five parts: the Yasna, which includes the Gathas (hymns) supposedly constructed by Zoroaster; the Vispered, an additional ritual; the Yashta, or hymns to angels and lesser divinities; the Vendidad, which is an account of the creation along with homiletic (preaching) material; and the Khorda Avesta, or a collection of short prayers used by the worshippers and priests.

The creation myth goes as follows: In the beginning there were two powerful deities or creative spirits, one good and one evil. This is similar to the Egyptian myths of Horus and Seth, and in another sense Jacob wrestling with God and Isaac against Esau. Aura Mazda (also called Ormazd) or the good spirit is in conflict with his twin, Angra Mainyu (Ahriman) who represents darkness, filth, death, and evil, all the corrupt parts of nature. Angra Mainyu translates as "evil-destructive." Around Ahura Mazda are immortal holy ones who act as aids; I will come back to one of his aids in a moment. They embody ethical ideas, that is, good, truth, perfection, immortality, and so on. Angra Mainyu also has his entourage who act as evil helpers.

The history of the world is the struggle between good and evil. Currently both good and evil are in a balanced state, but eventually Ahura Mazda will triumph, Angra Mainyu will be destroyed and thrown into a deep abyss, and all will transform into the good. Sound familiar? However, each person will be judged at the end of his or her life and have to pass over an accountant's bridge. If the individual has a balance of good over evil, he or she can cross the bridge into paradise. If the evil outweighs the good, then he loses his footing and falls into hell. If there is an exact balance of good and evil, he goes to some intermediate stage of existence (Limbo?) and awaits the final judgment.

In this belief system, man is central to this drama. That is to say, by his choices through free will he can render service to Ahura Mazda by doing good deeds. This idea of free will is very interesting because free will is not a central issue in Hinduism; there are too many rules to follow. The message is that, rather than evil behavior being attributed to a deity, you have the choice to do good or evil. This was the message to the ruler(s) and all other evildoers; do good and be rewarded in heaven while all evil deeds will be rewarded in hell.

Man, however, is blind and ignorant, and so Ahura Mazda's victory over Angra Mainyu has been delayed (a "second coming?"). Because of this, Ahura Mazda sent a prophet by the name of Zoroaster to deliver mankind. Zoroaster stated that he was in direct contact with Ahura Mazda, had visions, and so on. Zoroaster was tempted by Angra Mainyu. Remember that both Jesus and Buddha were tempted as well.

I mentioned earlier that Ahura Mazda has a number of immortal holy ones who aid him in his mission to destroy evil. His chief helper is Mithras. Between 1400 BCE and 400 CE, the Indians/Hindus, Persians, Greeks, and then Romans worshipped the god Mithras. Mithras may have originally been the Hindu sun god Mitra mentioned in the *Rig Veda*, the primary sacred texts of Hinduism dating to approximately 1500 BCE. During the Roman period, however, this worship of Mithras became a mystery religion and was mainly applied by the soldiers and imperial officials of Rome. In Mithraism, Mithras (or Mithra) slays the bull. According to Carl Jung, this is "self-sacrifice" in that Mithras is symbolic of the bull. The bull sacrifice is a symbolic release of the animal's energy (life's energy) into the world through death—out of death comes new life or renewal, which is the same symbolism involved in the crucifixion of Jesus and the death and resurrection of Osiris.

The Mithraic tradition also included baptism and the use of bread, water, and wine consecrated by priests (called fathers). The priests also used haoma (soma in the Hindu tradition), a mind-altering substance that was probably *Amanita muscaria* (although there are other possibilities, including combinations of substances), in their religious rites. Some nineteenth century authors suggest that if Christianity has faltered, we would probably be worshiping Mithras instead of Jesus.

Getting back to Zoroastrianism, we can find many parallels with Judaism and the later Christian cults. One of the legends surrounding Zoroaster (Greek rendering) or Zarathustra is that his birth is foretold. Sound familiar? His mother was only fifteen years of age (a virgin or young girl) at the time, and conceived Zoroaster (Zarathustra) after coming into contact with the sacred haoma plant (a plant-god impregnating a virgin). In Hinduism and Zoroastrianism soma (or haoma) is also a god, and this is more than likely the same plant-god Moses encountered "that would not burn." As soon as Zarathustra was born, he could converse with the good god, Ahura Mazda. At age thirty he had his first visions of the deity, after which he began to teach the Good Religion; this is the same age associated with the ministry of Jesus. The myth also states Zarathustra was beheaded while praying (a sacrifice like John the Baptist/Jesus?). After his death the magi, or the priests of the religion, modified his doctrines. According to Christian tradition, three of these magi, the three wise men, visited Christ as mentioned earlier, but some scholars think that this reference was to symbolize all races recognizing Christ rather than just Persia or Zoroastrianism.

Wouldn't it be nice if there were a gentle god who sent his son as a sacrifice in order to rid the world of sin and hate, war and strife? Wouldn't it be nice if we could just sacrifice someone or some helpless animal (like a lamb), please a deity, and all would turn to peace and harmony? Yes, it would. But there has been no peace. The problem with this sentiment is that the gentle god and sacrifice of his son is considered historical fact and that peace in the world comes from *outside* one's self; it is up to someone else to bring peace. If you are waiting for peace to come you will be waiting for a long, long time. Peace has to come through self-responsibility, which is not part of the Middle Eastern mind-set and takes second place to following orders from others, including deities. The common statement "Christ died for your sins" is a clear representation of this irresponsible sentiment. Your sins are *your* responsibility; this was a central message of Jesus. Reducing hate, war, poverty, and so on, is the responsibility of all, but it begins with *you*—"love thy enemy as thyself." If you were alive in the 60s, this should have a familiar ring to it.

In Judaism, Christianity, and Islam, God comes first and humanity last. God is all-knowing and all-powerful and in this condition is responsible for all good and evil in the world. This represents a contradiction, for if God is all knowing, then he knows that people will break His laws. But, when God comes first then all behavior (good and bad) can be blamed on Him—"God's will" or "the Devil made me do it." This mind-set does not seem to be the original intent of Jesus the Nazarene (or John the Baptist).

The Sacred Myth and the Secular

Separating sacred from secular history helps us to understand that the Bible is poetry. Like any historical novel, there can be names of real places and people but one interjects fictional characters and fictional places simply to fit the prevailing storyline. No reasonable, intelligent person can accept the Bible as the divine word of a deity, the God of Abraham. If this were the revealed word, then it would necessarily have to be perfect in every way, like a song with every note in harmony with the rest—the moon, the stars, the sun in the sky. Scientific and geographical mistakes, along with encounters with a supernatural being who has a special people, and so on, have brought the historical value into doubt. As any good novel is a reflection of the poet's world, so the Bible is a reflection of the life and troubled times between 600 BCE through 400 CE. Let's look at some errors in the New Testament.

In Matthew 4:8 we encounter one of Jesus' temptations, "Again, the devil took him [Jesus] up into a very high mountain, and showed him all the kingdoms of the world and their splendor." It would be impossible to see *all* the kingdoms of the world from the top of the tallest mountain unless the world was flat. Perhaps the devil, for this one temptation at least, flattened the world or, using mirrors, allowed Jesus to see the world in total, but there is no reference to such magical feats. The poets may have believed the world was flat, but I think this is simply the poetic metaphor making a point. "I will make you ruler over all you see," and, indeed, you would be able to see a long, long way. If this is the case, then truth is metaphoric and not historic.

In the King James Bible we read (John 1:28): "These things were done in Bethabara beyond the Jordan, where John was baptizing." The place called Bethabara, according to scholars, is a fabrication, as no such place exists. In the NIV (New International Version) the word Bethabara was changed to Bethany, which was a suburb of Jerusalem and not beyond the Jordan River.

In John 3:23, "Now John also was baptizing at Aenon near Salim, because there was plenty of water, and people were constantly coming to be baptized." There was no such place called Aenon near Salim until invented by the priest-poets.

Jesus, according to the account in the New Testament, was conceived in Nazareth, but Nazareth was not a place until created in the third or fourth century CE. Acharya S. (1999, 190–191) comments:

> The town of Nazareth did not appear on Earth until after the
> gospel tale was known . . . there is no such place as Nazareth
> in the Old Testament or in Josephus' works, or on early
> maps of the Holy Land. In fact, the town now designated as
> Nazareth is near Mt. Carmel, indicating it was the
> Carmelites who created it. Jesus, therefore, was not from
> Nazareth, which did not exist at the time of his purported
> advent. The real purpose for putting him there was to make
> him a Nazarene or Nazarite, as he was the same as the most
> famous Nazarite, Samson, a solar myth.

"Nazareth" refers to a sect. So Jesus of Nazareth, once again, is a confusion of the biblical poets.

To continue, his pregnant mother Mary, travels with Joseph to
Jerusalem for the Roman census, and Jesus is then born in Bethlehem,
several miles south of Jerusalem. Now in order to be the messiah, according the Old Testament, he must come from the lineage of King David.
If Jesus is the product of a deity seducing a human (Zeus, as you will
recall, did this on a regular basis), then Jesus cannot be of the House of
David. Joseph, however, is, according to the biblical poets, of the House
of David. Herod, the wicked king in those parts, hears that a divine
king has arrived and so goes about murdering all the male children in
them there parts (this is a replay of the Moses story). Joseph, Mary,
and baby Jesus escape to Egypt after Joseph hears what Herod is planning. So we have Jesus in Egypt. Herod dies when Jesus was around
three or so, the family moves back to "Nazareth," a non-place, where
Jesus spends most of his formative years. Here is an interesting point.
The demarcation between the old and new, that is B.C. and AD or the
beginning of the Christian era, appears to have happened when Jesus
left Egypt at age three. This may simply be some celestial recalculation
of the age of Jesus after the AD or anno domini, meaning "year of our
lord," was instituted. This dating reference was not implemented until

many centuries after his alleged death and was done to dramatically indicate a beginning of one phase of history and the end of another, which, by the way, was copied by the Muslims—the Islamic tradition begins with the *hijri* year or Muhammad's migration to Medina in 622 AD, and is represented as 1 A.H., which would be Friday, July 16, 622 in the Julian calendar (September 9, 622 in the Islamic calendar).

So, in the Islamic tradition, we have a replay of the biblical scholars who recalculated the myth, with Jesus born 3 BCE, but 1 AD representing the time frame or beginning *after* he left Egypt at age three. Again, this suggests the rebirth of King Tut, coming, as Jesus does, out of Egypt (see astrological data below). The importance here is that it may be a clue as to who Jesus represents, and this, again, just may be King Tutankhamun. Back to Nazareth.

According to the story, the Jewish community in "Nazareth" and the Galilee area was not strictly monotheistic in that it was near a major trade route from east to west and north to south, and could not afford to offend trading partners by being overly bound to a specific version of the supernatural world. Our mythic hero Jesus (and the poets who devised this tale), would then have been exposed to numerous ideas about the supernatural world coming from Hinduism, Buddhism, Zoroastrianism, the mother-goddess cults, and so on. The person who originally composed the storyline for Jesus, which then morphed into the Gnostic texts and Gospels we have today, was not an ignorant peasant. It was perhaps written by someone referred to as Mark (perhaps John Mark, a friend of Paul's). What is interesting is that John Mark and Paul had a falling out, probably for the same reason that Paul had a falling out with Peter—Jesus had not yet arrived but was on his way. The original Gospel of Mark, a remake of the Gospel of Q (see Powelson and Riegert 1996; Mack 1995) probably no longer exists. What we have today is a second, third, or fourth generation of Mark (pages wear out and are recopied), and then variations evolving in other geographies. As the scholars suggest, the Gospel of Q was similar in many way to the Thomas Gospel. What Mark did was add a storyline about who Jesus was and from whence he came, but maintained the Buddhist touch with

Jesus, as guru, responding to questions. Whoever wrote the original Mark would have known about mind-altering substances for communing with God or gods.

Jesus, as you will recall, is supposedly a very intelligent and inquisitive kid. When he was age twelve he traveled to Jerusalem to celebrate Passover, and took an interest in the teachers in the Temple; they were equally impressed by his questions and answers. So here we have Jesus drawing attention to himself through his wisdom. In other words, this is no ordinary person. He returned to Nazareth (remember that this is a non-place—it is a magical place, just like Happy Valley). The next time we hear of him is when he is baptized by John the Baptist; he just comes out of the desert. Eventually he went back to Jerusalem and tried to sell his ideas to a very conservative, monotheistic crowd, but because of his healing miracles he gathers a crowd from diverse segments of the population. His main followers were the commoners, those down and out. Tent evangelists these days do the exact same thing but with more glitter.

Jesus eventually goes on trial before Pontius Pilate and suggests (although this is not explicitly stated) that he is God. "Are you God?" Pilate questions. Jesus replies, "If you say so." The meaning here is subtle, that is, "I am only God if people recognize me or accept me as God." Obviously Pontius accepted Jesus as God, because his remark was a challenge to the political powers that be and Jesus had to go. Of course this is myth, and, just like in dreams, things don't have to be reasonable or logical, and this accounts for most of the errors in the Bible. Drugs can do strange things to people.

So here we have our hero Jesus, who has done magical healings and who promises peace and salvation in "heaven," if all will only follow him. Jesus suggests that he is the son of God and this is a statement of sedition in that time and place. In any case, as the story goes, he was either hung on a cross after much abuse or hung on a tree (Jewish law favored trees, and the Romans, the cross). The location of his crucifixion is Golgotha (the place of the skulls) or Calvary, a place that cannot be found in history (see Acharya S. 1999, 206–207).

He dies on the cross, is put in a tomb—the Holy Sepulcher—and comes back or arises from the dead in about a day and a half (not three days as prophesied). Three represents completion, while one and one-half represents one-half of the godhead. The three-day period, however, may have more to do with an astrological awareness. That is, the sun appears to stand still on December 22 (the shortest day of the year), but by December 25 the sun appears to "arise from the dead" (the days lengthens). Jesus also leaves Egypt when he is age three years. I will have more to say about astronomy, astrology, and religion in a future publication.

But one and one-half days as a time period between the death of Jesus and his resurrection may also represent that his job is only half-done: "I'll be back" or the "Second Coming" (see how easy it is to slap a layer on the mythic cake?). Thus, Jesus did not fulfill his own prophecy of "I'll be back in three days."

Shortly after saying goodbye to a few close friends, he ascends to heaven—skin, sperm, hair, bones, and all. Pope Pius, who like all popes is infallible in every way, declared in 1951 that "the Immaculate Mother of God, the ever Virgin Mary, when the course of her earthly life was run, was assumed in body and soul to heavenly glory." Amen. This is another example of how myth becomes layered over time. There are no relics of Mother Mary, and if we cannot find Jesus in history how can we possibly find his mother? If Jesus never existed, can he still have a mother or grandmother (St. Anna)? The geographical errors are clearly not mistakes but part of a poetic storyline full of magical places and people, and this is how the other "errors" should be read as well.

The religious clerics, the priests who could read and write, understood the power they had to literally create history ("So it is written, so it shall be"), and if the tale comes with authority (God's law, in the name of God, the will of Allah) then those in power can use that authority as they see fit. To the average person writing was magical; what was written could come alive, and if a priest or pharaoh said, "So it is written, so it shall be," it was.

Crucifixion and Atonement of Sin:
The Buddhist Touch

New, pristine storylines are difficult to find in our vast storytelling factories—the publishing and movie industries. It is difficult to find anything substantially new. In other words, there is a core cluster of symbols around which are assembled a matrix or storyline. Traveling from generation to generation, layers are added (or removed) so as to fit specific cultural needs. We find the core themes of life/death, good/bad, gods/demons, male/female, young/old, vegetable/animal, land/water/air, above/below, night/day, the four points of the compass, us/them, known/unknown, and so on, but this is not endless. There are simply variations of a limited number of themes, usually polarities. Dying on a cross or being sacrificed for the good of others is a common mythic theme (see Graves 1971). The story of Krishna (800 BCE), for example, contains many similarities to Jesus, especially the atoning part, where he is considered the Son of God, dies for your sins, casts out devils, cures lepers, the deaf, and the blind (all symbolic of healing society), and is crucified on a cross, with holes pierced in his feet. Many sayings are attributed to him which can also be found in the New Testament, such as, "Only the humble are beloved of God," "when the poor man knocks at your door, take him and administer to his wants, for the poor are the chosen of God," "look not upon a woman with unchaste desires," "above all things, cultivate love for your neighbor," and "do good for its own sake, and expect not your reward for it on earth." There are around fifty sayings attributed to Krishna that can likewise be found in the Bible. Krishna was crucified because he tried to purify the older religious tradition; Jesus attempted to do the same thing.

Then there is Sakia (600 BCE), also of the Hindu tradition, crucified for picking a flower in a garden. One of the accusations brought up against Jesus is that he broke the Jewish law by picking grain on the Sabbath. In some renditions of the story, Sakia was pinned to a tree with an arrow, which becomes a cross when looked at from the side.

Thammuz of Syria (1160 BCE) was crucified, another sin-atoning offering.

Hesus (Jesus?), a Celtic druid, 434 BCE was crucified with a lamb on one side and an elephant on the other, with the lamb symbolizing the innocence of the person and the elephant representing the magnitude of his crime. This was a sin-atoning event.

Atys of Phrygia, 1170 BCE, "was suspended from a tree, crucified, buried, and rose again."

Osiris, in the Egyptian tradition, is sacrificed, which reestablishes order in the world. His son Horus is born of a virgin (Isis was impregnated by Osiris after he was murdered) on December 25, just as Osiris' birthday is December 25, and it is Horus (the God of Light or the Holy Ghost) who is also the son of the Sun God Re (Osiris is the midnight sun and thus also Re) and identified with the pharaoh, a god on earth. Osiris is a generating god, whose disintegrating juices from his penis (that part of his body that was swallowed by a fish—see Rush 2007) fructify the land, and, as the Judge of the Dead in the Underworld, he becomes the counterpart of Re during his night journey through the Gates of the Underworld.

Then there are Aztec deities standing around a fire waiting for something to happen, for life to begin, when finally, out of frustration, one of the gods jumps into the fire, and the sun arises on the eastern horizon. That is a start. Finally, looking at each other in a moment of understanding, they all jump into the fire, things begin to move, and time and life commence. Thus, dying and placing one's energy into the world is a common mythic theme that certainly does not begin with the crucifixion of Jesus and is certainly not a local, unique event.

Virgin Birth

Is virgin birth a common theme? Yes. In the Egyptian tradition, Horus is born from Isis, who is magically impregnated by Osiris after his death at the hands of his evil brother, Seth. Buddha, like Jesus, was said to be born from his mother's side at the level of the heart, representing a spiritual/virgin birth. A dragon impregnated King Arthur's mother. Among the Navaho of the southwest United States, Sun and his counterpart Moon impregnate Changing Woman, the mother of the boys who go in search of their father. As mentioned earlier, Zoroaster, founder of the Zoroastrian tradition, was conceived of a virgin who came in contact with the sacred haoma plant, a plant-god. In ancient Greece the declaration of virgin birth, or impregnation by a god, was so common that a law was passed, under penalty of death, forbidding women to make such claims!

As My Grand Pappy Used to Say . . .

We are storytellers, and these stories not only entertain but also explain and create structure. Our stories seem to swing around truths or ideas that are universal, but that are expressed or structured in different ways. The Buddhists, for example, understand that we are all gods, and present a philosophy for acting in a god-like fashion. This is called the Four Noble Truths and the Buddha-dharma, and it goes like this:

1) All life is sorrowful (duhkah)
2) The causes of this sorrow and unhappiness are fear and desire
3) Your fear and desire can be overcome by
4) Following the Yellow Brick Road (Buddha Dharma), or the Eight Fold Path (ashtangika-marga), and you gradually cast away your fears and desires (your demons). These paths (remember Jesus said, "I am the way," zodiakos or path) are:

- Path of perfect view: Obtained by focusing on the Four Noble Truths (above) as an absolute truth around which is wrapped the eight-fold path.
- Perfect resolve: Harm to no one and good will to all.
- Perfect speech: No lying, and no judgments of others (gossiping) or slander of others (no negative incantations).
- Perfect conduct: Stay on task, do what you are supposed to do,

don't get tempted or sidetracked, and do unto others, as you would have them do to you.

- Perfect livelihood: Do not engage in activities that harm others (drug dealing, gun running, selling people celestial lies, strapping on bombs and killing others, etc.).
- Perfect effort: Avoid bad karma and do what is decent.
- Perfect mindfulness: Be aware of yourself and your surroundings.
- Perfect concentration (dhyana): Meditation or inward journey of absorption. There are numerous training exercises (such as yoga), but all have as a final goal the understanding that all is illusion and all is impermanent, thus eliminating fear, desire, and therefore ego.

Read the above again carefully and you will see the major ideas of Jesus/John the Baptist shining through. So let's take this a step further.

I mentioned earlier statements assigned to Krishna that are identical to those found in the New Testament. Let's take an in-depth look at these Hindu and Buddhist precepts. As Graves states (1971, 111–115; see also Borg 2004):

And many of the precepts uttered by Chrishna (or Krishna) display a profound wisdom and depth of thought equal to any of those attributed to Jesus Christ. In proof of the statement, we will cite a few examples out of the hundreds in our possession:

1) Those who do not control their passions cannot act properly toward others.
2) The evils we inflict upon others follow us as our shadows follow our bodies.
3) Only the humble are beloved of God.
4) Virtue sustains the soul as the muscles sustain the body.
5) When the poor man knocks at your door, take him and

administer to his wants, for the poor are the chosen of
God.

6) Let your hand be open to the unfortunate.

7) Look not upon a woman with unchaste desire.

8) Avoid envy, covetousness, falsehood, imposture and
slander, and sexual desires.

9) Above all things, cultivate love for your neighbor.

10) When you die you leave your worldly wealth behind
you, but your virtue and vice follow you.

11) Condemn riches and worldly honor.

12) Seek the company of the wicked in order to reform
them.

13) Do good for its own sake, and expect not your reward
for it on earth.

14) The soul is immortal, but must be pure and free from
all sin and stain before it can return to Him who gave
it.

15) The soul is inclined to good when it follows the inward
path.

16) The soul is responsible to God for its actions; God
establishes rewards and punishments.

17) Cultivate that inward knowledge which teaches what is
right and wrong.

18) Never take delight in another's misfortunes.

19) It is better to forgive an injury than to avenge it.

20) You can accomplish by kindness what you cannot by
force.

21) A noble spirit finds a cure for injustice by forgetting it.

22) Pardon the offense of others, but not your own.

23) What you blame in others do not practice yourself.

24) By forgiving an enemy you make many friends.

25) Do right from hatred of evil, and not fear of punishment.

26) A wise man corrects his errors by observing those of

others.

27) He who rules his temper conquers his greatest enemy.

28) The wise man governs his passions, but the fool obeys them.

29) Be at war with men's vices, but at peace with their persons.

30) There should be no disagreement between your lives and your doctrines.

31) Spend every day as though it were the last.

32) Lead not one life in public and another in private.

33) Anger in trying to torture others punishes itself.

34) A disgraceful death is honorable when you die in a good cause.

35) By growing familiar with vices, we learn to tolerate them easily.

36) We must master our evil propensities, or they will master us.

37) He who has conquered his propensities rules over a kingdom.

38) Protect, love, and assist others, if you would serve God.

39) From thought springs the will, and from the will action, true or false, just or unjust.

40) As the sandal tree perfumes the axe which fells it, so the good man sheds fragrance on his enemies.

41) Spend a portion of each day in pious devotion.

42) To love the virtues of others is to brighten your own.

43) He who gives to the needy loses nothing himself.

44) A good, wise, and benevolent man cannot be rich.

45) Much riches is a curse to the possessor.

46) The wounds of the soul are more important than those of the body.

47) The virtuous man is like a banyan tree, which shelters and protects all around it.

48) Money does not satisfy the love of gain, but only stim-

ulates it.

49) Your greatest enemy is in your own bosom.

50) The wounds of conscience leave a scar.

Graves (1971, 114) goes on to give quotes from the Hindu Vedas (1500 BCE):

1) He who is cursed by woman is cursed by God.

2) God will punish him who laughs at woman's sufferings.

3) When woman is honored, God is honored.

4) The virtuous woman will have but one husband, and the right-minded man but one wife.

5) It is the highest crime to take advantages of the weakness of woman.

6) Woman should be loved, respected, and protected by husbands, fathers, and brothers, etc.

Some scholars conclude that these philosophical quips are Greek (Cynic) in origin, but in my opinion these are fairly universal as they speak to our individual, small-group nature.

Briefly, comparisons with the above can be found in the Gospels (including Thomas). In Matthew 5, for example, we encounter some of the Hindu/Buddhist sentiments listed above. For example (Matthew 5:3–10—Sermon on the Mount):

Blessed are the poor in spirit,
for theirs is the kingdom of heaven.
Blessed are those who mourn,
for they will be comforted.
Blessed are the meek,
for they will inherit the earth.
Blessed are those who hunger and thirst
for righteousness, for they will be filled.
Blessed are the merciful,

for they will be shown mercy.
Blessed are the peacemakers,
for they will be called sons of God.
Blessed are those who are persecuted
because of righteousness,
for theirs is the kingdom of heaven.

Matthew 5:28, "But I tell you that anyone who looks at a woman lustfully has already committed adultery with her in his heart."

Matthew 5:33, "Do not break your oath."

Matthew 5:43, "Love thy neighbor. . . . Love your enemies."

Matthew 6:1, "Be careful not to do your 'acts of righteousness' before men, to be seen by them. If you do, you will have no reward from your father in heaven."

Matthew 6:5, "And when you pray, do not be like the hypocrites, for they love to pray standing in the synagogues and on the street corners to be seen by men. . . . But when you pray, go into your room. . . ."

Matthew 6:14, "For if you forgive men when they sin against you, your heavenly Father will also forgive you."

Matthew 7:1, 3, "Do not judge, or you too will be judged. . . . Why do you look at the speck of sawdust in your brother's eye and pay no attention to the plank in your own eye?"

I could go on and on, but the message we encounter is that many of the parables of Jesus found in the gospels of the New Testament and the Gnostic texts belong to more ancient traditions and predate the Gospels by over 1,200 years. Numerous parables and sayings of the Gnostic texts are found in Matthew, Mark, Luke, John, the Old Testament, the Talmud, and so on, but in the Bible gospels are usually connected to a wider story. And this is important to understand; you cannot sell the teachings of a cult leader without, at the same time, attaching a life history and personality.

We have no storyline for Jesus from age twelve to around ages twenty-eight to thirty; he and John the Baptist just come out of the wilderness. So what are the possibilities? Put yourself in the Baptist's place: 1) he defects from the Essenes; 2) this defection possibly happened after one of his wilderness trips, which may have been part of the secret rites of the Essenes; 3) he has a revelation that the essence of spiritual life has little to do with strict rules and regulations—this does not create a spiritual person; 4) he realizes that economics and politics interfere with the individual's spiritual quest and thus strips them away; 5) he understands the basic message for cooperative social living, "love thy neighbor," "don't judge," and so on; 6) through comparison he sees that these are central messages to many traditions, but also realizes that the Buddhist delivery system (you don't tell anyone anything until they ask a question) was the proper method for delivering the "good news." He could have obtained this comparative information talking with travelers on the Silk Road, he could have joined a caravan and journeyed to India (it really isn't that far away), or perhaps he hung around a lot of Cynics.

But there is another side to Jesus that is little talked about. There are many portions of the Gnostic texts found at Nag Hammadi that are just a step too far out to act as parables; their meanings are obscure at best. Although many of the parables in the Bible gospels were supposedly incomprehensible to the disciples, some portions of the Gnostic texts, more than likely, are the transcribed babblings of someone on cannabis or another mind-altering substance. "The Discourse on the Eighth and Ninth," (see Robinson 1990, 321–327) for example, most probably represents an introduction to a guided drug experience. The "Scribal Note" to "The Prayer of Thanksgiving" (Robinson 1990, 329) is an example of such babbling most probably stemming from a cannabis experience.

Within the babblings sometimes rather profound statements emerge that ring true to the right audience, especially to people who are suffering. "The meek shall inherit the earth," for example, or material things are just that and are of little use in heaven, and so on, act as psychological crutches for the down and out. With the Bible gospels, the priest-poets realized that these messages are more effectively received when imbedded in a larger storyline with the storyline supported and reinforced with parables. In a manner similar to a Buddhist monk or guru, Jesus does not remain simply a local phenomenon but moves about influencing a great many people through his message. And in most cases, like a Buddhist guru, he never tells you anything until a question has been asked or some manner of help is requested, after which a dialogue progresses designed to make some point(s). For example, in "The Parable of the Rich Fool" (Luke 12:13), "Someone in the crowd said to him, 'Teacher, tell my brother to divide the inheritance with me.'" Further down (Luke 12:41), a question is asked: "Peter asked, 'Lord, are you telling this parable to us, or to everyone?'" After this Jesus tells a series of parables. This is the gentle approach to conversion rather than conversion by fear and intimidation. This is not to say that the parables attributed to Jesus are pristine, for many can be found in rabbinic literature (see Evans 2005, 418–423). Again, and this needs emphasis, Jesus' general approach is to never say anything until help is requested, or the poets simply start off a chapter assuming that a question had been asked. This is the methodology of the Buddhist guru or monk and certainly not the *modus operandi* of Abraham, Isaac, Jacob, Moses, David, Muhammad, or the respective deities or angel connected to the Old Testament or the Qur'an. Jesus' approach to conversion or maintaining the law is very different from that of Judaism and Islam. In Judaism and Islam the message is acted upon, not willingly, but out of fear and threat of punishment. Imams, while teaching the Qur'an on Friday, often hold a sword, probably to terrorize those being indoctrinated (see Natan 2006, 31). During a recent trip to Xian, China, we visited the Great Mosque just prior to afternoon prayer. Close to the prayer room was a Chinese Muslim practicing swordplay in the court yard. He looked at my wife and me, and then did some speedy moves, I guess either to impress or intimidate. The scene of Indiana Jones' confrontation with the swordsman in the market square (*Raiders of the Lost Ark*) jumped swiftly to mind! At any rate, we, of course, were not allowed into the prayer room, and when prayer began this gentleman stood by the door with the sword by his side, looking very menacing, especially with his Fu Manchu mustache.

Comparing parables, we can see contradicting stories indicating that one or the other cannot be from the original philosophy of Jesus or John the Baptist. For example, an oft-quoted parable is of the sinner who repents, emphasizing the importance of *rewarding* the lost soul, symbolized by sheep, money, and prodigal son. These parables, how-ever, act as useful examples of confusion and reinforcement techniques used in clinical hypnosis. First, three renditions of the same story using different symbols in rapid succession serve to confuse the listener or at times promote questions. It is obvious to me that whoever wrote this was a showman, an artist. He or she understood how, in a position of no power or authority, to grab the attention of commoners and direct their thinking and energy without resorting to threats. Instead, he presents reason and usefulness through a non-threatening story, a parable, forc-ing the listener to question and actually take part in a divine process of reason and humanity. Logical arguments are not easily received by people under stress and down and out. Let's take a close look at this (Luke 15:1–31):

> Then drew near to him all the publicans and sinners to hear him.
> And the Pharisees and scribes murmured, saying, This man receiveth sinners, and eateth with them.
> And he spoke this parable to them, saying,
> What man of you having a hundred sheep, if he loseth one of them, doth not leave the ninety and nine in the wilderness, and go after that which is lost, until he findeth it?
> And when he hath found [it], he layeth [it] on his shoul-ders, rejoicing.
> And when he cometh home, he calleth together [his] friends and neighbors, saying to them, Rejoice with me; for I have found my sheep which was lost.

I say to you, that likewise joy shall be in heaven over one sinner that repenteth, more than over ninety and nine just persons, who need no repentance.

Most of the audience can understand this story, as it makes sense to gather up sheep that have wandered away from the herd. This is the first story of what is called a "yes set," where the audience is in agreement with the premise of gathering up one's possessions. But while the disciples are identifying with this story, Jesus connects the sheep to sinners by juxtaposing two totally *separate* ideas—this introduces a bit of confusion into the conversation. The sheep have not sinned; I'm not sure they are capable of sinning. Then the next story is offered.

Either what woman having ten pieces of silver, if she loseth one piece, doth not light a candle, and sweep the house, and seek diligently till she findeth [it]?

And when she hath found [it], she calleth [her] friends and [her] neighbors together, saying, Rejoice with me; for I have found the piece which I had lost.

Likewise, I say to you, There is joy in the presence of the angels of God over one sinner that repenteth.

A story is told about a search for a coin and abandoning all other interests, but once again it is attached to the idea of saving the lost sinner. This is once more part of the "yes set," wherein the listener can identify with the lost coin. As he agrees with that, the connection to the sinner is brought in so that the listener does not intellectually separate the two ideas—agreeing to the first also includes agreeing with the latter. The third story is designed to maintain the "yes set" and drive home the idea about repentance, but also to justify proselytizing and *not* rewarding virtuous behavior.

And he said, A certain man had two sons:
And the younger of them said to [his] father, Father, give

me the portion of goods that falleth [to me]. And he divided to them [his] living.

And not many days after, the younger son gathered all together, and took his journey into a far country, and there wasted his substance with riotous living.

And when he had spent all, there arose a severe famine in that land; and he began to be in want.

And he went and joined himself to a citizen of that country; and he sent him into his fields to feed swine.

And he would fain have filled his belly with the husks that the swine did eat; and no man gave to him.

And when he came to himself, he said, How many hired servants of my father have bread enough and to spare, and I am perishing with hunger!

I will arise and go to my father, and will say to him, Father, I have sinned against heaven, and before thee,

And am no more worthy to be called thy son: make me as one of thy hired servants.

And he arose, and came to his father. But when he was yet a great way off, his father saw him, and had compassion, and ran, and fell on his neck, and kissed him.

And the son said to him, Father, I have sinned against heaven, and in thy sight, and am no more worthy to be called thy son.

But the father said to his servants, Bring forth the best robe, and put [it] on him, and put a ring on his hand, and shoes on [his] feet:

And bring hither the fatted calf, and kill [it]; and let us eat, and be merry:

For this my son was dead, and is alive again; he was lost, and is found. And they began to be merry.

Now his elder son was in the field: and as he came and drew nigh to the house, he heard music and dancing.

And he called one of the servants, and asked what these things meant.

And he said to him, Thy brother is come; and thy father hath killed the fatted calf, because he hath received him in health. And he was angry, and would not go in; therefore his father came out, and entreated him.

And he answering, said to [his] father, Lo, these many years do I serve thee, neither have I at any time transgressed thy commandment; and yet thou never gavest me a kid, that I might make merry with my friends:

But as soon as this thy son had come, who hath devoured thy living with harlots, thou hast killed for him the fatted calf.

And he said to him, Son, thou art ever with me: and all that I have is thine.

It was meet that we should make merry, and be glad: for this thy brother was dead, and is alive again; and was lost, and is found.

The story of the prodigal son has little to do with being lost, and more to do with being desperate after making bad choices and maintaining a dependence on daddy for help. The sheep is lost only because the shepherd says so and the coin isn't conscious that it is lost. The stories are used as a "yes set" to obtain agreement that saving sinners is top priority, just as saving that one lost sheep or lost coin. An association is made between sinners, sheep, and coins and it does seem to have some sort of logic to it, but only the first two stories are about being lost, while the last is about being desperate because he got "lost," squandered his inheritance on fast living, and engaged in all kinds of sinning. The first two stories are there to get you in agreement with the third story and advance the idea of saving souls by proselytizing and spreading the word. Sinners usually do not know they are lost, and it is only through the judgment of others that a person is a sinner in the first place—not going to church, not accepting Jesus as your savior, screwing the neighbor's wife, and so on. The process in these instances is to obtain agreement for the punch line—people are worthwhile, even sinners. I doubt that Jesus or John the Baptist used this parable. Why? Buddhists don't go around saving sinners; you cannot save people until they understand they have a problem. This is the "pearls before swine" analogy; you can't have this both ways.

Another way of looking at this message is that those who sin seem to get more attention than decent people. And isn't that the way things work? Negative behavior gets more attention than positive behavior. But the author is attempting to make another point, that is, justifying the search for sinners and conversion (proselytizing). I don't believe that John the Baptist a.k.a. Jesus would have constructed parables to make the statement that decency is to be ignored in favor of the sinner. Sinners will be redeemed but only if they change their ways, not through baptizing or confessing sins.

The author of Mark, however, catches the Buddhist touch and does not promote the sinner (Mark 4:1–41).

> And he began again to teach by the sea-side: and there was gathered to him a great multitude, so that he entered into a boat, and sat on the sea; and the whole multitude was by the sea, on the land.
>
> And he taught them many things by parables, and said to them in his doctrine,
>
> Hearken; Behold, a sower went out to sow:
>
> And it came to pass as he sowed, some fell by the way-side, and the fowls of the air came and devoured it.
>
> And some fell on stony ground, where it had not much earth; and immediately it sprang up, because it had no depth of earth.
>
> But when the sun had risen, it was scorched; and because it had no root, it withered away.
>
> And some fell among thorns, and the thorns grew up, and choked it, and it yielded no fruit.
>
> And other fell on good ground, and yielded fruit that sprang up, and increased, and brought forth, some thirty, and some sixty, and some a hundred.

And he said to them, He that hath ears to hear, let him hear.

This is a very opposite message from the parable in Luke. In short, some people (sinners) will not get the message and thus attempting to save them is a waste of time. As the Buddha said, "Don't illuminate others until they are ready." This is more in line with statements coming from our mythic hero Jesus a.k.a. John the Baptist. Further:

And when he was alone, they that were about him, with the twelve, asked of him the parable.
And he said to them, To you it is given to know the mystery of the kingdom of God: but to them that are without, all [these] things are done in parables.

This is a clear statement that you cannot be direct with most people, sinner and non-sinner alike, and thus an approach designed to make the person think and come to his or her own conclusion is the proper course of action. Would such a person then turn around and create another Judaism with all the "Thou shalt nots" and rules? No, absolutely not. The other point is this: These parables were designed to make you think, but what you think about and the symbolic values are personal and not absolute. Paul's letters to the Corinthians are a clear statement that many Christians were thinking for the first time and not following some special path; there were many paths and Paul didn't like this. Paul wanted people to follow his peculiar brand of psychosis. Popes, bishops, ministers, imams, and other religious clerics would like you to believe that there is only one meaning—*their* assigned meaning. Jesus would never suggest such a thing, as reflected in the above parables about being lost and saving souls. That is to say, the meaning is determined by one's spiritual condition. When meaning turns to dogma, one's religious experience is determined by religious clerics, while the individual's religious experience is denied and short-circuited—to identify, communicate with, or become the deity becomes heresy and illegal.

Individual interpretation is instead replaced with an agenda designed by religious clerics. This is an important fracture because it helps us understand that what we call religions (Judaism, Christianity, and Islam) are, in reality, political systems specifically designed to control thoughts and behaviors, and direct them according to the purposes of the respective organizations. Conversations with God have to be controlled and/or made illegal lest such conversations challenge the power structure.

Finally, Jesus explains the parable and forces the listener into a bind of choosing between "closed and stupid" or "open and intelligent."

> That seeing they may see, and not perceive; and hearing they may hear, and not understand; lest at any time they should be converted, and [their] sins should be forgiven them.
>
> And he said to them, Know ye not this parable? and how then will ye know all parables?
>
> The sower soweth the word.
>
> And these are they by the way-side, where the word is sown; but when they have heard, Satan cometh immediately, and taketh away the word that was sown in their hearts.
>
> And these are they likewise who are sown on stony ground; who, when they have heard the word, immediately receive it with gladness;
>
> And have no root in themselves, and so endure but for a time: afterward, when affliction or persecution ariseth for the word's sake, immediately they relapse.
>
> And these are they who are sown among thorns; such as hear the word,
>
> And the cares of this world, and the deceitfulness of riches, and the lusts of other things entering in, choke the word, and it becometh unfruitful.
>
> And these are they who are sown on good ground; such as hear the word, and receive [it], and bring forth fruit, some thirty-fold, some sixty, and some a hundred.

He then grabs the crowd's attention with the candlestick riddle, referencing the fact that light (truth, knowledge, spirituality, etc.) cannot be kept secret. But then there is a word of caution—be careful how you interpret things.

> And he said to them, Is a candle brought to be put under a close vessel, or under a bed? and not to be set on a candlestick?
>
> For there is nothing hid, which shall not be manifested; neither hath any thing been kept secret, but that it should come abroad.
>
> If any man hath ears to hear, let him hear.
>
> And he said to them, Take heed what ye hear: With the measure which ye give, it shall be measured to you: and to you that hear shall more be given.

Next, a confusion tactic is offered:

> For he that hath, to him shall be given: and he that hath not, from him shall be taken even that which he hath.

After which he returns to a volley of analogies designed to keep the listener considering the possibilities of their own spiritual growth.

> And he said, So is the kingdom of God, as if a man should cast seed into the ground;
>
> And should sleep, and rise night and day, and the seed should spring and grow up, he knoweth not how.
>
> For the earth bringeth forth fruit of itself; first the blade, then the ear, after that the full corn in the ear.
>
> But when the fruit is brought forth, immediately he putteth in the sickle, because the harvest is come.
>
> And he said, To what shall we liken the kingdom of God? or with what comparison shall we compare it?

[It is] like a grain of mustard-seed, which, when it is sown in the earth, is less than all the seeds that are in the earth.

But when it is sown, it groweth up, and becometh greater than all herbs, and shooteth out great branches; so that the fowls of the air may lodge under its shade. [Note—a mustard seed will never grow into a tree.]

Finally, the narrator describes the scene of Jesus teaching his disciples through gentle stories and indirect insults to spur independent thought, probably for the first time.

And with many such parables he spoke the word to them, as they were able to hear [it].

But without a parable he spoke not to them: and when they were alone, he expounded all things to his disciples.

And the same day, when the evening was come, he saith to them, Let us pass over to the other side.

And when they had sent away the multitude, they took him even as he was in the boat. And there were also with him other small boats.

And there arose a great storm of wind, and the waves beat into the boat, so that it was now full.

And he was in the hinder part of the boat, asleep on a pillow: and they awake him, and say to him, Master, carest thou not that we perish?

And he arose, and rebuked the wind, and said to the sea, Peace, be still: and the wind ceased, and there was a great calm.

And he said to them, Why are ye so fearful? how is it that ye have no faith?

And they feared exceedingly, and said one to another, What manner of man is this, that even the wind and the sea obey him?

Not only are these parables theatrical in design, but I can imagine someone writing a screenplay about the life and times of Jesus. I would not be a bit surprised if these parables were acted out "on stage" before they became what we call the gospels. This gentle method of teaching was abandoned early on by the Orthodox Church, and replaced with strict interpretation of symbols and rites, an immense fracture and loss for humanity.

Let me summarize: Jesus used parables wrapped around yes sets, double binds, and confusion techniques to deliver a very simple message. His message was one of self-responsibility, independent thought, and compassion or basic human decency. He said to follow him because he was a decent human being as God intended, and if you follow him you will be like him, the Son of God; thus you *are* God. Because you are God, you don't need a priest or church; just be a decent human being and cast out your demons! Love thy neighbor and don't hold ill will toward others—you can make yourself sick and it sickens society with "leprosy, cataracts, boils, and plagues." Heaven is right here, not some other place, so why shit on the roses? Jesus had no threats (these were added by Paul and others) and very few rules for his followers, *unlike* Buddhism, Hinduism, Judaism, Islam, and what became Christianity. Why few rules? Because you need to be self-responsible and this is impossible if someone is always telling you what to think and how to behave; you don't have to be micro-managed. You simply have to have faith in your ability to act as a self-responsible, decent human being. The story of Jesus is not a story about God and it isn't a story about Jesus, and anyone who thinks that is a fool. His message was very secular but pointed toward a deep spiritual truth. The story of Jesus is about you, self-responsibility, and critical thinking; the parables are to personalize the message and make you think. If this wasn't the case, Jesus would have said, "Thou shalt not . . ." and that would be it.

Self-responsibility, as offered by Jesus, is also available in the Greek and Celtic/Germanic positions that a reasonable person knows right from wrong and does not need continual reminders or threats to be decent. In Christianity and Islam, the belief is that you need daily or weekly threats to keep you in line with the will of the deity. Early in the development of Christianity, much of the Greek philosophy, and certainly the scientific method and curiosity, were excised from the product (see Freeman 2002).

Jesus, Christianity, and Hallucinogens

It is well known that various plants and fungi have been used in rituals designed to connect the individual to the sacred, or the energy that informs all, for perhaps hundreds of thousands of years (see Chapter Two). I think that McKenna (1992) had it right when he suggested that various plants and fungi heavily influenced cultural insights, such as technology and magical/religious wondering. Our early ancestors, with a consciousness that allowed them to step back from nature, extract ideas, and press them back in (see Rush 1996, 1999), lived in very conservative groups. Ritual consumption of hallucinogenic substances would allow them, in times of crisis especially, to go beyond the bounds of society, obtain what was needed, and then return to the physical world. Johns (1999) makes a similar suggestion with respect to the development of medical systems. I recently heard that one of the geneticists responsible for unraveling the DNA structure used LSD to make this leap in perception.

Knowledge of plants for detox (purgatives), altering consciousness, wound healing, and so on, must predate hominids. Hominids may begin with *Orrorin tugenensis* or something similar, and that species goes back six million years. How can we say that use of plants for detox and altering consciousness predate our species? If you own a cat you have living proof. Felines are to the land mammal world as sharks are to sea life. They have a long season and branched away from our mammal line sometime after sixty-five MYA, and by sixty MYA they are known as *Miacia,* the first true mammal carnivores. The house cat we experience today went through many changes and from the start of their lineage they were deadly and successful small-group hunters. It is only by twelve MYA that we would notice them as felines, and by 500,000 years ago we encounter *Felis sylvestris* in northern climates. During several periods of global warming and cooling *Felis* was pushed into North Africa, and during warmer phases became isolated and evolved into *Felis lybica,* apparently the Adam and Eve of all the housecats on the face of the planet.

Getting back to my story, cats have some interesting behavioral patterns that must coincide with a carnivore lifestyle. Their complex is to eat meat, lick fur to clean and kill parasites, eat grass, and purge. I have at present twenty-four cats on our property—as many as thirty at times. This number is not likely to decrease as we rescue cats. Second, I have a very large herb garden (three quarters of an acre) containing anywhere from one hundred to 150 different herbs at any one time. I have watched the cats smell the leaves of virtually all the plants. They have tasted many, chewed the leaves of some, and really seem to enjoy sleeping next to or on top of specific plants, for example, *Phalaris* grass, a source of DMT—Dimethyltryptamine (although not orally active). And of course they love regular grass, preferring the tender new shoots in corners where they escape the lawn mower. Shortly after eating the grass they throw up (remember Puss in Boots in *Shriek II*?), and in the process remove hairballs acquired while licking their fur and cleaning themselves. They, unlike crocodiles and snakes, cannot digest hair and so remove it by throwing up on your new rug.

Humans are different. We wouldn't necessarily throw up after eating lawn grass, but we would if we ate the leaves of other types of plants (e.g., certain tobacco species, epasote or *Chenopodium ambrosioides, Cephaelis ipecacuanha,* etc.). Ingested toxins have an effect on the stomach and inner ear connection, vertigo follows, and then you vomit. This protective behavior would be very useful for a species that forages far and wide, and always bumps into new plants begging for a bioassay. Our ancestors did this for millions of years.

Cats, as is well known, are drawn to catnip (*Nepeta cataria*). I have to put tomato cages around most of my menthe plants or they will roll in them, sleep on them, and eat them; they apparently get pretty "stoned." They may also eat mint leaves to calm their digestive systems after being feed meat and veggies at the same meal, common with commercial cat foods. There is nothing in the *Menthe* family (excluding certain sage/salvia species) that would alter consciousness in humans, at least in the way it does cats; we have a long history with plants and our livers are able to conjugate the oils and other plant chemicals from which we acquire antioxidants and other necessary phytochemicals. A cat has a different liver designed to protect from the toxins generated after eating high levels of protein; cats don't need veggies because they produce copious amounts of antioxidants. At any rate, these oils, which give mints their distinctive aroma, apparently get into the bloodstream and pass the blood-brain barrier and *voila*—a stoned cat perhaps communing with ancestors like Puss in Boots. Cats actively seek out *Menthe* and it is not uncommon to see several cats waiting in line for access to a special plant, although there are patches all over the garden. Cats are not the only mammals that seek mind-altering plants, as such behavior has been seen with cows and datura. How much access a cat in the wild has to mint certainly is different from its availability in my backyard (perhaps I have enabled drug dependency in cats?), and thus the cats tend to pay attention to these plants on a regular basis. We have had dogs in the past that loved beer and in one particular case would growl at you if you didn't share.

In order for our ancestors to survive they could not afford to be stoned all the time (see Rush 1996); these would have been out-of-the-ordinary and unnerving experiences not to be trifled with. Remember that our ancestors lived in very conservative societies that changed little in behavioral patterns over thousands of years, and someone going berserk on the trail after consuming datura or falling down dead after consuming *Amanita muscaria,* only to arise again, could be absolutely upsetting. Mind-altering substances were restricted to special times or times of trouble, illness perhaps, or when there was a need to locate game and so on. These people had no need for addiction counseling. In other words, consumption of the "Host" would be placed within, and probably restricted to, a ritual context. Tobacco use among Native

American Indians is a case in point—because it is used ritually, addiction was not an issue. North American Indians did not, however, have a ritual context for alcohol and as with most people after continual use, became addicted.

Our type of consciousness (see Rush 1996, 1999), that is, the ability to be *part of nature,* step back and be *apart from nature,* could lead our ancestors to conclude that the plants and mushrooms were a conduit to some mysterious force, the abode of the ancestors, and so on. This was probably not an exclusive place where only few could travel, at least at first. In shamanic practices the shaman and the patient, or group, participate, with the shaman acting as a guide. A similar situation prevails to this day in many North American Indian groups with the Native American Church being the most visible. The Hindus used soma, the Zoroastrians used haoma (they also used cannabis, wine, and many other mind-altering substances), and the Hebrews used *Amanita muscaria,* definitely mandrake and wine, probably henbane, and lots and lots of cannabis. What about Jesus? A great deal of research has been devoted to the question of hallucinogens and their part in the development of Western religious tradition as well as those in the East.

Jesus, according to Ruck, et al. (2001, 143–234), was the "Drug Man." This is adequately displayed in the Canterbury Psalter (manuscript, 1300–1400 CE), stained glass in Canterbury Cathedral in Kent, England (1100–1200 CE), and in literally hundred of manuscripts, drawings and woodcuts readily available to anyone interested in the true development of Christianity. This leads one to ponder if the art historians and other interested scholars didn't notice the mushrooms or were simply ignorant of mushrooms and their importance in the development of Western Civilization. There are images, however, that without ambiguity show the connection between Jesus and mushrooms, and these occur among the outstanding mosaics in St. Mark's Basilica in Venice (built between 1094–1300 CE—begin with the back cover). One can see, in proud display, Jesus and mushrooms in the "Agony in the Garden of Gethsemane" on the south wall of the nave. In the left portion of the mosaic, but in back of a person (Mica, Peter?) who is seated in a contemplative posture (trance, ill?), is a curious plant that is obviously a mushroom. The middle cap is turned over to reveal the gills depicted by tree branches, while the other two caps are in side view (similar to the Tree of Good and Evil found elsewhere in the Basilica—see Rush 2005). Allegro (1970) displays one of several renderings of the mushroom in the form of a tree (mushroom-tree), but it is also found as a *tree-mushroom,* bush, or other plant. When displayed as a tree-mushroom (perhaps a pine tree?), the center "cap" will be turned toward the viewer, offering the underside blanches as analogues for the gills of the mushroom. This is also the mushroom-cross and halo (or nimbus). We must also include within this symbolic repertoire the sacrificial lamb (the sacrifice of the mushroom) and the dove-mushroom (the ascent to that spiritual geography) so beautifully displayed in the Rose Window, St. Brigit's Cathedral, San Francisco, California, dating back to the turn of the twentieth century.

To continue with Agony in the Garden of Gethsemane, the side caps, seen in side view, have dots all over them, just as do many of the mushroom-like flowers on other plants in the frame. If you look closely at the root base of this plant, you will see tipped to the left a mushroom in the rock structure. Directly in back of Jesus on the right is the cap of another tree-mushroom.

In this same mosaic there are other interesting plants surrounding the seated figure—one directly in back, one to his left, and one to his right. The plant to his back and right looks to be possibly a composite drawing, but the middle axial leaves and tulip-like flowers/pods appear to be henbane, Hyoscyamus niger (European and Middle Eastern), or Hyoscyamus muticus (Egyptian variety). This is a well-known hallucinogenic plant and the major component (along with belladonna) in witches' ointment and brew, and possibly the anointing oils described in Chapter Two. There are curious leaves/plants in the border under the scene, with one interesting "plant" to the left of the figure, a similar plant directly underneath, and then the same just past the foot of the seated figure. The three look to be mushrooms on a stalk, while other leaves in the border appear to be those of cannabis. There is little doubt as to the identity of the plant in the left center, to the left of the mush-room tree and below the kneeling Jesus. This is a cannabis "leaf-plant."

Above the figures is a phrase written in Medieval Latin: "And he rebuked them because of this." Is this a "bad trip," a warning from the plant-god that "purification must precede illumination"? If so, this would probably involve fasting for a few days. Are the plants-elements in this picture a sort of recipe for combining plants and fungi, that which is appropriate for an experience with God, or perhaps a warn-ing about combining elements? To interpret these mosaics without ref-erence to the plants, their importance, and use, obscures the origins and development of the Christian cult and much of Western Civilization.

These are perhaps the most beautiful mosaics in the world crafted by super-genius artists; this would have been very time consuming, exhausting, and expensive work. Moreover, these would be commis-sioned works wherein the priest, but more likely the Cardinal, Bishop, or perhaps even the pope, told the artist which symbols to include in the storyline, just as one includes specific symbols in the Mass or any Catholic ritual. The mushrooms and other mind-altering plants were not insignificant filler. If you pull these factors together, then you have to con-clude that what they portrayed must have been important to them. Prepare yourself for what comes next.

Another mosaic verifying these above observations occurs in the vault between the dome of the Ascension and the dome of the Pentecost (see front and inside front cover). Here, irrefutably revealed, is the meaning of Christ, the communion with God, and the perverted evo-lution of the church that followed (the rest of the New Testament mosaics in the basilica). In the first frame there is a picture of Jesus standing between what looks to be a female on his right (interesting that she is on his right side) and a male on his left, both kneeling, while on the rocks (probably stylized mushroom caps) to the left and right of these figures are all kinds of Psilocybe-type mushrooms, with little babies underneath. Centered between his feet, without doubt, is the *Amanita muscaria* mushroom.

Why mushrooms? Why not figs or apples? Why not beans or pota-
toes? They are mushrooms because they are the sacrament, or at least
part of the sacrament, the Body of Christ. To continue, if we assume
that the mushrooms are more than decoration, then we can suggest
that the small bush-like plant immediately in back of the woman, and
the larger bush which the kneeling man seems to be leaning against,
are pine trees; *Amanita muscaria* grows symbiotically on the roots of
conifers or pine trees. If you look closely, you will see that from the
knees down on these figures the tiles are white, but from the thigh up
they are brown, perhaps representing the stalk of the mushroom caps
mentioned above. The male and female could represent the cap, stalk,
and mycelium of the mushroom growing from a pine tree. More meaning is derived from the fact that both are in "prayer mode," looking
either at the mushroom between Jesus' legs or the holes in his feet. The
woman is pointing to Jesus and the man has his hands in an adoring position, most probably contemplating the mushroom between Jesus' feet—
Freud would have a field day with this! More about these holes or
openings in Jesus in a moment.

There has to be a connection between these symbols; these are not
simply bushes or trees, as these mosaics and their symbolic values were
commissioned and are just too costly to produce out of whimsy. Why
a pine tree when other types of trees were available? The pine cone is
a common symbol in Catholic cathedrals all over the world and it stands
for fertility, perhaps to produce more pine trees and more mushrooms.
The frame under the images is also composed of mushrooms more
closely resembling *Amanita muscaria*.

Now for the part that allows computation of the other symbols mentioned thus far. If you look closely at Jesus' left hand, you will clearly
see that he is holding a red mushroom cap with dots, *Amanita muscaria*. This is not blood from his piercing (piercing in his left hand is
clearly visible) nor is it his heart in his hand. This isn't artistic license;
it wasn't salted there by some deranged artisan pulling a fast one on a
despised pope, nor is it graffiti crafted by a pot-smoking hippie. It isn't
discoloration due to the encroachment of the sea. It is a mushroom cap,

Amanita muscaria, the sacred mushroom. But there is more. The careful juxtaposition of symbolic values tells the story, keeping in mind that this was time consuming, exhausting, and expensive work done by very clever people. Moreover, that which is rendered frequently, and especially in direct connection with Jesus, has to be more than important with respect to the overall tradition of Christianity.

Notice that Jesus is holding the Amanita cap upside down; you enter through the underside of the mushroom and then into Christ through the hole in his hand; the mushroom and Jesus are one and the same. His left index finger is pointing to the hole in his right hand; the hole is open to receive. There has to be some esoteric ritual in the Catholic tradition that represents this "going through the mushroom" (and this just might involve vaginal or anal sex), just as the mushroom goes through you. The mushroom, in one sense, is a paired opposite (the tree of Good and Evil), at the center of which is everything and nothing at the same time—a black hole, immortality. You go into its center just as it goes into yours when you consume it; "I and the Father are one." The Tree of Immortality and the Tree of Good and Evil are the same tree; it just depends on whether you go into it or it goes into you. The meaning of immortality is expressed in another mosaic described below. The Medieval Latin accompanying this mosaic says, "And do you believe that the rising contains the seed, even as Thomas tried to discover?" The reference is to the consumption of the Body of Christ. The "rising" refers to the emergence of the mushroom from the ground, and the seed (the fruit?) contains the mystery, "that to be discovered" even by someone as stubborn as Thomas. This is pretty spiritual stuff that does not come from ordinary awareness. This is the type of thing that certain mind-altering substances accomplish; they kick you out of the box and into another perception or experience.

In the central frame of the end portion of the vault, just past where Jesus is standing with the Amanita in his hand, we see Jesus now seated on his throne while converts are coming up, kneeling, and touching what appears to be "bread" (read mushroom) in his left hand. What he held in his left hand in the first frame (the dot covered cap of the *Amanita muscaria*) morphed into another rendition of the "body of Christ," symbolized by bread, which all take in and become one with Christ (see 1 Corinthians). Dried *Amanita muscaria* caps greatly resemble bread and this would be a code word, just as cannabis goes by many names, including marijuana, pot, weed, bud, dope, and so on. This also might symbolically represent the movement away from esoteric rites for only a few to exoteric rites for the many. This is the Golden Calf, perhaps, that Moses ground up for all to drink.

But there may be another possible meaning, although this is speculation. It was common practice for arctic shamans to consume the mushroom, have all the bad effects (death), return, and urinate in a pot for the patient to consume. This act appears to remove many of the negative effects of the mushroom. We know the Hindus did this; it was mentioned in the Vedas. The analogy is that Jesus/Christ went through the sacrifice for you, gave his body, paid the price, and now you can partake of the body (now "bread") because the ill effects have been removed (sin has been atoned). Urine drinking is a possibility; it also represents the Body of Christ—this is a very interesting purification rite.

There are onlookers (in the third frame on his right) who appear to be applauding; one appears to be holding more "bread." Also, the halos surrounding Jesus' head and the heads of other saints represent the sun, the Aten, the symbol of the path, and the gills of a mushroom. Again, the border under the three frames is composed of mushrooms. What part, then, did mind-altering substances play in the development and evolution of what we know today as Christianity? The major part. This being the case, how can these substances be excluded from scholarly analysis?

The image right above these three frames (inside front cover) shows the resurrected Jesus standing on the back of a dark-skinned man, who is handcuffed and surrounded by keys, a lock, and broken chain links. In back of Jesus is a very large mushroom cap. This is a reference to the keys of life and the absence of death, or breaking the chains of death, through the body of Christ. Jesus, or Christ himself, or perhaps the staff (cross, caduceus) is the stalk of the mushroom, in a fashion similar to that of Krishna (see Heinrich 2002, 36) and the mummy bundles of Ptah and Osiris in the Egyptian tradition. His sash is blowing back, perhaps another reference to the mushroom but definitely movement. The dark man appears to be giving the man a lift with his right hand under his left foot, while his left hand is ready to lift his right. We could also suggest that the dark man is the stalk of the mushroom representing earth, but more likely he represents time, which Jesus subdues by offering immortality through him. Jesus, then, is the conduit or the way to everlasting life. Looking closely at this image, right down to each individual tile, and you will see that the gentleman on the far right with the red cloak has *Amanita muscaria* for feet. In any case we are talking about mushrooms and fungi, and they are not there to accompany the steak and onions served at the communal meal.

Jesus is holding a man to his left by his left wrist and lifting him up off his knee; he is raising the dead (immortality) or perhaps offering enlightenment through the mushroom path. Under the right sleeve of this man is a mushroom cap with a stalk, apparently attached to the larger mushroom cap. In back of the man is what appears to be a woman dressed in red with a mushroom-shaped cap, and in back of her those waiting to be reborn. Again, these images of plants and mushrooms are not accidental, artistic license. Instead they instruct, without doubt or ambiguity, regarding the origins of Christianity as we see it today and the origins of much of Western Civilization. The Medieval Latin above the scene says, "I will be risen from death and for eternity among the company of God and God will rule over us." The larger translation is this: When you make the commitment, consume the mushroom, and complete the ritual, you will be one with God, "I and the Father are One," and our godly part will now rule over our "us," that is, our animal nature.

Through out the basilica there are representations of *Amanita muscaria* in its distinctive white-dot-on red configuration. We see this (inside back cover) in the angel's wings (dome of the Ascension), to the left of which is a mushroom hanging down from the ceiling, with Christ in the center holding a "book" in his left hand.

Are the plant-elements in these mosaics a sort of recipe for combining plants and fungi, that which is appropriate for an experience with God, or perhaps a warning about combining elements? To interpret these mosaics without reference to the plants, their importance, and use, obscures the origins and development of the Christian cult and much of Western Civilization.

On the inside of the back cover we are once again in Gethsemane. This time notice that some of the disciples are in a trance and others appear to "pass out" when they take in the wisdom of Jesus, the mushroom (determined by the pine tree at his back), and the mushroom-plant at the level of his shoulders and head. Attached to the pointed portion of Jesus' robe (laying on the rock) there appears to be a cross (ankh?), another determinative for Jesus and the mushroom (see Rush 2007).

These are perhaps the most beautiful mosaics in the world crafted by super-genius artists; these would have been very time consuming, exhausting, and expensive projects. Moreover, these would be commissioned at the request or demand of a priest, but more likely the cardinal, bishop, or perhaps even the pope. These religious clerics told the artist which symbols to include in the storyline, just as one includes specific symbols in the Mass or any Catholic ritual. The mushrooms and other mind-altering plants were not insignificant filler. When you pull these factors together, you have to conclude that what they portrayed must have been important to them.

In the eleventh through thirteenth century CE, the artisans knew of and consumed mind-altering substances and coded for us their use in the esoteric rites of the Jewish and Christian traditions. You might also wonder where all this beautiful art decorating the cathedrals came from. It came from the inspiration of God in the form of mushrooms and other plant substances. The mushrooms are in the mosaics as a means of giving credit to God, while the artist was simply a vehicle of God's expression. As I said in the preface, if mushrooms, cannabis, henbane, and so on are not factored into the analysis of who wrote what and why it was written, the reader gets a lopsided and very biased picture of the Bible's construction, and in this case, the true meaning of the Body of Christ.

Besides these mosaics (and there are many, many visual references at St. Mark's), there are hundreds of images of mushroom in stained glass, mosaics, wall paintings, and manuscripts around the world. We also have the more coded statements about drug use in the Bible. One revelation of this is to be found in Matthew 3:11–12. John the Baptist was asked if he was the Christ:

> I indeed baptize you with water to repentance: but he that cometh *after me* is mightier than I, whose shoes I am not worthy to bear: he shall *baptize you with the Holy Spirit, and [with] fire:* Whose fan [is] in his hand, and he will thoroughly cleanse his floor, and gather his wheat into the granary; but he will burn the chaff with unquenchable fire. [Emphasis added]

This is a reference to the use of some plant substance, possibly *Amanita muscaria* (see Ruck, et al. 2001), used to bring disciples (followers) to the godhead. The physical experiences manifesting during ritual use of mind-altering substances are often very unpleasant, and this is part of the process of purging or purification—essentially you have your hangover first. This purging can be seen as a form of celestial punishment. One has to purify before illumination can occur.

The above statement also reveals that John the Baptist never met Jesus, for he is the savior (Tut perhaps?) who *will* return, is *going to* return, the "second coming." In any case, John the Baptist/Jesus is no less than an urban shaman; he is the connection between the devotee and the other side. This would have been a powerful experience. Bennett and McQueen (2001) make the point that baptism is not simply the act of sprinkling or immersing someone in water to remove sin. This is the baptism for common folk these days. Baptism refers to "cleansing" and cleansing as a prelude to spiritual awakening, which means cleaning away the old in preparation for revelation. The consumption of *Amanita muscaria* would most certainly represent a cleansing process because the first part of the experience is "fire"—the initiate becomes very sick and in some cases "dies" or is thought dead. But then he returns, reveals images, and that he heard voices, messages from God or perhaps an archangel. These experiences still go on today, but only for a special few at the highest levels of the three Western traditions, that is, Judaism, Christianity, and Islam. People of a time past cannot be faulted for the assumptions they made about these mind-altering plants and fungi. It was not until Islamic and then European analysis of plant chemicals that the truth was revealed. I think it very interesting in the Catholic tradition that Cardinals wear those little red and white caps on their head, the Catholic version of the skullcap worn by Jewish rabbis. I've been told that this simply represents high rank or priest, but I have also been told by others in the Church that these are a reference to *Amanita muscaria* and represent the white and red dots on the mushroom's cap, with the white gowns a representation of the mummy bundle wrappings or the stem of a mushroom, most probably a reference to Osiris in the Egyptian tradition (see Rush 2007). These experiences with sacred plants and fungi were eventually restricted to a chosen few, for if the individual can commune with God using these substances, then what would be the purpose of the church and religious clerics? So they had to be outlawed with strict enforcement, lest the secret be known to all. Well, the secret is out. Many of the laws in the United States center on these original restrictions.

Disturbed Communication Patterns

Disturbed communication patterns are easy to detect because they lie outside of cultural expectations. In my opinion, many of the stories in Ezekiel, Zachariah, Daniel, and Revelation, as well as statements in the Gnostic texts, represent disturbed communication patterns as seen through a twenty-first century lens. No professional historian, anthropologist, clinical psychologist, or psychiatrist would ever consider these stories the product of a person actually communing with a god or demon. The visions reported in some scripture might actually reveal something of the storylines used in mystery cults while the initiate (disciple) was under the influence of some mind-altering substance. We can assume that the images suggested during the guided experience would be unusual to say the least and not about ordinary, everyday mundane stuff. The Eleusinian mystery cult in Greece provides an example of this procedure of leading the initiate through certain processes or rites, combining storyline and various images, from which the individual emerged profoundly changed. I believe (as do many others) that this is how Jesus (a.k.a. John the Baptist) illuminated disciples; this was the "real" baptism, the baptizing with fire, the consuming of the sacred flesh, the *Amanita muscaria* or other plant substances.

Psychologists have categorized Western perceptions of disturbed communication patterns (*DSM-IV—Diagnostic and Statistical Manual of Mental Disorders* 1994), and although these are artificial categories they do allow us to talk about these patterns with reference points. According to the creators of this document, most of what they categorize is universal now, as well as in the past (assuming our brains haven't changed in the past three thousand years), while there are a few pages at the end of the text considered "culture bound syndromes," or abnormalities specific to one culture or another (see Rush 1996). So, how do we explain these disturbed communication patterns in the Bible, the numerous occurrences of a deity communicating with special people? Are these just great stories fabricated by the creative mind? Were they for entertainment purposes or delivering moral messages and not to be taken literally? Were such conversations taken to be everyday occurrences, or were they considered unusual? How should psychologists and psychiatrists diagnose people who still believe these stories as historical fact? I think it is safe to say that these *were* common experiences for *some* people but not for others. People often develop disturbed patterns when outside of some preferred reference group, when they are abandoned or alone. Street people, in many cases, develop disturbed communication patterns that interface with the general communication patterns found at this level of the social hierarchy. The longer you stay on the streets or in the psychiatric ward interacting with other patients, the more disturbed the communication pattern becomes—usually. Why? This is called synchronicity—we tend to mesh with those with whom we most frequently interact. This meshing is not always positive.

Traumatic events can lead to disturbances in speech and content. But there are more possibilities. Not only was there a plethora of mind-altering substances available, but foods cooked in wine contained a great deal of lead during Roman times, and this could eventually lead to disturbed communication patterns. Much of the bizarre behavior of Roman rulers (Nero and Caligula, for example) might be connected to lead poisoning. Might this also be the case for priests and other religious clerics like Paul?

Then there are visions and auditory hallucinations caused by hypoglycemia and fevers. Some of these experiences would be taken as prophecy especially: 1) if the person was seen as important (a priest or rabbi), and/or, 2) if there had been previous visions or voices delivered in the right setting. In many instances a person goes away somewhere—to a mountain, tent, sacred grove, and so on—and consumes something, which suggests that these contacts were not spontaneous. Abraham's encounters with Yahweh are not necessarily spontaneous, knowing that He was Abraham's patron deity and the earlier name, El, is connected to the word *manna*. In a sense Abraham was always with El or Yahweh when needed.

As another example, Noah simply hears the voice of God telling him He is fed up with people and a flood is planned. It is as if the God is right there, all the time, and this is not in the least bit unusual. Noah is not too stunned to hear the voice and simply obeys. Although we get a similar play with Abraham, Moses is a bit different. His first contact with God was described as, well, a shock; certainly it was unexpected. This suggests perhaps his first experience with the mushroom, *Amanita muscaria* (Exodus 3:2), "And the angel of the LORD appeared to him in a flame of fire out of the midst of a bush: and he looked, and behold, the bush burned with fire, and the bush [was] not consumed. And Moses said, I will now turn aside, and see this great sight, why the bush is not burnt."

After this initial event Moses knows how to contact God by going up on the mountain, erecting the "tent of meetings" in the desert, and so on. Certain types of substances are likely to bring forth auditory hallucination (*Amanita muscaria,* high levels of THC) while others can produce visual hallucinations (datura, belladonna, mandrake, Syrian rue). For datura, henbane, belladonna, and mandrake, one of the constituents is scopolamine, a known hallucinogen; for Syrian rue, beta-carboline alkaloids (harmine, harmaline, tatrahydroharmine, etc.) are definite hallucinogens. Remember Aladdin and the Flying Carpet? The Persians dyed their carpets with harmaline and with great frequency "flew" with Aladdin on that magic carpet. God does not speak to Jesus in the same manner as the patriarchs probably because he is God, but certainly Jesus, according to Ruck, et al. (2001), introduces disciples to God through a cleansing with "fire" or some mind-altering substance(s); there is indisputable visual proof of this presented earlier.

I suspect that hearing voices or conversations with deities are not all plant or fungi driven, but I favor the use of plants and fungi in the reported events in the Bible. Why? Because their use is a time-honored shamanic practice for contacting the spirit world, and it was the shamans, and eventually the priests, who told the stories and wrote them down. Are we to believe that one day these substances just fell out of use and the "real McCoy," God, showed up? I can't accept this. For thousands of years in the Middle East dreams have been considered prophetic, revealing something to the dreamer or others. Many of the dreams reported by important people resulted from mind-altering substances and they led to social action. An example of this is Elijah (1 Kings 19:5–9), who is awakened by an angel and told to get up and eat. He looked around he saw "a round cake that had been baked over hot coals, and a jar of water to drink." This is secret coding in the Bible, that is, references to that which brings the prophet to the godhead and action; Elijah is instructed through his experience with the mushroom and sent on a journey.

Prophecy is also an out of the ordinary experience and because it is often "off the wall," it likewise fits into the mold of "disturbed communication." Prophecy refers to "global" events, but when I say global I do not mean our current idea of global. What to us is local would have been global to the ancient poet-priests.

Many ritual drug experiences are not all that pleasant and lead to disturbed communication patterns. This formerly was rationalized as proof of contact with the supernatural agency. Theatrics were certainly part of this—contrived disturbances caused by the powerful deities, and because people were very superstitious, John the Baptist and others played on this.

I also suspect the John the Baptist's disciples also helped with crowd control. From a logistic standpoint, Jesus could surround himself with only so many people, as shown in the fishing boat episode, where he tells stories from a boat offshore because there were lots of onlookers. The disciples would station themselves throughout the crowd (shills they are called) and these are the ones who ask the initial questions to break the ice. Evangelists and politicians are show people, and they are in the business of selling something that will never wear out, rust, bust, or corrode. They are selling you their truth—God perhaps, or a great society with a chicken in every pot—which you have to accept on faith. They all use shills.

The parable, as opposed to prophecy, is a little more down to earth, the here and now. Many of those most quoted are about getting along with people without all the glitter, thunderbolts, and wrath. The parable forces independent thought, which is really contrary to Christian teachings.

These stories also tell us that the main character of the story is having an experience with God, making him or her special. But the experience with God *is not* the purpose of the story; the story is to inform about social living, technology, government, and so on. Most people get hung up on the god and the message becomes secondary, if understood at all. Let's look at some disturbed communication patterns in the Old and New Testament.

We can start with Ezekiel 1:1–22:

> Now it came to pass in the thirtieth year, in the fourth
> [month], in the fifth [day] of the month, as I [was] among
> the captives by the river of Kebar, [that] the heavens were
> opened, and I saw visions of God.
>
> In the fifth [day] of the month, which [was] the fifth year
> of king Jehoiachin's captivity,
>
> The word of the LORD came expressly to Ezekiel the
> priest, the son of Buzi, in the land of the Chaldeans by the
> river Kebar; and *the hand of the LORD was there upon him.*
> [Emphasis added]

Let's pause here for a moment, moving past the astronomical/astro-
logical numbers. We read "the hand of the Lord was there upon him."
What is the reference? Is this simply metaphor or, literally, did this big
hand come down from the sky and grab him by the scruff of the neck?
No, that is not what is being said. Ezekiel was under the influence of a
powerful hallucinogen metaphorically referred to as the "hand" of god.
A synonym for hand would be "spirit." To continue:

> And I looked, and behold, a whirlwind came out of the
> north, a great cloud, and a fire infolding itself, and a bright-
> ness [was] about it, and from the midst of it as the color of
> amber, from the midst of the fire.
>
> Also from the midst of it [came] the likeness of four living
> creatures. And this [was] their appearance; they had the like-
> ness of a man.
>
> And every one had four faces, and every one had four
> wings.
> And their feet [were] straight feet; and the sole of their feet
> [was] like the sole of a calf's foot: and they sparkled like the
> color of burnished brass.
>
> And [they had] the hands of a man under their wings on

their four sides; and they four had their faces and their
wings.

Their wings [were] joined one to another; they turned not
when they went; they went every one straight forward.

As for the likeness of their faces, they four had the face of
a man and the face of a lion, on the right side: and they four
had the face of an ox on the left side; they four also had the
face of an eagle.

Thus [were] their faces: and their wings [were] stretched
upward; two [wings] of every one [were] joined one to
another, and two covered their bodies.

The above descriptions are classic drug-induced images—elaborations
of course—representing distortions of common experiences. The ox
and eagle, human faces, fire, wheels, and so on, are common reports
of those under the influence of powerful substances. Ezekiel (or whoever had the visions) probably consumed *Amanita muscaria,* felt deathly
ill ("the hand of god was on him"), and when that subsided he possibly looked at the moon or into a fire and generated all these images
and heard the voices. When I would hear these stories from people who
had "bad trips" after ingesting Morning Glory seeds, datura, psilocybin mushrooms, and so on, the connection to biblical ramblings, as
with the case of Ezekiel, was certainly a possibility. No respected psychiatrist, clinical psychologist, or anthropologist would ever consider
these real events prompted by a deity today or 2,500 years ago.

And they went every one straight forward: whither the spirit
was to go, they went; [and] they turned not when they went.

As for the likeness of the living creatures, their appearance
[was] like burning coals of fire, [and] like the appearance of
lamps: it went up and down among the living creatures; and
the fire was bright, and out of the fire went forth lightning.

Again, the above suggests that Ezekiel was looking at the moon or coals of a glowing fire in the dead of night. Or perhaps, when combined with the next sentence—

"And the living creatures ran and returned as the appearance of a flash of lightning"—

they suggest entopic images that usually accompany hallucinogenic experiences; the author of Ezekiel most surely had experiences with hallucinogens. If there are any archetypes in the human psyche, they are these entopic images—wavy lines, right angles, circles, flashes of light, and with the right substance or combination of substances, different color patterns caused by the rapid changes in brain chemistry. These types of images are not unusual as they are the platform for recognition of the world around us, that is, shading (in black and white and color), right angles, wavy lines, circles, and so on. Inside your head you own a complete instruction manual for how to apply geometry, calculus, and physics. You cannot possibly relate to your physical and social world without subconsciously knowing certain details. You wouldn't be able to throw a ball; forget about catching one. You would not be able to walk up stairs or sit on a toilet to take a poop. A class in geometry is simply digitalizing the information in order to consciously understand and manipulate nature. Back to Ezekiel.

Physical trauma and stress-induced psychosis can produce these images, as can fever and other types of chemical toxicity (lead, copper, etc.). There is no evidence in the story that Ezekiel had suffered trauma or that he was ill with fever. We do not know if he had some form of heavy metal poisoning, although the wine in those time periods may have contained lead as a coloring agent. We worry about lead-based paint and children chewing paint off toys, cribs, and so on; certainly this is a problem. I'm not sure that there was lead in the wine consumed in the sixth century BCE, but the Romans, a few hundred years later, were drinking lead every day in their wine as well as cooking with it in their food.

> Now as I beheld the living creatures, behold one wheel upon
> the earth by the living creatures, with his four faces.
> The appearance of the wheels and their work [was] like the
> color of a beryl: and they four had one likeness: and their
> appearance and their work [was] as it were a wheel in the
> middle of a wheel.

One of the more common methods of cult initiation involves having the initiate stand silently—hallucinating perhaps—while he or she is talked through a prayer that establishes a commitment to a new birth, a spiritual birth. He would then be instructed to turn around and when he does, he sees himself in a large, highly polished, parabolic bowl (nowadays this would be a mirror, perhaps concaved). What does he see? A distorted image *of himself,* and this can be quite shocking, especially when under the influence of some mind-altering substance. "Beryl," or bronze, was the color of the wheel, with four likenesses, with wheels in the middle of wheels. Ezekiel perhaps was experiencing an image of himself reflected from a concave surface that may have had circular indentations within. He was experiencing the center of himself, the center of the universe from which all things come and into which all things go. He is being talked through these images, or they are simply generated without prompting and written down the next day.

> When they went, they went upon their four sides: [and] they
> returned not when they went.
> As for their rings, they were so high that they were dread-
> ful; and their rings [were] full of eyes around them four.
> And when the living creatures went, the wheels went by
> them: and when the living creatures were lifted up from the
> earth, the wheels were lifted up.

This is more evidence of Ezekiel (or someone) being initiated into a cult, once again staring into that bowl. At the same time he was probably kneeling on a platform that could be raised and lowered along with the bowl. Ezekiel is the "living creatures." There is more of this below.

> Whithersoever the spirit was to go, they went, thither [was their] spirit to go; and the wheels were lifted up over against them: for the spirit of the living creature [was] in the wheels.
>
> When those went, [these] went; and when those stood, [these] stood; and when those were lifted up from the earth, the wheels were lifted up over against them: for the spirit of the living creature [was] in the wheels.
>
> And the likeness of the firmament upon the heads of the living creature [was] as the color of the terrible crystal, stretched forth over their heads above.

This type of initiation was part of the mystery cults of long ago. Ezekiel, recently exiled to Babylon (along with probably eight or nine-thousand countrymen and women), might have come into contact with Zoroastrians who ran him through one of their "training exercises." As we learned earlier, Zoroastrians were poly-drug users par excellence, but certainly the rites and rituals of the Israelites, probably learned from the Egyptians, would have sufficed. Again, these stories or prophecies may represent old storylines used for initiating members into mystery cults. You will recall that the Roman elite and military commanders belonged to the mystery cult of Mithras, a tradition that morphed from Zoroastrianism, and it is more than likely that they used mind-altering substances. These cults were all over the Mediterranean until banned by Theodosius around 380 CE, and their content, although secret, would have been preserved in some cases, especially as scripts for mind-altered initiation. If you want to consider another mind-altered trip that may represent another of these scripts, read the Book of Zachariah and Revelation.

What are we to make of Ezekiel's report? Certainly these are not normal, everyday sightings. Some see this as a spaceship from another world; others see this as a real, historical event of angels (Seraphim and

Thrones) descending from the sky and giving orders to "Son of man." Then there are some who see this as a drug experience. But perhaps Ezekiel was simply deranged. The central points are that he was respected, the dreams were experiences with the deity, and he had the ability to wrap them around an idea, in this case, the Israelites as a "rebellious house." The deity, with whom they formed an extensive behavioral contract, is pissed. The message that comes through, at least to me, is that the Israelites are not maintaining the covenant and God is not happy. One way to get people back in line is with fear. There is certainly another way of looking at this: Ezekiel (or whoever wrote this) simply has a vivid imagination. Would the deity really show up this way? Not an intelligent deity. An intelligent, all-powerful deity would simply put everyone to sleep and alter brain and memory so that His instructions were always followed, unless, of course, this is not what the deity really desires. To bitch and moan, spit fire, and sprout wings are the signs of an immature and frustrated tyrant who can't get his way, the "little child within," perhaps, who needs to be spanked. The message that shines through these types of antics and threats of punishment is that threats and fear from a deity, tyrant, king, pope, imam, and priest are designed to keep people in line, and if these approaches really worked we would have been beaten into submission thousands of years ago. Humans are a small-group animal designed to live in groups of between twenty-five to 125 individuals; greater numbers lead to increased conflict, and unless you control the politics and social relationships, tensions will increase and the group will fracture. To incorporate large numbers of people you need powerful symbols— gods and goddesses who set the rules while the leader is simply taking orders from these deities; everything that happens is the will of a deity. Cosmic laws are penned by the supernatural world, whereas secular laws are social agreements. Both contain threats and punishment. There seems to be some cosmic law in play that says once you begin a process of controlling people with threats and fear of punishment, this has to be kept in place with more rules, threats, and fear of punishment. Every once in a while there is public humiliation and violence toward subjects lest they forget their place—so you set an example. The Israelites are out of line and not in God's favor, indicated by the fact they are always getting beat up and pushed off their God-given real estate. Ezekiel is distraught; having been uprooted from his homeland and probably witnessed his kin killed, he is now in a strange place and with people from whom one could contract a spiritual disease. As a distressed stranger he probably has the option of staying with other exiles in a special area of the city, or perhaps he is disgusted with the behavior of his kin and he is alone. So he wanders and talks to people; Ezekiel is not a stupid person and realizes that if he is going to adapt and make a living he has to network. Culture shock can lead to depression and worse, and one of the best releases is to get out and mingle, observe, learn the customs, their stories, and so on. He is probably, by this time, out of pot and mushrooms, and his kin won't share theirs—especially the pot. But fortuitously he bumps into a proselyte of the Zoroastrian tradition. Proselytes are like the young men who ride up to your door on bicycles wearing a white shirt, tie, and black pants, selling God according to Mormon. (Jehovah Witnesses usually show up with a child hoping to get a better reception or at least not get beat up.) Our man Ezekiel, then, is promised an interview with God; as a good anthropologist he says, "Lead the way." The set was a defined ritual, the setting was a group with props, and his emotional set point was, "Why is God always picking on us?" Off he goes and his experience is coded in his book.

As mentioned above, the psychiatric community believes that the diagnostic categories in the DSM-IV are real entities, and except for the few pages considered "culture bound syndromes," the bulk are seen as universal. How should the psychiatric community approach Ezekiel? There are several possibilities. First, that Ezekiel was seeing a real event of God in a chariot. Second, he is schizophrenic with visual hallucinations (much rarer than auditory hallucinations). Third, he has experienced brain trauma or fever; perhaps it is lead poisoning or malnutrition. Fourth, this is just a good story from someone with a vivid imagination. And fifth, the most likely and reasonable with the data at hand,

304 | **Failed God**

he was using a time-honored procedure for touching the realm of the gods. I would say, in this light, that most clinicians would attribute Ezekiel's visions to mind-altering substances purposely consumed during a ritual process.

During a conversation with a minister from a liberal Protestant group (California has lots of these), I posed the question about hallucinogens and religion. The answer was intriguing. First, he admitted that it was probably true. He has studied ancient religions, and appreciated the point of shamanism and how the use of mind-altering substances translated to priests. Second, he was aware of some recent books about the use of mushrooms, cannabis, and so on. Third, he then eclipsed this with, "But the purest form of these experiences with God comes from simple devotion to Him and then He is there for you."

I needed some clarification, so I asked, "You mean that through prayer and meditation God is like the experiences in the Bible?"

"Well, no. Not exactly."

Realizing that I was not in a rational dialogue, I jumped in and asked, "Well, if they aren't like those in the Old Testament, then maybe they are just making it up?"

"No," he replied. "They are simply with a kinder, gentler God now."

"Is this a different god from the Old Testament? But more to the point, what if this person does have an experience with the God of the Old Testament, without using mind-altering substances? How would you deal with this person?"

"My first inclination would be that this person has a problem...."

"So the bottom line is that these monotheistic traditions have made it illegal to commune with God? The police can hold people seeing or talking to God against their will? So that which you are attempting to foster, that is, being with God or Jesus, is either disbelieved by the church when it happens, and/or is seen as aberrant?"

At this point the minister had an appointment and the conversation ended. The church, temple, or mosque patron is encouraged to be with God, Jesus, or Allah—but not too much. That is reserved for special people, the religious clerics with proper credentials and organic mushrooms; God loves organic and natural.

Props, Bells, and Whistles

Archaeologists and physical anthropologists rely heavily on artifacts/relics for interpreting our past. These objects are subjected to close scientific scrutiny to determine age, significance, how they were manufactured, and so on. Interpretations are open to change as new information becomes available; science is a self-correcting process of discovery. Christianity, beginning with the early writings of Paul, takes a different position, a position that places faith before reason (see Freeman 2002, 118). Again, St. Augustine, as mentioned earlier, presents a more telling stand (see Freeman 2002, vii) in which curiosity and critical thinking are demonized. The meaning here is quite clear: Do not think too deeply into our "truth;" throw out science and rely on faith.

As Freeman (2002) more than adequately points out, the only way Christianity can survive is by closing the mind to other possibilities. But just as they close the mind, they offer what naive people believe to be relics of mythical people, and this amounts to nothing less that fraud and deception. Yes, there are relics, the bones of early bishops and priests, but many of these—the bones of St. Anna, apostles, and others, and various objects (Jesus' cross or nails of the cross, the Holy Grail, the Shroud of Turin)—are inventions, fakes. The Grail, for example, is an invention of the Middle Ages, most noted in the Arthurian Legends. The Grail has been researched by Baigent, et al. (1982), Picket and Prince (1998), and others, with the most recent discussion coming by way of a novel, *The Da Vinci Code.* (Brown 2003) I find the research and the novel (based on this research) very interesting, but the bottom line is that the Grail is an invention during the layering of the Christ myth. Remember, Jesus is a mushroom, and all the stories are a personification of the fungi.

The Grail has several synonyms, including rose, lotus, cornucopia, octopus, magic harp, mushroom, book, and so on. The Grail is symbolic of that which brings forth everlasting life. The cornucopia has a long season and is represented by the Roman goddess Ceres, who causes living things to emerge from her breasts. The Greek goddess of fertility, Demeter, brings forth the grain year after year, and the Celtic

Cernunnos, also a fertility god, sits in a lotus position holding a cornucopia that pores forth "grain" or life into the world (see www.clinicalanthropology.com, World Myth Tattoo Gallery). The story of the Grail is a perfect example of how myth is constructed and layered by popes, priests, playwrights, and pretenders. Some historians, for whatever reason, seem to pander to the religious community, say little about these relics, assume that Jesus was a real person, and then conduct research geared to that assumption. What is created in the process is more myth about myth.

Religious traditions rely heavily on props or tangible items to create an illusion of authenticity. The ancient Egyptians and Greeks manufactured statues that could move, "talk," and dispense liquids. We have the Shroud of Turin and wood and nails from the cross upon which Jesus was crucified. There are many pieces of the cross, enough to construct several crosses! Relics make tangible that which can only be accepted on faith. Most are fraudulent and attempts to conduct scientific analysis (C^{14} testing, for example) are usually turned down for obvious reasons. The Shroud of Turin is an exception, but recent research shows this "relic" to be "a more recent product," in other words, a fake. The Greek Orthodox Church in Roseville, California, claims to have acquired a piece of bone from St. Anna, proudly announcing the acquisition to the news media (*Sacramento Bee*, July 26, 2005). Who was St. Anna? St. Anna is the mythic mother of Mary and mythic grandmother of Jesus. If Jesus has no historical visibility, then the same has to be said for his mother and grandmother. We cannot assume the existence of parents or grandparents for people we can't prove existed. In other words, in order for St. Anna to exist we need proof positive that Jesus existed.

Looked at from another angle, Jesus symbolized the *Amanita muscaria* mushroom. This being the case, St. Anna would have to be a pine tree, and Mary her roots (womb) from which come forth the fruit of the tree, *Amanita muscaria*, a.k.a. Jesus. And just as the Egyptian goddess Isis was the throne upon which the king (Horus) sat, so Mary is the throne upon which Jesus sat. Understand the connection. Isis is the root (throne) that brings forth the pharaoh (king, Horus, etc.). By the king's birth and death, he brings forth everlasting life by traversing the heavens as the sun during the day and fighting death at night, to reemerge (rebirth) as the morning sun (illumination). Jesus brings forth illumination (birth, light) and through him everlasting life, also defeating death in the underworld. Jesus, the mushroom, is a personification of the *experience* of the other side, of death and rebirth, an experience made illegal, restricted from the masses, and jealousy guarded by the few. The relic of St. Anna, then, is either a fake or a piece of 2,000–year old Lebanese Cedar. For thousands of years people worshipped trees and we should not find this unusual. The reason that the infallible Pope Pius declared, in 1951, that Mother Mary was assumed into heaven, bones, skin, hair, and clothing and all, was because, like Jesus, she has no historical visibility. What we are seeing is the business of constructed genealogy as part of Christology's mythical charter in a manner similar to the Jewish tradition. This is purposeful—not innocent—fraud. This desperation to find the "true" relics of Jesus (and of course the promise of wealth and fame), has led to the recently revealed ossuary box with the inscription, "James, son of Joseph, brother of Jesus," which the Israelis claim is also a clever fake. This box was brought to public attention by André Lemaire, an antiquities dealer suspected in many forgeries.

Some Protestant groups likewise sport relics. Mormons, for example, claim to have gold tablets sent down to Joseph Smith (Mormonism is a weak imitation of Judaism), who, by the way, was a habitual user of alcohol. Alcoholics experience all sorts of demons, deities, and bizarre apparitions. Many, many years ago a close friend of mine claimed to have met Jesus during one of our drinking bouts. I think that he was speaking to the porcelain telephone in the bathroom at the time; between flushes he was saying, "Oh, God. Oh, Jesus!" Perhaps, like Paul, my friend should be considered a "lesser apostle."

If these gold tablets did exist, you can rest assured they would be displayed, an admission fee charged, and we would all be Mormon. The Mormons claim to be so in touch with God and heaven that they have created special rooms in their temples where *paid up* members can see what heaven will be like. This is an example of social pathology and is a serious psychiatric issue, because it creates a fractured reality and promotes irrational thoughts, which can lead to irrational and dangerous behavior. Deception, rape, torture, slavery, and murder are justified in the name of God.

So why are these organizations allowed to continue this deception? It is called "freedom of religion," and the spokespersons for these traditions are permitted to say what they please and make outrageous claims; this is why there has to be total separation of Church and State. Religious personalities regularly back political candidates—this is pure politics. History has shown that when religion and State are conjoined, irrational beliefs are forced on the public offering pain and suffering to nonbelievers.

Many clergy have asked me, "Do you want to destroy people's faith in our Lord?" Besides the issue of Jesus being a mushroom displayed in Christian art commissioned and directed by priests, cardinals, bishops, and popes, the question indicates that the clergy, to maintain power and authority, are willing to deceive in order to have people maintain faith in a myth bandied about as historical fact. My answer over the years has been very simple: Systems that run on deception, fraud, intimidation, and fear do not serve the public good and, in fact, encourage immorality. Having "faith" in this instance is synonymous with believing a lie. In monotheistic traditions God comes first and humanity second; God is more important than being a decent human being. So not only are these systems involved in blatant fraud, they converted Jesus (*Amanita christos*) into a demon who condones deception and enslaves the minds and bodies of the unsuspecting—this is the nature of demons.

Jesus and Christianity

Our mythic hero Jesus had a very simple message for his followers: You don't need a church or a priest. Just follow his example and become God like him, in short, be a decent human being and treat others with compassion. This message was corrupted into what we now know as Christianity, a construction by the anti-Christ Paul and the early priest/poets. The idea of paying a minister or priest or giving money to the church or temple comes from Paul and is totally opposite from anything Jesus would have said. The building of a bureaucracy with all kinds of rules, restrictions, and wrath has nothing to do with the core message Jesus brought to the world.

Some suggest that religion and morality go hand in hand and that without church and religious clerics all would turn to rape and plunder. This is naïve and simply untrue. Morality and sensitivity to others come from the necessities of social living, that is, cooperation on the hunt, building irrigation works, care of others because you might need care yourself, and so on. Moreover, Judaism, Christianity, and Islam are responsible for some of the most immoral and horrendous acts, all committed in the name of their respective gods (drug-induced no less). Anytime you place God (Yahweh, Allah, etc., etc.) before humanity, you have a form of devil worship.

Taxes and the Church

Have you ever wondered why religious institutions are given tax-exempt status? And, yes, religious organizations do charity work, offer shelter, medical services, and so on, but this tax exemption didn't begin in that manner. The tax-exempt status is the keystone in the connection between religion and state. Here is what happened.

A long time ago (326 CE), in a place far, far away, there was a thug by the name of Constantine, who granted tax exemption to the "correct" or Catholic clergy. There were many Christian-type groups running around with their peculiar interpretation of the story of Jesus, who he was, and his life and times. The only way you can have truth is when everyone believes your side of the story. This led to arguments over interpretation—over who is who and what is what. Arguments between individuals and groups resulted in feuds that evolved into killings and retaliation. Constantine put out the word: "Either step up and solve

3

this in a reasonable manner, or I will solve this for you." So a large group of Christians, whose differences did not lead to blood feuds, stepped up and received as a reward no taxes. Eventually the land owned by clergy and/or church as an organization (corporation) was included in the exemption. The deferred tax status, which stems from this initial act by Constantine, has remained in effect ever since. This act, and the continued practice today, is for the explicit purpose of staying in step with the politic: "You support us, and we'll give you a break." It is interesting to note that the U.S. government keeps a close eye on *fringe* religious groups, and if they appear dangerous enough removes them from the landscape. Remember Waco? Religion is a business wrapped in politics and should be taxed like all other businesses.

Onward Christian Soldiers

How in this world did Jesus get connected to warfare? Here is another, very important connection between Christianity and the politic. A long time ago (372 CE), in a land far away, there was Ambrose, bishop of Milan. Keep in mind what is going on here. There are two types of rites within Church dogma or doctrines. There are the everyday rites priests administer to the public (exoteric) and then the esoteric rites, or those performed by certain grades of the priesthood involving mind-altering substances and the secrets of their use. Ambrose, through careful planning, altered states of consciousness, or psychosis, characterized Jesus as a general, a leader of the army conquering evil, especially the armies of others (see Freeman 2005, 177).

There are two references in the Bible used to build this picture (Psalm 91:13 and Revelation 19:11–16). In neither passage, however, is there any proof that the reference is to Jesus. Any reasonable person would conclude that the reference is to someone else, considering what is attributed to Jesus in the gospels and apocrypha. Making Jesus a soldier would be like having a poster of Buddha, Gandhi, or Martin Luther King, Jr. dressed in camo-garb, wielding an AK-47, and trampling adders and dragons underfoot. This is just plain "sacrilegious." So don't look for Jesus on the battlefield anytime soon. In fact, the purpose of the real story of Jesus is to be a decent human being, and it is difficult to sell that story if our hero is also trampling adders and dragons, which is not to say that adders and dragons must never be vanquished. I don't recall ever reading that Jesus was opposed to war, for he certainly suggested buying weapons (short swords) for personal protection. Jesus' message was not attached to the politic in a way that leads to personal wealth (tax deferred) or enhanced status (general of the armed forces, pope, bishop). His message was one of personal relationships and mental and social health, and then with the help of Paul and a plethora of pretenders, we revert back to reformed Judaism nowadays also known as Christianity.

Christian Conclusion

In my opinion, there probably was a person who came out of nowhere, who walked through the streets saying, "Hey man, let's get along. Follow my example and we will stop doing nasty things to each other, and all will be love and peace. You don't need a church, you don't need a priest, but you need to know yourself and your other side. Take some of this and you will experience the godhead." Jesus (a.k.a. John the Baptist or whoever) would lead the disciple through a mind-altering experience (the Spirit), a frightening experience for some, to remove the demons, that evil part of you, and to provide an introduction to the Father (the Son of the Sun, "Go into the light; go into the light!"). These would be powerful experiences and only those committed to truth need submit an application. All are not good students; "Only those who are right for the 'fire' need apply." Jesus is not really a hothead but he accepts that people are ignorant, and sometimes, in a manner similar to the "crazy shaman" posture, he does something outrageous to get attention. By overturning the tables of the money exchangers, he symbolically separated spiritual needs from politics and economics. This is clear evidence of Jesus "acting out" a parable rather than simply using words.

Once a disciple has the mind-altering, guided experience, he becomes a "true believer," an apostle or one who will spread the word. The spectacular way he (Jesus/John the Baptist) did this and the rumors that followed caused concern, as did any behavior that threatened the power structure. He and perhaps many others who engaged in the same activity were arrested and murdered. One or perhaps all of these episodes of crucifixion/murder left a memory that was worked into a mythic hero, about a nice guy who was brutally murdered. But why did this happen? There must be a purpose. No one can answer the question, but the event lingers in the group memory. Lots of bad dreams, no one wants to talk about it, the fear sinks in—this would have been a terrible time in which to live. One day an individual develops a story that puts meaning to these events, of a savior who rode into town one day on a donkey (not Clint Eastwood!); he was an average person who rejected none. He offered hope, worked magic, and tried to show people the way (zodiakos), the *Dao* to a better life, not in some other place, but here and now. It was this "here and now" emphasis that really attracted the attention of those in power because this was a clear challenge to the prevailing misery created and maintained by those in power. So, Jesus had to go, but he did this willingly as a cover for our sins; we can now start over and peace will prevail. Well, nothing changed, so it was added that Jesus said, "I'll be back." There will be a second coming, and then the evildoers will get their comeuppance. Amen.

The original story, of course, was not new, and was pieced together from popular themes. Hero stories always offer hope for the oppressed; they save us when in physical pain (torture) and prepare us for, and offer protection from, psychological shock (PTSD). The myth, designed to explain why people are so cruel to one another, goes from being just a story to truth, as layers and layers are added to the storyline. The original message of Jesus (a.k.a. John the Baptist) would fit all times. It appears to be the type of morality that can *only* mature in a free and open society engaged in a democratic process of electing rulers who promise a good life, and that disposes of rulers who don't keep their promises by voting them out rather than removal through assassination. The message of Jesus/John the Baptist never had a chance. Within a few years after the death of the Baptist, Paul managed to sew onto this simple but very threatening message all kinds of ancient mythic elements, rules, and regulations, reestablishing another brand of Judaism. I would place Paul on Axis I: 295.90/292.89 or Schizophrenia Undifferentiated Type and Hallucinogen Intoxication, and Axis II: 301.81, Narcissistic Personality Disorder—see DSM-IV.

In the next chapter we will take a close look at Islam, which, for all intents and purposes, is a replay of Judaism, an attempt to maintain a tribal form of life. Islam is also the most intolerant tradition in the world today and is on par with fascism and Stalinist communism.

CHAPTER FOUR

Islam

Qur'an, Surah 9:5: "When the sacred months are past, kill the idolaters wherever you find them, and seize them, besiege them, and lie in wait for them in every place of ambush; but if they repent, pray regularly, and give the alms tax, then let them go their way, for God is forgiving, merciful."

Introduction

I have heard many times that Islam is a religion of peace. I have read several translations of the Qur'an and many hadith; I have read many books on Islam written from the perspective of those who apologize or "spin" the sayings in the Qur'an or play down the pillars of violence and fear. Then there are opinions from Muslims I have interviewed, non-Muslims, news reports, and so on. Islam and many of its adherents are mired in a political and pseudo-religions system just as are Christianity and Judaism. Islam was originally connected to a violent period, a stance of defense, which turned to conquest. Islam, as it was known after 750 CE, has never been a religion of peace. Islam can only live in peace with its neighbors if it has no political power; this holds true as well for Judaism and Christianity. For once Islam (like Christianity) enters the politic, pain and suffering quickly follow. These political systems are not democratic; God or Allah is not democratic. "Peace" and "morality" in this system come not from piety or devotion to a deity, as some recent scholars have suggested (see Mahmood 2005). Peace comes from early indoctrination, using fear and threat of dire consequences if rules that control every part of one's life are not followed. Piety does not come from choice of devotion; it comes from fear of consequences (both here and in the hereafter) of not showing piety and devotion to a deity chosen *for* you. The origin of this fear is our primal fear of rejection, and rejection equals death (see Rush 1999).

Let me also say that Islam, as is the case for Christianity and Judaism, encompasses a wide range of views. There is large distinction between the tradition called Islam, and a person who calls himself or herself a Muslim. In Islam you are a slave to God; as a Muslim you are a follower of Muhammad. At one end we have those sincerely interested in peace and looking past our animal nature, a nature so elegantly described in both the Old Testament and the Qur'an (the real Muhammad). At the other end are those invested in war and conquering the world and committed to bringing us back to the Dark Ages of psychotic, insecure tyrants (the constructed thug). We could say that Muhammad and Jesus were cut from the same cloth, the differences being that Muhammad carried a sword representing a life and death struggle for independence—the reality of the world as it was—while Jesus carried a mushroom symbolizing a quest for an independent, personal, spiritual experience as it can only be. At this point in history, peace-loving Muslims lack visibility. Few will stand up and call for reform, and their silence is deafening. Many are afraid of retaliation. If nothing else, this silence has contributed to a perilous religious polarization with Islam on one side and Christianity and Judaism on the other. This is a dangerous time, even more so than the Cold War, and it has been brewing for a long, long time. Reason could surface at times in the Cold War; you cannot reason with terrorists, religious fanatics, or anyone who believes that God comes first and humanity second.

The Prophet of Islam

As with Jesus, the prophet of Islam, Muhammad, has no historical visibility. Warraq (2000, 75–78) informs us that the quest for the historical Muhammad bumps into similar problems as the quest for the historical Jesus. What we have for "evidence," Qur'an and hadith, do not offer proof of anything except that Islam is a composite of Babylonian, Zoroastrianism, Greek, Jewish, and Christian ideas, as well as astronomical concepts. I would add that there is a layer coming from Egypt, with a thick undercoat of ancient Arabic tribal deities and the laws of ritual performance, which, like roots, dig deep into the fabric of a people, into all aspects of their lives; Hinduism, Judaism, and Christianity do the exact same thing.

Muhammad is a figurehead, a focal point or hero, who, patterned after Moses, rallies the Arabs in an attempt to maintain tribal identity. The god of this tradition is simply a source of authority for directing and justifying the emotions and behaviors of illiterate and superstitious people, initially, again, to repel foreign ideas, beliefs, and customs. There is absolutely no evidence that suggests that Muhammad had any notion of creating a religion. Just as in the case of Jesus, he therefore cannot be the founder of Islam, but a reference point only. Moreover, it would be difficult to explain Muhammad's ability to move his men to action without reference to mind-altering substances, great storytelling, and psychosis.

As the story goes, Muhammad was born in Mecca on August 2, 570 CE. This is the twelfth day of the third month (*Rabi'u 'L-Awwal*) on the lunar (*Hijri*) calendar. The moon would have been full with Uranus at two o'clock (according to my astronomy program, REDSHIFT 5). *Rabi'* is an Indian word referring to "spring" and the planting of crops. What this indicates is that the religious clerics must have been aware of Indian (and certainly Greek) astronomical calculations. Their interest in astronomy was generated by a need for marking ritual events. The Muslim priest/mathematicians removed the astrological content (especially in the Hindu tradition), as this type of "large prophecy" was the provenance of the last prophet, Muhammad. By the twelfth century, they removed some of the philosophy. What I think we are seeing in the Qur'an, and certainly many hadith, is an astrological code, in much the same manner as the Old and New Testaments. Certainly it can be read that way, although the intent of the Qur'an and hadith was likewise political— as above, below. The conception of the heaven above has to be a reflection of the politic, so one should not be surprised to find it connected to ritual and especially ritual demands ("Thou shalt and shalt nots").

In any case, they didn't like what they were encountering in math and where it was leading, and by the sixteenth century the Arab world

moved into a "dark" age, one that disallowed philosophical exploration and examination of Islamic beliefs and practices (see Salbia 1994).

Of all the celestial objects, the lunar crescent (*hilal*) cannot be under-
stated as it is prominently displayed on the flag of Islam. Muhammad
represents the full moon that has grown out of the crescent and "all
should follow his example and you shall be full as well." As the story
goes, just prior to Muhammad's birth, an Abyssinian Christian army
attacked Mecca with the purpose of destroying the Ka'bah, the *pagan*
shrine which all Muslims are to visit at least once in their lifetime. At
the time the Ka'bah housed sacred images of gods and goddesses, but
now the pilgrim is privileged to kiss a black stone which is part of a
meteor that fell to earth some time in the pre-Islamic past. This is the
major relic of this tradition, supposedly given to Abraham by the
archangel Gabriel (possibly Samael—see below). It was not uncommon
practice to destroy the shrines of one's enemy, thus removing the god's
presence or influence from the battlefield. This is a reflection of an old
idea that gods hung around shrines and eventually temples, mosques,
and churches. These sacred geographies acted as portals, if you will,
for communing with the favored deity. People believed, and still do
today, that shrines, the embodiment or personification of a god or goddess, have power, spirit power. This type of belief is termed animism
and destroying idols removes some of the protective power.

But just as the army was approaching Muhammad's birthplace, the
elephants refused to attack. This is similar to the story of Buddha, who
was tempted by the God of Social Duty (Dharma), and the elephant
upon which he rode bowed in front of the Buddha. This temptation
for the Buddha is repelled by *inner will*, through personal illumination.
Muhammad's birthplace, and thus Muhammad, are protected, not by
some inner-directed illumination, but instead by an *outside* force showing special favor and privileges. Sound familiar? Thus, an outer will,
or God, controls all. The other message is that the elephants apparently knew of Muhammad's birth before anyone else. The elephant is
an important symbol, especially in Hinduism, where elephants (symbolized as clouds in the sky) represent a foundation holding up the

world. Their unwillingness to attack is a symbol of protecting the foundation of Islam, that is, Muhammad. The cavalrymen, as the myth continues, were decimated by birds who acted as a magical protective force for Muhammad. Birds, because they fly in the heavens, are more closely connected to the deity. Some researchers have suggested that the Abyssinian army was destroyed by smallpox instead of birds, as described in Surah 105. However, this is simply part of a mythical charter as there is no tangible, irrefutable evidence that the story is true.

Muhammad's birth is foretold by three angels who visit Muhammad's mother, Amina, in a dream, and instruct her to name the prophet Muhammad, which means "highly praised." Notice the name—Muhammad, "highly praised"; our hero has to have a credible name. It would never be "two goats humping" or "camel dung on his shoe." This "foretelling" of the birth is similar to Zoroaster, Oedipus, Buddha, John the Baptist, and Jesus. These angels also provide cover for Muhammad's birth by blocking out the sun, suggesting that this is not an ordinary vaginal birth. Shortly after his birth, angels instruct Muhammad in the ablution ritual performed before prayers. The only way to describe this (the Jewish purification rites are also extreme by any standard) is Obsessive-Compulsive Disorder (300.3 in the DSM-IV). And of course there is all the purification males have to contend with if they have contact with women (301.82, Avoidant Personality Disorder); these are very similar to those of the Jewish tradition. The belief in the polluting nature of women is very much alive in Islam and clearly indicates fear of women and rightly so, for it will be through the female energy (not warfare) that Islam will reform and then eventually fade away.

His birth being foretold, there is magic in the way it was carried out, but according to the myth the alleged father, Abdullah, died six months before he was born and his importance is marginalized. This is similar to the birth of Moses (who has a father-in-law but no father) and Jesus. Although Joseph is in the picture in the case of Jesus, he is there for genealogical reasons, that is, a connection to the House of David. From a social standpoint, Joseph is there for protection and probably to stem

322 | **Failed God**

gossip about Mary's pregnancy, and not as the father of Jesus, as one young Catholic cleric told me. Although the poets do not suggest he is the son of a god, Muhammad's birth is certainly very, very special, if not divine, or angels would not be involved. In many ways Muhammad is more important than Allah, which actually suggests a great deal of disrespect for this deity. So Abdullah, meaning "God's servant," stands in a similar relationship to Muhammad as Joseph stands to Jesus, that is, in the background but serving the deity in some special manner.

The above is all great mythic stuff. Muhammad's date of birth is revealing as it coincides with the planting season; his date of death is that liminal place where you are between the old and the new. Many deified individuals, like Jesus, Osiris, and Krishna, are said to have been born on December 25, which represents the lengthening of the day or the "blooming" of the sun. There is a three-day liminal phase (December 22–25) where the old drops away and the new takes its place (more about astrology and astronomy in a future publication). This is similar to Muhammad's liminal phase; let me explain.

As you recall, Muhammad was born during the third month, which would have been August in the Gregorian calendar. The Islamic calendar is calculated to the phases of the moon and shares many features with the Jewish calendar. Using the moon for ritual events has created problems in ritual performance because different geographical areas not only see the rising of the crescent moon at different times, but the beginning and end of religious observances can vary as much as a day or so. If the moon is not as useful as the sun for measuring time over the course of many years, then why has the moon been maintained for ritual observance? The main reason has to do with Muhammad's patron deity, the moon god of war, al Liah.

Second, they were emulating the Jews' use of the moon for ritual events. Third, the moon in many ways corresponds to human behavior and biology—our behaviors change from day to day and the moon is a good match for our biology, that is, menstruation and the birthing cycle, sleeping and waking, and so on. Fourth, and perhaps a more practical reason, another system could take years or decades to create.

The moon captivates us all. It is that which looks down on us and winks; unlike the sun, we can look back. You can't gaze at the sun without going blind, and that is why Zeus never revealed himself to the women he lusted after—well, maybe once.

Muhammad, as the story goes, died June 8, 632 CE. There was likewise a full moon, with Saturn to the right at about two o'clock. June 8th would have been the end the first month of the Islamic year (Muharram), and Muhammad's death can be seen as the start of another phase of Islam, with the liminal phase equal to the first month of the Islamic year. Muhammad has a tomb in the Mosque of the Prophet, Medina. Abraham is also said to have a temple at Ur on the banks of the Euphrates River. Moses, on the other hand, didn't get to see the "promised land" and has no monument because of an argument with the deity over water rights. He was buried anonymously in the desert or on a mountain because the Jews were afraid that people would come to worship him and thus detract from the radiance of the Lord, but this is just a layer to the overall story. The Muslims have a similar problem and this is one of several reasons why there are no pictures of Muhammad. And the Muslims are correct—you cannot have a picture of someone who did not exist.

There is no method, short of a time machine, of determining whether anyone named Muhammad existed until the writings of Ibn Ishaq (ca. 750 CE), and thus discussions of where he is buried, how he dressed, and what he said are all unverifiable. But there are some mythic connections. The dates of Muhammad's death and birth, for example, were constructed to coincide with: 1) the full moon; 2) the planting season (fertilizing the fields, in a way similar to how Osiris fructifies the fields along the Nile through his disintegrating penis—Osiris is the midnight sun or the moon); 3) and his death represents birth on the horizon, the beginning of Islam, just as the crucifixion of Jesus (not his birth) symbolically represents the birth or real commencement of Christianity. Out of death come life.

Muhammad is reported to have between twelve and thirteen wives, but it could be fourteen or one-half the phase of the moon. In one telling,

Osiris was cut into fourteen pieces (see Rush 2007). But most historians count twelve wives, equating the wives with the twelve tribes of Israel and the twelve apostles of Jesus, thus placing Muhammad in the realm of the sun god, to match the adjectives to describe the god of the Old Testament. This shows how the shift in just one wife can lead to an entirely different interpretation, just as including mind-altering substances changes our perspective. Muhammad is reported to have five, six, or perhaps seven children. Conveniently for those constructing hadith and the Qur'an, only one survived him, that is, Fatima—who may have been a wife and not one of his children. Having only one heir simplified the genealogy, at least for the Shi'ah. One would think that with twelve wives more children would be assigned to Muhammad. I would be curious as to where the children who died during his lifetime were buried, but they are not very important in terms of the overall story so they are simply minimized or deleted.

The Gods of Islam

Wars fought on the ground over territory and to repel aggressors have their counterpart in heaven, where gods fight over ideology or who is bigger, stronger, and smarter—Zeus fighting the Titans, for example, or Michael fighting Satan, Horus fighting Seth, or even Mickey fighting Willy. The patron god of a particular clan, tribe, or nation-state looked after his or her people, and when battles were won the victory was attributed to the deity. The losing side often saw the deity as more powerful than theirs. Again, the winners and losers quickly transferred their conquest or plight onto the patron deity, for it was only through devotion to this deity, male or female, that the war was won. The losers saw their deity as removing favor for some infraction, large or small. The gods have always been capricious.

The Middle Eastern mother-goddess, who went by many names, including Innana, Astarte, Astoreth, and so on, was extremely important and offered protection to her chosen people, whether a clan, tribe, or nation-state. The idea that a god would have a chosen people is a very old polytheistic, shamanic idea and was not invented by the Israelites and Ishmaelites or modern day Jews and Muslims.

Your identity in those times, as is the case today, is closely connected to tribal symbols often associated with astrological signs, including the sun and moon. These symbols were depicted as deities who look down upon the earth and all that transpires, and who will perhaps provide aid if properly addressed. Nomadic people usually emphasize a patriarchal deity but reference a pantheon composed of both males and females. The reason for the patriarchal emphasis is that nomadic people, just like the animals they herd, take what is in front of them. The males in the tribe are warriors who defend the group from other tribal groups and thus males are seen as more important than females. Nomadic people worship what is everywhere, including celestial objects and large geographic areas, a desert or mountain chain perhaps; deserts and mountains are forever and they hold the truth, but evil can lurk there as well—evil is also truth. Mountains, because they are closest to the heavens, act as "special purpose geographies" for contacting that which lies beyond human understanding. Both Muhammad and Moses make contact with their respective deities on mountains, Mt. Hira for the former, and Mt. Sinai or Mt. Horeb (in the Sinai) for the latter, both using mushrooms or other substances. Likewise, Hira and Horeb linguistically sound very similar. Recent archaeological research on Mt. Horeb has uncovered a temple to Hathor, the cow goddess, a fertility goddess who could just as well bring destruction in the form of Sekhmet the lioness.

Sedentary people, on the other hand, worship what is local, a rock or stream, but they also worship celestial objects because they appear local as well. Sedentary planting people usually have a mother-goddess emphasis, but always tied to the male energy. Nomadic tribes in the Arabian Desert would worship special tribal or patron deities who could fall out of favor, depending on who wins or loses a battle or other political issue. The patron god of Muhammad was not the god of the Jews or Christians, and one of the keys to the name of this god lies in the secret one-hundredth name attributed to the refurbished god, Allah.

The Real God of Islam

The ninety-nine characteristics attributed to Allah are exactly those attributed to the mythic hero Muhammad. All attributes, in most cases, are couched in a language of paired opposites—for example, *Ar-Raafi*, "the exalter, The Elevator, The One who lowers whoever He willed by His Destruction and raises whoever He willed by His Endowment." This is a clear statement of ego and nepotism, with the deity doing as he pleases for a special people, which is exactly the same for the god of the Hebrews. Nature likewise does what it likes.

These attributes for Allah are adjectives describing the possibilities of this energy that informs all. One of these endowments, *Al-Quddoos*, suggests Allah is "clear from children and adversaries," and is an interesting attempt to describe a deity that always was and has produced no other gods, and because he is IT, he trumps all and is final. The god of Islam, however, has daughters—Al lat, Al Uzza, and Manat (Qur'an, Surah 53:19–20).

Allah, as mentioned, has ninety-nine adjectives attributed to his character, although there are actually one-hundred. It is common in magical/religious traditions to withhold one's real name (birth name) for fear of being identified by demonic forces or, in the case of Allah, being identified for what He really represents. It is like someone knowing your social security number and stealing your identity, or, in the case of Allah, knowing his true identity and, from that, understanding the basic philosophy driving this tradition. Muhammad knew the one-hundredth name, but, according to legend, only whispered this to a camel. This is why the camel walks with its nose in the air. What could this one-hundredth name possibly be and why a camel?

The moon god was prominent among the Sabean, Minaean, and Qatabanian of southern and northern Arabia and was the god of war brandishing thunderbolts. The moon went by many names over time, for example, Kashku (Hattic), Arna (Luwian), Kushuh (Anatolia), Sin (Mesopotamia), Yarih (Ugarit), and al-Liah or Hiliah (Arabian Peninsula). According to Natan (2006), the moon god was Muhammad's patron deity justifying offensive warfare; Muhammad was most certainly not a monotheist. Muhammad, in short, is the prophet of the moon god of war. As the poets were constructing the Qur'an from bits and pieces of other mythic traditions, they saw an alignment with Abraham and Ishmael of the Old Testament and changed the god's name (but not his characteristics) for purely political reasons, from *al Liah* to *al La*, or "the god," and finally *Allah*.

As mentioned, Allah is only one of the one-hundred characteristics attributed to this energy. Ninety-nine are known, but to understand the one-hundredth name we must consider some basic tenets of Islam, that is, first, there is only one god, Allah (He comes first), and second, Muhammad is His mouthpiece. In this tradition, and in Fundamental Judaism and Christianity, God comes first and humanity comes second—if at all. According to many scholars, however, Allah has been from the beginning the same god of the Christians and Jews. In, *Al-Qur'an: A Contemporary Translation,* by Ahmed Ali (2001, 11), we read in the footnote: "Allah is the name of the same supreme Being who is called in English God and Khuda in Persian. He is the same God the Jews and Christians worship." There is never mentioned by most Islamic scholars of the deity's previous identity. But there is another serious issue. If the deities of the Old and New Testaments and the Qur'an are one and the same, then this god suffers from Dissociative Identity Disorder (Axis I – 300.14) with paranoid and narcissistic tendencies (Axis II – 301.0 and 301.5—see DSM-IV). This diagnosis represents the cap under which Islam resides.

Suggesting that Allah is Yahweh of the Jews and the God of the Christians is simply a failed attempt to usurp the Bible and create a Third Testament with all the entitlements. Some scholars believe that the God of the Old Testament is derived from El, and although there is some disagreement as to the characteristics of this god, El is not the moon god who went by a number of different names, including Sin (as in Mt. Sinai). The god of the Old Testament is Yahweh, the patron god of Abraham's tribe, who is also referred to as Elohim (thus El), but also as Adoni, derived from the ancient Egyptian sun disk, the Aten, promoted by the heretic Pharaoh Akhenaten (see Chapter Two). The God of Abraham presents himself in a very different manner than the God of Moses (see Chapters Two and Three), and the god of the New Testament bears little resemblance to the god of Abraham, Moses, or Muhammad. The god of the Old Testament is somewhat ambiguous, but the god of the New Testament is the *sun* god. Jesus is the Son of the Sun, and worship of this deity, in most Christian sects, is on *Sun*day. To equate the Muslim God Allah with the God of the New Testament and thus Jesus is absolutely absurd! The God of the New Testament does not instruct adherents to wage war, amputate limbs, suppress the rights of women, kill idolaters, stone people to death, keep slaves, and have multiple wives.

So how did the God of the New Testament become the vicious, insecure, wrathful, war mongering, self-serving God of Islam? Islam is a return to Judaism, and Jesus as a God on earth had to go. In order for Islam to be on equal par with Judaism and Christianity, the obvious references to the moon god were aligned with the God of the Old Testament. This was an easy alignment because the two gods had a great deal in common. The New Testament did not fit the agenda of the Islamic poets. Why? This is because of the stark reality that only war would accomplish their task. After all, look what happened to Jesus. The image and message of Jesus do not support a war god; there are few threats and few suggestions that one should fear God, at least coming directly from our mythic hero Jesus. Even if we leave Jesus out of the god category and see him simply as a prophet, the god in the New Testament is not the god of the Old Testament. The moon god of Muhammad was never suppressed—only relabeled for quick sale. There are numerous references to the moon in the Qur'an wrapped around several themes, a major one being an allusion to other gods. For example, in Surah 6:76–78:

When the night covered him [Abraham] over, he saw a star.
He said "This is my Lord." But when it set, he said "I do not
love those that set."

When he saw the moon rising in splendor, he said "This is
my Lord." But when the moon set, he said, "Unless my Lord
guides me, I shall surely be among those who go astray."

We could possibly interpret this as a dislike for stars and/or the sun
and its scorching heat, not that it sets. The second paragraph asks the
moon for guidance (night travel, advice, etc.), although this could be
interpreted as a reference away from both the sun and moon, with
"Lord" being another deity altogether. The moon, however, is just a
little too prominent in this tradition to be merely a logo. As I said earlier, this verse like many, many others represents an astronomical and
astrological footprint amongst many found in the Qur'an.

The earliest edition of the Qur'an of which scholars are aware was
not written down until around 750 CE (mythic Muhammad died in
632 CE). As we will see, the Arabian tribes were in the midst of an
identity crisis and in order to get in step with what they considered the
modern world they needed a mythical charter, a story that would justify whatever they did and whatever it took to meld an identity. In writing the story, however, traditions get combined simply because the older
traditions act as reference points for building the current story. The
unfortunate part is that in creating their mythical charter, the Arabs
threw away much of their secular history and many prehistoric connections.

As the poets were constructing the Islamic mythical charter, they
realized that war in the name of the moon god in 700 CE would simply
place the tribes in the category of barbarians. They had to be seen
instead as God's most recent chosen people, more special than the
Christians or Jews. Here is where the story of Abraham and Hagar
comes in and allowed them to align themselves with Yahweh. This is
done as *taqiyah*, that is, a lie that is allowed as a means to protect their
religion; they invented Allah, who morphed from al Liah to Allah—in

name only. Astronomically this could be seen as war between the sun, or Aten, and the moon, al Liah. In any event, you follow the footsteps of those who walked before and create a prophet (a shaman), who can go between the heaven and earth and bring the boon to the Arab people. The boon is an identity, inspired by the Jews and constructed around Abraham, the grand patriarch.

Continuing with the moon god, note that the symbol on the Islamic flag is the crescent moon (Surah 6: 96, "He it is that cleaves the day-break ...") with a "star" to the right. The star may be the planet Saturn, perhaps Uranus, but more likely Venus (two of al Liah's daughters, al Lat and al Uzza, represent Venus), which would appear to the ancients as a star. Moreover, crescent moons rest atop the minarets of most mosques. Why is this, if the god of Islam is related to El, or Adon, the sun god? This is what we today call political correctness. Mosques were, I might add, originally built as forts, and most still maintain that function.

Again, the belief that Allah has no pagan emphasis, with no offspring, no beginning or end, does not fit the archaeological and historical data. Al Liah or Allah was originally the moon god of the ancient Arabian Peninsula during our mythic Muhammad's time. He would not have been a monotheist any more than Moses was a monotheist. As stated at www.biblebelievers.org.au:

> The pagan Arabs worshipped the moon god Allah by praying toward Mecca several times a day; making a pilgrimage to Mecca; running around the temple of the Moon-god called the Kabah; kissing the black stone; killing an animal in sacrifice to the Moon-god; throwing stones at the devil; fasting for the month which begins and ends with the crescent moon; giving alms to the poor, etc.

The Muslim's claim that Allah is the God of the Bible and that Islam arose from the religion of the prophets and apostles is refuted by solid, overwhelming archeological evidence. Islam is nothing more than a revival of the ancient moon god cult. It has taken the symbols, the rites, the ceremonies, and even the name of its god from the ancient pagan religion of the moon god.

Again, the symbol for Islam is the crescent moon, a symbol representing the moon god of war. But we might be able to take this one step further. The word camel is Old English and comes from the Latin *camelus,* which comes from the Greek *kamelus.* In Hebrew the word is *gamal* (possibly meaning to bear or endure), and in Arabic *qamal.* Qamal might also be related through wordplay to *qisas,* meaning retaliation or revenge. The camel is important in that it was a symbol of war exploits, with Muhammad riding singularly into battle atop of one of these fast-moving beasties. This appears to be pure fiction for that time period; although several individuals might ride to the battle seated on a camel, fighting was mostly done on the ground, and the camel would be useful if they had to make a fast getaway. So what is the one-hundredth name for Allah? Is it camel, al-Gamal, or perhaps a sound alike? As Islam is a construction of bits and pieces of other traditions, I think it's legitimate to speculate.

In Judaism, Samael is the evil angel who becomes identified with Satan. Actually, Samael or Sam'al is the name of a kingdom of the Aramaeans, in the area of Syria, dating to the second and first millennium BCE (between 1073 BCE and 700 BCE). Sam'al is a city that means "circular." Their moon god was called Shahr. The Israelites were subjugated by the Assyrians and of course identified them with demonic powers. We know that the Qur'an is a composite of tribal religion and law, and Jewish and Christian personalities and beliefs, some of which became confused through the storytelling process. We also know that the Arabs were not worldly, in the sense of having a firm grasp of the literature and history of those surrounding them, as most people at the time the Qur'an was constructed were illiterate. Thus names of gods and people were confused. As Mingana (1998 [orig. 1914], 79) comments:

> The internal criticism of the Koran will easily show this elementary evidence of a foreign source; but what can by no

means explain, are the wonderful anachronisms about the old Israelite history. The only possible way of accounting for these would be distance which separated the moment of inspiration of the verses from the moment when the prophet received the oral communication. Who then will not be astonished to learn that in the Koran, Miriam, the sister of Aaron, is confounded with the Virgin Mary? (Surat 'Ali-'Imran, iii. 31 *et seq.*) And that Haman is given as minister of Pharaoh, instead of Ahasuerus? (Suratul-Qasas, xxviii. 38, Suratul-Mu'men, xl. 38 *et passim.*) The ignorance, too, of the author of the Koran about anything outside of Arabia and some parts of Syria makes the fertility of Egypt, where rain is never missed, for the simple reason that it is very seldom seen, depend on rain instead of on the inundation of the Nile. (Surat Yusuf, xii. 49.) Moreover, the greatest honor that the Israelite tradition bestows upon Esdras is found in Sanhedrin, xxi. 22, where we read that "Ezra would have been fully worthy to give the law, if Moses had not been before him"; but to state, as in Suratut-Taubah, ix. 30, that the Jews believed that Esdras was the son of God, as the Christians thought of the Messiah, is a grave error hardly justifiable. All these historical mistakes receive another and not less topical support from the utter confusion which is made between Gideon and Saul in Suratul-Baqarah, ii. 250. Such mistakes are indelible stains on the pages of the sacred book which is the object of our study . . .

If these errors were not telling enough, apologists inform us that you have to sing the Surahs. In other words, I have been told that these are not imperfection if they are sung! Some scholars have recognized that the ends of words are modified slightly for purposes of rhyme. This certainly could totally alter the meaning of a word and the context within which it is found. The point is that mistakes or changes creep in, intentional or not. Samael would have been known as an evil presence for the Jews, and the Mohammedans just might have seen Samael as their enemy's enemy, in which case he becomes their friend and conjoins with the moon god. Here is how this might have played out.

The Jews at some point would have asked for the name of the deity with whom Muhammad conversed. The response was Gabriel or perhaps Samael. The Jews then informed the Muhamadens that Gabriel was a "messenger of wrath and judgment" and he was an enemy (see Hughes 1994, 133) to the Jews as well as the Arabs. One can see how Samael and Gabriel could easily become interposed. Thus Camel, Qamal, Samael, and Gabriel, with a grafted connection to the moon god, become the one-hundredth name, a clever play on words. Samael, by the way, had *three* brides, one of which was *Lilith,* a blood sucking, seductive, baby-killing demon. Al Liah had *three* daughters (they are part of the satanic verses in the Qur'an—more below).

Imagine if you will a moon lit night where the ground is illuminated, allowing a cooler, safer travel. You stop for a moment to get your bearings and you see the shadow of the one humped camel or dromedary against a dune in the shape of a crescent moon. Let's look at the camel more closely.

Qisas refers to compensation for murder (purposeful or accidental) or perhaps wounding or cutting off someone's arm or hand. A person might have to forfeit his life, and, at least as stated in Islamic law, retaliation ceases once the life is given in compensation. In cases where there is retaliation "short of life" (wounding, property loss), a camel or camels could be given in payment to settle these lesser disputes. The camel might be sacrificed and divided in some way between the two parties, with the best or choice parts going to the injured party and the remainder to the injurer. This might be seen as a "cleaving of the moon." Most of the time retaliation led to more retaliation and long standing feuds, and compensation with camels, amber, hides, and so on, was not often satisfactory enough to avoid further tribal disruption. Qisas and camel, then, are connected in the sense of settling disputes, just as the moon dies and is reborn, thus reordering the world. In this sense the camel's death (the death of the moon) is a form of reordering the world, for the camel's blood will go into the sand and be reborn in another camel (rebirth of the moon—this rebirth is also part of the Jewish Kosher laws).

Thus we have Allah derived from the pre-Islamic, polytheistic moon god of war. Also, as mentioned, there is the crescent moon on the flag of Islam, the crescent moon on the minarets of mosques, and the numerous references to the moon in the Qur'an—Surahs x, 5; lxxi, 15; xxxv, 14; xxxix, 7; lxxv, 8; lxxiv, 35; lxxxiv, 18; xci, 2. Apologetic scholars attempt to connect Allah to El, the God of the Old and New Testaments. Why is this important? It is important because Allah, as the moon god of war, cannot then be connected to Abraham and his patron deity Yahweh. With this there can be no connection to Ishmael and Hagar. The Islamic mythical charter is seriously fractured, exposing the underlying foundation upon which it was built.

Islam as Misunderstood

Islam is not a pure "entity" with which all scholars or practitioners can agree, any more than there is a pure entity called Christianity. There are positions and "pillars" of Islam, in the generic sense, to which most would agree. Many apologists for this tradition simply claim that Islam is misunderstood, but I do not think that is correct. Islam is actually a very simple political system, but it becomes more and more complicated as academics construct new stories to explain this, that, or the other thing. When we dig deeper into the platform from which Islam evolved, we find it embedded in politics or control over people; you cannot build a successful army unless you can control and/or convince a large numbers of individuals to cooperate for some cause. The major tools of control are subordination, ritual to minimize idle time, judgment, along with threat and violence. This is basic barbaric stuff. To justify this you need a third party who is bigger and stronger than all others, and His rules or directives come only through a special, chosen people, in this case, Muhammad and his heirs.

Muhammad was probably a leader of war, a general, who took mind-altering substances, after which he said both insightful and stupid things that led people to action. Before he enlisted in the war business he might have been a caravan director, or *Qafilah-Bashi,* a wonderful occupation to learn strategies of war. In this case he would have traveled into Persia, and being an insightful and intellectual sort, learned local esoteric methods of contacting one's deities, although he probably had homegrown methods as well. It's like when dopers get together and sample each other's stash. As a war leader, he finds this useful for keeping his men motivated with divine instructions from his patron moon god. Orders come from the deity and Muhammad is merely a messenger, who will be in jeopardy if his men don't comply. He was a great man, a leader, who was not interested in creating a religion. Contrary to the claims of many historians, he was never the prophet or creator of Islam; he simply wanted to win battles in the name of his patron deity.

Muhammad dies, perhaps in battle, and his lieutenants take over and begin conquering one group after another. They are motivated in the name of their dead general, but someone needs to speak for him and here is where conflict starts. In a clever move, someone discloses the last wishes of Muhammad (or whatever his name was), that their allegiance should be directed to al Liah and not him. Their success came through al Liah, not Muhammad, but some sort of leadership had to emerge after Muhammad's death. Who should lead? It is at this point that stories, mostly verbal, some written, mysteriously show up, suggesting power should go to one side or the other—these are the Contendings of Abu Bakr and Ali in a similar fashion as the Contendings of Horus and Seth in the Egyptian tradition. I find it difficult to determine if such "contendings" really existed early on but suspect they may have been constructed in the early eighth century CE. What I see is a bunch of generals, many of whom were bullies, and initially it probably had less to do with genealogy or closeness to Muhammad and more to do with who is fit to lead, the Sunni ideal. Eventually, however, genealogy conveniently entered the picture as a means of both decreasing conflict (frequent assassination of generals is not a morale booster) and organizing groups in accord with standard principles.

In any event, around this evolved supportive sayings (hadith) and written documents in an attempt to give credibility by virtue of volume, suggesting some degree of contact, third or fourth-hand, with Muhammad, his prophecies, and his wishes. There is also a story about book burning, at the directive of Uthman (circa 643 CE), the Third Caliph, and alleged companion of Muhammad. This was in order to get some standard for the political charter. Uthman ordered all alternative copies or partial copies of this complied material destroyed. This is simply a story, a fabrication, to lend credibility, suggesting as it does that there *was* written material collected in Muhammad's time. "Uthman did a very bad thing. But what can you do? He is one of the relatives." Again, this is unlikely and certainly cannot be corroborated. Again, the burning is a story with a weak punch line, "to create a standard according to the will of Allah."

Uthman wasn't any more interested in creating a religion than was Muhammad; this came later, much later. Uthman was interested in power. Uthman, it must be noted, was assassinated by his own troops in 656 CE; assassinations are spiritual events in Islam. Time marches on, the authorized copies, according to the story, go missing, and the Islamic poets once again "gather up" (read this as fabricate or re-fabricate) written and oral material and retrofit the Old Testament. By 750 CE we have the Qur'an, *sort of* like we have it today, along with masses of hadith. The story about hadith existing at the time of Muhammad is a tall tale. That copies or partial copies of these early Qur'ans were burned is another chapter simply there to validate their existence—these never existed. Again, the story that authorized copies went missing is designed to validate the book burning and the existence of material during Muhammad's time. None of this can be substantiated; institutionalized lying begins early.

In review, hadith and book burnings are stories concocted to give more time depth to this document (Qur'an), suggesting that there were "teachings" of Muhammad that dispersed rapidly throughout the Middle East. Mohammedans did indeed disperse but their manuscripts did not, as there were none. What we have instead are echoes of another time, that is, the assembling of a mythical charter using the Old and New Testaments as a template. The Arabs would have been aware that the New Testament was a compiling of documents, while rejecting many and burning others. Uthman is somewhat analogous to the First Ecumenical Council, or Council of Nicaea held in 325 CE, where, through debate and vote, the various books of the New Testament were modified, created, and assembled. In the process they exclude and include.

With the construction of Islam, one thing was certain—the ruler had to be kept in power. Rapid turnover in leadership is demoralizing to the troops and a charter had to be instituted to give legitimacy for some to lead while excluding others. There were generals before Muhammad, but his importance rested in the fact that he received his directions from a higher power and won battles that he attributed to those powers. He was a great leader, he was a great warrior, and his troops were loyal to him and his patron deity (who wants to be on the losing side?); this is exactly the same scenario as Moses. Jesus would have been characterized as a sissy.

Putting the "pillars" of Islam aside for the moment, there is one aspect of Islam that is shared with Judaism and Christianity—God or Allah comes first and humanity comes second. The fundamentalists' rendering of these systems focuses on the deity and His appeasement. Humans and everything humans experience only exist because Allah is kind and beneficent. But as with Judaism and Christianity, Islam's placing of God first has always led to abuses of the most horrific nature, especially when the rulers are also the religious clerics or controlled by the religious clerics. Once again, in Islam as well as in Judaism and Christianity, belief in and slavery to God is more important than being a decent human being.

Monotheistic traditions are not democratic. In the case of Islam, there is a chain of command from Allah, to Gabriel, and then to Muhammad (or Shaitan to Muhammad, it makes no difference). There is a chain of command that God has established either by saying you are my chosen people, or by at least not denying the possibility as long as they are not "evildoers." In this tradition, one's evils are abolished by asking Allah's forgiveness—and you can apparently do this one hundred or more times a day. In my opinion, myths read as fact promote a great deal of personal irresponsibility and social neurosis. Praying to Allah because you fear His wrath if you do not promotes neurosis and psychotic behavior, such as torture, chopping off people's limbs, and homicidal bombings. Keep in mind that this tradition evolved out of the alleged conversations between Muhammad and supernatural powers, and is difficult to understand and appreciate without reference to mind-altering substances or self-generated psychosis.

Prehistory and History

Archaeological information regarding prehistoric Arabia (the Arabian Peninsula) is thin but very revealing in two ways. First, it provides information about animal use and domestication (camels, for example), trade routes, trade goods, statues of gods pointing to specific deities and where they were worshipped, and so on. Second, we begin to see a world that in large measure has been denied or covered up by the priest/poets who constructed Islam. This is unfortunate, because the prehistory would allow a greater understanding of the development of what today is called Islam. Living patterns, burial practices, foods consumed, patterns of feuding and warfare, and so on, tell us about ourselves and what our ancestors had to go through to get here. What information is available does help us to understand trade routes and the transmission of technology and belief systems.

But most importantly, it tells of polytheism and the periodic wars in heaven where one god or tribe conquers another god and tribe, and out of this emerges Big Daddy, the most powerful god of all. As we will see, people gathered around Muhammad not because he was a religious personality, but because he won battles. He, of course, denied winning the battles and attributed his success to his patron, "who guided my hand." It was Muhammad *and then* his patron deity that people rallied around. These were very superstitious people and conversations with Hubal (another possibility for Gabriel?), the oracle god, or al Liah would have been seen as aiding Muhammad's good fortune in war. You had to get everyone on the same page and some housecleaning (or god cleansing) was in order. As the story goes, Muhammad got in trouble with this as he attempted to convert tribal members to worship only one deity. This is the same story of Moses going to the mountain and obtaining the first edition of the Ten Commandments. As you recall, he was gone for some time, and when he returned he found his people still worshiping other gods, in this case, the golden calf. In Exodus 32:1–6 we read:

> And when the people saw that Moses delayed to come down from the mount, the people assembled themselves to Aaron, and said to him, Arise, make us gods which shall go before us: for [as for] this Moses, the man that brought us out of the land of Egypt, we know not what is become of him.
>
> And Aaron said to them, Break off the golden ear-rings which [are] in the ears of your wives, of your sons, and of your daughters, and bring [them] to me.
>
> And all the people broke off the golden ear-rings which [were] in their ears, and brought [them] to Aaron.
>
> And he received [them] at their hand, and fashioned it with a graving tool, after he had made it a molten calf: and they said, These are thy gods, O Israel, which brought thee out of the land of Egypt.
>
> And when Aaron saw [it], he built an altar before it; and Aaron made proclamation, and said, To-morrow [is] a feast to the LORD.

Moses is warned by God that His "stiff-necked people" were sinning all over the place and so he returned to his flock (Exodus 32:25–30):

> Then Moses stood in the gate of the camp, and said, Who [is] on the LORD'S side? [Let him come] to me. And all the sons of Levi assembled themselves to him.

> And he said to them, Thus saith the LORD God of Israel,
> Put every man his sword by his side, [and] go in and out
> from gate to gate throughout the camp, and slay every man
> his brother, and every man his companion, and every man
> his neighbor.
>
> And the children of Levi did according to the word of
> Moses: and there fell of the people that day about three
> thousand men.
>
> For Moses had said, Consecrate yourselves to-day to the
> LORD, even every man upon his son, and upon his brother;
> that he may bestow upon you a blessing this day.
>
> And it came to pass on the morrow, that Moses said to the
> people, Ye have sinned a great sin: and now I will go up to
> the LORD; it may be I shall make an atonement for your sin.

The story was changed for Muhammad at this point, because he was not that powerful or respected enough to give orders to kill all those who would not follow him. The story of Muhammad, then, could not accommodate this part of the Moses story, as this would antagonize the tribal leaders. Thus a substitute story is invented to bypass this problem (but it causes others). Gabriel (or Samael) came to him (third-person approach) and told him to "remember the daughters of al Liah, that is, al Lat, al Uzza, and Manat." These are the Satanic Verses made famous by Salman Rushdie. The compromise was that the tribes could still keep the shrines and goddesses, as well as accepting his tribal god al Liah. This is a conjoining of polytheism and monotheism, as was the case for Akhenaten a.k.a. Moses. The Moses and Golden Calf story illustrates the incompatibility of polytheism and monotheism; you can have one or the other but not both. But the Golden Calf story contains other meanings never suggested in Sunday school. The calf or bull refers to either the Apis Bull or, more likely, the Goddess Hathor. As mentioned, recent archaeological research on Mt. Horeb has uncovered a temple to Hathor the cow goddess, a fertility goddess. The calf ultimately was ground up and consumed (Exodus 32:19–20):

> And it came to pass, as soon as he came nigh unto the camp,
> that he saw the calf, and the dancing: and Moses' anger
> waxed hot, and he cast the tables out of his hands, and break
> them beneath the mount.
>   And he took the calf which they had made, and burnt it in
> the fire, and ground it to powder, and strewed it upon the
> water, and made the children of Israel drink of it.

What is the meaning of burning gold? Could they burn it, grind it up, and make a potion for all to drink? Some scholars (see Ruck, et al. 2001) suggest that this is a reference to *Amanita muscaria* and a communal experience with the godhead. This was their "Last Supper," for to burn *Amanita muscaria* would destroy its mind-altering properties. I suggest that this symbolically restricts the consumption or communion to only a special few who then administer to the congregation. Again, this is a separation of the Aaron priesthood from the masses. One might wonder why Aaron didn't get into trouble with this—after all, he was in charge. But, of course, he is the brother of Moses, you know, "like my dog, like his fleas." This conjoining of monotheism and polytheism is paralleled in the story of Muhammad. Back to Muhammad.

As the story goes, his attempt to instill monotheism so antagonized his fellow tribesmen that they ran him out of town (Mecca). So, like Jesus, Mickey, Donald, and Goofy, he goes to another place (the magical journey to Medina). For Muhammad, magical help continues to appear in the form of Gabriel (Samael and/or Shaitan), who gives Muhammad all kinds of instructions, to which, as a chosen person, he was obliged to follow. As time went on and as Muhammad won battles, the daughters of al Liah lessened in importance and they faded into the sunset. It is an unlikely story that Muhammad attempted to convert people to his patron deity. I'm sure that he would spare someone's life if he (or she) joined *his* cause (fought on his side) of uniting the Arab tribes. This most certainly happened before he faded from the scene—people would submit to Muhammad, for he was a great warrior. It was probably seen as an honor, but whoever took his place could not count on such fame and consequent loyalty, so they submitted to al Liah, just as they would Muhammad. The pitch is as follows, "Muhammad submitted to al Liah and won battles. Thus, if we serve the deity, we would be standing in Muhammad's boots."

By 750 CE the need to align themselves with the dominant traditions surrounding them (Judaism and Christianity) forced the Islamic poets to claim monotheism, just as the Israelites did around 560 BCE. For political reasons, competition between gods was eliminated by demonizing all other deities; all other gods, goddesses, and the rituals to support them were suppressed, violently at times, with the destruction of temples, artifacts, and books, and the murder of cult personnel (Buddhist monks, Christians, Jews—there is a long, long list). In Matthew 6:10, "your kingdom come, your will be done, on earth as it is in heaven"; as above, below. The ruler takes direct orders from Yahweh, God, or Allah, and just as God's word is final, the same applies to the king who manages in God's name and gives directions on earth. Muhammad's life presentation is that of a hero doing God's work, and fits neatly into the same framework as Moses, Jesus, Mickey Mouse, Rambo, and so on.

When it comes to history, we have two positions: The first is what scholars would call History with a capital "H," and the second is *sacred history* (see Nasr 2002, 42) with a small "h." Secular scholars, using both verifiable information and opinion about that information, construct History with a capital "H." Religious poets, using a combination of myth and legend wrapped around distorted historical places and people, construct sacred history. This construction is for political purposes, as we see in both Judaism and Christianity. The Qur'an and development of Islam can be seen as sacred history, and the only true, factual, verifiable aspect of the Qur'an is that it is a construction by poets assembled from tribal law and prevailing social situations, with much of its content patterned on the Old Testament; this amalgam was knitted together around 750 CE. Knowing how the Qur'an borrowed from major inauthentic and mythic players in the Bible, for example Abraham,

Isaac, Moses, Jesus, and so on, invalidates this document as the word of any intelligent divine being. Again, if the Bible does not stand as secular history, neither can the Qur'an.

Sturdy, clever, and resourceful people populated the pre-Muhammad Arabic world (consisting of the Arabian Peninsula and north into the Syrian desert). These people possessed an oral tradition and few could read or write. There are only limited areas suitable for any large-scale agriculture and sheep and goat herding. These two ecological specialists (farmers and herders) probably coexisted in a relatively peaceful manner around 3000 BCE. With population growth, the herding people move further and further away from growing urban centers out of necessity. There are very few areas for large-scale agricultural pursuits, with the remainder of the land comprised of mountains, desert, or desert scrub. Sheep and goat herders cannot provide all their needs—the same can be said for the agricultural/urban areas, and there were relationships between the sedentary agricultural communities and the nomads. Both groups were polytheists, with the different tribes having their special patron deity, while each settlement or city had its patron deities as well. They shared the same gods, perhaps not in name, but in duty, characteristics, or personification. People didn't argue too much about their religion; it was a personal experience. What they argued about were water rights, wealth, power over people, and territory.

For the little city-states on the Tigris and Euphrates River Valleys (that is, Ur, Uruk, and so on, with populations of 50,000 or more), there seems to have been a strong female emphasis as evident in the mother-goddess cults known to have existed in the Middle East with the advent of agriculture around 9,000–10,000 years ago. All was about to change. Around 2400 BCE, Semitic tribes begin raiding into the Tigris and Euphrates river valleys, bringing their polytheistic traditions but with a greater emphasis on male energy. After approximately 1,500 years of commingling, we see the emergence of exclusive, restrictive systems of monotheism in Egypt (1400 BCE), then dualism in Persia (Zoroastrianism around 700 BCE), and monotheism/dualism in Palestine (560 BCE). Akhenaten, as you recall from Chapter Two, established an oppressive monotheistic tradition in Egypt. With Zoroastrianism, around 700 BCE, we have *Ahura Mazda,* the good god, in battle with the powers of darkness personified by *Angra Manu,* his evil twin (this is the story of Osiris and Seth, and Able and Cain). Many scholars see Zoroastrianism as a dualistic system and somehow Judaism and Islam are monotheistic. For Christianity, it depends where you stand on the continuum, but the basic reference all share is the emphasis on male energy. Christians are told they have guardian angels, so I suppose we have all been assigned a patron deity. In this case there are billions upon billions of supernatural entities around and that alone qualifies as polytheistic.

Monotheistic Judaism (an emphasis on male energy) shows up at approximately 560 BCE and sports a supreme deity, but even He has helpers. Christianity comes into being between 150 to 400 CE, when Jesus becomes God on earth because he is the son of the Father, Deus, and the spirit—the light—that resides in all things (the Aten). Jesus is tempted by Satan, so there have to be at least two deities, and of course in Luke 1:1–55 we read about Zachariah being told by Gabriel (or Gabriela) that his wife Elizabeth would give birth to John the Baptist. Gabriel is pretty busy informing people of impending births, but only the important ones, like Mary, mother of Baby Jesus. So Christianity does not qualify as a monotheistic tradition other than as a reference to the male energy.

Islam (700–750 CE) is one of the more recent additions laying claim to monotheism. We know our mythic hero Muhammad talked to Gabriel (or Samael and definitely Shaytan), mentioned in Surahs 2:97 and 66:4, but the constructors of the Qur'an confused Gabriel with the Holy Spirit as conceptualized in Christianity (Surahs 2:81, 254; 5:109; 16:104). There are two other names that might apply, one in Surah 26:193, or Faithful Spirit, and "One Terrible in Power" (Surah 13:5). **So in Islam there is God, eight archangels, two of unknown name, and Shaytan makes twelve.** Also, there are many references at the popular level to Jinn and other demonic forces, which came into the system from pre-Islamic times.

As the mother-goddess erodes in importance from the Tigris and Euphrates west to the Mediterranean, so does the status of women. Women always had high status in Egypt (until the coming of the Christians and the Muslims). Most women among the Arab tribes were chattel, bought and sold. I'm not sure that we can trace the origins of this low status, but it may be because they have babies, especially girl babies, and they are a burden because they marry outside the group and take resources with them. Arab males seem to have an inordinate amount of psychological problems with women. It could have to do with "mouths to feed"; female infanticide was common, especially during times of famine. There does seem to be a correlation between the ability to obtain a specific social status and treatment of women. In other words, limited status, or lack of opportunities to obtain it, is often correlated with high levels of female (and child) abuse. I'm not sure anyone has the exact answer, but men who are insecure about their position in the group usually need someone (or group) to whom they feel superior. Looked at from another perspective, women are humankind's most valuable resource, for it is only through the female that human life comes into existence. Fights over females were common and is one reason that Islamic women conceal their identity with heavy garments. But the sale or gift of a woman, on the other hand, can cement intertribal relations through the offspring. Shortly after the time of Muhammad, laws and legal relationships with women change. Why did this happen? Let's consider this from a political perspective.

Hadith and eventually the Qur'an begin to show up between 700 and 750 CE, and the construction of these documents can be seen as a mythical charter for creating an identity in par with powerful cultural groups surrounding them, beginning with the Jews and Christians, and then a dash to create their own identity. The construction of the Qur'an by the early Islamic poets represents that early identity crisis (see Warraq 1998, 9–35). What we see are rulers and priest-poets constructing a political system for purposes of uniting the tribes under one house. Disagreements began early as to who should succeed Muhammad. This obviously wasn't well thought out, which strongly indicates that

Muhammad was not interested in anything long-term; he simply wanted to win battles or die. My opinion is that the mythic hero was probably a real person, a great warrior and organizer of people, and loved by his soldiers. Muhammad (or whatever the name of this legendary hero) was just waging war at the behest of one of the Ansar or Muhajirun warlords and he was probably killed in battle, which left a power vacuum. If they were to continue, another general needed to take his place; his name was Abu Bakr. This wasn't good enough for some, who felt that Abu Bakr. would favor some tribes over others. Assassinations followed. During this early conquest there does not appear to be much interest in religious dogma, but instead in winning battles and being top dog, the Alpha Male. Warraq comments (1998, 20–21):

> During the early years of the Umayyad dynasty, many Muslims were totally ignorant in regard to ritual and doctrine. The rulers themselves had little enthusiasm for religion, and generally despised the pious and the ascetic. The result was that there arose a group of pious men who shamelessly fabricated traditions for the good of the community, and traced them back to the authority of the prophet. They opposed the godless Umayyads but dare not say so openly, so they invented further traditions dedicated to praising the Prophet's family, hence indirectly giving their allegiance to the party of Ali supporters ... the ruling power itself was not idle. If it wished an opinion to be generally recognized and the opposition of pious circles silenced, it too had to know how to discover a hadith to suit its purpose. They had to do what their opponents did: invent and have invented hadith in their turn. And that is in effect what they did.

To establish a new religion, a religion that would fit all, these pious priest-poets took a very brave first step and began to question not only how women are treated, but how people in general are treated through the alleged sayings of Muhammad. Isn't that interesting—there appears to be a questioning about how ALL people are treated, a questioning drawn straight from the parables of Jesus. Women formerly treated as chattel were given rights through the manufactured words of Muhammad. Our mythic hero Muhammad then has a visitation with Gabriel and comes back with the boon: "Allah says, be nice to your women; let them own property; let them get divorced. Oh, yes, be kind to your slaves as well. But remember that men have an edge."

The underlying motive was simple: Although women are treated like chattel, they have a great deal of influence "in the bedroom" so to speak. Give them some rights and they can help get more and more men on board (join the movement). This is the old political game of giving premiums so the individual is more tempted to buy the product. The motive is a bit disingenuous but the potential result is a great deal of male/female equality, except amongst fundamentalists who interpret equality in peculiar ways. But the Muslims ebb and flow with this, one moment granting equality and the next suppressing human rights. When the rules are cosmic in origin they can be arbitrarily applied. We see this in Iran today, where women are so feared that they are micromanaged and thrown in jail if they show too much ankle. During the week of November 12, 2007, a nineteen-year-old Shi'ah woman was in Saudi Arabia, parked in a car with an old boyfriend. She was abducted and raped by seven men, but was sentenced to six months in prison and 200 lashes because she initiated the crime by being with a non-relative male. She was raped because women give men erections and men just cannot control themselves. She was originally sentenced to ninety lashes, but when her lawyer criticized the legal system this was raised to 200 lashes, which probably killed her. There is so much male fear of women that such outrageous acts are probably designed to set an example.

Why are Muslim men so afraid of women? The answer to this is simple; it is called emotional irresponsibility—Muslim men believe that women give them erections. Assigning the power of seduction to women, by virtue of uncontrolled sexuality on the part of men, translates into men being controlled by women. This justifies rape of women if they show too much skin; they must be kept covered from head to toe least men lose control. The unintended results of this, however, can lead to severe emotional and medical problems. Wearing so much clothing does not allow sunlight to convert cholesterol (fat under the dermal layer of the skin) into vitamin D. This results in higher incidences of osteoporosis as well as other health conditions (cancer, heart disease, and diabetes). Lack of exposure to the sun can also lead to decreased amounts of melatonin production in the penal gland, leading to sleep problems and depression.

To show this political connection to women's rights, a similar situation prevailed in the Unites States. Female property rights entered into California with the Spaniards, who borrowed this "unique" idea (except perhaps in ancient Egypt) from the Moors (Muslims in Spain). Not surprisingly, it caught on and spread eastward across the United States, and then, for political purposes (politicians needed voters), women were given the right to vote (first in Wyoming, 1869). Equality in Islam, however, means something very different than in the Western world. Islamic equality means people will follow the teachings/laws equally, not that the individual has an equal say in much of anything. Allah gave the laws, and there is no court of appeal outside of the arbitrariness of judges who, of course, act through the will of Allah; Islam is a form of fascism. The Qur'an, then, is a commingling of old Arabic tradition and law, the Old Testament Talmud, and New Testament, with elements added called hadith, conveniently invented to deal with troublesome day-to-day issues.

As mentioned, archaeological information regarding prehistoric Arabia (the Arabian Peninsula) is very thin. Through inscriptions and other artifacts there is a polytheistic tradition in play, with patron deities connected to specific tribes. Prior to the time of our mythic hero Muhammad, the Arab people in the area of Mecca and Medina were experiencing influences from both Judaism and Christianity but maintained a closer association with Judaism. They appear to have had an intense dislike for Christians from the start and this is understandable given Christian proselytizing. Christian missionaries in the South Pacific and the Americas show the culturally divisive nature of this tradition, and the need to totally destroy or undermine the "demonic" beliefs and practices of others. This is pure politics and not religion. The Christians destroyed shrines, smashed idols, raped and plundered, and Arab people were pissed. The irony is that today Islam is the most intolerant institution on the planet (see Spencer 2005).

In Medina, Muhammad (or someone like him) probably befriended Jews, perhaps protecting them in some fashion. And just like Jesus at age twelve wooing the rabbi in Jerusalem, our mythic hero Muhammad wooed the Jews in Medina; they liked him, he carried a very sharp sword, and had a crude but charismatic nature about him. He had the good "gift of gab." He knew how and when to flatter, he knew when to listen, and he knew the kinds of questions to ask without prying or offending. Whoever this person was—call him Muhammad if you like— he was smart, knew how to get to the top (he was a bully when need be), was flexible when weak, and overly determined when strong. He also—and this is very important for all the imams reading this—he kept his word and would not ask someone to do something he himself would not do. He would never, ever tell anyone to assassinate someone for him. To him life was personal, and if he had a grudge or heard criticism, he would deal with this in a personal manner. This is the only way to lead, as the other way (sending others to do your dirty work) implies cowardice. Muhammad was no coward; he was a leader—his men saw him every day. They respected him, went into battle with him, and died with him. Statements that he ordered people assassinated is an invention to create just a little paranoia, to prevent authority from being directly challenged, and an attempt to give credibility to his existence by painting a negative picture of his behavior. The Hebrews did the exact same thing with Abraham, Moses, and David. The statements that support assassination are unfortunately institutionalized and this became the prime method of dealing with critics and opponents. This certainly does not qualify as religion.

Back to the Jewish connection. Muhammad wins their trust and the rabbi tells Muhammad a secret, that the Arabic tribes are descendants of Hagar, the Egyptian slave girl, and Abraham, the grand mythic patri-

350 | **Failed God**

arch, the base of the Hebrew, Israelite, Jewish tradition, a very old tradition. This child of Hagar and Abraham is Ishmael, hence the names Hagarites and Ishmaelites. It must have been like learning that you are direct descendants of the King of England or perhaps Bill Clinton.

When the Jews were looking for the Messiah they were looking for someone who would wield a sword and liberate them from their enemies, an enemy defined as anyone who did not believe in their god (Yahweh), follow their rules, and so on. These were the chosen people set apart from everyone else. They were looking for someone like Muhammad, befriended him, and helped him with the initial mythic development, probably, again, informing him of the relationship of Abraham and Ishmael and many other secrets. I personally do not believe that any of the mythic charter involving Abraham and Ishmael materialized until the beginning of the eighth century CE (between 700 and 750 CE). Muhammad, initially at least, might not have been seen as a savior but at least he might be useful. Muhammad and the Jews had a falling out, most likely because he was an outsider with "backwoods" habits. It is unclear if this happened prior to or after he traveled to Palestine in particular Jerusalem (if any part of the story is true). Prayer initially was oriented toward Jerusalem but later was changed in the direction of Mecca, which represents maintenance of the moon god of war. Judaism, or at least the template, offered a storyline, a "history" or mythical charter, and preservation of tribal identity. The tribal leaders understood the erosion of their identity was politically based, with several proselytizing groups (Christians, Zoroastrians, etc.) vying for converts just as the Republican and Democrat parties in this country. So the Arabs fought back.

Islam, unlike Judaism (but in a manner similar to Christianity), is tribalism stripped for export—Islam is not tied to a particular territory as is Judaism (Israel) or Hinduism (India); one's loyalty is to Allah and the interpretation of Allah's will, and not to any particular government and the territory it occupies. This, in a sense, is the same position Christianity takes, which, like Islam, is not attached to any particular territory (the Vatican is just a reference point, as is Mecca). However,

Islam is not controlled by a central agency, as is the Catholic Church; councils control Islam, not a system of bureaucrats taking orders from a king or pope. With respect to Christianity, at least in the teachings of Jesus, there are no directives to engage violent acts for purposes of conquering territory or conversion. Certainly acts of violence toward others in the name of the Christian God happen but there is absolutely nothing in what Jesus said to justify violence and conquest, but there is a great deal of justification in the Qur'an.

What Would Muhammad Do?

Islam, like Judaism and Christianity, is complex in many ways but quite simple in others. The simple part involves the daily rituals of prayer, food taboos, and so on. What gets complex is the interpretation of treatment of people, both Moslem and non-Moslem; each group is dealt with using a different set of rules (see Spencer 2005). Nowhere is this more elegantly revealed than in the differing levels of hell to be occupied by Muslims, Christians, Jews, Magi, and so on. *Kafir,* a derogatory term for non-Muslims (remember that the Jews have their own derogatory terms), can never get out of hell and are doomed to torment forever, while Muslims go to different levels depending on their offenses. The greatest offense is ignorance of one's religion. Understand this: If you know your religion well, you go to heaven regardless of how many people you killed, maimed, cheated, lied to, and so on. In short, Allah comes first and humanity comes second; this is a serious form of psychosis. Muslim warriors who die in battle or through martyrdom receive the express ticket to paradise (Qur'an 3:169), these days usually riding on several pounds of high explosive at the instigation of some psychotic, self-righteous, cowardly imam.

Early in the development of Islam two factions emerged, Sunni and Shiite. There is a great deal of hostility between these two factions. The hostility and resulting bloodshed, as I explain below, stem from the same differences as those between Jews and Christians, that is, differences over divine word, Holy Scripture, substance abuse, and who is eligible to rule or interpret God's will. According to legend, before Muhammad's death there were already problems regarding who should rule with his passing. This suggests that Muhammad might have experienced a protracted death, or perhaps he died unexpectedly in battle, from assassination, or from another cause. However, if Muhammad was not a real person, this is simply another story. On the other hand, the intensity of the struggle over rule might indicate that Muhammad was only interested in the moment and not the future, or that his magical helpers, that is Gabriel (or Samael) and al Liah, were unaware of the impending conflict over succession and thus neglected to inform him. In any case, after Muhammad passed from the scene there was a jockeying for power as is common when the leader of any cult dies.

As the story goes, there were two candidates: Ali, a cousin who had married Muhammad's only surviving daughter, and Abu Bakr. These "contendings" probably did happen, but they were over who was bigger and stronger, not over any genealogical connection to Muhammad or some connection to a deity. In order to create stability and cut down on assassination and resulting power struggles, the field of who could rule needed to be narrowed; here we encounter the fabricated genealogical connections. Remember, if Muhammad is a non-person, then none of the genealogical connections can be factual. Shi'ah claim that Ali was the first legitimate Imam or Khalifah (successor) to the prophet. Shi'ah maintain that Ali had the divine right to rule because he was a cousin to the prophet and was married to his daughter, Fatimah. However, Fatimah may have been Muhammad's wife and not his daughter. If this is the case, then Ali's progeny have no genetic connection to Muhammad. As mentioned, things get really dicey if Muhammad never existed in the first place. Such discussions, however, are designed to make Muhammad a real person. Fighting over succession to rule is a parlor trick implying that there was a person named Muhammad, but it also narrows the playing field of who could rule in the future and adds credibility to their mythical charter.

But there is a theological issue at stake. If Muhammad was simply a conduit between God and humans, how does this make him or any of his biological heirs divine? This type of questioning was and is dangerous. God's choices of special people appear to be arbitrary. Certain passages from the Qur'an are used to show this divine connection or at least special privileges conferred by the deity in a fashion similar to Yahweh picking special people to carry on a genetic heritage. But there is a real problem with this. For example, Surah 2, verse 124, has been translated with at least two very different interpretations. One translation (by Abdullah Yusuf Ali 2004 orig. 1934) goes as follows: "And when his Lord tried Abraham with words and he fulfilled them, He said, 'I am about to make of the an Imam to mankind'; Abraham said, 'Of my offspring also?' 'My covenant,' said God, 'embraceth not evildoers.'" This statement does not say "yes" to Muhammad's question. In fact, the safest way to read this is, "Yes, your kin are included as well as everyone else," but clearly indicates that the deity will not promote evil people, although I'm not sure how to define evil in the Islamic tradition—I suspect that Islam has difficulty defining this slippery concept because it seems to change with circumstances.

On the other hand, a contemporary translation by Ahmed Ali (2001) reads, "Remember, when his Lord tried Abraham by a number of commands which he fulfilled, God said to him: 'I will make you a leader among men.' And when Abraham asked, 'From my progeny too?' the Lord said: 'My pledge does not include transgressors.'"

Something very different is said in the second translation. In the second translation he will be a leader among men, not humankind. As before, there is no divinity suggested, only special privileges, which may or may not include leading a nation or Islam. Again, Muhammad is only a leader among men and not leader of the world, a nation, or a tribe. The reference is to his *military* officers below him, his council. Both translations clearly state that bad, evil people—including the descendants of Muhammad—will not be leaders. This statement is a replay of Abraham and his relationship with Yahweh, his patron deity. Historians really do not know about these early genealogical connections with Muhammad nor is anyone really sure that

Muhammad was a real person. So, we have people arguing over power figures who were more than likely constructed by the Islamic poets. Also, there is the statement that Allah's covenant does not "embrace evildoers." The power struggle over which faction should rule, Abu Bakr or Ali, involved assassinations and a great deal of evil behavior, so how can either side claim to lead Islam? Again, it comes down to definition.

Sunni (Sunni comes from the Persian *Sunniyan,* meaning People of the Path), on the other side, say that Abu Bakr was the first Khalifah. This turmoil over succession is part of the mythic storyline and mirrors similar pre-Islamic events when a leader of a tribe died. Abu Bakr, as the story goes, was a trusted member of the Quraish (Khalifah) tribe and possible father of Ayishah, whom Muhammad married when she was age nine. This might have been done to cement a political relationship, or simply on the whim of Allah. Many on all sides attempt to make sense of Muhammad having sex with her at such a young age. Women were chattel and having sex with Ayishah would have been his right; no one would have paid any attention to this in those days. These stories, like most of the stories attributed to the Jewish patriarchs, are not angelic—"these are real people with faults;" this is an attempt to add credibility to the story. Jesus is too good to be true.

Abu Bakr is considered the first Khalifah of the Sunni, followed by Umar, and Usman. In this tradition, the one who should be Imam or Khalifah is the best ruler and not necessarily directly related to Muhammad. However, leaders are chosen from the Quraish tribe and no others because they trace their lineage back to Abraham, just as Jesus had to be of the lineage of David. Good luck, especially in the face of the fact that no one knows if Abraham was a real person; he most probably was not.

In both traditions (Sunni and Shi'ah), individuals and groups are attempting to gain control of the politic, including the military. As it turns out, in the Sunni tradition the first four Khalifahs received the Kutubu 's-Sittah or six "authentic" books of tradition; they also represent the four schools of law as formulated by Imam Abu Hanifah, Imam ash-Shafi'I, Imam Malik, and Imam Ahmed ibn Hambal. These people *represented* the law. But like Hammurabi (1792–1750 BCE) and Moses (1351 BCE), you do not simply present the law. The law has to come from a source more powerful than the imam, king, or prophet. In Hammurabi's case Shamash, the Sun God, gives the law. In the case of Moses, Yahweh is this ultimate power, and in the case of Muhammad, Allah. This justifies the law and those who administer it. So both the Shi'ah and Sunni create a mythical charter legitimizing their rule, and they have been killing each other ever since. What would Muhammad do about this if he were alive today? I can't help but think he would obsessively-compulsively wash his hands of the whole mess.

But there is another factor that sets Islam apart from Judaism and Christianity—Islam has never gone through reformation and is stuck in the Dark Ages. The storyline has not modified enough to bring it into alignment with the philosophy and technology of the twenty-first century. I'm not saying that the twenty-first century is the best, but it does seem to correspond with a scientifically-oriented, free enterprise-directed, self-responsible individual.

Outside of the two factions mentioned above (Shi'ah and Sunni), there are as many "Islams" or methods of submission as there are practitioners of this tradition, but they all turn on the interpretation of the Qur'an and hadith. Submission, however, is the key word—not submission by choice, but submission through indoctrination in early childhood and the use of fear and terror. Also keep firmly in mind that Islamic law favors Muslims, and another method of conversion is to have harsher punishments for non-Muslims. I'm sure that many non-Muslims threatened with death or having a hand removed convert to Islam in the courtroom. One is to fear Allah; as with Judaism and Christianity, Islam is truly a barbaric tradition when it gains the upper hand politically. Remember that Islam is the tradition, a Muslim is a follower, and there are many decent Muslims in the world.

Hallucinogens and Islam

Islam, like Christianity, is rooted in the troubled times existing between 560 BCE and 1000 CE. Don't misunderstand me; this trouble goes back to at least 2300 BCE and exists to this present day. The date of 560 BCE to 1000 CE represents urgency, perhaps never before felt, to stake out territory, to get absorbed into some "other" culture or die. Judaism, Christianity, and Islam are political/economic systems attempting to bring order to an unpredictable world. During this time period, monotheism was a way to bypass equality by attributing one's behavior to the will of a single god. When you eliminate the pantheon and reference only one deity, the channel of communication to that deity is restricted to a special few; that seems to be a main strategy in what are called "monotheistic" systems. In kingships and totalitarian systems in general, the head deities only speak through certain people; if God spoke to everyone, all would know His will, and religious clerics, churches, temples, and mosques would be superfluous—the power structure is compromised. Have you ever wondered why God only speaks through certain people, even though the delivered message is intended for all? This is the father-to-son transfer or delegation of *power*—this is not spirituality, this is not religion, for if there was a true, sensitive god who wished the best for his children, he would gather his creation, set them around a huge television screen (one of those new wrap-around, bendable types), and explain his plan. By the time of Muhammad you would think that any intelligent god would have caught on to the fact that you cannot expect one or two people to get the intended message, pass it on to everyone, and have total acceptance. Certainly if humans can invent trans-global communication where most people in the world can be informed in an instant about some event or issue, God could do the same, even better. Why doesn't He? That is not His purpose. Remember He invented evolution and we are supposed to work this out ourselves. We can do this brutally or we can do this with intellect and compassion; evolution, in time, simply does away with that which does not work or that which does not adapt. This is a cosmic rule. Brutality does not work well in the long run because most of your resources go toward fighting internal enemies, and the system implodes and/or becomes more and more vulnerable to attack from the outside. Democrats and Republicans playing politics in this country during a time of war are very, very foolish and dangerous.

Pre-Islamic tribal people were very superstitious and this attitude is alive and well. They knew about Jinn and how to interpret signs of supernatural presence and ritual procedures for counteracting evil. But there is more here. Muhammad, as mentioned earlier, may have been a caravan director and, as the story goes, took his future wife's caravan all over the place. The Arabs were herbalists and aware of certain hallucinogens because of the synergistic relationship between nomadic and agricultural people; they probably sold or traded such substances for hundreds if not thousands of years. Muhammad as a caravan leader is a good story because it places Muhammad in a wide geography, making him worldly and knowledgeable, dealing with diverse peoples and philosophies during his adventures, as well as in the art of war. Muhammad would have encountered and even traded numerous hallucinogenic substances in Persia, keeping in mind the Zoroastrians were quite heavily into haoma (soma in the Hindu—probably *Amanita muscaria*), Syrian rue (seeds are used to make dye for carpets and contain harmaline, a known hallucinogen—remember Aladdin?), and cannabis (and they probably would have sniffed glue if it was available). Muhammad would have known about these substances. Now, let's take this one step further.

People become leaders by being born into the job, voted in, or, in many cases, bullying their way to the top. In the latter case, the leader is bound to lose his power in time simply because of age and injuries. In short, people will question the leader's authority and eventually beat him up. However, if his authority comes from some higher power, like a god, and if the leader can sell this story to others, he can get people to act through the "will of God;" the leader is merely the "messenger." Muhammad, especially early in his military career, needed a higher power and his experiences with hallucinogenic substances would open that door. In my opinion, there probably was someone like Muhammad who did commune with the other side, but did so with mind-altering substances. This may have been a unique phenomenon, but I suspect that tribal leaders of by-gone eras did the same; he simply did it better.

Muhammad's descriptions of encounters with Gabriel, Samael, al Liah, and Shaytan/Iblis sound like experiences with hallucinogenic substances, and in many cases, bad trips. Muhammad's first encounter with Gabriel is interesting. Gabriel is misinformed about Muhammad's ability to take dictation (this is curious), so when Gabriel said, "Write," Muhammad said, "I can't," and he felt as if he was being squeezed to death. This happened three times before Gabriel caught on. There are other references in hadith to physiological reactions prior to or when communing with supernatural agencies, all of which highly suggest that these are purposefully drug induced. Keep in mind that Moses is the model on which Muhammad is based. Moses, as you recall from Chapter Two, spent some time hot boxing in "The Tent of Meetings," and also communing with the "Plant God." In fact, there is one incident where Moses has a bad trip (Exodus 4:24), symbolized as God trying to kill him. The priest poets try to explain this as the wrath of God because his son was not circumcised, but this appears unusual, out of context, and suggests confusion in the minds of the priest-poets. We read:

> And it came to pass by the way in the inn, that the LORD
> met him, and sought to kill him. Then Zipporah took a
> sharp stone, and cut off the foreskin of her son, and cast [it]
> at his feet, and said, Surely a bloody husband [art] thou to
> me. So he let him go: then she said, A bloody husband [thou
> art], because of the circumcision.

Ruck, et al. (2001, 166) suggests that the bloody foreskin is another reference to the mushroom, *Amanita muscaria*. We read in Mishkat, Book xxi, Chapter One, that Muhammad said, "Mushrooms are a kind of manna which God sent to Moses so that we can see." Some scholars translate this as some sort of eye wash for "sore eyes" (see Hughes 1994, 423), but this interpretation is difficult to sustain. The word *manna* (*mann* in Arabic and *man* in Hebrew) in the Qur'an always refers to some magical substance sent from God (Surah 2:54; 2:82, 7:160). Manna would perhaps look like bread, as was the case in the Bible, and something to eat, making a connection that goes beyond "breaking bread" with someone. The word manna, to my knowledge, never referred to some type of simple herbal remedy. Instead, manna was used to cure *spiritual* ailments, to convert, through the baptism of fire, the faithless nonbeliever, to make "real," through a hallucinogenic experience, that which can only be accepted on faith.

Again, the stories of Muhammad and his experiences with the supernatural world strongly indicate that, at least in some cases, hallucinogenic substances were involved. One author (Noldeke 1891, 598) has suggested that Muhammad had epileptic seizures, but he also could have been hypoglycemic or dehydrated. Keep firmly in mind that Muhammad always had enemies about and if he was an epileptic or suffered from hypoglycemia, he would have been vulnerable to, shall we say, "displacement." All politicians and leaders have rivals, and common practice is and was assassination (verbal or physical) of one's political rivals. In my opinion, the experiences that Muhammad related to Akisha and others were the physiological effects of a variety of substances (known to the poets), including manna or mushrooms, and undoubtedly cannabis, which he ate and did not smoke. Cannabis is connected to Muhammad's fondness for honey, which he used as an aphrodisiac among other things. In the Hebrew tradition we hear of "the land of milk and honey," and in both cases honey refers to something more than just sticky and sweet. "The land of milk and honey" was a psychological land of hope, with milk representing life (as in mother's milk) and honey representing that connection with the divine.

Leadership or the right to leadership has a great deal to do with the illusion we sell to self and others, and because you can't stay big and strong forever you need outside help—supernatural aid in the form of a supreme being who can beat up all the other gods, just as the leader beats up his enemies. All acts, however, are the will of Allah and the messenger takes no responsibility. And just as the shaman's revelations come through the unexpected—a contorted face perhaps, shaking, withering on the floor, and even strange utterances ("that could only be deciphered through the filter of others close by"), they create an illusion of one (Muhammad) possessed by the Spirit. It isn't the message so much as *where* it originates. Muhammad was just a messenger; he can never be the originator because he was always prompted by the divine. When the law comes from the authority of a supernatural being, one who will do terrible, terrible things if not obeyed, you pretty much have a captive audience. And of course this tradition is passed down from generation to generation, steering the mind of the masses in its "proper direction."

Muhammad, we've been told, was illiterate; he could neither read nor write. This is part of the myth. Why would anyone want to paint a picture of an illiterate Muhammad, a caravan leader who probably could read and write? Look at it this way: If he could write, then *he* would have written the Qur'an. There would have been linen or leather pages handed down, signed and certified; this would be valued and treasured stuff. Well, there are no such writings of which we are aware, so the simplest thing was for the poets to claim Muhammad was illiterate; we have the same story with Jesus, a god who should have been able to read and write. You would think that if you are going to send your son to impress people, you could at least make him literate. But, of course, Muhammad and Jesus are not about literacy; they are about saving identity (Muslim-physical) and saving your self (Jesus-philosophical). Back to Muhammad.

Because Muhammad never wrote anything, it is only reasonable to conclude that we do not know what he said and have to rely on the comments of others, that is, hadith and that which appears in the Qur'an. This is the third-person approach, attributing something to someone; you cannot argue with the messenger. None of this material (Qur'an) is pristine—it is all third or fourth-hand at best and most is likely imagined layering by the Islamic poets. However, we do have a great deal of legendary material about what Muhammad did—we know a great deal about his behavior, and it is through his behavior that we can understand what he believed and how he "convinced" others to follow his lead. I outlined earlier some characteristics of a real Muhammad.

The Muhammad in the Qur'an and hadith, however, is a murderous, psychotic, womanizing thug definitely on par with King David. It is quite apparent that Muhammad was intolerant of any criticism—he murdered his critics, and this attitude of intolerance of criticism is, again, a cornerstone of this tradition.

Many politicians in this country and others attempt to stay within a politically correct arena by making excuses for Islam. They have suggested that Bin Laden, a modern Muhammad, "hijacked a religion." Bin Laden did not hijack a religion. Bin Laden is acting on the contrived statements of Muhammad to convert the world to Islam. Islam is a policy or politic, not a religion, and the central message is conquest and control, not spirituality. This is a political-pragmatic tradition doing what it has always done. Muhammad, and certainly his continuers, were and are interested in world conquest. The mythic Muhammad, in short, had delusions of grandeur, but it goes much deeper than that.

Islam means submission to the divine will, a will generally (but not always) attributed to Allah, and religious clerics interpret His will. Yes, the individual is free to interpret God's will as long as it does not contradict Muhammad or Islamic religious clerics.

Muhammad is the self-proclaimed prophet of Allah, although as far as I can determine Muhammad usually spoke indirectly to this deity through an archangel like Gabriel or maybe Samael or Shaytan (Satan). Most in the Islamic community would agree that Muhammad came in contact with Shaytan during at least one of his altered states, but what really transpired is subject to interpretation. Shaytan, I might add, is given a pretty bad rap because he was told to serve humankind by God, refused because he only wanted to serve God, and was thus cast aside. I hope the reader got the point of that. Shaytan was doing what all good Muslims should do—*serve God only*—and he got screwed! Does anyone see the irony there?

One interesting comparison mentioned in the literature is that the constructed Muhammad, besides being a thug, fits many of the characteristics of a shaman. Briefly stated, the term shaman (shamaness, shamanka) comes from the Tungusic, Russian word, *saman*. Although not all anthropologists agree with this, I will use the term "shaman" to describe an activity that is more or less universal, although at the local level each culture has a different term for the practitioner and practices or techniques, which, although diverse, share some common elements. By definition, a shaman is a magician-religious specialist who acts as an intermediary between the members of his society and the supernatural world on the basis of self-acquired powers.

The key elements in the definition are as follows. A shaman is a contributing member of a group and is usually a part-time specialist and, at the same time, an intermediary between the community and the supernatural world. However, the spirit powers, the familiars of the shaman, are of his or her own making (or his or her tribe or family group). Shamans usually commune with these entities through trance behavior, either spontaneously or drug induced. Becoming a shaman often involves an initial psychotic split, often in their early youth, through a near-death experience or protracted illness. These experiences place individuals in direct involvement with the other world, making them good candidates for the role of shaman. Shamans heal the individual and community, and offer prophecies of future direction for the individual or group. I have found rare references that Muhammad cured the sick but not to the degree suggested for Jesus. The reason for this is that the moon god of war is not a healing god—he is a destroyer. To parallel the Bible, Muhammad had to at least have the healing capability even though it is infrequently mentioned; he was there to "heal" society. Healing of the individual was not Muhammad's responsibility; it was the "will of Allah."

A shaman is unlike a priest or imam, who is a functionary of an organized belief system. The superordinate powers do not come from him or her. These deities were there before this type of specialist (the priest or other modern religious cleric) entered the picture and will be there for the next generation. Al Liah was Muhammad's patron deity and his conception of this deity was of his own making—through the use of mind-altering substances. Al Liah has a general storyline, although it is also personalized by every member of the tribe.

By acting only as a messenger or conduit between his patron deity and his army, Muhammad's orders are more likely to be carried out and his authority less subject to challenge. To be a leader of men and not contend with rivals you have to win trust; you do not earn trust by being brutal and arbitrary. In this case you win trust by keeping your word and supporting your men in battle—on the front line. When a situation arose where you could not keep your word, it came by way of celestial decree. Politicians do this every day. They will make a promise or say something one day, only to disavow it and blame their behavior on some other politician or radio personality. In either way, "The Devil made me do it" or "It's the president's fault," a third person absolves one of all personal responsibility.

Islam and Science

The time period between the ninth and fifteenth centuries was, shall we say, the golden era of science in the Arab world. Through conquests in Persia, India, and Spain, the Arab world came in contact with new ideas about the universe and how it worked. There is an interest in astronomy (as opposed to astrology), mathematics and architecture, medicine, and any scientific endeavor that benefited or reinforced their celestial politics (Islam). Any realm of study or speculation that contradicted the teaching of Islam was shunned. Astrology, for example, claimed to be able to predict the future. If this was true, then it was in the power of the individual to manipulate the future by avoiding or embracing certain behaviors. In a tradition where the deity is all-powerful and all was predestined, astrology suggests otherwise (see Saliba 1994, 68).

Advancements in astronomy, certainly wrapped around religious observances, helped to correct some of the Greek ideas put forth by Ptolemy. Regulating when and where people were to worship became a top priority for two reasons: First, if you want to really control people, outside of promoting self-responsibility, they must be micromanaged through continual, habitual ritual observance on an hour-to-hour basis. Remember, "Idle hands are the Devil's workshop." From a behaviorist standpoint, this is operant conditioning on a grand scale; "Zig heil!"

Second, astronomy was important to the most ancient of cultures and thus one's place in the world was measured by what you knew or thought you knew about the world and the heavens above. Obviously they did not start from scratch and borrowed extensively from the Greeks, that is, the *Almagest* and Ptolemy's *Planetary Hypothesis* (see Salbia 1994). They also acquired Hindu astronomy texts, the best known being the *Sindhind*. Apparently Caliph al-Mansur of Baghdad received an embassy from India (province of Sind) and with them they had the Sindhind and an astronomer to decode and translate it into Arabic. This would have been sometime around 760 CE. There is a great deal of astrological coding in the Qur'an and this acquisition coincides with that coding. Salbia (1994, 72) states:

> If this tradition is true, it would explain why soon afterward several texts were written in Arabic based on the text of the Sindhind. Unfortunately, only one of these texts has survived in extensive form, that of Muhammad ibn Musa al-Khwarizmi, who was also distinguished as the originator of the discipline of algebra. That his text has survived only in a Latin version, and that the others have been all but totally obliterated, clearly indicates the quick neglect of the Indo-Persian tradition.

The loss of the original test is surely a great tragedy. Rather than the work being insignificant and ignored, perhaps it was the basis of Islamic astronomy; maybe it is a basic feature of the Qur'an. Moreover, Muhammad ibn Musa al-Khwarizmi is credited as the originator of the discipline of algebra. I find that an interesting coincidence and may suggest that algebra developed in India. It could also mean refinement of Hindu principles of astronomy by taking the practical and universal, sifting out the Hindu deities, replacing them with their own, and then tossing aside or destroying the original Hindu texts. Certainly there is a precedent in terms of destroying books, as was, in my opinion, the fictional case with Uthman discussed earlier (and below). They could not go about destroying the Greek texts because there were simply too many copies and too many literate Greeks. Moreover, we cannot be sure what is missing from that single surviving copy ("mainly in tack") of the Sindhind.

They made great strides in chemistry, inventing distillation. They had an intense desire to study herbs, as Muhammad stated that there was a plant for every ailment. Poisons were of special interest. They also made great strides in surgery, borrowing from the Greek and Indian systems.

Cult Development

Islam is a political system that developed over the course of about 1,100 years (700 CE to 1850 CE) with a number of esoteric offshoots (for example, Sufism) coming to the surface and maturing as well. In the later part of the nineteenth century, a cult emerged (probably brewing for 200 years or more) with a mission, that is, to return to the glorious days of yesteryear where all would adhere to the cosmic laws delivered through Muhammad. This cult bears the name of its alleged founder, Muhammad, son of 'Abdu 'l-Wahhab, or Wahhabi. What happened that brought out a hankering for the "good old days"? As is generally the case, extreme social stress. What was familiar to them gave reassurance of a better day, but only if they returned to the good old days of killing and taking what these fundamentalist Muslims considered their birthright—the world.

Warfare is the norm in the Middle East and has been for about 4,500 years; it is institutionalized just as it is in the United States. From about 800 CE to around 1600 CE there is something else going on besides warfare. There is a curiosity about the enemy's knowledge base. In other words, there seems to be a serious drive to find out about the enemy's technology and science. In order to do this, they had to minimize the book burning. For example, the Indian astronomical text mentioned above was quite possibly used as a basis for Arabic astronomy. I'm not so convinced the Indian text (Sindhind) was acquired in such a peaceful manner. Why would Hindu priests give up their sacred knowledge to non-Hindus, all of whom were considered less than the cows and rats running around the streets of Delhi. This might have been some sort of peace offering, but this doesn't make much sense either. The Hindus probably saw the Mohammedans as barbaric and the only fitting bribe or peace offering was a bordello. The Sindhind might have been traded for something considered of equal worth or acquired violently. In any case, they obtained this work, and with the *Almagest* and *Elements,* they added to astronomy and mathematics. Mathematics was refined mostly for the sake of their religious traditions but they came to unintended conclusions, which naturally lead to questions—evil questions.

Medicine was considered in the same light as astrology, but the tradition needed treatment methodologies. Thus, they began to distance themselves from certain practices and took a more pragmatic view—do what works. Also keep in mind that Indian medicine (Ayurvedic) was well advanced by the time the Muslims stormed into India. Parts of the *Susruta Samhita* (Bhishagratna 2002) must date back to 1000 BCE. This is probably where much of their knowledge came from. The Ayurvedic tradition included advanced surgery techniques, including plastic surgery. For the Arabs there is a concentration on herbal remedies, many of which were known since Egyptian times, along with improvements in patient care. Hospitals were clean and well kept, according to Islamic teachings of cleanliness by the prophet, and used as classrooms. There were also lecture rooms, libraries, a chapel and mosque, and sometimes musicians were hired as music therapists. They also served nourishing, clean food—something absent from modern Western hospitals.

The Arab people added immensely to our knowledge of math, medicine, and astronomy, all prompted by that dangerous temptation, curiosity. But that all came to an unfortunate but screeching halt sometime in the late fifteenth and early sixteenth centuries, for just as Europeans were extracting themselves from the Dark Ages, the Arab world was about to fall head on into that same pit of ignorance. And it was happening for the exact same reason it happened in Europe: those in charge ordered people, under the penalty of death, to stop thinking and questioning. The Arab scientists began to realize that things were a bit more complicated than some god in the sky. They realized that the earth was not the center of the universe, the universe was not static, and that things have not always been the way they are. But the real problem lay in a more critical and philosophic look at the sacred scriptures. Knowing how to read and write would have sent individuals to the head of the class, with an opportunity to study ancient philosophies with which connections are made. The same storylines and hero motifs were used in the Qur'an as in the Bible, Egypt, Mesopotamia, and so on, and this forced a question: "Oh, no! Was Muhammad a real person or simply a legend on which to hang a hat?"

This was so threatening to the religious clerics (the rulers) that science and independent thought were abolished. This ushered in the Dark Ages, in which many in the Middle East have lived for around 500 years. Islam is in a tight spot, a bind. On the one hand, if they modernize much further, and especially if they allow free access to information and different points of view, Islam as a viable political entity will cease to exist in one hundred years. Consider what is happening in Dubai, where many Islamic women from places like Saudi Arabia and Iran experience a great deal of freedom (and smile). If a tradition cannot meld with the prevailing social-economic times, it will eventually erode and end as a trace in some religious or political encyclopedia 1,000 years from now. The other option is to go to war and force a politic, a form of fascism, on the rest of the world. Then there is the question of, "Which is better: democracy or fascism?" The answer is by way of comparison. In fascism there are a few people telling everyone else what to do under threat of violence. This does not fit our small-group nature and leads to continual challenge. These systems run on ego, emotion, and arbitrariness, mixed with a large dose of paranoia.

Without the ability to challenge the politic, without fear of retaliation, how can a person or nation explore and challenge the universe to give up its secrets? Perhaps we shouldn't explore the universe and instead pray to Allah.

Western science, and the beliefs and liberal lifestyle that tumbles from it, offers a contradiction to Islamic beliefs about life, death, and the purpose of humanity. The purpose of Islam is servitude to God, but the real purpose of humanity might just be to explore the universe and experience God and His wonders. Ideas that suggest that the Qur'an's take on creation is bogus tend to invalidate the whole book, and once one ingredient is questioned the whole is open to the same criticism. There is a great deal of written material questioning the existence of people and places in the Bible and Qur'an. Monotheistic systems tend to be closed and exclusive in that they lay claim to certain truths that cannot be questioned, and the only way they can maintain their truths is through censorship and verbal and physical violence.

In any case, Islam will readily accept scientific advances from the West but not the philosophy surrounding their development. In many cases, advancements of an idea or technology can only go so far without speculation, which would certainly be the situation in math, physics, and astronomy. Without putting God on hold, there can be no discussion of what came before the Big Bang, quantum mechanics, and parallel universes. A tradition that devotes its time and resources to finding out what is possible is going to be very different from one that focuses resources towards limiting possibilities and censoring information from the outside world. These ideologies are in conflict and this spells danger for all of us.

Cults, Al Qa'ida, and Health: Hijacking a Religion and Muhammad's Modern Messenger

All political/quasi-religious traditions began as cults, with a cult defined as a group of people who come together to profess a certain creed or part of that creed, and who behave in a manner relevant to all; there are always some supernatural elements involved. If the beliefs and behaviors of the group are too far from the mainstream, we use the word "cult" in a pejorative manner. More recently, however, the term "spiritual psychology" is applied to these groups in North America.

Cults are usually considered regional. If the cult gains acceptance through proselytizing and/or violence, it can become sanctioned and move into a worldwide geography, as has Judaism, Christianity, and Islam. All have used war and violence, sanctioned in their myths, to gain political and economic advantage over others. There are numerous characteristics of newly forming and constructed cults. These include the following:

1) Often there is a charismatic leader, a prophet with a message that fits the needs of many of the society's members. Although all members of a society can be drawn to a cult's message because of individual or group circumstances, it is usually those who are confused about their direction in life, frustrated with life's condition, in need of someone to blame, and are easily led or insane. These individuals are most susceptible to leaving behind one life and taking up another. Many become "true believers" and enthusiastically support the group's continuance. Keep in mind that the charismatic leader becomes a "prophet" *only* if the movement succeeds. Also, a cult may not have a specific charismatic leader but numerous leaders acting with some authoritative status, and having a defined division of labor. A cult can even center on an imaginary person or figure, just as tribal leaders often trace their ancestry to powerful animals of one sort or another. Abraham, Moses, Jesus, and Muhammad represent examples of these mythic figureheads.

2) Through some type of information dissemination, a number of individuals get the message—with the Internet there is the possibility of a huge following. Islamic terrorists are certainly using the Internet to their advantage—a system that they could not possibly invent. In some situations, like Al Qa'ida, recruits

are composed of kin and often the dispossessed, although the message can attract a rather motley crew. Deranged imams in countries all over the world help recruit for Al Qa'ida. Some disenchanted U.S. citizens have joined, usually through the efforts of religious clerics preaching hate from the pulpit, sword in one hand and the Qur'an in the other, this, from the "religion of peace."

3) An organization begins to develop with disciples to train, many of whom become apostles and help the charismatic leader spread the word. The charismatic leader may not be available to the members of the cult (few early Christians would have personally interacted with John the Baptist). In some cases, the leader may only be known to a special few or personally known to no one, but *can* be known if the initiate shows promise, often through passing certain tests, ritual requirements, or through mind-altering or other rites-of-passage-type ceremonies.

4) A cult emerges. The cult members must be instructed in the beliefs and the behaviors related to the objectives of the cult—to return to a former golden time, to prepare for Armageddon, to do the will of God, military training to bring forth the objectives, personal growth (casting out your demons, clearing up your brain or relationship, and finding "it"), spirituality, and so on. The message has to be black and white, with no middle ground, and information from the "outside" is restricted in varying degrees. This can be as minor as restricting access to group members while going through ritual confrontation/indoctrination, or major, as, for example, being held in seclusion from friends and relatives. The most common form of message control in the world of politics is by controlling mass communication, as is seen in the news reporting of many countries as well as the liberal press in the U.S. The message sent is structured to the aims of the group. The organization has the truth and this truth can only be known by applying certain rituals and secret rites (praying to Allah, encounter-group type con-

frontations going late into the night, meditation, guided mind-altered experiences, etc.). Giving people ritual names as a symbol of rebirth, designating spiritual guides, handing out awards from God (a new gun, a badge or stripe, etc.) and the like, help guide the person to a new way of perceiving oneself and one's relationship to others and the world.

5) If the organization is to continue, it has to merge with the major organizations of the larger society and be recognized as legitimate. This is where most cults break down, because their message is different, authorities like the IRS, police, religious clerics, and so on examine them, and they are discredited.
Governments realize that "religious" groups are potential political rivals. In our own time, cults become obsolete, the message is not current, and membership wanes. Sometimes, as in the case of EST (a sensitivity-type cult of the 1960s and 1970s and nearly extinct by the 1980s), awareness-type cults pop up again but under different names.

Warfare would be one method of bypassing the IRS, religious clerics, and so on, but only if you win. This is how Islam was spread, through war and at the point of a sword. But the allegiance was to this general, Muhammad, or whatever his name might have been. By implication, the person now had an allegiance to Muhammad's patron deity, al Liah, in which case the person could expect the deity's protection in battle.

In short, the cult message and/or means are usually not tolerated by the dominant system(s). If the organization can merge and gain acceptance, then the cult's message could possibly transform the thinking and behavior of the culture/world. The message becomes routine in time, and a new steady state emerges.

Most messianic (deliverer oriented) movements collapse because their new message and methods are not accepted. There is a tremendous amount of rejection or perceived rejection, and this forces the group leader's hand. This rejection or perceived rejection (often amplified by the charismatic leader for purposes of control and separating the individual from the outside world, e.g., Jim Jones) serves to further convince the group that they are the chosen few (as Jesus was persecuted, so were his followers).

The world *is* coming to an end. This is symbolic, for, indeed, once you step out of the mainstream you are socially dead; you pass a point of no return. You must escape because the "world" is going to be destroyed. You must "die" and be "reborn" or resurrected. For some cults, however, that resurrection is within a "new kingdom," with the new kingdom these days perhaps on another planet or spaceship (Heaven's Gate) or at the right knee of Allah, with seventy-two virgins to look after your every need (seventy-two is a cosmological reference). For others, the death and rebirth are purely symbolic, as with Born Again Christians or New Age spiritual awakenings such as Wicca. For new cults, however, the rebirth-symbolism is often different from the prevailing ideologies, or distorted in some perverse or unorthodox manner. The symbolism and reference points are frequently more personalized and less abstract. They often involve a deity and his chosen few. This becomes a very exclusive group of people who indeed become even more separated emotionally (and sometimes physically—remember Jim Jones?) from the world. Bin Laden and his chosen few are considered outside the mainstream, at least in the eyes of Westerners, although there is ample evidence in the Qur'an and hadith to indicate that Bin Laden is perfectly within the range of practices connected to the Islamic tradition. There are 164 war verses in the Qur'an, and other statements and directives that legitimize violence towards all non-Muslims.

Al-Qa'ida fits all the characteristics of a cult and is really no different than any group aimed at a *revitalization* and bringing about an "old heaven, old earth." One has to assume that Bin Laden (like Hitler and Stalin before) has a plan with global consequences. Bin Laden, however, has made a fatal error. The longer the U.S. stays as a prominent feature in the Middle East, the more rapid the change in social values in that area of the world. But this is really no different from what has been happening for the past 4,000 years, with events culminating in tribal coalitions against a common foe; this aspect of human behavior has been very well studied in cultures throughout the world. This shows you the power of symbols.

We look at the world in terms of good and evil. Our loyalties are based on mutually recognized beliefs but, more importantly, behaviors that are right and wrong or good and evil. We might side with a traditional foe for something that fits within this moral arena. The U.S. saw Russia as an ally during World War Two, but Stalin was a psychotic monster. The U.S. sees Saudi Arabia as an ally but only because they have some territory we can use to stage air strikes (they also sell us lots and lots of oil), while the Saudis don't want Iran or Russia on their doorstep. Thus, loyalty against a common enemy is seen as healthy. Looked at from another direction, health can be perceived as having the right perspective on life, the right religious tradition, the right political arrangement, as well as the right diet and medical tradition. The political culture of Islam (and this applies to many Muslims in the U.S.) sees the U.S., in general, as unhealthy, decadent, and in need of revision.

Relationships exist on many levels, and sometimes we end up with strange bedfellows. In Islam, one's primary allegiance is to Allah and the second is to kin. There is no allegiance to a government. To pledge allegiance to the United States is a pledge to participate in an idea that you, the person making the pledge, can be part of and help build. Allegiance to Allah or Yahweh means the building has stopped and you are now a slave.

For Jesus, all were "kin;" there need not be strangers. For many groups, kin are specific and identifiable. Arab people can give you the names and characteristics of ancestors going back seven, perhaps ten generations; only under unusual circumstances would one oppose close kin in favor of a common enemy. This preoccupation with lineage and kin relationships is likewise connected to the control of women and reproductive access, although this is never explicitly stated. The reason for this is that women always know their children but a male can never be sure. Women were seen as a burden in pre-Islamic times, as chattel to be bought and sold like a goat or camel. They have their inconvenient periods, get pregnant, give birth to more women; people from other tribes get combative and attempt to steal them. Combining this with a pseudo-religious tradition that professes a supreme male deity to whom one must submit, it is not difficult to understand the suppression of women that is found in varying degrees in Judaism, Christianity, and Islam. All must submit to the male deity (Allah, for example) and, through analogy, women must submit to male kin and males in general. Women's rights are a central issue with which Islam must contend. In the West most see (we may not always practice this) the suppression of women's rights as socially unhealthy and spiritually/emotionally damaging, and most Muslims would probably agree.

There is a significant difference between the West and the Arab world in terms of determining trust. In the Arab world it is clear that you can think about trusting your kin (one, some, all), but the further you go out from that category, it is pretty likely that a stranger, an "outlaw," will try to get the better of you in a deal (just read Genesis). If the deal is too lopsided, this can lead to violence. Now you can appreciate a universal triad regarding neighbors who are seen as foreign and less than kin: fear them (tax them and apply different laws), join them, or kill them.

Osama Bin Laden can be characterized as a Muslim true to his faith. He has used Islam, that is, the Qur'an and hadith, to justify waging war on the U.S. and the civilized world. Al Qa'ida, and thus Bin Laden, is part of Wahhabism, a terrorist cult supported by the House of Sa'ud, Saudi Arabia (see Schwartz 2002). The goal of this cult is the revitalization of Islam and the true teaching of the Qur'an. This means a return to conquest. Recently prisoners from Guantanamo were returned to their native soil of Saudi Arabia, and immediately placed in a "terrorist rehabilitation center." Let me repeat that. The former prisoners, trained as terrorists (cold blooded killers) in Afghanistan, were taken to a rehabilitation center in Saudi Arabia. This was front-page news. How does one rehabilitate a terrorist using the Qur'an and hadith, which were originally used to promote terrorism in the camps at which they trained? Here's the rub: none of these ex-prisoners ever saw themselves as terrorists. This is like the Budweiser Beer Company attempting to rehabilitate alcoholics who don't believe they are alcoholics. Or, better yet, the Philip Morris tobacco company offering to help people quit smoking; this is really quite absurd.

Let's consider some definitions and how Bin Laden, to use President Bush's words, "hijacked a religion" (but, in reality, simply accentuated what was already in place). Before getting started, it is important to emphasize that the Muslim tradition as a whole has to take some responsibility for the fundamentalist Islamic tradition of war and conquest for at least three reasons.

First, the Islamic religious leaders in Saudi Arabia, Syria, Iran, and Egypt preach hate for Americans and all non-Muslims; all Americans are conceptualized as decadent and evil and in need of conversion.

Second, I have heard very little from Muslim religious leaders condemning Bin Laden and the violence instigated by Islamic religious clerics all over the world, including the United States. Why is this? One reason might be that, like all true believers, the Muslim leaders conclude that, for Islam to reign supreme and spiritual health to return to their world, conquest and warfare might indeed be necessary. The main reason, however, has to do with the sacred nature of the Qur'an, for if you discredit any of the Surah (chapters and verses of the Qur'an, for example, Surah 9:5), then that represents a questioning of the legitimacy of the Qur'an in general for instituting social action. This places many (if not most) in the Muslim community in a bind, that is, of perhaps wanting to step out of the Dark Ages, but not being able to eliminate the tradition of Holy War and intolerance of other non-Muslims. Islam, unlike Judaism and Christianity, has not experienced a Reformation and this accentuates a medieval mindset.

Third, and hinted at above, the Qur'an states that killing idolaters in the name of Allah is not only proper but necessary for spiritual health in the world (see Firestone 1999). In my opinion, there were many high level religious clerics in both the United States and the Middle East who knew that 9/11 was in the works. What they didn't know was the exact date of execution, but they knew. Why can I say this? It was Bin Laden's belief that the U.S. would attack Muslims in this country once it was learned who the perpetrators were and the reason for the attacks. It was Bin Laden's hope that this would touch off a "religious" war and leaders would have been informed beforehand. Mosques are forts and you can rest assured that mosques in this country are no different in content than those in Iraq. Remember, love thy neighbor, but don't be dumb and stupid.

Getting back to Bin Laden, he could be considered a Kharijite. These are followers of Islam who believe in an expansion of the Islamic empire through a continuous jihad or holy war. I am told that it is strictly forbidden to convert by force, but Surah 9:5 suggests otherwise. Conversion can also be anticipated as a by-product of expansion, wherein members of non-Islamic traditions are heavily taxed, subjected to different laws, and rejected or marginalized by the Muslim community, leading the next generation to submit to Allah—this is the shunning business found as well in Judaism and Christianity. The goal of conquest is acquisition of land and resources, and to do this you have to control large numbers of people through threat of divine punishment and violence. Those taxed or subjected to a different set of laws than Muslims, often by the second generation, submit and join the club. Once you join, you can't get out. The Islamic religious clerics are so insecure that even one doubter or apostate is too many.

The Kharijites were nearly destroyed during the wars of the eighth century CE, although obviously this ideological position is alive and well in Afghanistan, other areas of the Middle East, and now the world. The term Kharijite comes from the word *kharaju*, which means to withdraw. Certainly Bin Laden has withdrawn from the civilized world. Such a person can only be labeled psychopathic (Axis I: 301.7); the "religion card" cannot be played. Along with this, the religious clerics who support and promote a Holy War are delusional (Axis I: 297.1) and antisocial (Axis II: 301.7). You might wonder how an imam can justify instructing another human being to strap on a bomb, sacrifice himself to a god, and kill innocent men, women, and children. The justification is as follows: If those killed in the explosion were good Muslims, then they go to heaven—no problem. If they weren't good Muslims, or if they were non-Muslims, then they deserved it. One has to wonder if mind-altering substances are used in recruiting homicide bombers. What could possibly convince a person to become a human sacrifice? Let's look at some useful categories.

Imam—This means "true faith" and refers to divine unity of adherents to Islam in the submission to the deity, Allah (al Liah). Imam also refers to a religious specialist, a teacher, third level instigators of homicide bombers; they always take orders from someone interpreting the will of God.

Jihad—This means "fighting" or "striving," and refers to calling upon devotees to dedicate themselves to combating enemies of their political organization. Jihad requires "collective consent" before it can be initiated. Bin Laden, therefore, must have had collective consent. This, of course, is denied, but Islam, like all political systems condones lying and deception. It is institutionalized and called *taqiyah* (see more below). The jihad has been called upon currently and in the past to both justify violent activities and as a label to rally people to action and discredit opponents. Those dying in combat, according to the Islamic myths, become martyrs and are given a special place in paradise with seventy-two celestial virgins at their disposal and all the wine they can drink. (Seventy-two is connected to the concept of precession in astronomy, the approximately seventy-two years it takes the zodiac to move one degree of arc.) This has traditionally been a male prerogative, but recent events in Palestine and Iraq suggest that there is a movement toward female martyrs as well. Is this a move toward more equality with the males? Does the woman homicide bomber likewise acquire seventy-two celestial virgins (perhaps males) as a prize for martyrdom in the name of Allah? Or does she become one of the virgins? Islam seems to be the only current "religious" tradition still practicing human sacrifice to a deity. Moreover, one only has to understand the Muslim heaven to appreciate the male Muslim mindset of "striving" for sex, booze, and power. Islamic heaven is designed, at the popular level at least, to appeal to the Muslim's animal nature; Islam as a tradition is designed to appeal to one's animal nature.

Mind-altering substances—The original foundation of Judaism, Christianity, and Islam included the use of mind-altering substances (a variety have been suggested). Moses' encounter with the burning bush and a pillar of smoke (hot-boxing in a tent), references attributed to Jesus in the Bible, and supporting literature and mosaics all involve the use of the sacred mushroom, *Amanita muscaria* and/or other mind-altering substances like cannabis (see Bennett and McQueen 2001; Merkur 2000). Muhammad, according to Abu Hurairah (*Mishkat,* Book xxi, Chapter One), stated, "Mushrooms are a kind of manna which God sent to Moses, and it allows one to see." Either Muhammad was psychotic or on drugs.

Tha'r—This is related to *intertribal revenge*. Although we are told this has been abandoned by moderate Islamic adherents (recall taqiyah, or institutionalized lying, mentioned above—also see below), this attitude of "getting even" may prevent many in the Muslim community from speaking out against the fundamentalists, Al Qa'ida, and the Wahhabi for fear (a real fear) of reprisal, although this does not excuse the deafening silence from the Muslim community. A community that fears reprisal certainly can have little faith in the wisdom and protection of Allah. We see the revenge aspect when non-Muslims speak out against Islam. An Islamic devotee murdered Theo Van Gogh on November 2, 2004, because he had presented a play that placed Islam in a bad light. Again, fundamentalists are so insecure in their beliefs that emotional and physical violence is justified, if for no other reason than to obtain celestial credits from a deity/demon that condones such action.

Ijma—This means consensus. The Sunnis see the community as a source of consensus, while the Shiites believe that infallible knowledge can only come from Imam, or that which comes from God. With respect to consensus, the Sunnis believe that all humans are capable of obeying or disobeying God's law, a moral struggle—to do God's work and alleviate human suffering, or to live instead for self and personal gain (status and wealth). God's law, of course, is constructed by Islamic clerics, and it would be difficult if not impossible to alleviate human suffering by following these laws—they have more to do with submission to Allah and less with a healthy relationship to humanity. There are five sources (*usul*) for the doctrine of Islam: 1) the Qur'an; 2) Hadith, or sayings attributed to Muhammad; 3) the Sunna (traditions), 4) Ijma (consensus), and 5) Ijtihad (individual thought). Individual thought, however, has little to do with critical thinking but is, instead, directed toward submission to Allah. The totality of this tradition is submission to Allah, which means submission to rulers and/or religious clerics.

Umma—Refers to the Islamic community.

Hadith—Collection of sayings attributed to Muhammad and members of the early Muslim community. The plural is *ahadith*. None of these sayings can be considered authentic in light of the fact that Muhammad is a mythic hero and not a real, historical character. We hear of both authentic and inauthentic hadith, but this is just a ploy, for if there are inauthentic hadith there must then be authentic hadith. This is the same ploy used when placing Abraham, Jacob, Moses, and Muhammad in a bad light—this makes them real, tangible human beings. Again, Jesus is just too good to be true.

Sunnis—Those belonging to the largest branch of Islam and who consider themselves the legitimate heirs to the title of Caliph, that is, the *Quraish* tribe, to which our mythic hero Muhammad is assigned. The basic belief is that the Mohammedan theocratic state should have a leadership determined by political, on-the-ground realities, and not by divine order. The emphasis here is on the views and customs of the majority of the community, the consensus (Ijma). This consensus, however, is created by the religious clerics and the individual has little or no voice. The Sunnis are the majority in all Muslim nations except Iran, Iraq, and Bahrain. Bin Laden is a Sunni and a devoted follower of the Qur'an. The Saudis told him to leave Saudi Arabia, which is ironic in the face of the fact that the Saudi regime is based on the Wahhabists (see Ernst 1997).

Shi'ah—The smaller group of followers who broke away from

the mainstream in order to create their own political tradition. More specifically, they supported the son-in-law of Muhammad named Ali (murdered in 661 CE), the Fourth Caliph (a spiritual leader), for in their view, only a member of Muhammad's family could rule. Thus they see themselves as the lineal descendents of Ali (the Alids) and as the temporal and spiritual leaders. The Shiites became a major political power in Iran during the late 1970's, led the resistance in Lebanon against the occupation of the Israelis in 1980's and 1990's, and are currently major contributors (men and supplies) to the sectarian strife in Iraq. Iran's encouragement of sectarian violence in Iraq, since U.S. troops unseated Saddam Hussein in 2003, is understandable in terms of what is at stake. The Iranian President Mahmoud Ahmadinejad is personally signing the checks for this sectarian violence and he obviously has a disturbed communication pattern (DSM-IV: 301.7—Antisocial Personality Disorder). If Iraq became a stable, democratic state, then this would put pressure on the whole region to eventually follow suit. In a democratic, open society with freedom of speech and elections by the citizens, Ahmadinejad would be shown the door.

Mullah—This term is applied to religious leaders and teachers or those versed in canon law. They are also leaders in prayer in the Mosques and reciters of the Qur'an.

Taqiyah—This is institutionalized lying, where a person can protect lifestyle and Islamic beliefs by denying participation in Islam or even agreeing with critics about its diabolic objectives—as long as this is not apostasy or a real leaving of the tradition. Because Islam controls every aspects of a person's life, a Muslim can, in practice, lie about anything and everything.

Apostasy—This means quitting or leaving a tradition, in this case Islam. Apostasy is a death sentence in Islam, and to threaten members in this manner indicates great insecurity about Islam's continued existence without such threats. No reasonable person would ever willingly join this tradition unless down and out, insane, or threatened with torture or death.

Violence—Islam also contains institutionalized violence toward all non-Muslims and political opponents; assassination is an approved method of dealing with adversaries and critics. On December 27, 2007, Islamic extremists assassinated Benazir Bhutto, who twice served as Pakistan's prime minister between 1988 and 1996. She was President Pervez Musharraf's most powerful opponent. All nations resort to violence when dealing with adversaries; the deaths of Princess Diana (Christian) and Dodi al-Fayed (Muslim) are mighty suspicious. Assassination of political opponents seems to be the rule in fascist, communistic, and Islamic societies, and it is very openly performed with one side or the other taking responsibility loud and clear in order to get the attention of the deity. The different sects take great pride describing their animalistic acts. In the West we assassinate with words (usually); the others are done in secret.

Slavery—Slavery is still practiced in the Middle East (Saudi Arabia, for example) and mostly involves African or black women (see Segal 2002). One has to wonder if Muslims in the United States practice slavery; I suspect they do. Such slavery is even apparent in the Christian fundamental traditions, where many (both men and women) want out but would face shunning, loss of income, loss of their children, and so on. To me, this is a type of slavery.

Bin Laden and Al Qa'ida have not neglected the universal statements in Islam regarding the human condition, of how to bring it into a proper balance with the energy that surrounds us. The procedure is to convert everyone to Islam and there will be peace, but at the price of individual freedom, freedom of speech, and critical thinking—all would be abolished. With Islam you get poverty, misery, and a life lived in perpetual fear (see Gabriel 2004 for a personal experience). Of course, thinking that there would be peace if everyone was Muslim is bogus; the Shi'ah and Sunni spend a great deal of time and energy blowing each other up.

Let's put some of this information together. First, you have a charismatic leader (Bin Laden) who is able to convince others of his sincerity in a quest to return to a better day. Perhaps he communicated with Muhammad using mushrooms or Syrian rue.

Second, he has at his right arm Al-Zawahiri, his advisor (Bin Laden is the warrior chief and Ayman Al-Zawahiri is the magician priest or advisor), and the mullahs and imams to reinforce Bin Laden's messages with familiar rites and rituals, emphasizing the Imam ("true faith"), the unity that comes from their adherence to the creed as presented according to the needs of the charismatic leader. This is compounded and reinforced with the idea that each person is a member of a wider community, the Umma.

Third, the holy war called by the charismatic leader (apparently anyone can lead in the *Kharijite* tradition) is designed to eliminate anyone trying to get in the way of this glorious return to yesteryear. With our current technology and economic system, it is difficult indeed for people, with a choice, to return to living in tents and caves except on special occasions. However, and this is the point, if our technological, economic, and political structures are destroyed, people would become confused, fearful, cold, and hungry; they would be eager and desperate to join any system that promises some hope of survival, even at the cost of freedom. Perhaps the reader can see how the jihad worked in terms of "attracting" converts in those former days. Remember, once you give up your freedom it is difficult to get it back. Against the wall, many would rather be "Red than dead." This is the hope of Al Qa'ida—the base or the beginning, the starting point, or even the return—with the hope of destroying a decadent world.

You can see what the free world is up against, a cult-type revitalization movement, apparently speaking for the larger Islamic community, with lots of money, that uses terror as a means to an end (the end of civilization as we know it) and a return to the world in which Muhammad grew up. His was a time of warring tribes brought together with a new metaphor, a new set of symbolic reference points, that would unify at that level of social/technological/political/economic circumstances. Conversion at the point of a sword is the name of this bloody game—the Infallible Pope got that right. Issues are no longer local; they are global.

One definite failing of Bin Laden is that he could not come up with a new metaphor to help the helpless and improve the human condition. Instead, he creates the helpless (the base—Al Qa'ida) with a plan of keeping the helpless more helpless and dependent, using the authority of a ruling few—they (the cult leaders) will rule by consensus (Ijma). This would be a dark day if Al Qa'ida accomplishes its goals. We would be thrown back to the Dark Ages. I have been quite puzzled by many university professors suggesting that somehow the U.S. is responsible for the 9/11 terrorist attacks and all the intellectual apologies for this tradition. Nor do I understand the other professors and politicians who believe that somehow this situation with the terrorists is negotiable. How do you negotiate with the "will of God" or a *fatwa* (an Islamic legal ruling—death, etc., issued by a high religious ruler) with someone who has a different opinion? Remember Salman Rushdie? He wrote *The Satanic Verses,* and was cursed with a *fatwa*—yes, a *fatwa* is a religious curse. Rushdie's curse is worth $2.5 million dollars to anyone who kills him. High-level religious clerics in this system, this "religion of peace," can issue fatwas against anyone, Muslim or non-Muslim, which could include torture, murder, and rape. Bin Laden also issued a fatwa allowing the killing of all Americas. Show me in history where we have successfully negotiated with cults, let alone cult-terrorists.

If these cult-terrorists destroy the economic and political system in the U.S., these same professors and politicians will be living in caves and tents, bitching and moaning about why the Government didn't do more. There is only one way, with reasonable certainty in terms of outcome, to deal with this absurd brand of terror—kill the terrorists, disband the cult, reform Islam, and anticipate the next set of problems this world faces.

Finally, the two first tenets of Islam are: There is only one god, Allah, and He comes first, and Muhammad is His Prophet. In this tradition, and in fundamentalist Judaism and Christianity, God comes first and humanity comes second. This is a political statement allowing a special group of people to rule through the mouth of God. This has more to do with "who's on top," or "striving" (jihad) to be alpha male, and has nothing to do with religion.

Islam and Health

What are the social circumstances that open the door for political cult formation? Many people willingly join cults, and when the group gains enough power, conformity to certain types of celestial rules is forced upon the individual with little room for individual initiative. Social instability is usually the door that opens to cult formation. When expectations are stripped away, when there is frequent or violent change of government, violent and/or unexpected loss of social relationships, and so on, this can lead to emotional and social insecurity—people feel stuck, they can't see a future, everything is immediate, they can't plan, etc. Add to this famine, brought about by an interruption of food or food sources, and out of this springs disease—emotional, physical, and social. Part of the disease process involves entropy or the loss of energy. The human body (life) and the social system in which it resides are perhaps best seen as systems of *negative* entropy. Entropy is the gradual and systematic degradation of everything: ashes-to-ashes and dust-to-dust, hot to cold, burnt out, and so on. Negative entropy would represent a slowing of the process. A political cult, therefore, could be seen as a symptom of a "dis-eased" social state, a strange attractor, a signal of social decay and death. A new order must be installed; there is urgency about this. All one has to do is study the myths associated with most cult activity in order to understand their position—lots of doom, gloom, and "dis-ease." Bin Laden's cult activity and attack on the United States is a clear indication of the dis-eased state of Islam, *not* the United States.

Political cults of the type promoted by Bin Laden and Islam do not breed health; they cultivate death, both physical and spiritual. Al-Wahhab, an attribution to Allah, means "the bestower of gifts," and true to the Wahhabi tradition these gifts are disease and death in the name of a deity. All cults, however, are also a statement about the power of symbols and how they can be manipulated for the purpose of health and/or disease.

The health or continuance of the fundamentalist aspects of these political systems, more specifically Judaism, Christianity, and Islam, relies on the censoring of information and the limiting of critical thinking about the existence of a male god who controls the world and every aspect of human life. These fundamentalist traditions maintain an attitude of male superiority, the male interpretation of the will of this god, and the subservience of women to male rulers and males in general. In a world where information about competing myths is more and more available, even in those countries where there is the belief that the average person cannot and should not think for him or herself (i.e., Saudi Arabia, Syria, Iran, etc.), we may actually be witnessing the "illness" and eventual "death" of these traditions; we may be seeing a last ditch effort to keep this archaic political system alive.

Because the West has been more or less open to new ideas, philosophies, and technological advances, we have a society that promotes exploring and analyzing. We expect new ideas and new technology; we expect change. Vast numbers of Christians and Jews have opened themselves to other possibilities and few take as historical fact much of what is written in the Bible. There is more and more leaning toward a personal interpretation, even if one regularly goes to temple or church. Very few intelligent Christians or Jews would kill in the name of God; and killing in the name of Jesus would be like killing in the name of Buddha. We might go into battle thinking that God is on our side, but few if any would say, "This one's for the Gipper." Islamic fundamentalists kill and torture in the name of Allah every day. The Wahhabi cannot survive in nations where people are self-responsible and support themselves and their families. Wahhabi attracts the disenfranchised, those without a profession, and those misdirected by religious clerics.

Prevarication and Apostasy

Surah 16:106: "Whoever denies having once believed—unless he is forced to do so while his heart enjoys the peace of faith—and opens his mind to disbelief will suffer the wrath of God. Their punishment will be great." The first and last parts refer to apostasy, and the middle part allows a person to lie about his/her religious conviction if in danger of having one's religious beliefs criticized or being forcefully converted. As Islam means submission, a person who submits dedicates his or her whole life to this tradition. In this sense, and taken to extremes, a person can lie about anything if it is seen as a threat to one's beliefs and practices. *Taqiyah*, as it is called, means "guarding oneself." When Muslims are confronted with specific questions about slavery, woman's rights, homicide bombers, and even where they are from, the answers are couched in excuses, diversion techniques, and outright lies. So there is an issue of trust. It is difficult to trust a tradition and its adherents who condone institutionalized prevarication; it is difficult to trust politicians in this country for the very same reason.

Apostasy, or leaving the Islamic fold, is a death sentence. Defectors are seen as a threat to Islam because if just one person is allowed to defect, then maybe others will want out as well. I have it on good authority that there are many, many Muslims who want out of Islam. For those who want a close, personal look at some brave people who said "no more" and walked away, see Gabriel (2004) and Warraq (2003). If Islam has the truth, the right way, why are people forced to join and prevented or discouraged from leaving? The answer to this is simple: No one would willingly join this tradition unless threatened, mentally challenged, or desperate.

Apologies for Islam and the Qur'an

If the Qur'an represents the word of God, then one would not have to apologize for its content, let alone suggest how someone read or approach this document. Any intelligent deity would dictate instructions that would be self-evident. Suggesting that God needs humans to instruct in how to approach the Qur'an is absurd. The message of the Qur'an is self-evident but the tradition needs apologists (see Zarabozo 1999 and Esack 2005) to cover up the true agenda of controlling people through fear and threat of violence.

Conclusion

The stages in the development of the Qur'an and hadith are clear enough, although some of the details are speculation. The Jews, Christians, and others are pushing the Arabs. The various tribes define a common enemy and a war leader emerges. They begin to win battles. Muhammad, in the role of a warrior-priest (shaman), communes with the spirit world, which allows him to give orders in the name of his patron deity, al Liah. Muhammad is very successful and gradually wins people over to his patron deity, and although still polytheistic, it opens the door for monotheism, just as Moses' patron deity, Yahweh, opened the door to monotheism in that tradition.

Muhammad dies, perhaps in battle, perhaps eating bad mushrooms, but it might have been a slow death over the course of many weeks. His recovery was assumed, but when death was inevitable someone had to take his place. Through conquest and pillaging they just couldn't let a good thing go, so they need a new leader to take Muhammad's place with his inevitable death approaching. As the story goes, this is the beginning of hadith, or statements attributed to Muhammad. Actually, what is now called hadith was borrowed from a very old tradition used in settling inter- and intra-tribal disputes. Tribal chiefs, in attempting to solve a problem or enact a sentence, would pull into the picture precedents from the past that often referred to an enlightened elder. This is the "third person" information delivery approach (just as when I reference sources in this work); you can argue with the message but not the messenger. As hadith adds up they become law or dogma; most law is based on precedent but can change depending on new circumstances. Dogma is often times very resistant to change even in the face of new circumstances. Whatever Muhammad was reputed to have said came by way of al Liah through Gabriel/Samael or Shaytan, and thus his message can't be challenged or changed except through Muhammad's "new prophecies for old" formula. Of course Muhammad is dead, so there can be no new major prophecies. As time went on, a new system was attached to their old tribal polytheistic beliefs and practices, laws, and so on, which included an intricate legal system, with laws about women, food restrictions, and dress codes that would fit all tribes. Once the door was opened to monotheism, in stepped the Old Testament with its guidance for building a mythical charter through Abraham,

Hagar, and Ishmael. They did exactly as the Jews did; they created so many ritual and social requirements that they separated themselves from everyone else. Much of their ritual and mythic tale is based on the Old Testament, and so it was a matter of what would Moses do, just as we ask, "What would Jesus do?"

If we are to believe the stories that Uthman had alternate collections of hadith destroyed in order to create a single script, Uthman would have destroyed valuable documents. However, as it is difficult to verify early Muslim political history, this has to be treated as just another story. I do not believe that Muhammad had any idea at all that he would be used as a focal point, a third person to whom all kinds of behaviors and wise, prophetic statements were attributed. Muhammad may indeed have been an orator, but at the very least he was much smarter then most. In my opinion, again, if there was a person like Muhammad, he was introduced to shamanic ritual processes most likely through the Zoroastrians, who supported the use of mind-altering substances as a conduit to God and social control.

By approximately 700 CE, the Arab people had been united under several rulers who continued to wage war, but by this time the patron god of Muhammad, the moon god of war, becomes connected to the God of the Jews as a means of justifying conquests far and wide. Using the Abraham, Hagar, and Ishmael connection to Yahweh, they slightly altered the pronunciation of al Liah to Allah with an emphasis on the first syllable. During this time period the identity with the Jews had coalesced to the point that Jerusalem became their new ritual focal point or base. I have come across no proof-positive evidence that Muhammad really went to Jerusalem but his followers did.

This, however, was short lived, because the Jews did not welcome these new converts into the fold and the reasons for this are quite simple—they would have eventually been absorbed into the Arab tribes, the very thing they fought against in the first place. Social or group rejection is very powerful; the Arab-Israeli conflict, in part, stems from this. As a reaction to this rejection, the Islamites have placed themselves above everyone else (the chosen few—a sure sign of an inferiority complex), much the same as occurred with the Israelites 1,000 years earlier. They can do this because Ishmael was first born. By 750 CE, a document now referred to as the Qur'an came into existence. It is a composite of legends, both prior to and concurrent with Muhammad, and sayings constructed for political-social reasons after his death. Much of the material represents opinions, interpretations, and poetry of individuals, but is attributed to our third-person hero, Muhammad, and a fourth-person source, Gabriel or Samael, and then fifth, Allah.

Islam, like the other monotheistic traditions, appeals to our animal nature, places Allah and Muhammad before humanity, and is intolerant of all other monotheistic and polytheistic traditions. Islam is stuck in the Dark Ages, is not a religion, and certainly not a religion of peace. And, in my opinion, it is currently engaged in a last ditch effort, through terrorist activity, to disrupt the world economy. Terror is Islam's main method of conversion because no one in his or her right mind would willingly join. Finally, any tradition that places God before humanity is demonic; there are many gentle Muslims in the world but they still worship a demon. I will say one positive thing about Muhammad. According to hadith, he liked cats: "Cats are not impure, they keep watch around us." (*Mishkat,* Book iii)

Islam has been unable to move into a modern world and remains, for the most part, anchored in an ideology that believes that people have to be lead by the nose or micromanaged. Subjects are to do what they are told without question, worship without question, eat without question, dress without question, and kill without question. As with Judaism and Christianity, one is to submit to a god, which means submission to the king and/or religious cleric, on faith. This type of philosophy squashes independent thought and creativity; thinking outside the narrow box of Islam can be dangerous. The major reason for this stems from the Islamic community's inability to approach the Qur'an and hadith in a scholarly/poetic fashion, rather than maintaining that the Qur'an is the divine word of God and therefore not subject to historical/linguistic analysis. By maintaining this unyielding position the Islamic community misses out, in a way similar to fundamentalist

Jews and Christians, on a renaissance of thinking and possibilities.

Islam is best defined as a tyrannical political system (fascism) with a thin veneer of what one might consider religion because of references to supernatural beings. This tradition demands absolute submission to Allah. In a fashion similar to fundamentalist Judaism and Christianity, the deity comes first and humanity comes second. Why, we might ask, is absolute submission to the deity necessary? Here is where the political weight of Islam comes in—as above, below. When you submit to the deity you are also submitting to the Caliph, the ruler, and/or the religious cleric who pretends to interpret the will of God.

We are also treated with cries that Westerners lack understanding of Islam. Nasr's (2002) outline of Islam is a case in point. It is an apologetic attempt to spin Islam into something that it is not, although it may be his experience of this tradition. Any "enduring values for humanity" in Islam can be found in the necessity of cooperative social living and not in religion proper; morality and religion are two entirely different things. Moreover, any humanitarian values presented in Islam are far, far overshadowed by the millions murdered and tortured in the name of Allah. No forgiveness can be issued for this, any more than the Catholic Church can be forgiven for the torture and murder of innocent men, women, and children throughout the centuries. Why no forgiveness? Because of their claims (and continued claims) of infallibility and that they act according to the will of a god—a demon.

The Qur'an tells its followers to kill or convert all non-Muslims, which includes me, and thus I perceive Islam as a personal threat. Many academics and followers of Islam attempt to turn this around by saying the reference is, instead, to the "struggle" with one's own evil impulses, but this is pure taqiyah, a lie. Perhaps through reform this might become the case, but in its present condition I am at risk of being tortured and/or murdered by the mindless, cowardly thugs who do the dirty work of insecure imams in a fascist political system. I have also been told that I'm not showing respect or enough religious tolerance, but I have little tolerance for this or any tradition constructed on lies and deception, and which places a deity—a demon—first and humanity second.

CHAPTER FIVE

Conclusion

Introduction

All mammals are engaged in the enterprise of eating, sex, and clinging to life. This 200 million year enterprise is based on a process called evolution, that which was created by the energy that informs all. We, *Homo sapiens,* arrived on the scene around 130 KYA and are a direct descendent of *Homo erectus,* dating to 1.8 MYA. This may have all happened by divine will; certainly, some energy informs all we experience.

Humans are a special animal, in the sense of being culture bearing to a degree unknown in the rest of the animal kingdom on this planet. As small-group animals, we learned to cooperate as family units, with both males and females engaged in the process of raising and enculturating the child, a very different behavioral pattern than seen in our nearest primate relative, the chimpanzee. There are many blank pages in the book of human evolution, but this is not the case with other species, such as plants, insects, horses, cats, and so on. We must have evolved just as other plants and animals; we have the bones of our most recent ancestor, *Homo erectus,* and a close cousin, *Homo neanderthalensis.*

All cultures are wrapped in stories about ourselves—who we are, why we are, and where we are. In times past, these stories would recalibrate as circumstances demanded, for it was through stories that culture directs the thoughts and behaviors of the cultural carriers. Hunter-gatherers have their own inflection, while agriculturalists have theirs. Humans are a small-group animal—methods of social control in groups ranging from twenty-five to 125–150 individuals are accomplished through face-to-face contact. Deviant behavior is minimized because everyone knows what everyone else is doing. Magico-religious traditions in these small societies are designed to connect the individual and the group to the imagined spiritual world. No one was left out—all were involved in this spiritual endeavor, orchestrated by a part-time specialist called a shaman in popular parlance. Hallucinogenic plants and fungi were usually part of this, especially during curing ceremonies and other crises. What is needed is not available locally, so the shaman travels to the spirit realm and returns with that which is needed to heal or bring the system into balance. The shaman fits the hero model. Moses, Jesus, and Muhammad are cultural heroes. The mind-altering plants altered perception and for hundreds of generations allowed these individuals or heroes to go outside the bounds of normal reality and experience another truth or possibility.

As agriculture along the Tigris and Euphrates rivers developed, food surpluses allowed more people to live within a much smaller geographical area and, with food surpluses, populations increased. This came with an unexpected problem—all are not in face-to-face contact, there are strangers around, and deviant behavior increases (see Rush 1996). If this hydraulic adventure was to survive, a new type of political organization had to emerge. The shaman morphs from a part-time specialist into a full-time priest, who might also be the ruler of the community or perhaps a co-regent, with the magician-priest ruling alongside the chief or the person with a mythical charter, legitimizing his (or her) right to rule. Because face-to-face contact with all members of the community is strategically impossible, the chief would make a point of moving from group to group, acting as a mirror for proper behavior, settling disputes, and giving advice. The priest, for his part, helped maintain order through various and frequent rituals that served to enhance group bonding and maintain direction for the populace. The original "policing" for these early populations was at least threefold: First, the rituals bound the group together; second, the priest's ability to predict seasonal variation gave him magical power or credibility; and third, the gods supported the ruling class and their right to rule by giving orders, punishing, and rewarding (recall the story of Adapa and Anu in Chapter One). The gods were also capricious; bad things happen (floods, drought, infant death, etc.), but it was the will of the gods. The concept of an underworld or geography to which the individual was assigned after death was long established, and initially did not (as far as can be detected) involve punishment, as it was more like a holding tank (see Rush 2007). This underworld was not exactly a bad place, but it required that relatives maintain shrines where food was placed on a regular basis. This accomplished two things: respect for the ancestors and, through analogy, respect for the living.

As time went on cosmologies became more complex, and this upper world or heaven was constructed as a mirror for the living to emulate, complete with a stratified bureaucracy. The king was a caretaker and the priests were administrators. Punishment for deviance became more extreme, lest such activities unbalance the universe and the gods unleash a flood and destroy all humankind; their stories told of celestial brutality in the past. With more impersonal and brutal leadership, the underworld takes on a new dimension—punishment. This is a direct result of thuggish rulers and priests who dispense punishment arbitrarily and brutally, just as the deities bring rain and drought at their convenience. The myth of a tormenting hell, originally a reflection of brutal leadership, is the hope of the oppressed, but is likewise used to threaten and control the oppressed. The gods at this point are impersonal and do not appear to have a direction or purpose for a special people.

Eastern traditions, such as Hinduism and Buddhism, evolved in a cultural landscape that remained relatively stable over a long period of time, mainly because India is difficult to invade. These spiritual traditions turned inward with the realization that the individual is God, and the energy that informs all, Atman, is not separate from Its creation; heaven and hell, and all the gods and demons, are inside the mind and not separate from it. The Middle East, on the other hand, is open to invasion from strangers with different beliefs and behavior, and these invasions have continued to this day. God becomes the other, existing outside the individual, the one who conquers and then rules with an iron fist. This god is like a king who is unapproachable except for immediate advisors or magician-priests, and any suggestion that you are a god likewise suggests you are a king (or at least in a position to tell the king what to do). This is very, very bad; just consider what happened to Jesus.

With the development of Zoroastrianism we see the first moral religion, where good is pitted against evil and it is up to the individual to follow the laws and enter heaven; by not following the rules you go to hell. Scholars suggest that this tradition, as well as others developing at about the same time (800–600 BCE), was a statement or message to brutal rulers that, unless they showed more concern for their subjects, they would get their comeuppance at death. At this point, however, there does not seem to be a plan constructed by the good god (Ahura Mazda) for a special people, outside of eliminating evil in the world.

Judaism as we know it today begins around 560 BCE. This is a monotheistic tradition only in the sense that the male energy is dominant and female energy suppressed. There is one male god and a male bureaucracy; this is the definition of monotheism, which refers to an accentuation of male energy and not simply the existence of one god. This is not exactly rule by council as in nomadic Arab traditions, indicating that poets separated from nomadic life for a long time constructed the Old Testament. At this point in time the Israelites begin a political process of separating themselves from the surrounding Canaanite tribes, as a means of maintaining their tribal identity rather than being absorbed into an urban center. This fear exists today (Telushkin 2002, 17–18). To do this, they construct a mythical charter with time depth and connections to royalty through Abraham, Joseph, and Moses. They promote the patron god Yahweh to first place, who has a special people (the Hebrews) with a special plan (land ownership), to build a nation unto itself. These chosen people create rules upon rules (food restrictions, clothing styles, rules related to work, marriage, sex, and purification) specifically designed to separate themselves from others. Their written mythical charter was unique. It had historical references and hero storylines, with the heroes being told by the deity they had special status with land ownership. Through their stories they became better than all other groups around them. They believed that written words come to life and what they wrote would come true: "As it is written, so it shall be." They demanded special privileges, and in the process alienated other Canaanite tribes and became despised.

The political climate in the Middle East becomes intolerable by 200 BCE and a secret Jewish sect, the Essenes, prophesizes the end of the world brought about by their special deity. All the evil in the world will be removed, with evil referring to evil rulers and all non-Jews. There will be a return or second coming of Esau, the Son of the Father, and he will set things straight. Scholars have suggested that the Essenes are an ancient sect who migrated from Amarna in Egypt to the Sinai, and eventually into Canaan, shortly after Amarna was abandoned. As Aldred (1988, 306) states:

> After the Amarna interlude, the life of Egypt resumed its
> flow through familiar channels. Yet perversely, the idea to
> which Akhenaten had sacrificed so much did not wholly die
> with him. They continued to haunt the minds of others, and
> eventually prevailed as the ordinances for the conduct of
> Man *vis-à-vis* God in the Decalogue that was part of another
> "Teaching."

This other "teaching" is Judaism. They worshipped the Aten/Yahweh, saw Akhenaten as a god on earth, and Tutankhamun (his son) as the Son of the Sun. Notice how Aldred worded his statement so as to not stray too far from political correctness. The probable synonym for King Tutankhamun was Joshua (another term for Esau or Jesus), Son of Nun, with Nun referring to the Egyptian primal abyss out of which all comes and into which all goes.

Sometime around 28 CE, John the Baptist defects from the Essenes and brings a message to the common people. His message came without the usual "Thou shalt," but instead with an emphasis on core human needs presented through parable, forcing people to think about their life situations and basic human needs, that is, compassion and love toward others, judge yourself before judging others, do unto others as you would have done unto you, love thy neighbor, and so on; churches and priests are unnecessary because you are God. John the Baptist also reintroduced mind-altering substances, so the individual could personally commune with the energy that informs all. John also realized that he came with no authority, and so he used the time honored, third-person approach by revealing that the message came from Esau, Son of Nun, Son of God, Son of Man, from which all things come and go. "Esau is coming, Esau is coming! Clean up your lives. Don't worry about what you eat or wear, start being nice to people so that when He arrives you will already be in heaven. Heaven is here and not some other place; live it, and when you die you will already be there."

John became a very successful street performer; he had many followers and some he baptized with fire (*Amanita muscaria* and other substances), making "tangible" what could only be accepted on faith. He became a little too successful. At the same time Herod lost a battle with Aretas, the king of Arabia Petrea, and some Jews (the Essenes) saw the destruction of Herod's army as a sign from God and a mandate for the populace to rise up and overthrow the government. John was arrested and executed. This left his followers with a leader, Peter (perhaps), who knew full well that it was the Baptist who preached the second coming of Esau. Peter was not a charismatic leader, and the disciples were losing motivation and drifting away. Up stepped Paul, an early persecutor of Christians, a contemporary of Esau (Jesus) and John the Baptist (although he never met them), and with only Peter as an informant. Paul had a mind-altering experience on the road to Damascus, possibly prompted and led by some Gnostics, and he became a convert fully believing (perhaps) that there was a person named Jesus. He then came in contact with Peter and obviously Paul didn't like what Peter had to say. Here is the actual conversation.

> "That's the truth, Paul, Jesus hasn't landed yet, but we are told he is coming soon."
>
> "You mean that I drove all the way out here, and there is no Jesus? What kind of bullshit is this? I meet up with those Gnostics . . ."
>
> "What's the matter with you, Paul? Can't you take a metaphor?"

"You sarcastic little prick! Go peddle your metaphor somewhere else . . . although you are quite cute. I've got a better idea—I'll write some letters to the editors and get this whole thing cleared up."

This is precisely what Paul did. He took the initiative to write and obtain commitment to *his* ideas, ideas fostered and matured through the uses of cannabis, *Amanita muscaria,* henbane, or maybe combinations. There was no Jesus; it was John the Baptist who was selling the story. But Paul, after his experience on the road to Damascus and telling all his friends, refused to believe Peter; he could not distinguish the difference between "drug real" and "real real." Paul was of an unstable mind to begin with and his drug experiences didn't help. Through his own mental gymnastics and drug trips, he because a pseudo-apostle and stepped into the shoes of Jesus. A probable statement of his contact with Jesus through hallucinogenic substances is brought out in 1 Corinthians 9:1, "Am I not an apostle? Have I not seen Jesus our Lord?" Later in 1 Corinthians (15:8–9) we read, "Last of all, as to one untimely born, [Christ] appeared also to me. For I am the least [i.e, most recent] of the apostles." Because his statement was not disputed, it implies that use of mind-altering substances was the *standard modus operandi* for contacting the spiritual world, and those with whom he corresponded couldn't very well fault Paul for what they themselves were doing. I suspect, however, that not everyone had experienced Jesus during these hallucinogenic trips. Paul, according to scholars, was an emotionally disturbed individual from the start. He had an inferiority complex, absolute fear of women, and was a guilt ridden homosexual, a behavior demonized when the Israelites distanced themselves from the mother-goddess cults of the Canaanites.

Paul almost single-handedly corrupted the message of John the Baptist, perverted the universal message of love and compassion, and it all sank back into what we know as Christianity, a form of reformed Judaism. Paul is the anti-Christ. His message, corrupted further by his continuers, told people to follow like sheep and not to think. Once out of the hands of John the Baptist, Christianity fractures at every turn and falls back into a political abyss designed to control and severely punish non-believers, either in this world or another. Catholicism maintained control for over 1,200 years, until the first quarter of the sixteenth century CE when Martin Luther condemned the Church for its numerous activities, like accepting money to clear people's sins and open the gates to heaven, and so on. On May 25, 1521, the Holy Roman Emperor Charles V officially declared Martin Luther a criminal and heretic for refusing to recant his position at the Diet of Worms. Thus we begin the reformation of a tradition born out of love and compassion, which became twisted and perverted first by Paul and then by every one of his continuers—popes, bishops, priests, ministers, and evangelists. All the Christian religious clerics had a hand in this, and still do. What started as a spiritual endeavor ended as a political and economic system masquerading as "religion." The immorality of this tradition is well documented in history. The Protestants ("protest-ants") haven't faired much better, and many of these groups (Mormons, Seventh Day Adventists, Jehovah's Witnesses, etc.) have almost totally reverted to Judaism, with outrageous claims of special people with special privileges. The Mormons have even gone so far in their deception as to invent gold tablets sent down from heaven, thus justifying their status as "top dog." Their original leader, Brigham Young, is their focal point, the born-again Moses, for it is he who led them west to their promised land. Brigham Young was an insecure, womanizing thug who had many of his followers murdered in the name of their god. There are other Protestant groups, however, who are a bit more liberal in their interpretations of the scriptures and are likely to survive into the twenty-second century. I prophesize that those groups that control parishioners with threat and intimidation, shunning, and general lack of compassion will, like Islam, go the way of the dinosaur within the next one hundred years. Any system that maintains membership through threat, intimidation, and shunning is obsolete, and sends a clear message of insecurity and lack of faith in their own message. Scientologists should take note of this as well. When these systems enter the politic, when they become a force able to dictate rules and regulations, pain and suffering, poverty and misery are quick to follow. Critical thinking was abolished in Christianity and Islam; logic, reason, and human decency come second to believing in God. This is clearly illustrated in contemporary Christmas music, where God or Jesus is praised and statements about human decency are minimized. Santa usually has nice things to say; Santa is a pagan deity with characteristics borrowed from shamanism. Jesus can be characterized as a shaman as well. Under the Christmas tree is the gift, a mushroom for communion with God (*Amanita muscaria* grows symbiotically on the roots of conifer or pine trees). Jesus did the exact same thing, except he didn't bring the tree into the house; he went to the tree.

Like Judaism and Christianity, Islam emerged during times of extreme social stress. Emerging as it did almost 1,000 years to the day after Judaism and around 300 years after the coalescing of Christianity, it enjoyed precedents on which to build its own tradition and align with the world as it then existed. In short, Islam needed to join the world community and yet maintain its own identity, for loss of land and identity is what the future held in store. The tribal groups in the Arabian Peninsula were always feuding with one another over water and grazing rights, and the Jews and especially the Christians took advantage of this. The Jews were not particularly looking for recruits but land and wealth are okay. The Christians wanted land, wealth, and converts. I suspect that their proselytizing efforts, attacks on shrines, and destruction of idols are what pushed the Arabs too far, although some scholars insist that Islam was born out of radical Christianity. I think this unlikely.

There was distaste for Christianity early on and I think the answer to this is twofold. The first part is related to their proselytizing efforts. But as they were constructing Muhammad's personality and behaviors, they knew that Jesus' behavior had to be a construction as well. The poet/philosophers were not stupid people. They were the cream of the intellectual crop. Most of the poets, I suppose, believed Jesus to be a real person, and they also thought that he was a nice guy—period. But their myth, if they wanted to enter the world community, couldn't be based on a "nice guy." You cannot remove foreign invaders from your soil by being gentle and philosophic—as Gandhi said, "You can't kill Hitler with love." They chose as their focal point a real general, and his name might have been Muhammad, the praised or glorified one. Although the name Muhammad has been very popular over the centuries, during the time period it might have been rare. Why can I say this? Well, if you want to set this general apart from the masses, you need an uncommon name or to invent one, befitting the status and position desired by the Islamic poets.

Islam is a replay of Judaism. The poets used the story of Hagar and Abraham to construct their genealogical rights and privileges. While the Jewish poets were attempting to remove the genealogical connection to Egypt by consigning Hagar and Ishmael to the desert, they probably never considered that the Arab peasants would ever learn to read and write, use this as part of their own mythical charter, and demand their land back.

Muhammad was very successful in vanquishing these interlopers (Jews, Christians, and others) and went on to conquer area after area. It is unlikely that Muhammad was the least bit interested in creating Islam. He had his patron god, al Liah, with whom he communed in a time-honored fashion using mind-altering substances. He credited his triumphs to al Liah and he attracted followers. He was a clever man who could build trust, as he did by riding into battle side by side with his men. Muhammad did not die of old age. He is wounded in battle, at which point there is conflict as to who should take his place; Muhammad neglected to assign the role to any person or group of his followers. The biggest and strongest took his place, only to be displaced by someone bigger and stronger, resulting in great brutality to critics and pretenders to power. Thus we get the two pictures of Muhammad— his ability to develop trust and loyalty (the real Muhammad), and then the brutality-toward-critics, a sort of a philosophical Hell's Angel (the invented Muhammad). A way of preventing assassination was to construct hadith to legitimize one individual's right to rule as opposed to another, and out of this came the Sunni and the Shi'ah, who represent two very antagonistic divisions in Islam. The demon al Liah (Allah) seems to very much enjoy the conflict between these two groups of Muslims, and probably orgasms every time a homicide bomber hits the switch. You can see this fat demon licking up the blood and bones of his victims, in a fashion similar to the Hindu god of dark time, *Mahakala,* standing there with eight arms, a weapon in each, while human bodies smash against his teeth, with blood, guts, and gore splattering into his open mouth, or Nun, the primal abyss.

The Arabs reach a point where it is difficult to expand their territory and hold it, and beginning in the early part of the eighth century the priest-poets realized that they had to reorganize and put meaning to what they had accomplished. This took many years and required that they construct a history of events using very limited data. So they call forth hadith and likewise construct their own; they wrap this around existing charter material, the Old Testament, and the auxiliary writings connected to the Jewish tradition. Jesus is pretty much neglected, perhaps because they found little evidence for his existence as well, but more likely because Jesus was a model of peace and this did not fit the Arab agenda. By 750 CE there is now a document called the Qur'an, a mythical charter that allows this tradition to do anything it wants to Muslims and non-Muslims, for all is done in the name of Allah, that third-person trickster with a very large knee.

New areas of conquest include India and other parts of Africa, but they dare not storm too far into Europe, at least not yet. During their smashing they are seeing another world, a more sophisticated world, with different philosophies and knowledge about the universe. Soldiers who could grasp the import of certain writings preserved them, and over time added greatly to the sciences of astronomy, math, and practical medicine. But just as the Christians before them, they reach a point where science confronted them with difficult questions and consequent answers. Their quest for knowledge ceases in most quarters and they tumble into their Dark Age. There is a yearning in some quarters for a return to those exciting years of yesterday, riding into battle on camels, brandishing swords, and slaying the infidels. These days, the promoters of Islam, Al Qa'ida, and the Wahhabists are a clear reminder of how far this tradition will go to install Islam in every corner of the world. This will be their last chance, for the future is hostile to their continuance, at least in a non-reformed tradition that closely resembles fascism. Remember, I am referring to the tradition of Islam, and not to all people who call themselves Muslims. Just as Christianity and being a Christian or a follower of Jesus are two different things, the same applies to Islam and Muslims who follow the original Muhammad, who was probably as decent as Jesus, but had another mission and carried a sword.

Hallucinogens and Religion

Most anthropologists would agree that shamanic behavior and ecstatic rites often involve the use of mind-altering substances, or manna, which include *Amanita muscaria,* the various *Psilocybe* species found all over the world, Syrian rue, henbane, datura species, belladonna, cannabis, mandrake, ergot fungus, and opium, along with wine and beer; in the New World, these include tobacco, San Pedro, peyote, ipomoea species, tree datura, *Banisteriopsis caapi,* yopo, the coca plant, and so on. Combinations of these plants, fungi, and brew can have striking effects and lead to some very bad trips, complete with monsters and flying beasts. Anything you have ever seen, heard, or created in your mind is available, along with unimaginable monsters and deities. The intensity and even the colors of the experience can also change when various plants are combined. In our own time, cannabis is often mixed with alcohol, thus enhancing the "trip." Many using prescription tranquilizers and other substances, like Prozac and Zoloft, often combine them with alcohol to enhance the effects. Let's take a more detailed look at manna, as revealed by the biblical poets.

In Bialik and Ravnitzky's *The Book of Legends (Sefer Ha-Aggadah) from the Talmud and Midrash* (1992, 75–76), we encounter discussions and descriptions of manna, and how biblical passages were interpreted many centuries after they were written. I'm going to engage this in detail, commenting on specific parts, to suggest a different meaning as gathered through a twenty-first century lens, once mind-altering substances enter the picture.

> 3. "Moses said: 'It is the Lord who will give you flesh to eat in the evening, and bread in the morning to the full.'" (Exod.16:18) R. Aha bar Jacob said: At first Israel were like hens, randomly pecking away in a heap of refuse, until Moses came and fixed definite mealtimes for them.

Jacob's rendering is unlikely to be the meaning of Moses' statement. Instead, it is a statement that the Lord will provide and that we should be thankful. His statement suggests, however, some of the humor (sarcastic in this case) deeply imbedded in this tradition.

> 4. "The disciple of R. Simeon ben Yohai asked him: 'Why did the manna not come down for Israel just once a year?' He replied: 'Let me answer you with the parable of a mortal king who had a son. When the king provided him with this sustenance once a year, the son visited his father only once a year. When the father began to provide him with his sustenance daily, the son had to call on his father every day. So it was with Israel. If the Israelite had, say, four or five children, he would worry, saying: Perhaps the manna will not come down tomorrow, and all my children will die of hunger. And so [because the manna was coming down daily], the Israelites were compelled to direct their hearts to their Father in heaven [every day].'"

Mushrooms have interesting characteristics, one of which is the ability to grow rapidly, even overnight, as if they had fallen from the sky. In geographies with noticeable seasons, some mushrooms, like many plants, are seasonal. In climates without dramatic temperature changes (the Mediterranean, for example), mushrooms appear on a day-to-day basis. However, the disciple understands manna to be food and, like grain, it is seasonal—you have one big harvest. The rabbi's answer clearly indicates that this is not food, for it is a connected to the Father. Here is my logic. Even if you have one harvest, you do not consume the harvest all at once. If the reference was to food, then you could simply thank the Lord each time you meet and be with the Lord with each meal. So manna is not food; it is that which connects to the godhead. This is the original Christian meaning of "breaking bread" (the "body of Christ") and partaking in a communal identity with God by becoming God. This is clearly illustrated in the mosaics at St. Mark's Basilica.

> Another reason [for daily manna]: They were able to eat it while it was still warm.
>
> Still another reason [for daily manna]: To lighten the burdens that had to be carried during the journey.

These above reasons are simply guesses as to why manna is a daily affair. They possibly confuse manna and food, are being used to humor a novice, or perhaps to encourage dialogue. I suspect that the rabbi knew full well the meaning of manna, but the disciple was not ready for that enlightenment. The next paragraphs begin to bring to light the real meaning of manna.

> 5. Manna is described in Scripture as "bread," as "honey," and as "oil." How are the differing descriptions to be reconciled? Young men taste in it the taste of bread, old people in the taste of honey, and infants in the taste of oil.

Manna is simply a generic term for mind-altering substances. Bread refers to dried mushroom caps, honey is used to mute the taste of mushrooms and cannabis (among other substances), and the oil is a reference to anointing oils discussed in Chapter Two. The connection to the sensory experience of manna is probably a reference to the age or stage of training at which a student or disciple was introduced to these substances. Again, the rabbis knew full well the meaning of manna, and these statements are designed to make people think and are not to be taken literally. Those who could honestly and respectfully question the comment are likely to go to the head of the class.

> 6. It is written, "When the dew fell in the camp in the night, the manna fell upon it" (Num. 11:9); it is also written, "The people shall go out and gather," etc. (Exod.16:4); and it is also written, "The people went about to and fro to gather it" (Num. 11:8). How are these three statements to be reconciled? For the righteous, it came right down to the doors of their tents; ordinary people had to go out and gather it; but the wicked had to go about to and fro to gather it.

Without specifics as to what manna was, then the poetic interpretations of statements in Exodus and Numbers are simply ways of layering a story with meaning and new meaning. Mushrooms can grown is patches, especially where there is sufficient moisture (dew). Not understanding the life cycle of a mushroom, that a mushroom is built from an itsy, bitsy spore, and they grow very rapidly, the belief was that they must have come from the heavens.

Manna is also described as "bread" (Exod. 16:4) and as "unbaked dough" (Num. 11:8), and Scripture also says, "They ground it" (ibid). How (do we) reconcile the differing descriptions? Well, the righteous received it as [baked] bread, ordinary Israelites as unbaked dough, and the wicked as grain yet to be ground in a hand mill."

How the "bread" is received definitely says that manna is not food (nourishment of the flesh). In our day when people have bad trips on mind-altering substances, we usually attribute this to some prevailing mental problem, inappropriate set and setting, and so on. In the time period in which the Bible and commentary were written, physical and emotional illnesses were often attributed to gods and demons. Thus, a bad trip suggested that "the gods are angry."

"Grinding in a hand-mill" was probably a metaphor for a bad trip, definitely not a pleasant experience. I find it interesting that the word "Gethsemane," of Aramaic origin, means "an oil press." Remember that Jesus is arrested in Gethsemane, a non-place; he and his disciples spent a great deal of time there. And what were they doing? They were in "the oil press" or "grinding in a hand-mill," having "wheat separated from the chaff," or purification or preparation for the experience with the mushroom god, Jesus. "And if not pure of mind, if you have not had your purification before the revelation, I rebuke you." This "coming home to Jesus" speech (see back cover and Chapter Three) is telling disciples to smarten up and treat people decently. If you do not, your guilt and your negative mental set will make you sick in God's place; you will not be worthy. Again, this may suggest a bad trip, which must have happened for a variety of reasons, at least occasionally. Thus setting and set were extremely important; this was not recreational drug use. This was serious business.

> 7. Our rabbis taught: "Each [Israelite] ate the bread of the mighty" [abbirim] (Ps. 78:25), the same kind of bread, so said R. Akiva, as [mighty] ministering angels eat.
> When these words were reported to R. Ishmael, he said: Go and say to Akiva: Akiva, you are mistaken. Do ministering angels really eat bread? Did not Moses [after being in heaven] say, "I ate no bread"? (Deut. 9:18)

How then should one interpret "bread of *abbirim*"? Read rather "bread of *evarim*," bread that was directly absorbed by the 248 parts (*evarim*) of the body.

The reference to bread/manna and "abbirim" (mighty) is surely "food of the gods." The last sentence, read rather "bread of *evarim*," bread that was directly absorbed by the 248 parts (*evarim*) of the body, might be a reference to anointing oils, another type of manna absorbed through the skin.

8. "And the taste of it was the taste of a cake (*leshad*) baked with oil" (Num. 11:8) R. Abbahu said [Read not *leshad*, "cake," but shad, "breast"]. Hence, just as an infant, whenever he touches the breast, finds many flavors in it, as it was with manna. Whenever Israel ate it, they found many flavors in it.

Mind-altering substances can have a multitude effects on the sense organs, but it also has to do with how the substance was prepared, for example, soaked in honey or perhaps a little olive oil. But there is more here. Some read *leshad* as *le-shed*, "of a demon"—even as the demon changes himself into many shapes, so manna changed into many flavors.

Juxtaposing "demon" (le-shed) and "cake" (leshad) is quite a stretch, but I think the message is that this "cake" is supernatural stuff and bad trips are caused by opening a door and letting in a demon.

9. "Thou preparest a table before me in the presence of mine enemies" (Ps. 23:5). Issi ben Judah said: "The manna that came down for Israel piled up to such a height that all kings of the east and the west could see it."

This is clearly saying that we have no fear of our enemies; god is on our side and He reaches to the heavens.

10. "And the sun waxed hot, it melted (Exod. 16:21). When the sun shone upon the manna, it began to melt and formed rivulets which flowed into the Great Sea. Harts, gazelles, roebuck, and all kinds of other animals would come and drink from the rivulets. The nations of the world would then hunt these animals, eat them, and, tasting in them the taste of the manna that came down for Israel, say, 'Blessed is the people who have it so.'" (Ps. 144.15)

There are two references in the above, one to an actual observation that certain psilocybe species of mushrooms do appear to melt in sunlight and disappear into the soil. One of the kosher laws involved allowing all the blood of the animal to go back into the ground to bring forth another animal. The reference is that the mushroom melts into the ground, becomes the grass upon which animals feed, animals that are then consumed by the Israelites, who, in turn, taste the "food of the gods" through the animal. God is responsible for all life, and manna is that which brings it forth.

Amanita muscaria does not exactly melt. Instead, flies lay their eggs in the underside of the moist cap, the cap rots, and it looks like slime melting into the ground. Slugs also love Amanita, leading to the same "melting" effect.

> 11. It is taught that R. Yose said: Just as a prophet can tell Israel what might be hidden in holes and clefts, so would the manna reveal to Israel what was hidden in holes and clefts. How so? When two men came before Moses with a lawsuit, one saying, "You stole my slave," the other saying, "You sold it to me," Moses would say to both of them: Judgment will be pronounced tomorrow. The next day, if the slave's measure of manna was found in the house of the claimant, it was clear that the respondent had stolen him; if it was found in the house of the respondent, it was clear that the claimant had sold to slave to him.

This is a curious parable in that the word manna may have been substituted for another in different renderings of this story. What I believe is being conveyed is that God knows who is "naughty and nice," and that God will reside in the home of the righteous.

> 12. "He subjected thee to the hardship of hunger when He gave the manna to eat" (Deut. 8:3). R. Hananiah and R. Jonathan asked Menahem the Baker: Can this verse possibly

intimate that the manna the Holy One gave to Israel was
food that left them hungry? How did Menahem answer
them? He set before questioners two cucumbers, one whole
and the other crushed, and asked, "How much is the whole
one worth?" "Two silver zuz." "But is not the crushed
cucumber just as large as the whole one?" asked Menamen,
and then, answering his own question, said, "Even as a man
derives enjoyment from the taste of food, so he derives
enjoyment from the appearance of food." (Footnote: 7.
Though the manna had all kinds of flavors, it always looked
the same, and so those who ate it did not have the pleasure
of seeing the different foods that they tasted in the manna.
Eccles. R. 5:10, P. 1.)

What is being said in Deuteronomy 8:3 is that manna is not food.
It is not designed to nourish the body, but, instead, connect the individual to the deity. The complete rendering of Deuteronomy 8:3 is:
"And he humbled thee, and suffered thee to hunger, and fed thee with
manna, which thou knewest not, neither did thy fathers know; that he
might make thee know that *man doth not live by bread only, but by
every word that proceedeth out of the mouth of the Lord doth man
live.*" [Emphasis added]

Manna is special food, non-caloric, that allows you to hear the word
of God. There is no doubt in my mind that the legendary patriarchs
and biblical heroes communed with God in a time-honored fashion,
that is, through mind-altering substances. I am also of the opinion that
the rabbis knew full well what manna was and indirectly commented
on its use.

As mentioned, shamans in the new urban setting morph into full-
time specialists or priests, and with time and resources they experimented and worked out new doses and ritual performances. At least
initially these rites were communal, where the goal was to connect the
individual to the energy that informs all. This energy was personified,
giving rise to Innana, Ea, Enki, El and his brother Baal, and so on. Then

there were the patron or household gods; one communed with the cult god of the household and the patron god of the town or village.

With respect to Judaism, beginning with the institution of monotheism sometime after 560 BCE, there is a restriction of esoteric rites to the priesthood of Aaron. The surrounding Canaanite tribes were involved in mother-goddess rituals, which included numerous mind-altering substances as well as ritual sex, both hetero- and homosexual. Although these mind-altering substances (especially cannabis, formerly burned in temple braziers by the bushel as well as being used for medicinal purposes) continued to be used by Israelite priests, the practice was demonized and the knowledge of ritual process restricted to the priesthood. The cannabis laws in the United States are based on this demonizing.

John the Baptist created a movement that was initially wrapped around human decency without a bunch of rules, priests, and the necessity of a church; this was short lived. His message fit everyone—no discrimination. In the short span of perhaps two years he attracted a large following because of his appeal to basic needs and the way he delivered his message. He turned "Thou shalt not" to "I will not," a personal choice that made sense, that is, "Do unto others as you would have done to you." This message and others were twisted and turned by Paul (the anti-Christ) and his continuers, reverting back to a form of conservative Judaism. The Baptist's message fractured soon after his murder and resulted in the Catholic tradition, which led hundreds of thousands of people headlong into the filth and hopelessness of the Dark Ages.

Mind-altering substances were used within ritual contexts to make tangible that other side, and Jesus was metaphoric of the portal or doorway. In hundreds of renditions of Jesus in Christian art, over a time period of almost fifteen-hundred years, Jesus is graphically connected to mushrooms, held in his hand or surrounding him. All the players in the New Testament are a reference to Jesus, and to find mushrooms connected to Mary as well as the Apostles and Saints is likewise a reference to Jesus. The mushrooms of the *Amanita muscaria* and *Psilocybin* species are adjectives describing his characteristics—He, Jesus (the mushroom), is the source, the path, the way to knowledge and life ever-lasting. Using associated images was common practice in Egyptian hieroglyphs, where Isis, for example, is depicted with a throne on her head. She is the throne upon which the pharaoh sits. Jesus, the mushroom, "sits" on the roots of the pine tree (Mary). Isis, remember, is the image that came into Christianity as Mother Mary or the Madonna figure.

Islam was created as a justification for conquest and, only after the fact, a justification for unification. The character of Muhammad was patterned after the mythic heroes David, Solomon, and Moses—complete with mind-altering substances. Moses was a non-person patterned after Akhenaten, the heretic pharaoh. If Abraham and Moses are non-persons in the Jewish tradition, they fare no better in Islam.

Muhammad also assumed the role of a shaman, communicating as he did with his patron deity, who would have been al Liah, the moon-god of war. Muhammad was possibly a general who died unexpect-edly in battle, which then led to numerous power struggles. The successes in battle prompted military councils, and of course clerics whose job it was to construct a mythical charter justifying conquest, that is, hadith and Qur'an, which appear somewhere around 750 CE. Muslims become the chosen people with the truth, and because there can only be one truth all other traditions are in their gun sights.

When Judaism, Christianity, and Islam have no political power, when they cannot sponsor or lend support to politicians or legislation in favor of their agenda, they live in peace—sort of. These traditions support untenable philosophies of a supernatural world, a world con-structed through the use of a plethora of mind-altering substances. These traditions have duped people into believing that they and only they preach and teach morality. They would like us to believe that they invented morality and are the true moral watchdogs of society. They claim that if these traditions did not exist, people would become immoral and some (see Mahmood 2005, 140–145) insist that it is the fear of God's punishment that leads to moral behavior. This is another of the "Big lies" associated with these traditions. Morality stems from social necessity; morality does not begin when you become a Jew, Christian, or Muslim. With respect to morality, these traditions preach some of the thickest, greasiest, and smelliest hypocrisy in the world.

People live in a fractured world with one foot standing on a rational platform of science and the other in the irrational arena of spooks and demons—the fracture between them widens every day. Alongside one foot are stories of supernatural beings who talk to humans and promise land holdings and special privileges. All you have to do is follow Yahweh's rules and place him in front of all others. Then there is the all-loving and caring savior, Jesus, who died for your sins because you can't take ownership of them yourself. He arose from the dead and went to heaven with the message, "I'll be back!" And then there is Islam, whose prophet is Muhammad, who went to the mountain and communicated with supernatural beings who gave him the rules that all humankind should live by. These supernatural beings, however, were demons not by accident but by choice. Abraham did not have to accept God's offer, Moses didn't have to commune with the sacred plant, and Muhammad didn't have to keep going to the mountain and commune with Gabriel or Samael. They all made pacts with a demon. Each tradition believes it has the truth, or the right god, the right method of worship, and the right answers to living. How can there be only one god standing in back of all these traditions? If scholars continue to maintain this belief, then this one god is surely psychotic.

Alongside the other foot is science, which looks at gods, demons, and spooks with a very skeptical eye, and which sees the events in the Bible and Qur'an as sacred history or myth representing charters of legitimacy for interpreting the will of God. People desire explanations for their experiences, and the simple truth is that the person with the most compelling story wins. Science has a much better story grounded in math, physics, and open dialogue; it is also self-correcting. We are almost at a point where people in many areas of the world, through reason or reticule, will have to emotionally select one side over the other simply because they are so contradictory. And as has been noted by many scholars, the more one leads toward science, the less personal God becomes. God become energy, something to understand, not fear.

This brings us to a point where using fear tactics is less effective for promoting faith and continued belief in a supernatural world as promoted by the three Western traditions. Piety out of fear is not the same as piety out of choice. As fear of God falls away, it is being replaced, slowly but surely, with self-responsibility, where the individual maintains morality through compassion for others, friends, and strangers alike. When morality and compassion are personal choices, they are enacted with a higher level of commitment.

There is nothing right or wrong about mind-altering substances. But when they are the basis of the experiences in the Bible and Qur'an, leading to the construction of Judaism, Christianity, and Islam and thus the basis of Western Civilization, they would be important to include in the scholarly texts recounting the history of the West. Out of political correctness, famous scholars have compromised the truth.

Psychiatry and Religion

A middle-aged man was walking along a major city street, and to each person he passed he said, "I have seen God. I have talked with God!" Thinking he was having a psychotic split, the police were called and he was transported to the nearest psychiatric ward. The admitting staff determined that there was no obvious brain damage, he was not combative, and seemingly in good health. The attending psychiatrist was called. Here is the conversation that followed.

Dr. Jones: Good evening, Mr. Smith.

Mr. Smith: Hello, Doc. Why was I arrested?

Dr. Jones: Let's see. It says in the accompanying police report that you were walking along hallucinating, saying you were seeing God.

Mr. Smith: I don't understand. What is wrong with seeing God?

Dr. Jones: There is nothing wrong with seeing God. But you were under the influence of . . .

Mr. Smith: DMT. It opens one to the experience.

Dr. Jones: In your understanding, Mr. Smith, your conversation, or rather your psychosis, was caused by a chemical.

Mr. Smith: Why do you refer to it as "psychosis" when bishops and Ayatollahs claim to have these experiences every day? These experiences were reported in the Bible and Qur'an. Were these people also psychotic? When faith healers lays on hands and act as conduits between God and the troubled individual, are they psychotic?

Dr. Jones: But, Mr. Smith, you can't wander the streets and annoy people with your revelations. You were disrupting pedestrian traffic.

Mr. Smith: Well, isn't this the case on Sunday, when people go to church and disrupt traffic? Or are you saying *that* situation is okay because the parishioners only hope to experience God but most never do? What you are saying that as long as people only hope to experience God but never do, that makes them normal? But when a person sees or communicates with God that is a form of psychosis?

Dr. Jones: Mr. Smith, you are getting defensive and are in denial. Your experience of God was an illusion, a hallucination caused by drugs . . .

Mr. Smith: Are you saying that drug-induced experiences with God don't count, that the experience has to be spontaneous? If I was having this experience without DMT, I would not have been arrested, is that correct?"

Dr. Jones: No, I'm not saying that.

Mr. Smith: Well, what are you saying? Let me guess. You are saying that all experiences of God are a form of psychosis, and therefore popes, priests, ministers, and imams who promote this are also psychotic, and those who go to temple, church, or mosque are stupid for listening to psychotics and believing such things?

Dr. Jones: No, I'm not saying that . . .

Mr. Smith: Well, Doc, you can't have it both ways. Either believing in God is an antiquated form of insanity or experiencing God is normal.

Dr. Jones: You are missing the point, Mr. Smith. Your experience was drug induced . . .

Mr. Smith: You're talking in circles. If I have the experience *without drugs* I'm psychotic and with drugs I have *induced* psychosis. But yet these traditions that *support* contact with God are normal and okay?

The psychiatrist went silent at that point and Mr. Smith understood he had made his point. It is "illegal" for the individual to have an ecstatic experience or to be in touch with the energy that informs all. Those who try to get there, by praying and going to church, are normal until they communicate with God. But isn't the person who prays to God, or any deity in order to obtain special favors, just as insane as the individual who breaks through and has that personal conversation? Of course the psychiatric community believes that going to church and wanting prayers answered is just part of our culture, while actually taking with God is unusual and thus abnormal.

The religious community, as a political entity, has made the experience of God illegal unless the experience comes through special people with special credentials. The average person can only worship the deity—never can he or she identify with, communicate, or become the deity without being shot in the head or ushered onto a psychiatric ward.

As we look back at these traditions, we can excuse these people for believing that gods rule our lives and communicate through special people; children will believe almost anything you tell them and maintain those "truths" all their lives. People believed in spirit possession and that the gods could manifest through trees, rocks, clouds, and plants. The reports in the Bible and Qur'an do not represent the usual; they represent the unusual. Good stories are always the different stories, and it is the good story that somehow survives the individual memory. Those people who most likely had the reported experience from which the stories evolved were those who could also afford the time and money to have these experiences. For example, getting drunk and managing the hangover is at least a two-day affair. Some of the substances used by shamans and priests could consume more time than that, especially if mind-altered trips were part of a larger ritual context performed on a regular basis. You have to have provisions to do this, especially in urban areas. The priest, then, is an ideal candidate. He has the time and community support to work through his psychosis spontaneously or drug induced.

A debate went on for years in the anthropological community as to whether shamans as a group were just a little different from all the rest (I think "crazy" was the scientific term). This led to wondering if psychiatrists as a group, assuming that shamans and psychiatrists had a great deal in common, were at least as "crazy." Most psychiatrists (Carl Jung and Milton Erickson would be two notable exceptions) have more in common with priests and little in common with shamans. In any event, many of the major players in the Bible exhibit very disturbed communication patterns using today's standards, and this would have been considered just as unusual in that time or place or these stories would not have been seen as significant enough to write down.

Thus, we are left with several possibilities or interpretations of what prompted these stories about supernatural beings and supernatural events. First, these stories are factual, historical renderings of real events. Second, gifted storytellers had great imaginations. Three, these people were psychotic. Four, these stories were purposely constructed by creative poets to build a mythical charter. And five, these stories were induced through the use of powerful mind-altering substances. Take your choice. In modern times we see a form of dependent neurosis that develops from the belief that God actually spoke to special people, where the believer has to be constantly reassured, week after week, that these magical things did happen. The cure to this neurosis is to tell people the truth; these are just stories and it is the message that counts, not the supernatural being(s) or the person who had the experience.

Religion and Politics

I was told at a young age that you should not argue politics or religion. At the time I did not understand why. I originally thought that religion and politics were two separate entities. After all, two different nouns were used as reference points, sort of like dog and cat. But then I realized that dogs and cats, although they come in genetically different packaging, were still mammals.

A political tradition is one designed to control people using rules, regulations, and threats of punishment if the individual does not comply.

Except in democratic systems, the individual has little part to play other than to follow the rules. To see, talk to, or identify with the deity is dangerous for all political systems (polytheistic as well as monotheistic) because such connections could possibly place the individual in a position of interpreting the deity's will, undercutting the ruler's authority and affecting public policy. The creators of the Islamic tradition fully realized this, and that is why Muhammad is considered the "seal of the prophets," for to do otherwise encourages more prophecy, new lamps for old, and change that could alter the power structure. Again, for the individual to have direct contact with an all-powerful deity represents a possible challenge to the power structure and for this reason anyone making claims of contact with God is considered a heretic, a psychiatric case, or a criminal. This is why our mythic hero Jesus a.k.a. John the Baptist had to go.

We also noted in Chapter Three that close political ties with these pseudo-religious traditions assures that the challenge is minimized. The United States is considered a Christian country and silently, in the background, Christian clerics influence political action. There is reference to God in our Pledge of Allegiance and on our money ("In God we trust"). Our courts still resort to swearing in on the Bible, government meetings are opened with prayer, and so on. In the larger sense, there is little difference between what scholars term political systems and the Western "religious" traditions. They have the same objective, that is, control over the populace and the power to direct emotion and energy. And just like political systems, these three Western traditions appeal to our animal nature and have little or nothing to do with religion as defined earlier, or spiritual endeavors in general.

Going deeper, we can construct similarities between politicians and religious clerics, for example priests and imams. Both politicians and priests claim to speak for their constituents or subjects, and both claim to act in the best interests of a power greater than them (Nature, State, God).

They both claim to have the truth but can change that truth when convenient. In Islam, for example, there is institutionalized lying; lying is also institutionalized in politics. Both systems are invested in holding onto their truths even in the face of tangible evidence to the contrary. All politicians as well as all religious clerics answer to someone in the hierarchy, and both will do what it takes to obtain and maintain power.

Both politicians and religious clerics sustain themselves on money taken from a general fund, and both have expense accounts. Politicians and religious clerics as a group often become very wealthy. Both accept money on false pretenses—the priest takes money so that he will have a job and the parishioner will get to heaven, and the politician takes money to get reelected with the promise of creating heaven here and now, especially for those who donate the most to the individual's election or re-election. Again, both are known to take bribes or contributions, money designed to obtain political favor or favor with God. Although Catholic priests take a vow of poverty, most certainly do not live an impoverished lifestyle. For both politicians and religious clerics, position or status becomes more important than the people they administer to.

Both politicians and religious clerics tell their "congregations" what they want to hear even through there is a low probability that they can deliver the goods; anything they tell you has to be taken on faith. Much of what they tell you is a distortion of the facts or issues.

Both proselytize in an attempt to gain supporters, both are engaged in maintaining power over their constituents, both attempt to influence secular rules or public policy, and both belong to organizations that are tax exempt.

Both attempt to cover up misuse of the systems they represent, both, viciously at times, attack opponents with different points of view, attempting to promote their own morality while tearing down the morality of others. Both claim to have the truth and the ability to predict the future.

So where is the religion? People simply going to church, temple, or mosque and praying? Is that religion? Or is it simply political activity using God as a third-person power source? Again, the Christian god is written all over the face of the United States, "One Nation under God," "In God we Trust." If Islam is a religion, then democracy, as practiced in the United States, must also be a religion.

And then we encounter apocalyptic politicians. Doomsday cults or cults supporting the idea that the world is coming to an end go back at least to the Essenes. Statements of gloom and doom are the product of people who have been disenfranchised or under the thumb of those in power. On one level, these beliefs foster urgency and preparation for the end of the world. On another level, however, such statements are also designed to create an atmosphere of fear, for the disenfranchised have no power beyond symbols or stories often dramatically sold to others. John the Baptist probably stood on street corners preaching the impending destruction of the world. Charlie Manson's Family, the Branch Davidians, the People's Temple, Heaven's Gate, and many others, in their own way, have done the same thing. Few would accept that David Koresh (Branch Davidians) or any of these recent cult figureheads were in touch with God. Today we would consider these people just plain nuts, on drugs, or both.

When politicians and political parties are on top the message from the pulpit is usually one of hope and good deeds, but when the political party is on the bottom, gloom and doom is the mantra. During the Bush administration, many of the most vocal senators and representatives in the Democrat party preached a sermon of gloom and doom, especially Al Gore's position on global warming, which symbolically represents the condition of the Democrat party. Yes, the world may be warming up, just as it has done many times in the past, but the message presented by Gore and others in the party is that this has been created by "sinful humans," a metaphor for George Bush.

So what is the real difference between politics and religion? It depends on how you define religion. Returning to the original definition for the term, that is, identity, communication with, or becoming the deity or deities, one would have great difficulty seeing the Western traditions of Judaism, Christianity, and Islam as religions. To identify, communicate with, or become the deity is against the law.

We are at a crossroads of choice, of selecting a path to further enlightenment through science and a need to understand the energy that informs all, or maintaining ignorance and darkness, and following the superstitious road of a day long past.

Does God Have a Sense of Humor?

Clowns and jesters are necessary parts of the king's court. They can tell the truth, slander your enemies, and otherwise present a point of view not experienced by others. They are similar to tricksters found in many cultures, for example, Juha and certain jinn-type entities in Arab folk humor who cause trouble and at other times teach lessons. In their own way, all these categories draw attention to some matter that can be a threat to cosmic and social order.

Humor and jokes can also inform and serve as symbolic outlets for anger, frustration, and social "dis-ease" in general. People have reportedly laughed themselves well. There is a psychological rule that says we block or defend against contrary ideas, beliefs, and values, and just like the parables of Jesus, jesters, and clowns, humor and jokes have easier access to the subconscious mind; this can be very threatening to fundamentalist Jews, Christians, and especially Muslims.

An interesting point about the Old Testament is that there are many missing parts to the storylines and a singular lack of humor. The lack of humor is of interest, especially for a tradition that excels at poking fun at itself, politics, and so on. The story of Job, for example, originally had wonderful, humorous punch lines added as the rabbi told the story.

Islam as a tradition is without a sense of humor and this is understandable—there is nothing funny about fascism. Humor forces into existence oppositions and a mirror of one's self. Now, I emphasize an important distinction. Islam is what you are ordered (laws) to do, but a Muslim is a human being with faults, aspirations, fears, concerns, compassion, and a sense of humor. This humor may not be obvious to an outsider or non-Arabic speaking observer (see Helmke 2007), but some of the stories spin equally as well in Israel and Toronto, Canada. Why? This is because they speak to our humanity, not Judaism,

Christianity, or Islam. To make clear the threat humor poses to Islam, the following was taken from www.islamisforyou.com/ islamicjokes:

> Some people joke too much and it becomes a habit for them. This is the opposite of the serious nature, which is the characteristic of the believers. Joking is a break, a rest from ongoing seriousness and striving; it is a little relaxation for the soul. 'Umar ibn 'Abd al-'Azeez (may Allaah have mercy on him) said: "Fear joking, for it is folly and generates grudges."
>
> Imaam al-Nawawi (may Allah have mercy on him) said: "The kind of joking which is forbidden is that which is excessive and persistent, for it leads to too much laughter and hardening of the heart, it distracts from remembrance of Allah, and it often leads to hurt feelings, generates hatred, and causes people to lose respect and dignity. But whoever is safe from such dangers, then that which the Messenger of Allah (peace and blessings of Allah be upon him) used to do is permissible for him."
>
> Sa'd ibn Abi Waqqaas said: "Set a limit to your jokes, for going to extremes makes you lose respect and incites the foolish against you."
>
> The amount of joking should be like the amount of salt in one's food.
>
> The Prophet (peace and blessings of Allah be upon him) said: "Do not laugh too much, for laughing too much deadens the heart." (Saheeh al-Jaami', 7312)
>
> 'Umar ibn al-Khattaab (may Allah be pleased with him) said: "Whoever laughs too much or jokes too much loses respect, and whoever persists in doing something will be known for it."
>
> So beware of joking, for it "causes a person to lose face after he was thought of as respectable, and it brings him humiliation after esteem."

A man said to Sufyaan ibn 'Uyaynah (may Allah be pleased with him), "Joking is not right, it is to be denounced." He replied, "Rather it is Sunnah, but only for those who know how to do it and do it at the appropriate time."

Nowadays, although the ummah needs to increase the love between its individual members and to relieve itself of boredom, it has gone too far with regard to relaxation, laughter, and jokes. This has become a habit which fills their gatherings and wastes their time, so their lives are wasted and their newspapers are filled with jokes and trivia.

The Prophet (peace and blessings of Allah be upon him) said: "If you knew what I know, you would laugh little and weep much." In Fath al-Baari it says: "What is meant by knowledge here has to do with the might of Allah and His vengeance upon those who disobey Him, and the terrors that occur at death, in the grave and on the Day of Resurrection."

The attitude in Islamic tradition is quite clear; there is nothing funny in life or death. This, however, is a very curious situation, in that the Arab people have a wonderful literary tradition containing a great deal of humor. This goes much deeper and shows the perhaps universal difference between male and female storytelling, as well as the different presentations of stories. Commenting on collected tales from Palestine and Lebanon, Nuweihed (2007, vi) states:

It was fascinating for me, reading these stories now, to recall how different my aunt's treatment of them from my mother's. My aunt stressed the *moral significance of a story,* its *ethical message,* its more *serious aspects.* My mother's treatment was *romantic, fun-loving, humorous, and light.* But both were always humane, emphasizing the importance of *self-reliance and personal achievement.* Yet, as the reader will see, they are tales that celebrate *cleverness* too, the capacity of the protagonists, *especially the women, to save themselves and their own in the face of life's dilemmas and puzzling surprises.* These stories are certainly many centuries old, yet they almost *always portray women as doers, achievers and movers, capable of independent decisions.* I think this had a great influence on several of the female cousins nourished on the stories. The *patience and persistence with which the characters, especially the women,* dealt with life's problems also left a strong impression on me. [Emphasis added]

I have emphasized those aspects that are contrary to Islam, and this may be one of the reasons that Western culture is almost totally ignorant of Arab literature. This ignorance does not issue from lack of interest but more likely a need by the Islamic clerics to restrict these stories from the West. When people can laugh at their follies, it is only a matter of time until political folly will be held up to the mirror as well.

But there is a larger issue. Arab folklore communicated orally alters to fit the situation, as noted above by Nuweihed (2007), just as the stories connected to the Qur'an (and Bible) would alter to fit a particular situation. Thus the idea that the stories in the Qur'an have always been the way they are presented is unlikely.

The emphasis on the women in these stories, their patience and cleverness, is exactly what one finds in the Jewish tradition (see Chapter Two). There is an undercurrent of self-responsibility and independent thought, not strongly emphasized in the Qur'an and Islam. And, as prophesied in Chapter Four, it will be the female energy that will eventually rise to the surface and alter Islam, displacing the exclusive male agenda.

Without the ability to laugh at ourselves and comment about our behaviors and beliefs in tales and stories, we become robotic and one's direction in life goes unquestioned. At the institutionalized level, that is, Islam, there is hopelessness, despair, and fear. But at the popular level, out of earshot of religious clerics, there is a wonderful sense of humor and practicality in the Muslim world that will, at some point, rise to the surface. An example of that humor is as follows:

> There was an old storekeeper in Medina who had recently lost his right-hand man, Abdula, who helped him stock shelves, wait on customers, and close at night. He was run down by a camel the night before, while gazing at the moon and not noticing that the animal had backed into a curtain rod used to separate the kiosks. He came to his heavenly reward, may Allah be merciful, before his time. No matter. Akram now had to find a replacement, someone who would be there when needed, his right-hand man.
>
> There was interview after interview and with each disappointment his wife Anmar would ask, "What was wrong with him? Why don't you try someone out?" They would discuss all prospects, but the one thing they wanted most of all was someone who was honest, certainly not a thief.
>
> Finally Akram interviewed Bassam, and being desperate hired him on the spot. When Akram presented Bassam to his wife she asked, "Why did you hire him? His left had has been cut off—he's a thief!"
>
> "Yes, a thief" Akram agreed, "but not a good one."

Sigmund Freud (1963) commented years ago that jokes and stress were interrelated, and that jokes were important for stress release. An example of this would be jokes leveled at President Bush during his eight years in office. Such symbolism is stress reducing and allows citizens and other politicians to comment or work things out symbolically (frustration, anger, disappointment) without resorting to assassination.

Fundamentalist Christians cannot tolerate humor—they are very gloomy people, and remarks suggesting that Jesus is not responsible for all the good in the world come under harsh attack. A recent example was Kathy Griffin's statement about Jesus. From Reuters News Service:

Tue Sep 11, 2007 7:31pm EDT

LOS ANGELES (Reuters) - Comic Kathy Griffin's "offen-
sive" remarks about Jesus at the Creative Arts Emmy
Awards will be cut from a pre-taped telecast of the show, the
Academy of Television Arts and Sciences said on Tuesday.
Griffin made the provocative comment on Saturday night as
she took the stage of the Shrine Auditorium to collect her
Emmy for best reality program for her Bravo channel show
   "My Life on the D-List."
   "A lot of people come up here and thank Jesus for this
award. I want you to know that no one had less to do with
this award than Jesus," an exultant Griffin said, holding up
her statuette. "Suck it, Jesus. This award is my god now."

The idea of attributing all one's successes to Jesus or God is a leftover from kings and tyrants attributing successes and failure to gods.
Assigning all one's successes and failure to a third party is a very powerful defense mechanism, but it leaves one powerless and naked in the
world.

Humor opens a system and fractures a prevailing mood, it juxta-
poses unanticipated connections and exposes new possibilities, and this
is contrary to fundamentalists. Fundamentalists live in a dark world
without change and only limited possibilities. If God did not intend
laughter it would not have to be suppressed, but we live in a world of
paired opposites in which laughter unites us with our follies, it flips the
coin, and offers us a mirror to our real selves.

Imagery connected to religious art is extremely important, and a
tradition's art forms are many times all an anthropologist has to work
with when suggesting meaning and use. For example, we can only guess
at the specific meanings of the cave paintings in France and Spain, but
they do inform on a general level. A more modern rendering of cave
art is found in the cathedrals scattered about the globe, with stories in
mosaics, stained glass, and statuary; read them carefully, especially
those in St. Mark's Basilica, Venice. As with the cave paintings, there is

no intimation of humor or play; God is serious. Sacred places are not circuses with live comedians (except in some very liberal Christian churches). As expressed earlier, there is nothing funny about Islam, and thus this tradition has a lot of catching up to do. Keep in mind, however, the distinction between Arabic/Muslim as opposed to Islamic lack of humor. Any humor about Islam that enters the mainstream information channels is quickly denounced. As an example, a sex shop in jolly old England (February 2006) featured a sex toy, "Mustafa Shag," sporting a seven-inch penis. This was "very upsetting" to the Islamic authorities. As reported in the February 9, 2006 edition of *The Sun*, a spokesperson stated:

> You have no idea how much hurt, anguish and disgust this
> obnoxious phrase has caused to Muslims. We are asking you
> to have our Most Revered Prophet's name "Mustafa" and
> the afflicted word "shag" removed.

The reader will recognize immediately the emotional irresponsibility in the above statement. The Islamic community might have felt offended, but that is their own personal experience. The toy in itself is neutral, for the meaning, thus emotion, is in the eye of the beholder. Muhammad, at least in one of the legendary stories, became so sexually aroused during a battle that he returned home to have sex with one of his wives. Of course, this is a story of Muhammad's virility on the battlefield and in the bedroom, while the sex doll, even with a seven-inch penis, is considered disgusting. For me, the story of Muhammad becoming sexually excited during battle presents him as a psychotic pervert. The sex doll is simply a joke; I am sure there are sex dolls of many important people. I notice you can obtain a George W. Bush puppet with twenty-five sound clips in his voice. There is a magnetic paper doll ensemble where you can take off George's clothes and replace them with high heels, garter belt, and girl's panties—pretty tasteless stuff, but I don't recall Bush ever demanding a recall of the product, proposing a law suit, or reporting his annoyance to the press.

The *Jyllands-Postem's* September 30, 2005, publication of Cartoons of Muhammad ("The Face of Muhammad") represented political satire similar to that aired about Hitler during his reign of terror. After these cartoons ran, there was worldwide, orchestrated protest, with attacks on the Norwegian and Danish Embassies in Syria and elsewhere, and burning of lots of Norwegian and Danish flags. Are these flags so popular that shop owners had stockpiles of flags ready to be handed out and burned? The reactions to speaking out against Islam and fundamentalism in general, especially with humor and wit, are telling of a system that is so insecure that it dare not hold a mirror up to itself lest it shatter. Islamic activists in the United States are currently attempting to make it illegal to say anything negative about Islam, which is an infringement of free speech. Systems not open to criticism attempt to stifle critical thinking, questioning, and especially humor; this is politics.

Over the years I have collected numerous religious action figures, some used to reenact hero myths of the Bible, for example, Moses with staff and tablet and David slaying Goliath. I have a plastic "Buddy" Jesus for my car's dash, mechanical renditions of a Catholic nun (one that shoots sparks from her mouth), and "Jesus wrapping tape" to keep packages safe. I have a "Jesus Saves" coin purse and Jesus Adhesive Bandages for cuts and scrapes. I have some "Wash Away Your Sins" breath spray for "Liars, Cheaters, and Wrong-Doers," "Wash Away Your Sins Towelettes" with "Anti-Bacterial Formula" that "Kills Sins on Contact," Jesus Air Freshener, Jesus Saves Candy Mints ("Blessed Be Thy Breath"), Last Supper After Dinner Mints, and Messiah Mints. Then I have Jeez-Its Sticky Notes, Commandments Sticky Notes, and a statue of the Pope John Paul II as a duck. I can find nothing in the Bible or Qur'an that forbids images unless they are worshipped. One then must wonder why are there no Muhammad, Abu Bakr, and Ali dolls, Uthman burning books, or action heroes representing the Islamic glory days of conquest. The answer to this is simple and in three parts.

First, all the images of prophets had been taken and Muhammad would simply be a replay. By disallowing images, they separate themselves from Judaism and Christianity. Second, the original poets knew that Muhammad was a construction and having images was just too disingenuous. Realistically, one cannot have an image of a non-existent person. Third, because Islam is claimed to be a non-changing tradition, images of Muhammad, or any of the other players, are likely to change simply because new artists have different abilities, likes, and dislikes, and alteration in the art could imply changes in Islam. For example, there were no images of Buddha until around 50 BCE, signaling a different type of Buddhism, one in which anyone could join.

Looking Back . . .

Cultures are composed of symbols which, although relatively stable over time, nonetheless change or evolve. Genes, on the other side, are very conservative because of complexity, an intricacy thought so great by some groups (Intelligent Designers) that only a god could have created them. They may be correct, but this is of little use in terms of understanding that "god" and our survival. In short, if we expect our genes to survive in some recognizable form a few million years from now, we have to alter our metaphor, or storyline, of who we are and our purpose in the universe. It is not so much what the storyline contains, as long it leads to a respectful, self-responsible, decent individual. This is not the mantra in Judaism, Christianity, or Islam. The mantra, instead, is directed to Yahweh, God or Jesus, or Allah—"Glory, Glory, Glory." God comes first.

"All is illusion, all is impermanent," the Buddha informs; all things change. Social systems that do not adapt fall by the wayside and then are absorbed into the fabric of history. We are in a paradigm shift, a shift away from an irrational observation of cause and effect, and movement toward a more rational, scientific point of view. This cannot be stopped. Even destroying the world economy, blowing up buildings, and murdering innocent men, women, and children can only delay the inevitable. In fact, the more destructive Islamic terrorists become, the more rapid Islam will fade into the sunset, and unless fundamentalist Christians can keep the science of evolution out of high school or isolate themselves from the real world, they will fade into the sunset as well. The Jews live in Israel.

The War in Heaven

Periodically, perhaps every 500 to 1,000 years, there is housecleaning in heaven. Gods, as everyone knows from reading the myths from Mesopotamia, Egypt, Greece, the Mayans, the Aztecs, and so on, are displaced; there are wars in heaven where one god unseats or attempts to unseat another. We have Zeus against the Titans; with help from a Titan, Prometheus, a god-prophet, who knew what the future held. Seth, in the Egyptian tradition, murders his brother Osiris, who, in his death brought fourth everlasting life in the form of Horus, the Holy Spirit. Yahweh competes with and replaces Baal, a wrathful god of fecundity represented as a human or bull. God displaces Yahweh, at least for many, and then the Christian god (Jesus) comes into confrontation with al Liah (Allah). In each case we see a separate god looking after his people. In each case the god is political, and concerned with and appeals to our animal nature. But for as long as these gods have been at war, another tradition—a tradition of inquiry and a need to understand that which we experience—has brought forth a new interpretation of who, what, and where we are. The new god—call it Energy, Force, or Nature—has a new congregation of disciples called scientists, who seek to understand this impersonal force. The methodology is different, as outlined in Chapter One, but the goal in many, many cases is very spiritual. That is to say, much of what the scientist studies, whether it is the cosmos or insects, does not involve clinging to life, sex, or food to maintain life, or status and money. Yes, status and money might be a by-product of scientific inquiry, but it is the knowledge or understanding of the workings of the universe that underlines the pursuit.

We also encounter the ancient gods and goddesses in "new age religions," for example, Wicca. I exclude this from the "spiritual psychologies" (Scientology, EST, etc.), which are an instant replay of oppressive monotheism, including lots of rules and regulations crammed down your throat over the course of several weekends. These new age traditions (e.g., Wicca), however, usually offer a personal experience with this energy, where there is an identity and communication with and/or becoming the deity. This has little to do with politics except, in some cases, a rebellion against the male agenda.

Using the beliefs in Yahweh, God, or al Liah (Allah) as a reference point for social action has only a limited life expectancy, unless they evolve away from an emphasis on God and scriptures as historical truth and move toward an emphasis on the individual and self-responsibility. Why is this so? This is because we are in the midst of a true world economy with the sale and import of goods far and wide. Market economies emphasize individual consumption of goods and services, within which the individual is presented a choice. Choice includes everything from the shoes you wear to the type of art on your walls, and this extends to personal choices regarding the supernatural. But there is another issue lurking in the background. Terrorism is supported by money and much of that money comes from oil, the current source of energy running capitalism and world economics. This dependency on oil will gradually lose its importance and be replaced by unlimited energy from the sun. By 2025, houses will be energy self-sufficient, with the introduction of inexpensive solar cells at a fraction of the current cost. This same technology promises to replace the need for gasoline-powered cars. Solar "cells" will be used in place of paint on cars and trucks powered by electric motors. Cars and trucks will be made lighter through the use of carbon fiber and titanium instead of steel. Electric devices (TVs, computers, radios, electric lights, etc.) are becoming more and more efficient. Mining Helium[3] on the moon for fusion reactors on earth, which might start as early as 2017, holds promise of unlimited, inexpensive energy. I predict that within one hundred years those countries supporting themselves through the sale of oil could be reduced to poverty unless they develop other trade items. The handwriting is on the wall and the political system called Islam will have great difficulty sustaining itself without money and violence. Bin Laden and al Qa'ida are a "first thrust" of this revitalization and there will be more violence to come.

Humor Has the Last Say

As mentioned earlier, humor has a therapeutic and cleansing effect; it exposes our follies, dissects our faults and shortcomings, and is more likely to remain in a culture's memory. I will end this work with political satire and cite several stories that say a great deal about the nature of Judaism, Christianity, and Islam.

JUDAISM

Judaism as a tradition has survived for two and one-half millennia in part due to its ability to hold a mirror up to itself and see human frailty—and joke about it. The ability to work out frustration, rejection, and discrimination through humor is a key to our humanity. When a chimpanzee gets angry he or she often acts out violently. For humans, when we are laughing and talking, we are not hitting and killing. Political satire, acted out, verbally expressed, or in cartoon form, is, in many cases, all that a person or group has for expression.

In 1939, a Viennese Jew enters a travel agent's office and says, "I want to buy a steamship ticket."

"Where to?" the clerk asks.

"Let me look at your globe, please."

The Jew starts examining the globe. Every time he suggests a country, the clerk raises an objection. "This one requires a visa. . . . This one is not admitting any more Jews. . . . The waiting list to get into that one is ten years."

Finally the Jew looks up.

"Pardon me, do you have another globe?" (Telushkin 2002, 108)

Christians use the issue of who killed Jesus to discriminate against Jews. If such a crucifixion took place the Romans would have conducted it, and the use of Judas in the caper is a symbol lending credibility to "the Jews killed Jesus story." Christianity began (after Paul entered the picture) as a cult, a sect that broke away from Judaism. You have to have some good reason, that is, some event that sparks the split, and what better way to do this than an accusation that the Jews, with the help of a Jew (Judas), killed their god. This says two things: Jesus and/or God of the Christian tradition is not the god of the Jews, because if he were, the Jews would not have killed their own god. And second, the death of Jesus represents an irreparable act that allows Christians to use the platform of Judaism to get on their own path. That death had to happen, and the Jews had to be blamed to create antagonisms and the irreparable split.

A Christian woman and a Jewish woman get into a fight in a post office line. The argument escalates and the Christian woman yells at the Jew, "Christ-killer!"

"You're right," the Jewish woman says. "And if we could kill your God, imagine what I can do to you." (Telushkin 2002, 110)

CHRISTIANITY

There are as many jokes about Christians, Jesus, St. Peter, and God in Christianity as there are in Judaism. The nature of the humor is often very different, as usually the jokes are an attack on Christianity and not a defense of ethnicity. Here are several examples:

What should a good sermon be about? Answer: It should be about God and about ten minutes.

What was the first thing Noah said when he stepped off the ark? I should have killed those mosquitoes when I had the chance.

Three friends died and went to heaven at the same instance. Saint Peter meets them at the gates and says to the first, "Welcome to heaven! Here is your reward." After that, Saint Peter immediately handcuffs him to an extremely unattractive woman.

"Saint Peter! Why is this my heavenly reward?" the man asked.

Saint Peter replied, "When you were five years old, you killed a bird with a stone." Saint

Peter then turned to the next guy and did the exact same thing for the exact same reason. Finally he turned to the third guy and said, "Welcome to heaven! Here is your reward," and he was immediately handcuffed to a beautiful girl. Shocked but not complaining, the man walked away. The other two, who stayed around to see what their friend's fate would be, aggressively asked, "How come he gets a beautiful girl and we're stuck with these? We can name a few things that he did that were worse than ours!"

Saint Peter said, "When she was five, she killed a bird with a stone."

A preacher went to a convention were he was scheduled to talk for fifteen minutes, the time allotted for the other ministers as well. When he started off, those preachers from his district cheered him on, throwing in an occasional, "Amen." The preacher, however, talked on and on, encouraged as he was and thinking that he had something important to say. Twenty minutes passed, thirty minutes, forty minutes, sixty-five minutes, and finally a brother sitting on the front row threw a songbook at the preacher. But being of quick eye, he noticed the book sailing toward him, ducked just in the nick of time, but kept right on talking. A preacher seated to his rear was not quite so lucky and took the book right in the head. As the man was going down, you could hear him say, "Hit me again, I can still hear him preaching!"

ISLAM

Jews and Christians, at least in the non-fundamentalist condition, can laugh at themselves and their beliefs and practices. No one calls foul, no one goes to the authorities, and no one goes to the United Nations complaining of religious insensitivity. The Jews certainly have their Anti-Defamation League, but this organization is not about stopping humor but discrimination and stereotyping for economic and political purposes. Jokes about God, rabbis, money, sex, and so on are very much part of this tradition. The Islamic tradition, as noted above, has a singular lack of humor and has little toleration for satire. So as not to disappoint, I recently heard a variation on the *Jyllands-Postem* Muhammad cartoon.

Recent homicide bombers, smoldering and smelling of C4 and splattered flesh, are standing in a row waiting to be greeted into heaven, a reward for their martyrdom to Allah. Finally a celestial imam walks across a puffy white cloud and in a downcast voice says, "I'm sorry to inform you that we have run out of wine and beer, although there is a little schnapps left from when Adolph came through. And, yes, the rumor is correct; we've run out of virgins. I know the promises; we are usually well supplied, but the traffic through here lately . . ."

Abdula, in the back of the row, raises his hand and steps forward, bowing slightly, and says in a whimsical voice, "I brought my own, and as far as the virgins, I've kinda had my eye on young Al-Bara here, and Alim." Alim then whispers to Al-Bara, "Abdula must be from Iran."

As the story goes, Muhammad became so sexually excited during one of his battles and multiple sword fights that he left his men and raced home for a quick go with one of his wives. After a short time, one of his men came banging at the door, "Muhammad, Muhammad! You are needed back at the battle! Come quickly! Things are going badly!"

Muhammad, on his back and with his wife on top still wearing her veil, shouts, "Give me another minute or so, Babu. I'm still not sure if it is Gretchen or Ingrid!"

Acharya, S. *The Christ Conspiracy: The Greatest Story Ever Sold.* Kempton, IL: Adventures Unlimited Press, 1999.

Albrektson, B. *History of the Gods: An Essay on the Idea of Historical Events as Divine Manifestations in the Ancient Near East and in Israel.* Lund, Sweden: CWK Gleerup, 1967.

Aldred, C. *Akhenaten: King of Egypt.* London: Thames & Hudson, 1988.

Ali, Ahmed. *Al-Qur'an: A Contemporary Translation.* Princeton, NJ: Princeton University Press, 2001.

Ali, Abdullah. *The Qur'an: Translation.* New York: Tahrike Tarsile Gur'an, 2004.

American Psychiatric Association. *DSM-IV: The Diagnostic and Statistical Manual of Mental Disorders.* Washington, DC: American Psychiatric Association, 1994.

Armstrong, K. *Muhammad: A Biography of the Prophet.* San Francisco: Harper, 1993.

Asad, T. *Genealogies of Religion: Discipline and Reasons of Power in Christianity and Islam.* Baltimore: The Johns Hopkins University Press, 1993.

Baigent, M., R. Leigh, and H. Lincoln. *The Holy Blood and the Holy Grail.* London: Jonathan Cape, 1982.

Bashear, S. *Arabs and Others in Early Islam, Vol. 8, Studies in Late Antiquity and Early Islam.* Princeton: Princeton University Press, 1998.

Basheara, S. "Riding Beasts on Divine Missions: An Examination of the Ass and Camel Traditions." *Journal of Scientific Studies* 37, No. 1 (1991): 37–75.

Bennett, C., and N. McQueen. *Sex, Drugs, Violence and the Bible.* British Columbia, Canada: Forbidden Fruit Publishing Company, 2001.

Bialik, H., and Y. Ravnitzky, Y., eds. *The Book of Legends Sefer Ha-Aggadah): Legends from the Talmud and Midrash.* New York: Schocken Books, 2001.

Bickerton, D. *Language and Species.* Chicago: University of Chicago Press, 1990.

Bhishagratna, K. K. *Susruta Samhita, Vols. I-III.* Varanasi, India: Oriental Publishers & Distributors, 2002.

Borg, M., ed. *Jesus and Buddha: The Parallel Sayings.* Berkeley, CA: Ulysses Press, 2004.

Brophy, T. *The Origin Map: Discovery of a Prehistoric, Megalithic, Astrophysical Map and Sculpture of the Universe.* New York: Writers Club Press, 2002.

Brown, D. *The Da Vinci Code.* New York: Doubleday, 2003.

Cameron, R., ed. *The Other Gospels: Non-Canonical Gospel Texts.* Philadelphia, PA: The Westminster Press, 1982.

Campbell, J. *The Masks of God: Occidental Mythology.* New York: Penguin, 1991.

Campbell, J. *The Hero with a Thousand Faces.* Princeton, NJ: Princeton University Press, 1949.

Collins, A., and C. Ogilvie-Herald. *Tutankhamun: The Exodus Conspiracy.* London: Virgin Books, 2002.

Devereux, P. *The Long Trip: A Prehistory of Psychedelia.* New York: Penguin/Arkana, 1997.

Doniger, W., ed. *Merriam-Webster's Encyclopedia of World Religions.* Springfield, MA: Merriam-Webster, Inc., 1999.

Drosnin, M. *The Bible Code.* New York: Touchstone, 1998.

Dudley, M., and G. Rowell, eds. *The Oil of Gladness: Anointing in the Christian Tradition.* London: Liturgical Press, 2003.

Duffy, E. *Saints and Sinners: A History of the Popes.* New Haven, CT: Yale University Press, 2001.

Elaide, M. *Shamanism: Archaic Techniques of Ecstasy.* Princeton, NJ: Princeton University Press, 1972.

Eller, C. *The Myth of Matriarchal Prehistory.* Boston: Beacon Press, 2000.

Ernst, C. *Sufism: An Essential Introduction to the Philosophy and Practice of the Mystical Tradition of Islam.* Boston: Shambhala, 1997.

Esack, F. *The Qur'an: A User's Guide.* Oxford, England: One World, 2005.

Evans, C. *Ancient Texts for New Testament Studies.* Peabody, MA: Hendrickson Publishers, 2005.

Faulkner, R. *The Egyptian Book of the Dead: The Book of Going Forth by Day*. San Francisco: Chronicle Books, 1998.

Festinger, L. *When Prophecy Fails: A Social and Psychological Study of a Modern Group That Predicted the Destruction of the World*. New York: Harper-Torchbooks, 1956.

Field, M. *Search for Security*. Evanston IL: Northwestern University Press, 1960.

Firestone, R. *Jihad: The Origins of Holy War in Islam*. New York: Oxford University Press, 1999.

Freeman, C. *The Closing of the Western Mind: The Rise of Faith and the Fall of Reason*. New York: Vintage Books, 2002.

Freud, S. *Jokes and Their Relation to the Unconscious*. New York: W. W. Norton, 1963.

Gabriel, M. *Jesus and Muhammad: Profound Differences and Surprising Similarities*. Lake Mary, FL: Charisma House, 2004.

Gadalla, M. *Historical Deception: The Untold Story of Ancient Egypt*. Greensboro, NC: Tehuti Research Foundation, 1999.

Galanter, M. *Cults: Faith, Healing, and Coercion*. New York: Oxford University, 1999.

Gellette, P. *The Complete Marquis de Sade, Vols. I and II*. Los Angeles: Holloway House Publishing Co., 1967.

Goodison, L., and C. Morris. *Ancient Goddess*. Madison, WI: The University of Wisconsin Press, 1998.

Graves, K. *The World's Sixteen Crucified Saviors: Or Christianity Before Christ*. New York: University Books, 1971.

Greenberg, G. *101 Myths of the Bible: How Ancient Scribes Invented Biblical History*. Naperville, IL: Sourcebooks, Inc., 2002.

Hamburger, J. *St. John the Divine: The Deified Evangelist in Medieval Art and Theology*. Berkeley: University of California Press, 2002.

Hamer, D. *The God Gene: How Faith is Hardwired into Our Genes*. New York: Doubleday, 2004.

Harris, M. *Cows, Cannibals, and Kings: Origins of Culture*. New York: Vintage Press, 1989.

Heinrich, C. *Magic Mushrooms in Religion and Alchemy*. Rochester, VT: Park Street Press, 2002.

Helmke, M. *Humor and Moroccan Culture*. Fez, Morocco: Derby & Whettam, 2007.

Hughes, T. *Dictionary of Islam.* Chicago, IL: KAZI Publications, 1994.

Ingermanson, R. *Who Wrote the Bible Code?* Colorado Springs, CO: WaterBrook, 1999.

Irvin, J. 2008. *The Holy Mushroom.* Riverside, CA: Gnostic Media, 2008.

Irvin, J., and A. Rutajit. *Astrotheology and Shamanism: Unveiling the Law of Duality in Christianity and Other Religions.* San Diego, CA: Book Tree, 2006.

Jaynes, J. *The Origins of Consciousness in the Breakdown of the Bicameral Mind.* New York: Houghton Mifflin, 1990.

Johns, T. "The Chemical Ecology of Human Ingestive Behaviors." *Annual Review of Anthropology,* Vol. 28. Palo Alto, CA: Annual Reviews, 1999.

Josephus, F. *The New Complete Works of Josephus.* Translated by W. Whiston. Grand Rapids, MI: Kregel, Inc., 1999.

Juergensmeyer, M. *Terror in the Mind of God: The Global Rise of Religious Violence.* Berkeley: University of California Press, 2003.

Kimball, C. *When Religion Becomes Evil.* New York: HarperCollins, 2002.

Klein, R., and B. Edgar. *The Dawn of Human Culture.* New York: John Wiley & Sons, 2002.

Leach, E. *Genesis as Myth and Other Essays.* London: Jonathan Cape, 1969.

Lester, T., "What is the Koran?" In *What the Koran Really Says,* ed. I. Warraq. New York: Prometheus Books, 2002.

Mack, B. *Who Wrote the New Testament? The Making of the Christian Myth.* San Francisco: Harper/Collins, 1995.

Mahmood, Saba. *Politics of Piety: The Islamic Revival and the Feminist Subject.* Princeton, NJ: Princeton University Press, 2005.

Manniche, L. *An Ancient Egyptian Herbal.* Austin, TX: University of Texas Press, 1989.

Marett, R. *The Threshold of Religion.* London: Methuen, 1909.

McKenna, T. *Food of the Gods.* New York: Bantam Books, 1992.

McKinsey, C. *The Encyclopedia of Biblical Errancy.* Amherst, NY: Prometheus Books, 1995.

McQueen, C. and N. McQueen. *Sex, Drugs, Violence and the Bible.* Gibsons, BC: Forbidden Fruit Publishing Company, 2001.

Merkur, D. *The Mystery of Manna: The Psychedelic Sacrament of the Bible.* Rochester, VT: Park Street Press, 2000.

Merker, D. *The Psychedelic Sacrament: Manna, Meditation, and Mystical Experience.* Rochester, VT: Park Street Press, 2001.

Miller, P. *Dreams in Late Antiquity: Studies in the Imagination of a Culture.* Princeton, NJ: Princeton University Press, 1994.

Mingana, A. "Three Ancient Korans." In *The Origins of the Koran,* ed. I. Warraq. Amherst, NY: Prometheus Books, 1998.

Müller, M. *The Sacred Books of the East,* Vols. 1–50. London: Oxford, 1879–1910.

Nasr, S. *The Heart of Islam: Enduring Values for Humanity.* San Francisco: HarperSanFrancisco, 2002.

Natan, T. *Moon-O-Theism: Religion of a War and Moon God Prophet,* Vol. 1–111. Morrisville, NC: Lulu.com, 2006.

Nigosian, S. *The Zoroastrian Faith: Traditions and Modern Research.* Montreal: McGill—Queen's University Press, 1993.

Nuweihed, J. *Abu Jmeel's Daughter and other Stories: Arab Folk Tales from Palestine and Lebanon.* New York: Interlink Books, 2007.

Osman, A. *Moses and Akhenaten: The Secret History of Egypt at the Time of the Exodus.* Rochester, VT: Bear & Company, 2002.

Pelikan, J. *Whose Bible Is It?* New York: Viking, 2005.

Perlmutter, D. *Investigating Religious Terrorism and Ritualistic Crimes.* Boca Raton, FL: CRC Press, 2004.

Picknett, L. and C. Prince. *The Templar Revelation: Secret Guardians of the True Identity of Christ.* New York: Touchtone, 1998.

Powelson, M. and R. Riegert, eds. *The Lost Gospel Q: The Original Sayings of Jesus.* Berkeley, CA: Seastone, 1999.

Prichard, J. *Ancient Near Eastern Texts Relating to the Old Testament.* Princeton: Princeton University Press, 1969.

Rosenberg, D. *Abraham: The First Historical Biography.* New York: Basic Books, 2006.

Rudgley, R. *Essential Substances: A Cultural History of Intoxicants in Society.* New York: Kodansha International, 1994.

Ruck, C., B. Staples, and C. Heinrich. *The Apples of Apollo: Pagan and Christian Mysteries of the Eucharist.* Durham, NC: Carolina Academic Press, 2001.

Rush, J. *Clinical Anthropology: An Application of Anthropological Concepts Within Clinical Settings.* Westport, CT: Praeger, 1996.

Rush, J. *Spiritual Tattoo: A Cultural History of Tattooing, Piercing, Scarification, Branding, and Implants.* Berkeley, CA: Frog, Ltd., 2005.

Rush, J. *Stress and Emotional Health: Applications of Clinical Anthropology.* Westport, CT: Auburn House, 1999.

Rush, J. *The Twelve Gates: A Spiritual Passage Through the Egyptian Books of the Dead.* Berkeley, CA: Frog, Ltd., 2007.

Saliba, G. *A History of Arabic Astronomy: Planetary Theories during the Golden Age of Islam.* New York: New York University Press, 1994.

Sapir, E. *Culture, Language, and Personality: Selected Essays.* Berkeley: University of California Press, 1966.

Schwartz, S. *The Two Faces of Islam: The House of Sa'ud from Tradition to Terror.* New York: Random House, 2002.

Scranton, L. *The Science of the Dogon: Decoding the African Mystery Tradition.* Rochester, VT: Inner Traditions, 2006.

Scupin, R., ed. *Religion and Culture: An Anthropological Focus.* Upper Saddle River, NJ: Prentice-Hall, 2005.

Segal, R. *Islam's Black Slaves: The Other Black Diaspora.* New York: Farrar, Straus and Giroux, 2002.

Shaw, I. and P. Nicholson. *The Dictionary of Ancient Egypt.* New York: Harry N. Abrams, 1995.

Shulman, D. and G. Stroumsa, eds. *Dream Cultures: Explorations in the Comparative History of Dreaming.* New York: Oxford University Press, 1999.

Singh, S. *The Code Book: The Science of Secrecy from Ancient Egypt to Quantum Cryptography.* New York: Anchor Books, 1999.

Sparks, K. *Ancient Texts for the Study of the Hebrew Bible: A Guide to the Background Literature.* Peabody, MA: Hendrickson Publishers, 2005.

Spencer, R. *The Myth of Islamic Tolerance: How Islamic Law Treats Non- Muslims.* Amherst, NY: Prometheus Books, 2005.

Sviri, S. "Dreaming Analyzed and Recorded: Dreams in the World of Medieval Islam." In *Behind Closed Eyes: Dreams and Nightmares in Ancient Egypt.* Wales: The Classical Press of Wales, 2003.

Telushkin, J. *Jewish Humor: What the Best Jewish Jokes Say About the Jews.* New York: Perennial, 2002.

Thompson, T. *The Messiah Myth: The Near Eastern Roots of Jesus and David.* New York: Basic Books, 2005.

Van der Toorn, K., B. Becking, and P. van der Horst. *Dictionary of Deities and Demons in the Bible.* Grand Rapids, MI: William B. Eerdmans Publishing Company, 1999.

Vermes, G. *The Changing Faces of Jesus.* New York: Penguin Compass, 2000.

Vermes, G. *The Authentic Gospel of Jesus.* New York: Penguin Compass, 2003.

von Eschenbach, W. *Parzival.* New York: Penguin Classics, 1980.

Von Strassburg, G. *Tristan.* New York: Penguin Classics, 1982.

Warraq, I., ed. *The Origins of the Koran.* Amherst, NY: Prometheus Books, 1998.

Warraq, I., ed. *The Quest of the Historical Muhammad.* Amherst, NY: Prometheus Books, 2000.

Warraq, I., ed. *Leaving Islam: Apostates Speak Out.* Amherst, NY: Prometheus Books, 2003

Whorf, B. *Language, Thought, and Reality.* Cambridge, MA: MIT Press, 1964.

Wilkinson, J. *Oannes According to Berosus: A Study in the Church of the Ancients.* London: James Speirs, 1888.

Wilkinson, T. *Genesis of the Pharaohs.* London: Thames & Hudson, 2003.

Wills, G. *Papal Sin: Structures of Deceit.* New York: Doubleday, 2000.

Zarabozo, J. *How to Approach and Understand the Quran.* Boulder, CO: Al-Basheer, 1999.

John A. Rush, PhD, ND, is Professor of Anthropology at Sierra College, Rocklin, California, teaching Physical Anthropology and Magic, Witchcraft, and Religion. Dr. Rush's publications include *Clinical Anthropology: An Application of Anthropological Concepts within Clinical Settings* (1996), *Stress and Emotional Health: Applications of Clinical Anthropology* (1999), *Spiritual Tattoo: A Cultural History of Tattooing, Piercing, Scarification, Branding, and Implants* (2005), and *The Twelve Gates: A Spiritual Passage through the Egyptian Books of the Dead* (2007). He is also a naturopathic doctor and medical hypnotherapist in private practice.